HUMAN
RIGHTS
WATCH

NO ESCAPE

MALE RAPE IN U.S. PRISONS

Human Rights Watch

NEW YORK · WASHINGTON · LONDON · BRUSSELS

PHOTO CREDITS/CAPTIONS:

Cover photo: © James Nachtwey/Magnum Photos. Razor wire frames Alabama prisoners on
    their way out to work.
Page ii: © Chris Cozzone. A prison guard tower.
Page 2: © Chris Cozzone. A prisoner's hands outside of the bars.
Page 26: © Aurora Photos. Prisoners exercising outdoors in the prison yard.
Page 44: © Aurora Photos. Guard walking through a cell block.
Page 80: © Aurora Photos. Shanks, knives, screwdrivers: weapons confiscated from prisoners.
Page 108: © Chris Cozzone. Spiraling razor wire.
Page 128: © James Nachtwey/Magnum Photos. Prisoners lying down on their bunks.

ISBN 1–56432–258–0
Library of Congress Catalog Number: 2001088989

ADDRESSES FOR HUMAN RIGHTS WATCH

350 Fifth Avenue, 34th Floor, New York, NY 10118-3299
Tel: (212) 290-4700, Fax: (212) 736-1300, E-mail: hrwnyc@hrw.org

1630 Connecticut Avenue, N.W., Suite 500, Washington, DC 20009
Tel: (202) 612-4321, Fax: (202) 612-4333, E-mail: hrwdc@hrw.org

33 Islington High Street, N1 9LH London, UK
Tel: (171) 713-1995, Fax: (171) 713-1800, E-mail: hrwatchuk@gn.apc.org

15 Rue Van Campenhout, 1000 Brussels, Belgium
Tel: (2) 732-2009, Fax: (2) 732-0471, E-mail:hrwatcheu@skynet.be

Web Site Address: http://www.hrw.org

Listserv address:
To subscribe to the list, send an e-mail message to majordomo@igc.apc.org with "subscribe hrw-news" in the body of the message (leave the subject line blank).

Human Rights Watch is dedicated to protecting the human rights of people around the world.

We stand with victims and activists to prevent discrimination, to uphold political freedom, to protect people from inhumane conduct in wartime, and to bring offenders to justice.

We investigate and expose human rights violations and hold abusers accountable.

We challenge governments and those who hold power to end abusive practices and respect international human rights law.

We enlist the public and the international community to support the cause of human rights for all.

Human Rights Watch

Human Rights Watch conducts regular, systematic investigations of human rights abuses in some seventy countries around the world. Our reputation for timely, reliable disclosures has made us an essential source of information for those concerned with human rights. We address the human rights practices of governments of all political stripes, of all geopolitical alignments, and of all ethnic and religious persuasions. Human Rights Watch defends freedom of thought and expression, due process and equal protection of the law, and a vigorous civil society; we document and denounce murders, disappearances, torture, arbitrary imprisonment, discrimination, and other abuses of internationally recognized human rights. Our goal is to hold governments accountable if they transgress the rights of their people.

Human Rights Watch began in 1978 with the founding of its Europe and Central Asia division (then known as Helsinki Watch). Today, it also includes divisions covering Africa, the Americas, Asia, and the Middle East. In addition, it includes three thematic divisions on arms, children's rights, and women's rights. It maintains offices in New York, Washington, Los Angeles, London, Brussels, Moscow, Dushanbe, and Bangkok. Human Rights Watch is an independent, nongovernmental organization, supported by contributions from private individuals and foundations worldwide. It accepts no government funds, directly or indirectly.

The staff includes Kenneth Roth, executive director; Michele Alexander, development director; Reed Brody, advocacy director; Carroll Bogert, communications director; Barbara Guglielmo, finance director; Jeri Laber special advisor; Lotte Leicht, Brussels office director; Michael McClintock, deputy program director; Patrick Minges, publications director; Maria Pignataro Nielsen, human resources director; Jemera Rone, counsel; Mal-

Contents

ACKNOWLEDGMENTS xiii
PREFACE xv

I.
SUMMARY AND RECOMMENDATIONS 3

Case Histories: S.M. and C.R. 19

II.
BACKGROUND 27
The Size and Growth of the U.S. Inmate Population 27
The Structure of Imprisonment 28
Characteristics of the U.S. Prisoner Population 30
Conditions and Abuses 31
Grievance Mechanisms 37
Oversight of Treatment and Conditions 38

Case History: R.G. 39

III.
LEGAL CONTEXT 45
National Legal Protections 45
International Legal Protections 54

Case History: Rodney Hulin 61

IV.
PREDATORS AND VICTIMS   63
Age   64
Size, Physical Strength, Attitude, and Propensity toward Violence   67
Sexual Preference   70
Race and Ethnicity   71
Criminal History   73
Relationship between Victim and Perpetrator   75

Case Histories: L.O. and P.E.   77

V.
RAPE SCENARIOS   81
Consent and Coercion in Prison   83
Violent or Forcible Assaults   85
Coerced Sexual Abuse   87
Continuing Sexual Abuse   90
Slavery   93
Sex, Violence and Power   96

Case Histories: S.H. and M.R.   99

VI.
BODY AND SOUL
The Physical and Psychological Injury
of Prison Rape   109
Physical Effects and the Threat of HIV Transmission   110
Psychological Impact   112
Inadequate Treatment   122

Case Histories: P.N. and L.T.   123

VII.
ANOMALY OR EPIDEMIC
The Incidence of Prisoner-on-Prisoner Rape   129
Chronic Underreporting   130

Low Numbers Reported by State Correctional Authorities   133
High Numbers Estimated by Correctional Officers   135
Findings of Empirical Studies   136

Case History: B.L.   140

VIII.
DELIBERATE INDIFFERENCE
State Authorities' Response to
Prisoner-on-Prisoner Sexual Abuse   143
Failure to Recognize and Address the Problem—and the Perverse
    Incentives Created by Legal Standards   144
The North Carolina Pilot Program   146
Lack of Prisoner Orientation   147
Improper Classification and Negligent Double-Celling   148
Understaffing and the Failure to Prevent   150
Inadequate Response to Complaints of Rape   151
Failure to Prosecute   154
Internal Administrative Penalties   156
The Failure of Mechanisms of Legal Redress   157

Case History: W.H.   159

Appendix I: Excerpts from Prisoners' Letters   163

Appendix II: Miscellaneous Documents   233
1. U.S. Department of Justice, Federal Bureau of Prisons,
    "Program Statement: Sexual Abuse/Assault Prevention and
    Intervention Program," Directive 5324.04 (December 31, 1997)   234
2. Excerpts from Arkansas Department of Correction, "Sexual
    Aggression in Prisons and Jails: Awareness, Prevention and
    Intervention" (undated)   252
3. Curriculum outline from the Illinois Department of Corrections,
    "Inmate Sexual Assault" (February 1, 2000)   288
4. Declaration of Plaintiff's Counsel in the case of Dillard v. Decker,
    Case No. CV F-94 5048 AWI SMS (E.D. Ca. 2000)   295

5. Sample letter from Human Rights Watch to correctional
   department regarding rape prevention and prosecution strategies.   311
6. Sampling of responses from correctional departments to
   Human Rights Watch's survey of rape prevention and
   prosecution strategies.   312

NOTES   343

Acknowledgments

Joanne Mariner, deputy director of the Americas Division of Human Rights Watch, is the author of this report, which is based on research conducted from 1996 to 1999. The research was a collective effort requiring the assistance of a number of Human Rights Watch staff members, interns, and others. Among those who gave generously of their time and ideas were Sahr Muhammedaly, former program associate; Gail Yamauchi, program associate; Kokayi K. Issa, former Leonard Sandler Fellow; Rae Terry, former New York University law student; Anna-Rose Mathieson, former Everett Intern; Emma Algotsson, former intern; Zoe Hilden, former intern; Caroline Flintoft, former intern; Marcia Allina, program associate; and Ali Ehsassi, former intern. Professor Michael Mushlin of Pace University offered helpful suggestions regarding the report's legal section.

During informal discussions on prison issues with Associate Counsel Jamie Fellner, the author gained many insights that inform this report. She would also like to thank Cynthia Brown, former program director of Human Rights Watch, who was a steadfast supporter of the project.

The report was edited by Michael McClintock, deputy program director of Human Rights Watch, and Malcolm Smart, program director. Jamie Fellner also provided invaluable editorial comments. Dinah PoKempner, general counsel of Human Rights Watch, reviewed it for legal accuracy.

Generous financial assistance for the research was provided by the Edna McConnell Clark Foundation, the Public Welfare Foundation, and John Kaneb.

The author wishes to thank the many prisoners who contributed to the report, both by recounting their personal experiences and by offering their thoughts and recommendations on the topic. The report is dedicated to the memory of two exceptional men: the late Justice Harry Blackmun, a former member of the U.S. Supreme Court, notable, among other things, for his eloquent concern for the humane treatment of prisoners, and the late Stephen Donaldson, a former prisoner and tireless activist whose ground-breaking work drew needed attention to the human suffering that is the subject of this report.

I've been sentenced for a D.U.I. offense. My 3rd one. When I first came to prison, I had no idea what to expect. Certainly none of this. I'm a tall white male, who unfortunately has a small amount of feminine characteristics. And very shy. These characteristics have got me raped so many times I have no more feelings physically. I have been raped by up to 5 black men and two white men at a time. I've had knifes at my head and throat. I had fought and been beat so hard that I didn't ever think I'd see straight again. One time when I refused to enter a cell, I was brutally attacked by staff and taken to segragation though I had only wanted to prevent the same and worse by not locking up with my cell mate. There is no supervision after lockdown. I was given a conduct report. I explained to the hearing officer what the issue was. He told me that off the record, He suggests I find a man I would/could willingly have sex with to prevent these things from happening. I've requested protective custody only to be denied. It is not available here. He also said there was no where to run to, and it would be best for me to accept things. . . . I probably have AIDS now. I have great difficulty raising food to my mouth from shaking after nightmares or thinking to hard on all this . . . . I've laid down without physical fight to be sodomized. To prevent so much damage in struggles, ripping and tearing. Though in not fighting, it caused my heart and spirit to be raped as well. Something I don't know if I'll ever forgive myself for. [1]

The letter excerpted above was one of the first to reach Human Rights Watch in response to a small announcement posted in *Prison Legal News* and *Prison Life Magazine*, two publications with a wide audience in U.S. prisons. Having been alerted to the problem of prisoner-on-prisoner rape in the United States by the work of activists like Stephen Donaldson of the organization Stop Prisoner Rape, we had decided to conduct exploratory research into the topic and had put a call out to prisoners for information. The resulting deluge of letters—many of which included compelling firsthand descriptions such as this—convinced us that the issue merited urgent attention. Rape, by prisoners' accounts, was no aberrational occurrence; instead it was a deeply-rooted, systemic problem. It was also a problem that prison authorities were doing little to address.

The present report—the product of three years of research and well over a thousand inmate letters—describes the complex dynamics of male prisoner-on-prisoner sexual abuse in the United States. The report is an effort to explain why and how such abuse occurs, who commits it and who falls victim to it, what are its effects, both physical and psychological, how are prison authorities coping with it and, most importantly, what reforms can be instituted to better prevent it from occurring.

The Scope of This Report

This report is limited in scope to male prisoner-on-prisoner sexual abuse in the United States. It does not cover women prisoners, nor does it cover the sexual abuse of male prisoners by their jailers. Human Rights Watch investigated the problem of custodial sexual misconduct in U.S. women's prisons in two previous reports and the issue has been a continuing focus of our U.S. advocacy efforts.[2] As to custodial sexual misconduct against male prisoners, we decided not to include that topic within the scope of this report even though some prisoners who claimed to have been subject to such abuse did contact us. An initial review of the topic convinced us that it involved myriad issues that were distinct from the topic at hand, which is complicated enough in itself.

Even though the notices that Human Rights Watch circulated to announce our research on prisoner-on-prisoner sexual abuse were written in gender-neutral language, we received no information from women prisoners regarding the problem. As prison experts are well aware, penal facilities for men and women tend to differ in important respects. If the problem of prisoner-on-prisoner sexual abuse exists in women's institutions—a possibility we do not exclude—it is likely to take somewhat different forms than in men's prisons.[3]

For several reasons, the primary focus of this report is on sexual abuse in prisons, rather than jails.[4] Most importantly, all of our information save a handful of letters came from prison as opposed to jail inmates. Many of these prisoners did, however, describe sexual abuses they had suffered when previously held in jails, allowing us to gather some information on the topic. Nonetheless, the bulk of our prisoner testimonies and documentation—and all of the information we collected from state authorities—pertain specifically to prisons. Already, with fifty separate state prison jurisdictions in the United States, the task of collecting official information was difficult; obtaining such information from the many thousands of local authorities responsible for city and county jails would have been infinitely more so. Yet we should emphasize that our lack of specific research on jails should be not interpreted as suggesting that the problem does not occur there. Although little research has been done on sexual assault in jails, the few commentators who have examined the topic have found the abuse to be similarly or even more prevalent there.[5]

It is evident to Human Rights Watch, even without having completed exhaustive research into the jail context, that the problems we describe with regard to prisons generally hold true for jails as well. This conclusion derives from the fact that most of the risk factors leading to rape exist in prisons and jails alike. We therefore believe that our recommendations for reform are largely applicable in the jail context, and we urge jail authorities to pay increased attention to the issue of prisoner-on-prisoner sexual abuse.

While this report does not deal specifically with juvenile institutions, we note that previous research, while extremely scanty, suggests that inmate-on-inmate sexual abuse may be even more common in juvenile institutions than it is in facilities for adults.[6] Indeed, a case filed recently by the U.S. Justice Department in federal court to challenge conditions in a Louisiana juvenile institution includes serious allegations of inmate-on-inmate rape.[7]

Finally, our choice of U.S. prisons as the subject of this research, over prisons elsewhere in the world, in no way indicates that we believe the problem to be unique to the United States. On the contrary, our international prison research convinces us that prisoner-on-prisoner rape is of serious concern around the world. We note that several publications on human rights or prison conditions in other countries have touched on or explored the topic, as have past Human Rights Watch prison reports.[8] Interestingly, researchers outside of the United States have reached many of the same conclusions as researchers here, suggesting that specific cultural variables are not determinative with regard to rape in prison.[9]

Methodology

The report is primarily based on information collected from over 200 prisoners spread among thirty-seven states. The majority of these inmates have been raped or otherwise sexually abused while in prison, and were therefore able to give firsthand accounts of the problem. Numerous inmates who were not subject to sexual abuse also provided their views on the topic, including information about sexual assaults that they had witnessed. A very small number of inmates who had themselves participated in rape also contributed their perspectives. Much of the information was received via written correspondence, although Human Rights Watch representatives spoke by telephone with a number of prisoners, and personally interviewed twenty-six of them. Prisoner testimonies were supplemented by documentary materials such as written grievances, court papers, letters, and medical records.

Prisoners were contacted using several different methods. Human Rights Watch posted announcements in a number of publications and leaflets that reach prisoners—including *Prison Legal News, Prison Life Magazine* (which has since ceased publication), and *Florida Prison Legal Perspectives*—informing them that we were conducting research on the topic of prisoner-on-prisoner sexual abuse and that we welcomed their information. Several organizations that work with prisoners, including Stop Prisoner Rape, put us in contact with additional inmates.

The prisoners who collaborated in our efforts were thus a largely self-selected group, not a random sampling. Previous researchers have conducted quantitative studies using statistically valid techniques in certain U.S. prisons—most recently, in 1996 in the Nebraska prison system—but, given that there are some two million prisoners in the United States, this would be difficult to achieve on a national scale. The research on which the present report was based was thus qualitative in nature: it sought to identify systemic weaknesses rather than to quantify actual cases of abuse. The result, we believe, sketches the outlines of a national problem, bridging the gap between academic research on the topic and the more anecdotal writings that occasionally appear in the popular press.

The prisoners with whom Human Rights Watch was in contact, we should emphasize, did not simply serve as a source of case material. Rather, their comments and insights—based on firsthand knowledge and close observation—inform every page of the report.

Besides prisoners, we also obtained valuable information from prison officials, prison experts, lawyers who represent prisoners, prisoners rights organizations, and prisoners' relatives. Written materials including academic studies, books, and articles from the popular press supplemented these sources. In addition, Human Rights Watch conducted an extensive review of the case law relevant to prison rape in the United States.

NO ESCAPE

SUMMARY AND RECOMMENDATIONS

A **Florida prisoner whom we will identify only as P.R.** was beaten, suffered a serious eye injury, and assaulted by an inmate armed with a knife, all due to his refusal to submit to anal sex. After six months of repeated threats and attacks by other inmates, at the end of his emotional endurance, he tried to commit suicide by slashing his wrists with a razor. In a letter to Human Rights Watch, he chronicled his unsuccessful efforts to induce prison authorities to protect him from abuse. Summing up these experiences, he wrote: "The opposite of compassion is not hatred, it's indifference."

P.R.'s bleak outlook is not unjustified. Judging by the popular media, rape is accepted as almost a commonplace of imprisonment, so much so that when the topic of prison arises, a joking reference to rape seems almost obligatory. Few members of the public would be surprised by the assertion that men are frequently raped in prison, given rape's established place in the mythology of prison life. Yet serious, sustained, and constructive attention to the subject remains rare. As Stephen Donaldson, the late president of the organization Stop Prisoner Rape, once said: "the rape of males is a taboo subject for public discussion. . . . If ever there was a crime hidden by a curtain of silence, it is male rape."

Without question, the hard facts about inmate-on-inmate sexual abuse are little known. No conclusive national data exist regarding the prevalence of prisoner-on-prisoner rape and other sexual abuse in the United States. Indeed, few commentators have even ventured to speculate on the national incidence of rape in prison, although some, extrapolating from small-scale studies, have come up with rough estimates as to its prevalence. With the staggering growth of the prison population over the past two decades, such ignorance is more unjustifiable than ever.

Prison authorities, unsurprisingly, generally claim that prisoner-on-prisoner sexual abuse is an exceptional occurrence rather than a systemic problem. Prison officials in New Mexico, for example, responding to our 1997 request for information regarding "the 'problem' of male inmate-on-inmate rape and sexual abuse" (the internal quotation marks are theirs), said that they had "no recorded incidents over the past few years." The Nebraska Department of Correctional Services informed Human Rights Watch that such incidents were "minimal." Only Texas, Ohio, Florida, Illinois and the Federal Bureau of Prisons said that they had more than fifty reported incidents in a given year, numbers which, because of the large size of their prison systems, still translate into extremely low rates of victimization.

Yet prison authorities' claims are belied by independent research on the topic. Indeed, the most recent academic studies of the issue have found shockingly high rates of sexual abuse, including forced oral and anal intercourse. In December 2000, the *Prison Journal* published a study based on a survey of inmates in seven men's prison facilities in four states. The results showed that 21 percent of the inmates had experienced at least one episode of pressured or forced sexual contact since being incarcerated, and at least 7 percent had been raped in their facility. A 1996 study of the Nebraska prison system produced similar findings, with 22 percent of male inmates reporting that they had been pressured or forced to have sexual contact against their will while incarcerated. Of these, over 50 percent had submitted to forced anal sex at least once. Extrapolating these findings to the national level gives a total of at least 140,000 inmates who have been raped.

"The opposite of compassion is not hatred, it's indifference."

An internal departmental survey of corrections officers in a southern state (provided to Human Rights Watch on the condition that the state not be identified) found that line officers—those charged with the direct supervision of inmates—estimated that roughly one-fifth of all prisoners were being coerced into participation in inmate-on-inmate sex. Interestingly, higher-ranking officials—those at the supervisory level—tended to give lower estimates of the frequency of abuse, while inmates themselves gave much higher estimates: the two groups cited victimization rates of roughly one-eighth and one-third, respectively. Although the author of the survey was careful to note that it was not conducted in accordance with scientific standards, and thus its findings may not be perfectly reliable, the basic conclusions are still striking. Even taking only the lowest of the three estimates of coerced sexual activity—and even framing that one conservatively—more than one in ten inmates in the prisons surveyed was subject to sexual abuse.

It is evident that certain prisoners are targeted for sexual assault the moment they enter a penal facility: their age, looks, sexual preference, and other characteristics mark them as candidates for abuse. Human Rights Watch's research has revealed a broad range of factors that correlate with increased vulnerability to rape. These include youth, small size, and physical weakness; being white, gay, or a first offender; possessing "feminine" characteristics such as long hair or a high voice; being unassertive, unaggressive, shy, intellectual, not street-smart, or "passive"; or having been convicted of a sexual offense against a minor. Prisoners with any one of these characteristics typically face an increased risk of sexual abuse, while prisoners with several overlapping characteristics are much more likely than other inmates to be targeted for abuse. Yet it would be a mistake to think that only a minority of extremely vulnerable individuals face sexual abuse. In the wrong circumstances, it should be emphasized, almost any prisoner may become a victim.

The characteristics of prison rapists are somewhat less clear and predictable, but certain patterns can nonetheless be discerned. First, although some older inmates commit rape, the perpetrators also tend to be young, if not always as young as their victims—generally well under thirty-five years old. They are frequently larger or stronger than their victims, and are generally more assertive, physically aggressive, and more at home in the prison environment. They are "street smart"—often gang members. They have typically been convicted of more violent crimes than their victims.

The reality of sexual abuse in prison is deeply disturbing. Rapes can be almost unimaginably vicious and brutal. Gang assaults are not uncommon, and victims may be left beaten, bloody and, in the most extreme cases, dead. One of the most tragic and violent cases to come to the attention of Human Rights Watch was that of Randy Payne, a twenty-three year old incarcerated in a Texas maximum security prison. Within a week of entering the prison in August 1994, Payne was attacked by a group of some twenty inmates. The inmates demanded sex and money, but Payne refused. He was beaten for almost two hours; guards later said they had not noticed anything until they found his bloody body in the dayroom. He died of head injuries a few days later.

Another Texas inmate, who had deep scars on his head, neck, and chest, told Human Right Watch that the prisoner who inflicted the wounds had raped him eight separate times from July through November 1995. The first time M.R. was raped—"which felt like having a tree limb shoved up into me"—he told the prison chaplain about it, and the chaplain had him write out a statement for the facility's Internal Affairs department. According to M.R.'s description of the events, the Internal Affairs investigator brought both the victim and the perpetrator into a room together and asked them what had happened. Although M.R. was terrified to speak of the incident in front of the other inmate, he told his story, while the perpetrator claimed the sex was consensual. After both of them had spoken, the investigator told them that "lovers' quarrels" were not of interest to Internal Affairs, sending them both back to their cells. "The guy shoved me into his house and raped me again," M.R. later told Human Rights Watch. "It was a lot more violent this time."

M.R. spent several months trying to escape the rapist, facing repeated abuse. He filed grievances over the first couple of rapes in an effort to draw the attention of prison officials; they were returned saying the sexual assaults never occurred. On the last day of December, the rapist showed up on M.R.'s wing and threatened to kill M.R. with a combination lock. "I was in the dayroom. I remember eating a piece of cornbread and the next thing I knew I woke up in the hospital," M.R. recalled. A room full of prisoners saw the rapist nearly kill M.R. and then rape him in the middle of the dayroom. The rapist hit M.R. so hard with the lock that when M.R. regained consciousness he could read the word "Master"—the lockmaker—on his forehead. Four years later, a Human Rights Watch researcher could still see the round impression of the lock on the right side of his forehead. In all, M.R. suffered a broken neck, jaw, left collarbone, and finger; a dislocated left shoulder; two major concussions, and lacerations to his scalp that caused bleeding on the brain. Notwithstanding the extreme violence of the attack, and despite M.R.'s best efforts to press charges, the rapist was never criminally prosecuted.

Yet overtly violent rapes are only the most visible and dramatic form of sexual abuse behind bars. Many victims of prison rape have never had a knife to their throat. They may have never been explicitly threatened. But they have nonetheless engaged in sexual acts against their will, believing that they had no choice.

Although Human Rights Watch received many reports of forcible sexual attacks, we also heard numerous accounts of abuse based on more subtle forms of coercion and intimidation. Prisoners, including those who had been forcibly raped, all agree that the threat of violence, or even just the implicit threat of violence, is a more common factor in sexual abuse than is actual violence. As one explained:

"If ever there was a crime hidden by a curtain of silence, it is male rape."

> From my point of view, rape takes place every day. A prisoner that is engaging in sexual acts, not by force, is still a victim of rape because I know that deep inside this prisoner do not want to do the things that he is doing but he thinks that it is the only way that he can survive.

Once subject to sexual abuse, whether violently or through coercion, a prisoner may easily become trapped into a sexually subordinate role. Prisoners refer to the initial rape as "turning out" the victim, and the suggestion of transformation is telling. Through the act of rape, the victim is redefined as an object of sexual abuse. He has been proven to be weak, vulnerable, "female," in the eyes of other inmates. Regaining his "manhood"—and the respect of other prisoners—can be extremely difficult.

Stigmatized as a "punk" or "turn out," the victim of rape will almost inevitably be the target of continuing sexual exploitation, both from the initial perpetrator and, unless the perpetrator "protects" him, from other inmates as well. "Once someone is violated sexually and there is no consequences on the perpetrators, that person who was violated then becomes a mark or marked," an Indiana prisoner told Human Rights Watch. "That means he's fair game." His victimization is likely to be public knowledge, and his reputation will follow him to other housing areas, if he is moved, and even to other prisons. As another inmate explained: "Word travels so Fast in prison. The Convict grape vine is <u>Large.</u> You cant run or hide."

Prisoners unable to escape a situation of sexual abuse may find themselves becoming another inmate's "property." The word is commonly used in prison to refer to sexually subordinate inmates, and it is no exaggeration. Victims of prison rape, in the most extreme cases, are literally the slaves of the perpetrators. Forced to satisfy another man's sexual appetites whenever he demands, they may also be responsible for washing his clothes, massaging his back, cooking his food, cleaning his cell, and myriad other chores. They are frequently "rented out" for sex, sold, or even auctioned off to other inmates, replicating the financial aspects of traditional slavery. Their most basic choices, like how to dress and whom to talk to, may be controlled by the person who "owns" them. Their name may be replaced by a female one. Like all forms of slavery, these situations are among the most degrading and dehumanizing experiences a person can undergo.

> **"A prisoner that is engaging in sexual acts, not by force, is still a victim of rape because I know that deep inside this prisoner do not want to do the things that he is doing but he thinks that it is the only way that he can survive."**

J.D., a white inmate in Texas who admits that he "cannot fight real good," told Human Rights Watch that he was violently raped by his cellmate, a heavy, muscular man, in 1993. "From that day on," he said, "I was classified as a homosexual and was sold from one inmate to the next." Although he informed prison staff that he had been raped and was transferred to another part of the prison, the white inmates in his new housing area immediately "sold" him to a black inmate known as Blue Top. Blue Top used J.D. sexually, while also "renting" his sexual services to other black inmates. Besides being forced to perform "all types of sexual acts," J.D. had to defer to Blue Top in every other way. Under Blue Top's dominion, no task was too menial or too degrading for J.D. to perform. After two and a half months of this abuse, J.D. was finally transferred to a safer environment.

Six Texas inmates gave Human Rights Watch firsthand accounts of being forced into this type of sexual slavery, having even been "sold" or "rented" out to other inmates. Numerous other Texas prisoners confirmed that the practice of sexual slavery, including the buying and selling of inmates, is commonplace in the system's more dangerous prison units. Although

Texas, judging from the information received by Human Rights Watch, has the worst record in this respect, we also collected personal testimonies from inmates in Illinois, Michigan, California, and Arkansas who have survived situations of sexual slavery.

Rape's effects on the victim's psyche are serious and enduring. Victims of rape often suffer extreme psychological stress, a condition identified as rape trauma syndrome. Many inmate victims with whom Human Rights Watch has been in contact have reported nightmares, deep depression, shame, loss of self-esteem, self-hatred, and considering or attempting suicide. Serious questions arise as to how the trauma of sexual abuse resolves itself when such inmates are released into society. Indeed, some experts believe that the experience of rape threatens to perpetuate a cycle of violence, with the abused inmate in some instances turning violent himself.

Another devastating consequence of prisoner-on-prisoner rape is the transmission of HIV, the virus which causes AIDS. Several prisoners with whom Human Rights Watch is in contact believe that they have contracted HIV through forced sexual intercourse in prison. K.S., a prisoner in Arkansas, was repeatedly raped between January and December 1991 by more than twenty different inmates, one of whom, he believes, transmitted the HIV virus to him. K.S. had tested negative for HIV upon entry to the prison system, but in September 1991 he tested positive.

It must be emphasized that rape and other sexual abuses occur in prison because correctional officials, to a surprising extent, do little to stop them from occurring. While some inmates with whom Human Rights Watch is in contact have described relatively secure institutions—where inmates are closely monitored, where steps are taken to prevent inmate-on-inmate abuses, and where such abuses are punished if they occur—many others report a decidedly laissez faire approach to the problem. In too many institutions, prevention measures are meager and effective punishment of abuses is rare.

Prisoner classification policies include among their goals the separation of dangerous prisoners from those whom they are likely to victimize. In the overcrowded prisons of today, however, the practical demands of simply finding available space for inmates have to a large extent overwhelmed classification ideals. Inmates frequently find themselves placed among others whose background, criminal history, and other characteristics make them an obvious threat. Indeed, in the worst cases, prisoners are actually placed in the same cell with inmates who are likely to victimize them—sometimes even with inmates who have a demonstrated proclivity for sexual abusing others.

Another casualty of the enormous growth of the country's prison population is adequate staffing and supervision of inmates. The consequences with regard to rape are obvious. Rape occurs most easily when there is no prison staff around to see or hear it. Particularly at night, prisoners have told Human Rights Watch, they are often left alone and unsupervised in their housing areas. Several inmates have reported to Human Rights Watch that they yelled for help when they were attacked, to no avail. Although correctional staff are supposed to make rounds at regular intervals, they do not always abide by their schedules. Moreover, they often walk by prisoners' cells without making an effort to see what is really happening within them. The existence of difficult to monitor areas, especially in older prisons, compounds the problem. As one Florida inmate summed up: "Rapes occur because the lack of observation make it possible. Prisons have too few guards and too many blind spots."

An absolutely central problem with regard to sexual abuse in prison, emphasized by inmate after inmate, is the inadequate—and, in many instances, callous and irresponsible—response of correctional staff to complaints of rape. When an inmate informs an officer that he has been threatened with rape or, even worse, actually assaulted, it is crucial that his complaint be met with a rapid and effective response. Most obviously, he should be brought to a place where his safety can be protected and where he can set out his complaint in a confidential manner. If the rape has already occurred, he should be taken for whatever medical care may be needed and—a step that is crucial for any potential criminal prosecution—where physical evidence of rape can be collected. Yet from the reports that Human Rights Watch has received, such responses are rare.

The criminal justice system also affords scant relief to sexually abused prisoners. Few public prosecutors are concerned with prosecuting crimes committed against inmates, preferring to leave internal prison problems to the discretion of the prison authorities; similarly, prison officials themselves rarely push for the prosecution of prisoner-on-prisoner abuses. As a result, perpetrators of prison rape almost never face criminal charges.

Internal disciplinary mechanisms, the putative substitute for criminal prosecution, tend to function poorly in those cases in which the victim reports the crime. In nearly every instance Human Rights Watch has encountered, the authorities have imposed light disciplinary sanctions against the perpetrator—perhaps thirty days in disciplinary segregation—if that. Often rapists are simply transferred to another facility, or are not moved at all. Their victims, in contrast, may end up spending the rest of their prison terms in protective custody units whose conditions are often similar to those in disciplinary segregation: twenty-three hours per day in a cell, restricted privileges, and no educational or vocational opportunities.

Disappointingly, the federal courts have not played a significant role in curtailing prisoner-on-prisoner sexual abuse. Despite the paucity of lawyers willing to litigate such cases, some inmates do nonetheless file suit against the prison authorities in the aftermath of rape. They assert that the authorities' failure to take steps to protect them from abuse violates the prohibition on "cruel and usual punishments" contained in the Eighth Amendment to the U.S. Constitution. Such cases are often dismissed in the early stages of litigation. Moreover, the rare case that does survive to reach a jury typically finds the inmate plaintiff before an audience that is wholly unreceptive to his story. While there have been a few generous damages awards in prison rape cases, they are the very rare exceptions to the rule.

Unfortunately the legal rules that the courts have developed relating to prisoner-on-prisoner sexual abuse create perverse incentives for authorities to ignore the problem. Under the "deliberate indifference" standard that is applicable to legal challenges to prison officials' failure to protect prisoners from inter-prisoner abuses such as rape, the prisoner must prove to the court that the defendants had *actual knowledge* of a substantial risk to him, and that they disregarded that risk. As the courts have emphasized, it is not enough for the prisoner to prove that "the risk was obvious and a reasonable prison official would have noticed it." Instead, if a prison official lacked knowledge of the risk— no matter how obvious it was to anyone else—he cannot be held liable. In other words, rather than trying to ascertain the true dimensions of the problem of prisoner-on-prisoner sexual abuse, prison officials have good reason to want to remain unaware of it.

> "Once someone is violated sexually and there is no consequences on the perpetrators, that person who was violated then becomes a mark or marked."

Recommendations

The existing situation, marked by a wholesale disregard for prisoners' right to be free of violent rape and other forms of unwanted sexual contact, must be reformed. Human Rights Watch calls on the United States authorities to demonstrate their commitment to prevent, investigate, and punish prisoner-on-prisoner sexual abuse in men's prisons and jails, as required under both international and national law. We make the following recommendations to the federal and state governments, urging them to step up their efforts to address this gross violation of human dignity.

Recommendations to Federal Authorities

I. To the U.S. Congress

- Congress should amend or repeal those provisions of the Prison Litigation Reform Act (PLRA) that severely hinder prisoners, nongovernmental organizations, and the Department of Justice in their efforts to remedy unconstitutional conditions in state correctional facilities. The following changes should, at a minimum, be considered:

  - the repeal of 18 United States Code Section 3626(a)(1), which requires that judicially enforceable consent decrees contain findings of federal law violations;
  - the repeal of 18 United States Code Section 3626(b), which requires all judicial orders to terminate two years after they are issued; and
  - the restoration of funding for special masters' and attorneys' fees to the levels that prevailed before the passage of the PLRA.

- Congress should pass legislation conditioning states' eligibility for funding for prison construction and equipment purchases on efforts by state correctional authorities to combat prisoner-on-prisoner sexual abuse. Such efforts should include comprehensive protocols to govern staff response to cases of prisoner-on-prisoner sexual abuse, the establishment of a sexual abuse prevention program that includes inmate orientation and staff training, and the collection of data on prisoner-on-prisoner sexual abuse.

- Congress should appropriate the funds necessary to enable the Department of Justice to conduct increased and thorough investigations of prisoner-on-prisoner sexual abuse and to enjoin prohibited conduct pursuant to the Civil Rights of Institutionalized Persons Act (CRIPA).

- Congress should pass legislation requiring states to certify that their prisoner grievance procedures satisfy the requirements of the Civil Rights of Institutionalized Persons Act (CRIPA). It should also review CRIPA provisions pertaining to the certification of prisoner grievance procedures to ensure that certified procedures will function effectively for complaints of prisoner-on-prisoner sexual abuse.

- Congress should hold hearings on the problem of male inmate-on-inmate sexual abuse.

- Congress should adopt legislation to withdraw the restrictive reservations, declarations and understandings that the United States has attached to the ICCPR and the Torture Convention.

- Congress should adopt legislation to implement the ICCPR and the Torture Convention within the United States, and, in particular, to establish that the provisions of these treaties are legally enforceable in U.S. courts.

II. To the Civil Rights Division of the U.S. Department of Justice

- The Special Litigation Section of the Civil Rights Division should investigate reports of prisoner-on-prisoner sexual abuse to ascertain whether they rise to the level of a "pattern or practice." Any allegations that meet this standard should be vigorously prosecuted. Allegations that do not meet this standard should be forwarded to state authorities for investigation.

- When investigating conditions in any men's correctional facility, the

Special Litigation Unit should be extremely attentive to the issue of prisoner-on-prisoner sexual abuse and cognizant of the difficulties of obtaining information on the issue. One member of every investigative team, preferably someone with particularized expertise in the area of sexual abuse, should be named as the point person on this topic.

• The Special Litigation Section should name an attorney to be responsible for overseeing its investigations of prisoner-on-prisoner sexual abuse, including formulating proactive strategies for obtaining information on such abuse. All complaints lodged with the section that are relevant to this topic should be copied to this person. The person should familiarize him- or herself with the complexities of the topic by meeting with experts and reviewing relevant studies and reports.

III. To the National Institute of Corrections

• The National Institute of Corrections (NIC) should develop training programs on the topic of male prisoner-on-prisoner sexual abuse for both high-level corrections officials and line staff. In drafting a curriculum for the training, the NIC should consult with outside experts who have studied the topic. The object of these programs should be to sensitize corrections officials as to the importance of taking effective steps to prevent and remedy prisoner-on-prisoner sexual abuse, and to provide them with the tools needed to do so.

• The NIC should draft model investigatory procedures for allegations of prisoner-on- prisoner sexual abuse.

• The NIC should make an effort to collect, maintain and disseminate data relating to prisoner-on-prisoner sexual abuse.

Recommendations to State Authorities and the Federal Bureau of Prisons (BOP)

I. To State Departments of Corrections (DOCs) and the BOP

- DOCs should draft comprehensive protocols to govern staff response to cases of prisoner-on-prisoner sexual abuse. Such protocols should contain guidelines on investigation, evidence collection, outside reporting, and medical and psychological treatment of victims of abuse. The guidelines should emphasize the importance of the prompt collection of evidence, and the immediate medical care of victims.

- DOC staff, particularly line staff, should be vigilant and attentive to the problem of prisoner-on-prisoner sexual abuse while being cognizant of the difficulties of detecting it. In particular, line officers should react appropriately to signs of abuse. Any inmate claiming that he has been subject to sexual abuse, or that he is in imminent danger of such abuse, should be immediately removed to a holding cell in another area, and a prompt investigation of his claims should be instituted.

- All prisons should at all times be staffed with sufficient numbers of correctional officers to ensure effective monitoring and control of the prison population. Officers should make regular rounds, closely monitoring prisoners' treatment and ensuring that abuses do not occur.

- DOCs should routinely report all cases of rape or other criminal sexual abuse to local police and prosecutorial authorities for possible criminal prosecution. They should make clear to such authorities that such reporting is not merely a bureaucratic formality—rather, that they expect cases to be fully investigated and, if the evidence warrants it, prosecuted to the full extent of the law.

- In addition to referring cases out for criminal prosecution, DOCs should take appropriate disciplinary actions against the perpetrators of sexual abuse. Administrative proceedings should be instituted, a prompt and thorough investigation should be conducted, and if guilt is established an appropriately serious punishment should be imposed. In no instance should the perpetrator simply be transferred to another unit.

- A section of the orientation programming provided to incoming male prisoners should be dedicated to educating them about the issue of prisoner-on-prisoner sexual abuse. It should emphasize, in particular, the right not to be subject to such abuse, and how that right can be enforced. It should also inform prisoners of how and to whom to report such abuse; what scenarios commonly lead to sexual abuse; what to do if abuse occurs (mentioning, in particular, the importance of prompt reporting and evidence collection); and options such as protective custody.

- DOCs should never hold minors together with adult prisoners. The two groups should be kept entirely separate from each other.

- Prisoners who, by virtue of the risk factors discussed in chapter IV of this report, are clear potential targets for sexual abuse should be warned of their possible vulnerability and offered protective custody or other protective options.

- DOCs should avoid double-celling prisoners. If double-celling is unavoidable, corrections authorities should take extreme care in selecting appropriate cellmates, giving due regard to the risk factors described in chapter IV of this report and to inmates' preferences. Prisoners with a known history of committing sexual abuse or harassment should never be double-celled, whether or not they have been subject to disciplinary proceedings or prosecution.

- All DOC employees, from high-level officials to line staff, should receive detailed and realistic training on the issue of prisoner-on-prisoner sexual abuse. Line staff, in particular, should be trained regarding how to respond to inmate complaints or fears of sexual abuse, risk factors increasing prisoners' likelihood of being subject to such abuse, and common scenarios leading to such abuse. Particular attention should be paid to the problem of staff homophobia, a problem that frequently reveals itself in an unsympathetic and unprofessional response to the problem of prisoner-on-prisoner sexual abuse, particularly when gay inmates (or inmates perceived as gay) are the target of such abuse.

- Appropriate classification policies should be instituted and strictly followed to separate at-risk inmates from potential aggressors. Particular attention should be given to the risk factors described in chapter IV of this report.

- The conditions of protective custody and safekeeping units—areas in which vulnerable prisoners are held—should not be punitive in nature. Although heightened security concerns may entail additional restrictions on inmate movement, conditions should otherwise be kept as normal as possible. In particular, educational, vocational, and other program opportunities should be made available to inmates held in such units.

- Psychological counseling should be promptly provided to all victims of prisoner-on-prisoner sexual abuse.

- Given the element of racial bias in many instances of prisoner-on-prisoner sexual abuse, steps should be taken to address racial tensions in the inmate population. DOC staff should receive racial sensitivity training. Racial slurs and other forms of harassment—whether from inmates or staff—should not be tolerated.

- In the design of correctional facilities, attention should be given to the problem of prisoner-on-prisoner violence and sexual abuse. All areas should be easily monitored by and accessible to DOC staff. Cells should be designed for a single inmate.

- Effective data collection should be undertaken. Statistics on prisoner-on-prisoner sexual abuse must be disaggregated from statistics on overall prison violence. Information on disciplinary actions and criminal prosecutions of perpetrators of prisoner-on-prisoner sexual abuse should also be collected. Data should be compiled and made public on an annual basis.

- In general, abusive prison conditions, marked by overcrowding, custodial abuse, lack of work, vocational, and educational opportunities, etc., should be remedied, as such conditions encourage inmate-on-inmate violence and sexual abuse.

II. To State and Local Prosecutors

- Strictly enforce state criminal laws prohibiting rape by investigating and prosecuting instances of prisoner-on-prisoner rape. Do not abdicate responsibility for prison abuses by allowing corrections authorities to handle them via internal disciplinary procedures.

S.M.

Two of them held me down while the other raped me . . . . I stayed in my cell all day, skipped lunch. I didn't say anything to my cellmate about it. I was so embarrassed I had let it happen to myself.[1]

Q. Do you know that if you would comply with the T.D.C. [prison] rules on shaving and cutting your hair, then you would be released from closed custody, right?

A. I feel after so much amount of time, and in that time period I would be assaulted. And the reason for my continuing to disobey the rules is to be placed in special cell restrictions where I stay in my cell basically 24 hours a day.[2]

S.M. was only eighteen when he entered Texas prison; he was twenty-one when he was first raped. But from the very beginning predatory inmates targeted him. S.M.'s strategy for avoiding victimization was to violate prison rules—to refuse to shave, to cut his hair, or go to work—so that, as punishment, he would be kept safe in a locked cell. For three years, he managed to protect himself in this way.

S.M. started out in March 1994 at High Tower Unit, a safe minimum security prison. He only stayed there for a few months and then was transferred to another unit to get psychiatric treatment for depression. Within a week, other prisoners were threatening him, trying to coerce him into giving up his allowance for the prison commissary. Although S.M. is six feet tall, he is not a fighter. He has a gentle, subdued personality and a young face.

S.M. was on the minimum custody level, but he was exposed to closed custody (maximum security) prisoners at his job working in the fields.

Fearful because of threatening notes he had received, S.M. refused to go out to work one day and was punished by being placed on special cell restrictions, essentially, being forced to stay all day in his cell. But the disciplinary violation he received made his custody level drop down to closed custody, where he ended up with a much more violent set of prisoners. When S.M. entered the general population of closed custody after his thirty days under special cell restrictions, "the inmates swarmed me. They all wanted me to pay protection: the blacks, whites and Mexicans. I didn't know how to fight, couldn't stick up for myself."[3]

S.M. was forced to "ride"—to pay protection—but to escape to a locked cell he began violating prison rules by refusing to shave, to cut his hair, and to work. He spent nearly all of his three years at this facility locked in his cell under special cell restrictions. Sometimes other inmates were placed together with him but he spent much of the time alone.[4] Having complained to guards about his problems with other inmates, to no avail, he thought this was the best way to stay safe.

In January 1997 S.M. was transferred to another unit and placed on a medium custody wing. He wanted to manage with other prisoners and for a month or so this seemed possible. But soon some prisoners who knew him from his previous facility were moved to his wing. "They spread rumors about the fact that I rode," S.M. related. "Then the inmates started swarming. They knew I was easy."[5]

Under threat of assault, S.M. had his family deposit money into the bank accounts of people named by some Crips gang members who had targeted him. "And that apparently wasn't enough," S.M. later testified under oath. "And I had three of them run in my cell and sexually assault me."[6] Two of the gang members held him down while the other anally raped him. It was morning, and S.M. could hear the television on in the dayroom; although he yelled he knew the officers outside would not hear him. Before the prisoners left his cell they warned that if he told anyone they would eventually "get" him, no matter where he went.

S.M. was stunned, "in shock," he later said.[7] He skipped lunch, and then at dinner approached a sergeant to try to explain the situation, but he could not manage to describe it directly. He simply told the sergeant that he was having "serious problems"; he claims that the sergeant dismissed him.

The very next day he refused to go to work in order to be placed on special cell restrictions. He was locked in a cell with a Mexican gang member who, S.M. said, "had heard rumors" about him. One night a few days later, the other prisoner attacked S.M., pointing a shank at him and threatening to kill him. Out of fear, "I let him do what he wanted," S.M. said. "It was impossible to tell a CO because I was still locked in the cell with the guy. The CO could walk away and I'd get stabbed. It went on for three days in a row: we had anal sex two times—whenever the guy wanted."[8]

After the first rape, S.M. filled out a form requesting to see a psychiatrist, stating that he was contemplating suicide. Three days later, S.M. was brought in to see him. S.M. immediately broke down and started crying, telling him what had happened. After a medical examination, S.M. was brought to speak to investigators working for the prison's gang intelligence division. He told them exactly what happened. They asked if he wanted to prosecute the case and S.M. responded no. He was afraid of being labeled a snitch—of increasing the likelihood of being assaulted again.

The psychiatrist put him on single-cell restriction for his protection. At a hearing of the Unit Classification Committee (UCC) a few months later it was recommended that S.M. be placed on safekeeping in another prison. For four months, S.M. was in a single cell in "transit status," waiting for state officials to review the UCC's decision about safekeeping. In July 1997, the state authorities rejected S.M.'s placement on safekeeping, and he was placed back in medium custody with a single cell restriction.

The last time S.M. was raped was the worst, he later said: the most violent and the most painful. It was in October 1997, and the prison officials were insisting that S.M. return to the general population of closed custody. S.M. tried to refuse but they placed him in handcuffs and brought him to a cell. His new cellmate, an African American prisoner, told S.M. that he had "'heard about him'"—that he knew that S.M. was a "willing homosexual"— but that even if S.M. wasn't willing, they were still going to have sex.[8] S.M. was terrified but he tried to stall. He pretended to go along with his cellmate but put off having sex. At breakfast time, after his cellmate had left, he told the guards what was happening: that he was being threatened with rape. The guards locked him in a shower and called a sergeant. When the sergeant arrived, S.M. explained his situation, but the sergeant said, "that he didn't care, that he would force me back into the cell if he had to, that if I didn't come out of the shower that he would beat me himself."[9]

S.M. agreed to return to his cell but when the officers unlocked the shower he ran to the dayroom at the front of the wing. The sergeant then escorted S.M. to the front desk and handcuffed him, saying, "'you're going back to the cell whether you like it or not.'"[10] The officers placed S.M. in the recreation yard for a time, then informed him that he could either return to his cell voluntarily or be forced to return. S.M. replied that he was refusing housing.

> I was begging them: "Take me to prehearing detention." They refused; they handcuffed me and carried me back to the cell, and threw me in it. By then it was around 3 a.m. My cellie started hitting me. He was a huge guy. I gave up.[11]

By then, because of his past assaults, S.M. was aware that proof of rape could be obtained by the use of a rape kit. He desperately wanted the prison authorities to collect evidence of the rape. Early in the morning, when his cellmate left the cell, he reported the rape to a guard, who told him that he would tell the sergeant what had happened. But for several hours, no one came to investigate. When S.M. was released from his cell for lunch, he found a sergeant and reported the rape. The sergeant handcuffed S.M. and left him on the recreation yard for an hour; finally around noon S.M. was brought to the infirmary and examined for rape. He was later informed that the examination showed no evidence of rape—unsurprising given the amount of time that had elapsed since the assault occurred.

"Two of them held me down while the other raped me . . . . I stayed in my cell all day, skipped lunch. I didn't say anything to my cellmate about it. I was so embarrassed I had let it happen to myself."

Since the last rape, S.M. has been held in a single cell. When Human Rights Watch interviewed him, he was in a psychiatric unit, having tried to commit suicide in late January 1999. Because of the countless disciplinary cases he had accrued for violating prison hygiene rules, he still had several years of his ten year sentence left to serve, and was feeling depressed and scared about the future. His projected release date was August 2003.

C.R.

i am a gay Spanish male. . . . back in "92" i was on the Hightower unit and i was Beating and Raped By Texas Syndicate gang members. So the officers Shipped me to Ferguson and Placed me on safe-keeping . . . . Then in "94" i got Removed From safe-keeping because i had "3" fights in "9" months. Then i was Placed on Close-Custody Population and i was beating in the Cell Several Times by Mexican Mafia gang member's and then They Started Saling me to The Black inmate's and if i Refused i got Beat up. Well During this Time i Contracted HIV by a Black inmate . . . . Where in the middle of may i was Beating and "Raped" agian. i Reported it and went to the Doctor 2 Day's later and the Doctor Did not even Do a "Rape Kit." Then i Was moved to a Different Cell with a hispanic inmate who on August of "95" attacked me and Beat me for not Participate in sexual act's with him. Then i was moved to another Close Custody wing where i was Raped and was Paying Protection to another inmate. So That's when i Decided to Protect Myself and was Placed in seg for it. [12]

C.R. was only nineteen when he was sent to prison in Texas for violating his probation restrictions. He was first placed in a minimum security unit, which he remembered as a relatively easy, relaxed place. Because of disciplinary problems, he was soon transferred to a higher security facility. "I messed up," he admitted. "It was easy to get into trouble, so I did." [13]

A handsome, outgoing bisexual man, C.R. is originally from San Antonio, Texas. When he arrived at the new unit, he quickly understood that his origins would be a defining factor for his treatment there. Hispanic prisoners grouped themselves by hometowns: for each locality, the dayroom had a separate bench, or benches, controlled by inmates from the area. Unfortunately for C.R., he was the only prisoner on his wing from San Antonio. While other Hispanic prisoners had to fight once or twice—to be tested—before they were allowed to sit on a bench, C.R. was forced to fight constantly.

C.R. told Human Rights Watch that one day about a month after his transfer to the wing, when he was asleep in his cell, a group of six Hispanic prisoners slipped into his cell and raped him. They beat him up with locks and canned goods, and then held him down on the bed. Afterwards, C.R. told a guard what happened. According to C.R.'s account, he was not brought to a doctor for any testing, nor was any investigation done into the incident, but he was transferred to another prison and placed on safekeeping status.

Prisoners in "safekeeping," although they live in their own separate housing areas, still have a fair amount of contact with regular inmates; they meet them in the showers, the cafeteria, and at work. As many safekeeping inmates have emphasized to Human Rights Watch, these encounters are the opportunity for inmates from general population to harass and threaten them. The general population inmates generally despise prisoners in safekeeping, viewing them as weak, cowardly, and homosexual. C.R. explained:

> If you were on safekeeping, the Hispanics didn't want anything to do with you. You couldn't even claim a hometown. They'd say you were disgracing their hometown. . . . Whenever we were around them, they'd tell us, 'get your ass out of here.'[14]

Prisoners from C.R.'s previous unit had been transferred to the general population of his new unit; he said that they were particularly aggressive toward him. C.R. ended up getting into several fights with general population inmates, he said, including one time in the cafeteria when a prisoner from general population tried to stab him. "I was young," C.R. remembered. "I didn't like being disrespected by the dudes in general population."

In mid-1994, C.R. was transferred out of safekeeping because of these fights. The hearing officers told him that if he was able to fight then he could handle general population. They placed him in a close custody (maximum security) unit. There, C.R. was constantly having to fight to protect himself.

> I broke my hand fighting and lost my two front teeth. It was a very, very violent camp. You had to box; you weren't allowed to wrestle. I had to fight lots of guys back to back—one after the other. You get tired; you make mistakes. If you're knocked down and don't get up, you a 'ho'; you have to ride. The bosses will stand there and watch it.[15]

C.R. said that Mexican Mafia gang members ended up making him "ride" with them, then they "sold" him to a group of African American inmates. C.R. believes that he contracted HIV during this period. He claims that he reported the sexual abuse several times and finally, in March 1995, he was transferred to another prison unit. At his initial classification hearing at the new unit, C.R. said, he requested safekeeping, telling the warden that he was gay and vulnerable to abuse, but the warden replied that he "didn't care." C.R. was again placed in close custody.

In mid-May, C.R. said, he was beaten and raped again. A Hispanic inmate "popped" the door to his cell in the middle of the night, entered and anally raped him. A few hours later, C.R. reported the rape to guards who were making their rounds, but they did not remove him from his cell. The next morning, he went to the infirmary, but was not able to see a doctor for two days. By that time, it was too late to conduct a rape examination.

If you're knocked down and don't get up, you a 'ho'; you have to ride. The bosses will stand there and watch it.

C.R. was moved onto a different wing where his problems continued. On August 31, 1995, he said, his cellmate badly beat C.R. because he refused to have sex with him. C.R. was then transferred to another wing, where he said he was extorted for money and was again raped. He filed a life endangerment grievance toward the end of the year but prison officials again denied him safekeeping. Finally, in February 1996, prison officials confiscated two homemade weapons from his cell and placed him in administrative segregation, where he was given a single cell.

C.R. filed suit against prison officials in federal district court, challenging their repeated failure to protect him from sexual assault. In a hearing before the court, C.R. testified that he wanted the court to "'make it known' to prison officials that they need to do a better job of investigating such incidents and to order prison officials to place him in safekeeping."[16] The court reviewed C.R.'s disciplinary history, agreeing with prison officials that "he was not a good candidate for safekeeping."[17] Without disputing the fact that C.R. had been subject to a year and a half of violent sexual abuse, the court then conclusorily stated that C.R. had "failed to allege facts showing the Defendants disregarded an excessive risk to his safety."[18] Not only did the court dismiss C.R.'s claim, the court deemed it "frivolous": lacking any basis in law.

BACKGROUND

With one out of every 140 people in the United States behind bars, the question of prisoner-on-prisoner sexual abuse can no longer be ignored. The staggering numbers of people filling the country's prisons and jails mean that what happens in these institutions is necessarily of consequence to society, for most prisoners do, finally, return to the communities from which they came. Over half a million people are released from prison each year, and many millions more are cycled through local jails.[1] To disregard the egregious abuses that affect these people is to forget that prisons are not cut off from the world outside.

The Size and Growth of the U.S. Inmate Population

By any measure, the U.S. inmate population is enormous—in absolute numbers, in the proportion of U.S. residents behind bars, and in comparison with global figures. With the country's prisons and jails holding some two million adults—roughly one in every 140 persons—the rate of incarceration in the United States is about 727 prisoners per 100,000 residents.[2] No other country in the world is known to incarcerate as many people, and only a small handful of countries have anything approaching a similar rate of incarceration.[3] Most European countries, for example, imprison fewer than 100 people per 100,000 residents, a rate more than seven times lower than that of the United States.

These high figures do not represent longstanding patterns of incarceration, but instead are the consequence of radical changes in criminal justice policies over the past two decades. Incarceration rates remained relatively stable at much lower levels through most of the twentieth century, rising and falling according to factors such as economic growth and depression, but remaining within reasonable limits. Rates began to climb somewhat in the mid-1970s, with the growth rate accelerating in the 1980s and particularly the 1990s. In 1985, the inmate population stood at three-quarters of a million; by 1990 it was over 1.1 million. Since that time, on average, the inmate population has grown 6.5 percent annually, with the federal prison population growing at an even faster rate than that of the states.[4]

These increases reflect an important overall shift in state and federal sentencing rules. In particular, they are indicative of a general trend toward longer prison terms, more stringent parole policies, mandatory minimum sentences and, most recently, "three strikes" laws.[5] The sentences handed out in the United States for a variety of crimes, including nonviolent crimes, are now among the longest anywhere.[6]

The Structure of Imprisonment

Rather than a single national system of imprisonment, the United States has a federal correctional system, separate state correctional systems, and thousands of jails managed at the local level. They make up a complex network of people and institutions, involving thousands of correctional and detention facilities, hundreds of thousands of employees, and billions of dollars in operating costs.

The conceptual distinction should be recognized between correctional facilities—i.e., prisons—which are designed for convicted inmates—and detention facilities—i.e., jails—which are designed to hold unsentenced inmates on a relatively short-term basis after arrest and pending trial. In practice, nonetheless, there is a degree of overlap between the two types of facilities. Inmates serving sentences of a year or less normally remain in local jails and, due to prison overcrowding, even some inmates serving long sentences may be housed there.[7] The resulting mixing of convicted and unconvicted prisoners contravenes international human rights standards.[8]

As of July 1999, slightly more than two-thirds of all U.S. prisoners were incarcerated in federal or state prisons, with the remainder detained in local jails.[9] The federal inmate population was estimated at 129,678, of which

117,331 were housed in facilities operated by the federal Bureau of Prisons.[10] These facilities held persons convicted of federal crimes, that is, crimes prosecuted in the federal court system under federal law. The state prison population—consisting of persons convicted of state crimes—totaled more than 1.1 million. The single largest state correctional systems were those of California, with over 150,000 prisoners, and Texas, with over 130,000.[11] Nationally, there are some 1,375 state-operated penal institutions (mostly prisons but including other types of facilities).[12]

The expansion in prison capacity in recent years, via new prison construction, has not kept pace with the growth in the inmate population. Overall, in mid-1995, the nation's 1,500 adult correctional facilities had a capacity of 976,000 beds, well short of the number needed. The degree of overcrowding varied from system to system, with some state prison systems operating at up to 89 percent over their design capacities, and the federal correctional system at 19 percent over its rated capacity.[13]

Nearly one-third of all U.S. inmates are held in jails and other short-term detention facilities operated by the county or local governments where they are located.[14] Such facilities are normally managed by county sheriff's departments, city police, or other local-level law enforcement agencies. There are approximately 3,300 jails in the United States, most of which are small in size. Indeed, according to a 1988 survey, two-thirds of local jails had daily populations of fewer than fifty inmates. Although overall jail capacity figures appear roughly sufficient, numerous jails are woefully overcrowded.[15]

Another trend over the last fifteen years affecting both prisons and jails is that of "privatization," by which states pay private companies to construct and manage their penal facilities. As of May 1999, private correctional facilities in the United States had an overall capacity of 132,933 beds.[16] Leading the way toward the corporate management of corrections was the state of Texas, with forty-three such facilities. It is likely that privatization, unless accompanied by stringent public oversight, brings with it an increased risk of inmate mistreatment and abuse.[17]

With or without private prisons, the costs of incarceration in the United States are enormous. Nearly $40 billion annually is spent on prisons and jails, making corrections one of the largest single items on many states' budgets, above their spending on higher education or child care.[18]

Characteristics of the U.S. Prisoner Population

A review of U.S. inmate statistics discloses certain conspicuous facts. To begin with, the prisoner population of the United States is largely male: as is true around the world, men make up more than 90 percent of all prisoners.[19] Also, in comparison with people outside prison, the inmate population is heavily weighted toward ethnic and racial minorities, particularly African Americans. Overall, African Americans make up some 44 percent of the prisoner population, while whites constitute 40 percent, Hispanics 15 percent, with other minorities making up the remaining 1 to 2 percent.[20] Relative to their proportions in the U.S. population as a whole, black males are more than twice as likely to be incarcerated as Hispanic males and seven times as likely as whites.

Some two-thirds of U.S. prisoners are held for nonviolent offenses, many of them drug offenses. Indeed, the number of prisoners incarcerated for drug crimes has increased sevenfold in the last twenty years.[21] To a large extent, the disproportionate impact of incarceration on African Americans reflects the impact of the country's drug war, as arrest rates for drug offenses are six times higher for blacks than they are for whites.[22]

The majority of prisoners are between eighteen and forty years old, but the trend toward longer sentences and more restrictive parole policies has swelled the ranks of elderly inmates.[23] At the same time—and in violation of international standards—there has been a notable increase over the past decade in the numbers of juveniles held in adult penal facilities.[24] As of 1995, an average of 6,000 juveniles were held in adult jails on any given day.[25] If found guilty of a crime, such juveniles were normally sent to adult prisons, which housed several thousand young offenders by the late 1990s.[26] Indeed, in 1997, an estimated 7,400 juveniles were admitted to state prison.[27] A 1995 survey of state prison practices found that twenty-seven correctional departments held such juveniles in adult prisons; since then these numbers have likely risen.[28]

Conditions and Abuses

Overcrowded and understaffed, filled with too many idle prisoners facing long terms of incarceration, many U.S. penal facilities are rife with extortion, violence, and other abuses. Due to public reluctance to spend any more than necessary to warehouse the criminal population, inmates generally have scant work, training, educational, treatment or counseling opportunities. A small minority of correctional staff physically abuse inmates; many more are simply indifferent to abuses that inmates inflict on each other.

Guard violence, if not endemic, is more than sporadic in many penal facilities. In 1999, for example, news stories detailed a series of horrific stories of guard abuse—stories of inmates being beaten with fists and batons, fired at unnecessarily with shotguns or stunned with electronic devices, slammed face first onto concrete floors, and even raped by correctional officers.[29] In some instances, entire state prison systems are found to be pervaded with abuse. A March 1999 federal court decision concluded, for example, that the frequency of "wholly unnecessary physical aggression" perpetrated by guards in Texas prisons reflected a "culture of sadistic and malicious violence" found there.[30]

Inter-prisoner violence, extortion, harassment, and other abuse is even more common. Indeed, it has been estimated that as many as 70 percent of inmates are assaulted by other inmates each year.[31] In 1998, the most recent year for which national statistics are available, seventy-nine inmates were killed and many thousands more were injured so severely that they required medical attention.[32] In 1997, 10 percent of state inmates and 3 percent of federal inmates reported being injured in a fight since entering prison.[33] Recognizing the problem, a recent study of New York state prisons focusing on criminal conduct by inmates spoke of the "extraordinary amount of crime committed in state prisons annually," and concluded that rather than preventing crime, in many cases incarceration "merely shifts the locus of criminal activity away from neighborhoods to correctional facilities."[34]

As in the streets, gang activity is an inescapable fact of present-day U.S. prisons. Gangs exist in every prison system and every large jail.[35] In 1992, the American Correctional Association (ACA) conducted a national survey of prison gang activity, identifying over 1,000 different gangs (labeled "security threat groups") with a total membership of over 46,000.[36] The actual numbers are probably much higher, however.[37] The large majority of prison gangs have counterpart groups on the street; indeed some of them, such as the Crips and the Bloods, are primarily known as street gangs. Gang members are much more likely than other prisoners to be involved in violent and extortionate activities.[38]

Personal antagonisms are the cause of some inter-prisoner violence, but financial incentives probably drive a larger proportion of it. Not only are significant numbers of inmates indigent, they are generally not compensated for prison jobs or are paid extremely low wages, leaving prisoners without outside financial support to seek other ways to obtain money. Extortion is common in many penal facilities, with many inmates being forced to pay "protection" money in order to be safe from physical attack. In addition, almost every prison has an illegal economy based on contraband goods and services: everything from sex to drugs to alcohol to weapons. Much prisoner-on-prisoner violence, particularly gang-related violence, centers around efforts to seize or maintain control of this economy.[39]

Abuses against inmates, whether committed by other prisoners or by guards, are rarely effectively prosecuted. Because police do not patrol prisons to monitor crime there, prison abuses are only prosecuted when they are reported. Although inmates nominally enjoy the right to file complaints with local police and prosecutors regarding prison crimes, Human Rights Watch's research suggests that local officials generally ignore complaints made by prisoners.[40] Nor do prison employees often report crimes that occur in their facilities.[41] Although overall figures are lacking, it is evident that criminal charges are brought only in the most egregious cases—or in instances of prisoner violence against guards—and that many instances of violence, extortion or harassment do not even result in administrative sanctions against the responsible party. The rule of impunity holds true both for inter-prisoner abuses and abuses committed by guards against inmates. In California, for example, not a single local prosecutor has ever prosecuted a guard for prison shootings that have killed thirty-nine inmates and wounded more than 200 over the past decade.[42]

Punishments meted out by internal disciplinary mechanisms—prison justice systems—are the only sanction prisoners are likely to face for committing prison abuses. All penal facilities have administrative rules and some form of disciplinary procedure for adjudicating violations of those rules. Sanctions for violations range from simple reprimands to long-term confinement in disciplinary isolation to loss of good-time credit.[43]

As will be described in detail below, those prisons most conducive to inter-prisoner violence—because of lax supervision, poor inmate classification, a failure to prosecute abuses, few work, training or educational opportunities, intense racial antagonisms, and other problems—are also those most likely to be plagued by inmate-on-inmate sexual abuse.

PRISONER CLASSIFICATION AND SEPARATION

Most prisons, and even some jails, have a system of prisoner classification by which the inmate population is divided into groups. At the institutional level is the well known distinction between minimum, medium and maximum security facilities, with prisoners assigned to a given security level according to variables such as the severity of their offense, their perceived dangerousness, their expected length of incarceration and their history of escapes or violence.[44] Within a given facility, similarly, prisoners may be divided up among different security levels, housing placements, programs, etc. Initial classification decisions are normally made when the prisoner enters the prison system; the prisoner's conduct is then supposed to determine subsequent decisions as to changes in classification status. The goal of classification is to address security and program needs—reducing violence, limiting security risks, and facilitating rehabilitation efforts.

In the nineteenth and much of the twentieth century, racial segregation was commonplace in U.S. prisons and jails—indeed, in some cases segregation was statutorily required. In the South, blacks and whites were typically housed in separate prisons, while in northern states prisoners were segregated by race within the same facility.[45] A Supreme Court decision banned the practice in 1968,[46] but nonetheless many penal facilities continue to separate inmates by race, sometimes relying on surrogate variables such as gang affiliation or following inmate preferences for self-segregation.[47]

Prisons and jails typically have a protective custody classification for isolating and protecting prisoners believed likely to be victimized by others. Prisoners assigned to this status are usually housed in separate areas of the facility, in which conditions are often highly restrictive. Nationally, nearly 2 percent of prison inmates are being held in protective custody, although the average in a few states is over 5 percent.[48] In addition, some states have devised statuses similar to protective custody such as "safekeeping" in which vulnerable inmates may be held. Texas, for example, makes little provision for protective custody, but keeps a few thousand inmates in safekeeping.[49] Yet another common management technique is to transfer threatened prisoners to another facility, away from the inmates seeking to victimize them.

As one court explained, proper classification "is essential to the operation of an orderly and safe prison . . . . It enables the institution to gauge the proper custody level of an inmate, to identify the inmate's educational, vocational, and psychological needs, and to separate non-violent inmates from the more predatory."[50] Conversely, the failure to properly classify and separate prisoners is a significant contributing factor to prison violence.

> **"I hate to say this but if you weren't racist when you came to prison more than likely you will be when you leave."**

State correctional departments generally have written policies that set out the criteria relevant to classification decisions. Many prison systems have a central classification office that oversees such decisions, but the primary decision-makers are the classification committees in each institution. Given the importance of proper inmate classification, these decisions are frequently hotly disputed: prisoners often see them as arbitrary and unfair. Yet there are very few legal constraints on the classification powers of correctional departments. In general, prisoners have no legal basis for challenging such decisions, as due process protections are deemed to apply only when the changed conditions are extraordinarily harsh.[51]

RACIAL TENSIONS

Racial antagonisms are another important contributing factor to prison violence and abuse. In the prison context, it bears emphasizing, the racial tensions that pervade U.S. society are significantly magnified. Even though in prison, more so than in the surrounding society, members of different racial groups are placed into close contact with each other, racial divisions are one of the dominant features of inmate life. Prisoners' social relationships are largely determined by race; their gang affiliation, if they have one, is racially defined; and whatever racist beliefs they may have held prior to their imprisonment are likely to be significantly strengthened over the course of their stay in prison.[52]

In their correspondence with Human Rights Watch, both black and white prisoners emphasized the importance placed on racial distinctions in prison. A white prisoner asserted: "I hate to say this but if you weren't racist when you came to prison more than likely you will be when you leave. In Texas prisons *race* is the main issue and until people wake up and realize that nothing will change!"[53]

Describing the prevalence of racist beliefs in prison, an African American prisoner who described himself as relatively oblivious to racial distinctions before entering prison said:

> Most blacks see whites as "The Man" or "The Law!". . . . I may be beating a dead horse when I say this, but black men as a whole do not trust white law officials, male or female, from judge to lawyer. Most feel that the legal system is fundamentally racist and officers are the most visible symbol of a corrupt institution & with good reason . . . . So is it any wonder that when a white man comes to prison, that blacks see him as a target.[54]

The resentment voiced by this inmate was echoed by numerous other African American prisoners. Many were acutely aware of racial disparities in imprisonment, and of incidents such as the Rodney King beating and the police shooting of Ghanaian immigrant Amadou Diallo. One inmate went so far as to assert:

> The prison system is just a stage of the final solution to get rid of America's so-called problem, especially the Blacks and the Latinos. I ask the question [is it] bad luck, good luck or a set up that the prison system in the U.S. is half filled with Blacks when in fact they don't even make-up half of the population of the U.S.?[55]

The anger of many black inmates toward whites is met by white inmates' hatred of blacks. The white supremacist movement has many adherents in the prison system. Many white prisoners told Human Rights Watch that they were uncomfortable with blacks and would prefer to live in a racially segregated environment. A few espoused virulently racist views. More so than African American prisoners, many whites asserted that the prison experience had made them racist—or, as they tended to put it, "racially aware."

An African-American inmate sent Human Rights Watch a racist pamphlet that he said was circulating among white prisoners. Explaining his view of why many incarcerated whites were attracted to white suprematist groups, he said:

> Because of the lop-sided ratio of whites to minorities, most whites in T.D.C.J. rush into the A.B. or A.C. (Aryan Brotherhood & Aryan Circle, respectively) . . . . The A.B. & A.C. create humoungous propaganda to subtly turn non-racist incarcerated whites into bigoted fanatics. Believe it or not, the Protocols of Zion are still making the rounds real regular with the Turner Diaries & this [pamphlet] I'm sending you.

Whatever the causes, race has become the great divide in prison. Not only whites versus blacks, it is also Hispanics versus blacks, whites versus Hispanics, and so on. The names of many prison gangs—the Mexican Mafia, the Black Gangster Disciples, the Aryan Circle, the White Knights, the Black Guerrilla Family, the Aryan Brotherhood, and the Latin Kings, among others—indicate their racially exclusionary nature, while even gangs with non-racially-defined names, such as the Bloods, are nonetheless largely restricted to a single racial group. Many prison riots are racially motivated, sometimes pitting one racially defined gang against another.[56]

The level of racial antagonism appears to vary from jurisdiction to jurisdiction, with prisons in many Southern states being particularly tense. Certain prison systems seem to have almost no positive social interaction—not even the most trivial—between members of different races. A white prisoner in Texas, where racial tensions are particularly acute, summed up the situation there:

> On maximum security wings, blacks and whites don't even sit together. The Blacks have there own benches and the Mexicans have theres and the Whites if there are enough to fight for one has theres. And if a white went to sit on a Black bench he would be jumped on ditto for blacks and Mexicans. Even in celling assignments the whites will refuse to live with a colored or a mexican

because there cellie who has friends will steel there stuff or they will jump on the white dude so they refuse to live with them. And if a white dude kicks it or talks to blacks or mexicans a lot of the whites will run court on him (court means an ass whoppin). Its the same for blacks and mexicans.... The whites hate the Blacks and Mexicans because those two races have a lot of people in here and take advantage of us by making the small and week ones ride or turn them out, and the big ones have to fight all the time.[57] If you come in here as a non-racial white man and you fight for your proporty more than likely when you leave you'll be a full fledge KKK member! There are a lot of racial groups here and with the way the whites get treated, they get mixed up in those groups and become haters. Prison is the best recruiting ground the white power movement has![58]

Grievance Mechanisms

Prisoners nominally have the opportunity to complain of abuses and other unfair practices using internal grievance mechanisms. Such mechanisms typically involve a great deal of paperwork—with many forms and several-stage appeals processes—often to little practical effect.

Grievance procedures are usually initiated with the filing of a grievance form by a prisoner. These forms often include a box that can be marked if the situation is of an emergency nature. Emergency grievances are supposed to be handled immediately, while normal grievances are supposed to be processed within a set period, usually fifteen days or a month.

The flaws of grievance mechanisms will be discussed in greater detail below, but in general they tend to be plagued by a lack of confidentiality, which may expose the complaining prisoner to retaliation by others, a bias against prisoner testimony, and a failure to seriously investigate prisoners' allegations. Grievances are frequently denied with rote responses that show little individualized attention to the underlying problem.

Under the Prison Litigation Reform Act, passed in 1996 (see discussion below), prisoners must exhaust the remedies open to them via internal grievance procedures before they are allowed to file suit in federal court to challenge prison abuses.[59] This change in the law makes the deficiencies of grievance mechanisms all the more troubling.

Oversight of Treatment and Conditions

A great many prison abuses occur because prisons are closed institutions subject to little outside scrutiny. Such abuses become much less likely when officials know that outsiders will be inspecting their facilities and that ill-treatment and poor conditions will be denounced. Regular access to penal facilities by outside monitors—from judges to national and international human rights groups to independent government bodies—can thus play an immensely positive role in preventing or minimizing human rights abuses. Recognizing this principle, international standards of good prison practice emphasize the need for independent and objective monitoring of penal facilities.[60]

Prison monitoring in the United States falls far short of what is needed. Unlike some countries, the U.S. has no official prison monitoring body. Instead, responsibility for outside oversight of detention conditions varies from state to state, with some jurisdictions having few if any monitoring mechanisms. The American Correctional Association (ACA), a private nonprofit organization, administers a voluntary accreditation program for U.S. prisons and jails under which conditions and policies are evaluated, yet the majority of state and local penal facilities choose not to participate in this scheme.[61] Some states have inspector generals or other outside ombudsmen who visit penal institutions, while others have investigatory bodies within corrections departments that operate with a degree of independence. A few states, such as Illinois and New York, allow certain nongovernmental groups to visit their prisons.[62] Human Rights Watch has, however, found that some states routinely deny requests for access made by it and other nongovernmental bodies.

Local jails, even more than state correctional facilities, tend to escape outside oversight. Some states have established state jail standards by which to evaluate the conditions in their jails, but compliance with them is largely unenforced.

The lack of comprehensive and effective outside monitoring mechanisms has meant that the federal judiciary has become, however reluctantly, a sort of default national prison oversight body. But as described in detail in chapter III, judicial monitoring of prison abuses has declined in effectiveness over the past decade, just as the inmate population has grown dramatically.

R.G.

*My abuse started in the County Jail where I was raped by four inmates . . . .
[In prison, a few years later,] I was put in a cell with a gang member who
made me give him oral sex. . . . . [After reporting the incident to two officers,] I went to see a psychologist who told me that I'd caused that inmate
to sexually abuse me because I walked around thinking that I was better than
the others. He said that I should come down out of the air . . . . [After being
transferred to another facility and sexually abused again,] I was put back in
that same building, in a different cell. Still I was being asked for sex and told
that I would have to give myself over one way or another; at this point (looking back on the matter), I can see that I was going through a brake down
mentally. Anyway that night I'd made up my mind that I was taking my life
for it seemed as if that was the only way out of that Hell. So the sleeping
medication they was giving me, I saved for 8 days which came to 800 mg and
I took them . . . . It is truly impossible to put into words what goes through
one's mind when becoming a victim of rape. Being made into a person of no
self worth, [being] remade into what ever the person or gang doing the raping wants you to be.*

R.G., California inmate, October 1, 1996

*Inmate is an effeminate with a proclivity toward being sexually assaulted. He
cannot mainline at San Quentin.*

Date: 01/02/91   P. Hicks, M.D., Chief Psychiatrist

R.G. is a gay, middle-aged, African American prisoner whom prison psychiatrists have classified as "effeminate." Skinny and of medium height, R.G. weighs only 135 pounds and sports thick, black-rimmed glasses. Outside of prison, his looks might peg him as a nerdy intellectual: bookish but not necessarily effeminate. Rare among inmates, he claims two years of college education, having worked for a time as a substitute teacher in Baltimore. All of his crimes are nonviolent: car theft, burglary, etc.

Although R.G. was raped in prison, it was in jail that he suffered the most vicious sexual abuse.[1] The first incident occurred in 1988, when he was confined at a Los Angeles jail for tampering with a vehicle—charges that were later dropped. R.G. was placed in a two-man cell, and on his first night there was awakened at about 1 a.m. by his cellmate and three others. Sticking a sharpened mop bucket handle into the soft skin of his neck, they warned him, "You're going to do what we want or you're going to die." They pulled him off the top bunk, where he had been sleeping, and threw him onto the bottom bunk, where they spent over an hour taking turns orally and anally penetrating him.

That morning in the inmate dining hall R.G. reported the rape to a lieutenant and said he refused to return to his cell. The lieutenant showed no interest in discovering who had committed the rape, but he did move R.G. to the "softie tank" on the thirteenth floor of the facility, where R.G. had no further problems during the four months he was held there.[2]

In 1993, R.G. was arrested on burglary charges and confined at the Los Angeles County Jail. There he was placed in a large overcrowded dormitory that held at least 500 people. Due to a bunk shortage, R.G. had to find a place to sleep on the floor, near a corner of the room. He was awakened at about 4 a.m. by six members of the Crips gang. They held a razor to his throat and forced him to give them oral sex. At 6 a.m., when all of the prisoners were brought out for breakfast, R.G. tried to report the rape to the sergeant on duty, for whom "it was a laughing matter." The sergeant forced R.G. to return to the dormitory, where he broke down, sobbing hysterically. "I just fell apart; I was scared that the situation would continue, and what really got me was the coldness of the CO when I told him what happened, that he didn't care. I was crying and crying and couldn't stop shaking."

R.G. kept banging on the window of the dormitory and finally a different officer brought him to see a lieutenant. After hearing his story, the lieutenant said he never should have been placed in that ward. He sent R.G. to a medical facility, where he was again placed in the "softie tank."

That August R.G. was transferred into the California prison system. In his initial interview with a classification officer, he explained that he was gay and had been raped by gang members, and that he needed to be housed with another gay person, or someone of small build, or a first-timer—in his words, a "softie"—and not a gang member. The sergeant on duty that night was concerned about R.G.'s safety and assigned him to a single cell, but the sergeant on duty the next night placed him in a two-man cell.

R.G.'s new cellmate was an African American gang member who became immediately aggressive, bragging about his gang connections and his violent crimes. He soon grabbed R.G. by the collar and told him, "You can do this the easy way or you can do it the hard way." Fearing that he would be badly beaten, R.G. submitted to performing oral sex. Afterwards he threw up and sat on his bed awake all night long. The next morning he told a white correctional officer what happened and the officer did nothing, saying "I don't have time to be baby-sitting you." When the prisoners were let out of their cells for dinner that evening, R.G. approached an African American officer and told him what happened. The officer brought him to a sergeant, who moved him to a single cell. His former cellmate was transferred to another prison, but no disciplinary investigation of the incident was ever conducted.

> **"On maximum security wings, blacks and whites don't even sit together. The Blacks have there own benches and the Mexicans have theres and the Whites if there are enough to fight for one has theres."**

In December 1993, R.G. was transferred to a correctional facility in Calpatria, where he again explained his vulnerability to the classification staff. He was held for about two weeks in a single cell, but was moved to a two-man cell on the evening of January 5, 1994. As the door to the cell closed, standing before R.G. was a huge African American inmate who explained that he had "bought" R.G.: that he had "paid two caps of weed and two sacks of heroin" to have R.G. moved to his cell. "'My homeboy that's the clerk in the program office saw you and made out a 154 for the lieutenant to sign to get you here. You're my property now.'"

The inmate was a prison drug dealer, and to impress R.G. he pulled out bags of narcotics: marijuana, heroin, and embalming fluid used on cigarettes. He said he made $1,700 a month selling drugs, and "if I 'sexed him up'—those were his exact words—I wouldn't have to worry about a thing. . . . He was friendly, a friendly demon, but I knew I was in a very vicious situation." That evening the cellmate offered R.G. a cup of coffee:

After my third swallow my system started feeling funny, and I knew that it was laced. I threw the rest of the coffee away and got in bed, then I threw up all over myself . . . . I'm feeling really sick, and he starts saying get up out of bed and have sex with him. I said I'm sick; he said "you don't have to do much, just take your pants off." (I go to bed fully dressed now.) I told him, "I can't, I'm sick." "Well just look down here," he said. I did, and saw him masturbating. Then he came. I stayed up all night, depressed, scared. I just couldn't face more abuse. I thought I'd rather die. In the morning when he woke up I had tied the end of my sheet around my wrist to get my veins bulging and I held a razor in my hand. I said I'd kill myself if he didn't let me leave. He knew I wasn't kidding and he said "don't worry, I'll get you out of here." He couldn't afford for me to kill myself because there'd be an investigation and he had all those drugs. He called the guards and said "get him out of here." They saw me in that setup and took me to a room with nothing in it but a rubber mattress. They kept me there for fourteen days, giving me Benedril. Every day the doctors would come in and ask me how I was feeling and then talk amongst themselves as if I wasn't there. I had nightmares that the night nurse noticed. . . . I had no chance to explain my situation to anyone. They weren't concerned about why I wanted to commit suicide, just that I wanted to.

A few weeks later, after being placed back out into the general prison population, R.G. attempted suicide:

I saved up eight days' worth of Benedrils. I drank them with some Kool-Aid and wanted to die. A CO woke me up; he was a Christian; he told me God had a better plan for me. He got the MTA [medical technician] and they pumped my stomach.[3]

After recuperating from his suicide attempt, R.G. was transferred to a protective custody unit at another California prison where he stayed for over a year. Later, he was moved to another facility, and then to another, staying in several prisons in all. He has been sexually pressured on several occasions, but only once since Folsom, in December 1997, was he forced to orally copulate another prisoner.

In late 1994, R.G. filed suit against the prison authorities for allowing him to be sexually abused and for failing to provide him with appropriate psychological treatment after his suicide attempt. His attempts to obtain legal assistance were unsuccessful: the judge denied his motion for appointment of counsel and public interest lawyers turned him down, saying that they only litigated class actions. Acting without legal counsel, he drafted his own legal papers, charging prison officials with showing "deliberate indifference" for his well-being. He asserted that their indifference was manifested in "the fact that they housed plaintiff under conditions they knew put [him] in danger, [placing] plaintiff in a cell with a inmate who had just received two (2) life sentences consecutively, this action then resulted in plaintiff being assaulted sexually."[4] The case was summarily dismissed in late 1996.

LEGAL CONTEXT

Prisoners are legally protected from human rights abuses under both U.S. and international law. Domestic legal protections include U.S. constitutional provisions, notably the Eighth Amendment, and statutory provisions such as the Civil Rights of Institutionalized Persons Act (CRIPA). International legal protections include binding treaty standards as well as a plethora of interpretative guidelines, the most comprehensive of which are the U.N. Standard Minimum Rules for the Treatment of Prisoners.

The weakness of these protections, both national and international, lies less in their substantive shortcomings than in the fact that they are not properly enforced.

National Legal Protections

Several U.S. constitutional provisions bar the abusive treatment of prisoners, primary among them the Eighth Amendment, which prohibits cruel and unusual punishment. In reviewing these protections, it is important to remember that their enforcement depends on the combined efforts of an array of governmental authorities, including the courts, Congress, and numerous federal and state executive officials. Unfortunately, actual practice in this area falls far short of authoritative pronouncements.

THE RISE AND FALL OF FEDERAL COURT SUPERVISION OF PRISON CONDITIONS

It was not until the late 1960s that U.S. courts began to take an active role in monitoring prison conditions and mandating their reform. Until then, the judicial branch had assumed an extremely deferential posture with regard to state and federal correctional authorities, leaving them to administer prisons as they saw fit.[1] As Supreme Court Justice Clarence Thomas once pointed out, in advocating a return to past practice: "For generations, judges and commentators regarded the Eighth Amendment as applying only to torturous punishments meted out by statutes or sentencing judges, and not generally to any hardship that might befall a prisoner during incarceration."[2] Indeed, the "hands off" approach advanced by Thomas held sway through the mid-twentieth century.

Nominal advances in the recognition of prisoners' rights were made in the 1940s and 1950s, but only in the 1960s and 1970s did the federal courts begin to make meaningful inroads against the abuses that plagued the nation's correctional institutions. The animating sentiments of the era, which tended to favor rehabilitation over punishment, made abusive prison conditions appear unjust, unnecessary, and counterproductive. Tragedies such as the 1972 rioting and subsequent killings at New York's Attica prison galvanized public attention to prison abuses. Following the pattern set with regard to school desegregation and other civil rights issues, a generation of prison reformers looked to the courts to rectify abuses, garnering an impressive string of legal victories.[3]

From the 1980s through the 1990s, in contrast, the pendulum swung back toward harsher, more punitive treatment of prisoners. Effective judicial oversight of conditions, in particular, was greatly reduced. Several factors encouraged this trend. In general, the rehabilitative view of incarceration was increasingly called into question by commentators who, focusing on high recidivism rates, advocated in its place a more explicitly retributive model of imprisonment.[4] At the same time, numerous conservative judges appointed by President Ronald Reagan joined the federal bench, most of them anxious to repudiate the "activist" approach represented by close judicial monitoring of prison conditions.[5] A series of Supreme Court rulings cut back on prisoners' rights, imposing difficult to meet requirements of showing intent and actual damages.

Meanwhile, public outrage over crime and criminals gave rise to the stereotype of the "pampered" prisoner living in a college campus-like setting, watching television all day, and filing frivolous lawsuits over petty grievances. Catering to such sentiments, officials shifted toward "tougher," more punitive forms of incarceration: building so-called supermax units, discontinuing inmate college programs, stripping prisons of weight equipment, even reinstituting chain gangs in several states.[6] Prisoners' right of access to the courts came under particular attack, as government officials vied with each to find the most outrageous legal claims to compile into lists of "Top Ten Frivolous Inmate Lawsuits."[7]

The backlash against prisoners' rights culminated in the 1996 passage of the Prison Litigation Reform Act (PLRA). The "reform" of the statute's title was a misleading reference to the severe limitations the PLRA placed on the possibility of challenging and remedying abusive prison conditions through litigation. A comprehensive set of constraints on prison litigation, the PLRA invalidates all settlements that do not include explicit findings that the challenged conditions violate federal law or the constitution. Since prison authorities are reluctant to admit to such findings, this requirement makes it much more difficult for the parties to a prison conditions suit to reach a negotiated settlement. In addition, the PLRA requires that prospective relief in prison conditions suits, such as consent decrees (judicial orders enforcing voluntary settlements), be "narrowly drawn."[8] It also arbitrarily terminates court orders against unlawful prison conditions after two years, regardless of prison authorities' degree of compliance with the orders. Further, it restricts the grant of attorneys' fees for successful prison conditions suits, severely reducing the financial viability of even the most sorely-needed prison reform efforts. Other objectionable provisions of the act limit prisoners' access to the courts by imposing court filing fees on certain indigent prisoners, and bar the recovery of damages for pain and suffering not accompanied by physical injury.[9] In short, without explicitly cutting back on prisoners' substantive rights, which are constitutionally protected, the PLRA creates formidable obstacles to the enforcement of these rights.

The PLRA has been challenged as unconstitutional in several jurisdictions, but to date the federal courts have upheld its restrictive provisions.[10]

CONSTITUTIONAL PROTECTIONS
ON PRISONERS' RIGHTS

Lawsuits challenging physical abuses against prisoners, including those in which prison authorities are sued for failing to protect inmates from attack by other inmates, usually rely upon the protection of the Eighth Amendment to the U.S. Constitution and its prohibition on "cruel and unusual punishments."[11] In cases involving pretrial detainees, as opposed to convicted prisoners, the Fifth Amendment's Due Process Clause is applicable; courts have ruled that it guarantees pretrial detainees similar protections as those provided convicted prisoners under the Eighth Amendment.[12]

In interpreting the Eighth Amendment, the courts have generally held that it requires prison officials to provide "humane conditions of confinement" and to take "reasonable measures to guarantee the safety of the inmates."[13] As the Supreme Court explained in 1989, "when the State takes a person into its custody and holds him there against his will, the Constitution imposes upon it a corresponding duty to assume some responsibility for his safety and general well being."[14] Not every discomfort or injury suffered by prisoners is legally actionable, however. Instead, as the Supreme Court has emphasized, the Eighth Amendment only bars "punishments"— not just poor treatment in itself, but "the unnecessary and wanton infliction of pain."[15] Therefore, to prove an Eighth Amendment violation, plaintiffs must show not only objective injury, either physical or psychological, but also a subjective intent on the part of authorities to cause that injury.

To pass the requirement of objective injury, the prisoner's pain must be so serious that it violates contemporary standards of decency.[16] The subjective intent requirement—that the responsible prison official acted with a "sufficiently culpable state of mind"—is somewhat more complex.[17] To begin with, the applicable standard varies according to whether the suit alleges excessive physical force or abusive policies or conditions of incarceration. In cases alleging excessive physical force by correctional staff, a prisoner must prove that prison officials acted "maliciously and sadistically for the very purpose of causing harm."[18] In cases challenging abusive policies or conditions of incarceration, a prisoner must demonstrate that officials acted with "deliberate indifference" in subjecting him to such conditions.[19] The latter standard is normally applied in cases of prisoner-on-prisoner rape.

It is well established that the Eighth Amendment not only bars direct guard brutality, it also requires prison officials to protect prisoners from violence inflicted by fellow prisoners.[20] A number of federal courts have specifically examined the protections provided by the Eighth Amendment in the context of prisoner-on-prisoner sexual abuse. In *Farmer v. Brennan,* a 1994 decision involving the rape of a transsexual inmate, the Supreme Court ruled that a prison official violates the Eighth Amendment if, acting with deliberate indifference, he exposes a prisoner to a substantial risk of sexual assault.[21] Confirming the previous holdings of a number of lower courts, the *Farmer* court acknowledged that prison rape is constitutionally unacceptable; indeed, the court stated explicitly that being sexually abused in prison is "not part of the penalty that criminal offenders pay for their offenses."[22]

While the Supreme Court's rhetorical stand against prisoner-on-prisoner violence and sexual abuse is encouraging as a statement of principle, it ignores the formidable legal barriers to the success of suits challenging such abuses. The primary obstacle to such cases is the subjective intent requirement, mentioned above. As will be described in greater detail in chapter VIII of this report, proving terrible conditions or terrible abuses is not enough; the prisoner must also prove that the prison official who is sued knew of and disregarded the conditions.[23]

Notably, this "actual knowledge" requirement is imposed not only in cases in which prisoners seek damages for past abuses, but also in cases in which prisoners seek remedial action to prevent continuing abuses.[24] In other words, a court will allow the infliction of abusive conditions if such conditions cannot be shown to be the result of prison officials' deliberate indifference. As noted in the concurrence to the leading Supreme Court decision on this question, such a rule means that inhumane conditions can easily go unredressed due to the courts' "unnecessary and meaningless search for 'deliberate indifference.' "[25]

The failure of prison authorities to provide proper treatment for the physical injuries, communicable diseases, and psychological suffering that often accompany sexual abuse is also subject to scrutiny under the Eighth Amendment. The courts have held that the medical care a prisoner receives is just as much a "condition" of his confinement as the food he is fed, the clothes he is issued, and the protection he is afforded against other inmates.[26] Although the inadvertent failure to provide adequate medical care is not legally actionable, the deliberate deprivation of proper medical treatment is.[27]

THE ROLE OF THE U.S. DEPARTMENT OF JUSTICE IN ENFORCING THE U.S. CONSTITUTION

Constitutional protections on prisoners' rights may be enforced by the U.S. Department of Justice (DOJ) acting under statutory authority. The DOJ may criminally prosecute a person "acting under color of state law"[28] for violating a prisoner's constitutional rights, under Sections 241 and 242 of Title 18 of the United States Code.[29] The DOJ also may investigate allegations of unconstitutional conditions in a state's prisons under the Civil Rights of Institutionalized Persons Act and bring a civil suit against a state. In addition, the Violent Crime Control and Law Enforcement Act of 1994 added Title 42, United States Code, Section 14141, under which the DOJ also may enforce the constitutional rights of prisoners through civil suits. All of these statutes are, however, subject to prosecutorial discretion. The DOJ has no affirmative obligation to enforce them in every instance, nor, it should be emphasized, does it have the resources to do so.

Criminal Enforcement: Title 18, U.S. Code, Sections 241 and 242

The evidentiary burden imposed under Title 18, United States Code, Sections 241 and 242, makes it extremely difficult to convict someone under criminal law for violating a prisoner's constitutional rights. To convict a public official, the DOJ must not only prove beyond a reasonable doubt that a constitutional right has been violated, but also that the public official had the "specific intent" to deprive the prisoner of that right.[30] The specific intent requirement creates a substantial burden for the DOJ to meet because it must show that an official knowingly and willfully participated in violating a prisoner's constitutional right.[31]

The U.S. government has provided only limited resources for the prosecution of such suits.[32] According to official data, the DOJ's Criminal Section receives some 8,000-10,000 complaints annually, the majority involving allegations of official misconduct, and files charges in forty to fifty criminal cases—less than 1 percent of complaints.[33] Only some of these cases involve correctional officials; the rest involve other law enforcement officials.

Civil Enforcement under CRIPA

The DOJ may also institute civil suits for abuses in state and local prisons which violate the civil rights of prisoners under the Civil Rights of Institutionalized Persons Act (CRIPA).[34] Congress passed CRIPA in 1980 to enable the federal government to investigate and pursue civil suits against state institutions that the attorney general suspects of violating the U.S. Constitution. Prior to CRIPA's enactment, the government had only limited authority to intervene in private lawsuits alleging a violation of constitutional rights inside state institutions.[35] Before suing a state under CRIPA, the DOJ must have "reasonable cause to believe" that a state institution is engaging in a pattern or practice of subjecting prisoners to "egregious or flagrant conditions" that violate the U.S. Constitution. Reasonable cause may be obtained through an investigation of a prison. According to the DOJ, it decides to investigate when it acquires a "sufficient body of information" to indicate the existence of abuses that may rise to the level of a constitutional violation.[36] The DOJ receives information from a variety of sources, including individual prisoners, public interest and defense attorneys, and corrections staff.

Once the DOJ decides to investigate, it must first file a letter with the state and the prison's director stating its intention to investigate and giving state officials seven days' notice. During an investigation, DOJ investigators—attorneys with the DOJ and consultants—conduct personal interviews with prisoners, tour the facilities, and review documentation and institutional records to determine whether unconstitutional conditions exist. The DOJ takes the position that its authority under CRIPA to determine whether unconstitutional conditions exist necessarily includes the right to enter state prisons to examine such conditions.[37] In 1994, one federal court in Michigan refused to issue a court order giving the DOJ access to investigate.[38] This decision, however, appears to reflect the exception rather than the rule.[39]

Once the on-site investigation is complete, the DOJ must issue a letter to the state that summarizes its findings and sets forth the minimum steps necessary to rectify any unconstitutional conditions found. Under CRIPA, forty-nine days after this letter is received by the state, the DOJ may sue the state to remedy the constitutional violations. The U.S. attorney general must personally sign the complaint and, according to DOJ representatives, all possibility of a settlement must be exhausted. As a result, suits are generally filed well after the forty-nine-day period has passed. The DOJ has said that CRIPA contemplates that the state and the DOJ will attempt an amicable resolution of the problem and that many cases are, in fact, resolved through negotiated settlements and consent decrees.[40]

The Special Litigation Section of the Civil Rights Division of DOJ, the unit responsible for enforcing CRIPA, does not have nearly enough staff to fulfill its mandate.[41] Made up of twenty-six lawyers (including supervisors), it handles a handful of cases involving a tiny minority of the country's prisons.[42] In all, in fiscal year 1999, the Special Litigation Section opened three new jail investigations; sent findings letters to seven correctional facilities, including two prisons; and settled three cases involving prisons or jails.[43]

THE ROLE OF CIVIL LITIGATION
IN ENFORCING THE U.S. CONSTITUTION

Unsurprisingly, given the inadequacies of official enforcement efforts, most attempts to prevent or redress prison abuses are initiated by prisoners. The usual method for challenging abusive practices or conditions is via civil litigation under Section 1983 of Title 42 of the U.S. Code. Because of constitutional rules barring suits under federal law against states as such, individual corrections authorities are generally named as defendants in Section 1983 actions.[44]

Section 1983 is a civil rights statute dating from the post-Civil War era that was revived in the 1960s as a tool for enforcing the U.S. Constitution.[45] A 1964 Supreme Court decision confirmed that prisoners could rely upon Section 1983 in challenging conditions that violated their constitutional rights.[46] All or nearly all of the landmark prison conditions precedents that followed were litigated under the statute.

Prisoners' lack of legal representation

Because most prisoners are indigent and unable to afford the costs of litigation, they must look either to public interest lawyers who work for free or private lawyers who work on a contingency fee basis to obtain legal representation in suits challenging prison abuses.[47] Both options are exceedingly limited.

A 1996 law greatly reduced the number of public interest lawyers available to litigate on behalf of inmates by barring the federal Legal Services Corporation from funding legal aid organizations that represent prisoners, adding prisoners to a list of forbidden clients (along with undocumented aliens and women seeking abortions).[48] Those public interest organizations that continue to handle prison cases are generally so overburdened that they rarely accept individual suits, focusing instead on reforming overall prison policies via class action litigation.[49] A few states have legal services organizations specifically directed toward inmate lawsuits, such as New York's Prisoners' Legal Services, but these too are normally short-staffed and often suffer chronic funding shortages.[50]

Nor do private lawyers handle many cases involving prison abuses. The difficulties of winning such cases and of obtaining reasonable damages awards, given popular animosity toward prisoners, has meant that the field of prison litigation has never been very lucrative, and thus never very attractive to private lawyers. In addition, the fact of incarceration—especially with so many prisons located in remote rural areas—makes attorney-client communications more difficult and expensive, requiring attorneys to travel long distances to interview their inmate clients. The passage of the PLRA, with its additional disincentives to litigation, has made private lawyers even less willing to represent inmates on a contingency fee basis.

Inmate pro se litigation

Because of the many obstacles to obtaining legal representation, the vast bulk of prison conditions litigation arises via complaints filed by prisoners acting pro se, that is, without professional legal counsel.[51] Indigent inmates file many thousands of pro se lawsuits each year.[52] Indeed, much of the case law pertaining to prisoner-on-prisoner sexual abuse is the result of suits initiated by pro se plaintiffs.[53]

Like all persons lacking legal training, pro se inmate plaintiffs face a very difficult time in court. Not only are they unfamiliar with the law, both substantively and procedurally, and often uneducated, but being incarcerated makes it much harder for them to do the factual and legal research necessary to successfully litigate a case. Most inmates even lack access to a typewriter on which to draft their pleadings, instead filing handwritten—or scrawled—documents with the court.[54] More fortunate prisoners have the aid of do it yourself legal manuals that sketch out the legal rules applicable in the prison context and walk the prisoner through the relevant legal procedures.[55] Others obtain assistance from "writ writers" or "jailhouse lawyers"—inmates who have trained themselves in law and procedure. Yet all too many prisoners have no knowledge of the law, no legal assistance, and no possibility of successfully pursuing a legal case, no matter how egregious the abuses they suffer while incarcerated. While a few inmate plaintiffs manage to negotiate monetary settlements with prison authorities or even win their cases, most of them fail in their efforts.[56] Their complaints are often dismissed for procedural errors or other legal shortcomings in the early stages of litigation. Their legal failures, however, may have little to do with the validity of their underlying claims.[57]

Under the U.S. Constitution, prisoners are guaranteed a right of access to the courts. The landmark case of *Bounds v. Smith*, decided in 1977, was an important step toward making this guarantee more than a hollow one: it purported to insure that inmate access to the courts was "adequate, effective, and meaningful."[58] Specifically, it held that prisons must provide inmates with adequate law libraries or adequate assistance from persons trained in the law. Yet more recent judicial decisions—in particular the case of *Lewis v. Casey*—have greatly eroded the constitutional duty imposed on prison authorities to facilitate prisoners' legal efforts.[59] The passage of the PLRA, designed in part to hinder "frivolous" inmate litigation, has placed additional burdens on inmate plaintiffs. Finally, numerous state legislatures have passed similar laws to limit prisoner lawsuits by, for example, requiring inmates to pay filing fees or sanctioning inmates found to have filed frivolous suits.[60] While such laws may discourage unnecessary and groundless litigation, they are equally likely to prevent inmates with valid claims from asserting their rights in court.

International Legal Protections

The overriding weakness of the national legal protections described above—the lack of effective enforcement—is even more glaring with regard to international legal protections. International human rights law reflects ample concern for prisoners' rights. Even more than U.S. domestic law, international legal norms are directed toward the humane treatment and rehabilitation of prisoners. Yet, no mechanism exists to ensure their enforcement in U.S. prisons and jails, and there are very few official avenues even for monitoring their implementation.

TREATIES AND AUTHORITATIVE GUIDELINES

The chief international human rights documents binding on the United States clearly affirm that the human rights of incarcerated persons must be respected. The International Covenant on Civil and Political Rights (ICCPR) and the Convention against Torture and Other Cruel, Inhuman or Degrading Treatment or Punishment, both ratified by the United States, prohibit torture and cruel, inhuman, or degrading treatment or punishment, without exception or derogation. The ICCPR mandates that "[a]ll persons deprived of their liberty shall be treated with humanity and with respect for the inherent dignity of the human person."[61] It also requires that the "reformation and social rehabilitation" of prisoners be an "essential aim" of imprisonment.[62]

Several additional international documents flesh out the human rights of persons deprived of liberty, providing guidance as to how governments may comply with their obligations under international law. The most comprehensive such guidelines are the United Nations Standard Minimum Rules for the Treatment of Prisoners, adopted by the Economic and Social Council in 1957. Other relevant documents include the Body of Principles for the Protection of All Persons Under Any Form of Detention or Imprisonment, adopted by the General Assembly in 1988, and the Basic Principles for the Treatment of Prisoners, adopted by the General Assembly in 1990. Although these instruments are not treaties, they provide authoritative interpretations as to the practical content of binding treaty standards.[63]

These documents reaffirm the tenet that prisoners retain fundamental human rights. As the most recent of these documents, the Basic Principles, declares:

Except for those limitations that are demonstrably necessitated by the fact of incarceration, all prisoners shall retain the human rights and fundamental freedoms set out in the Universal Declaration of Human Rights, and, where the State concerned is a party, the International Covenant on Economic, Social and Cultural Rights, and the International Covenant on Civil and Political Rights and the Optional Protocol thereto, as well as such other rights as are set out in other United Nations covenants.[64]

Endorsing this philosophy in 1992, the United Nations Human Rights Committee explained that states have "a positive obligation toward persons who are particularly vulnerable because of their status as persons deprived of liberty" and stated:

> [N]ot only may persons deprived of their liberty not be subjected to [torture or other cruel, inhuman or degrading treatment or punishment], including medical or scientific experimentation, but neither may they be subjected to any hardship or constraint other than that resulting from the deprivation of liberty; respect for the dignity of such persons must be guaranteed under the same conditions as for that of free persons. Persons deprived of their liberty enjoy all the rights set forth in the [ICCPR], subject to the restrictions that are unavoidable in a closed environment.[65]

"Except for those limitations that are demonstrably necessitated by the fact of incarceration, all prisoners shall retain the human rights and fundamental freedoms set out in the Universal Declaration of Human Rights."

No international law provisions specifically pertain to rape in prison, but international tribunals and other bodies have established that rape is covered by international prohibitions on torture or cruel, inhuman or degrading treatment.[66] Although there is no general definition of rape in international human rights law, rape has been authoritatively defined as "a physical invasion of a sexual nature, committed on a person under circumstances which are coercive."[67] It is important to note, in addition, that sexual abuse that falls short of rape—aggressive sexual touching, etc., that does not involve physical penetration—may also violate international protections against ill-treatment.[68]

Somewhat more complicated is the question of prison authorities' responsibility for preventing prisoner-on-prisoner abuses such as rape. On this point, the language of the Convention against Torture is instructive. In defining torture and cruel, inhuman or degrading treatment or punishment, it includes not only acts committed *by* public officials, but also acts committed with their "acquiescence."[69] That is, international human rights law bars the state from tolerating rape and perpetuating conditions conducive to its occurrence. In the prison context, where most conditions are directly attributable to the state, and where inmates have been deprived of their liberty and the means of self-protection, the prohibition on torture and other ill-treatment translates into an affirmative duty of care. With regard to rape, as with other inter-prisoner abuses, correctional authorities must take reasonable measures to protect inmates from other inmates.[70] Although not every incident of prisoner-on-prisoner rape necessarily proves a failure to fulfill this duty, a pattern of rape indicates that the official response to the problem is inadequate.

THE PROHIBITION ON SLAVERY

Sexual slavery is a form of slavery recognized as such under international law and prohibited under both treaty law and customary international law.[71] Notably, "[t]he crime of slavery does not require government involvement or State action, and constitutes an international crime whether committed by State actors or private individuals."[72]

The 1926 Slavery Convention, to which the United States is a party, describes slavery as "the status or condition of a person over whom any or all of the powers attaching to the right of ownership are exercised," a definition that includes, as modern commentators have noted, "sexual access through rape or other forms of sexual violence."[73] The Convention specifically calls on states to impose "severe penalties" for instances of slavery in order to accomplish the goal of eradicating the abuse "in all of its forms."[74] Other international treaties ratified by the United States also bar slavery, including the ICCPR.[75]

In its more extreme cases, prisoner-on-prisoner sexual abuse can constitute a form of sexual slavery. As is described in detail below, some prisoners have been raped on a repeated basis; forced to work for other prisoners by cleaning their cells, washing their clothes, cooking and running errands for them; deprived of almost all independence and autonomy; forced into prostitution, and even bought and sold by other prisoners. Each of these abuses, let alone all of them at once, suggests a situation of slavery.[76]

BARRIERS TO THE IMPLEMENTATION
OF INTERNATIONAL PROTECTIONS

The United States has long been resistant to subjecting itself to scrutiny under international human rights law, demonstrated both by its failure to ratify numerous key human rights treaties, and by its insistence on attaching limiting reservations, declarations and understandings to any instruments that it does ratify. The limiting provisions that the U.S. attached to its ratification of the ICCPR and the Convention against Torture—which are among the longest and most detailed of any country that has ratified the two instruments—work both substantively, by restricting the scope of the treaties, and procedurally, by restricting their usefulness in court proceedings.[77] In all, they are indicative of U.S. reluctance to allow international protections to make any real impact in broadening or extending the rights granted its citizens.

The primary substantive limitations on prisoners' rights are the U.S. reservation to Article 7 of the ICCPR, by which it declares that the treaty's prohibition on torture and cruel, inhuman or degrading treatment or punishment applies only to the extent that the provision covers acts already barred under the U.S. Constitution, and its similar reservation to Article 16 of the Convention against Torture.[78] In effect, the U.S. government has chosen to nullify these standards to the extent that they grant broader rights than those already guaranteed under the U.S. Constitution. Such reservations are extremely controversial. Indeed, several other governments have explicitly protested them.[79] As these governments have pointed out, reservations like these, which are incompatible with the object and purpose of a treaty, are void.[80] In 1995, the U.N. Human Rights Committee, charged with monitoring the implementation of the ICCPR, also found the U.S. reservation to Article 7 of that instrument to be incompatible with its object and purpose.[81]

Human Rights Watch agrees with this analysis, finding that the U.S. attempt to narrow these treaties' coverage is incompatible with the treaties' goal of preventing a wide range of human rights abuses.[82] We therefore hold the U.S. to the full scope of the prohibition on torture and other ill-treatment contained in the ICCPR and Convention against Torture. Notably, this broad prohibition—which bars abusive *treatment* as well as punishment—lacks the stringent intent requirement that U.S. courts have found in the Eighth Amendment, which bars only abusive punishments. The distinction is of particular relevance in cases of prisoner-on-prisoner sexual assault, where prison authorities are frequently exonerated because they lacked the necessary intent.

"The crime of slavery does not require government involvement or State action, and constitutes an international crime whether committed by State actors or private individuals."

In ratifying the ICCPR and the Convention against Torture, the U.S. government did not limit itself to attempting to impose substantive restrictions. Procedurally, the U.S. government attempted to limit the effectiveness of both treaties by declaring that their provisions are "non-self-executing." In other words, the government declared that the treaties cannot be directly relied upon in U.S. courts, but require enabling legislation before violations of their provisions can serve as the basis of a lawsuit. To date, no U.S. court that has considered the issue has found either treaty to be self-executing, nor has legislation been passed to fully implement their provisions within the United States.[83] The effect of the declarations, therefore, has been to greatly diminish the practical usefulness of the treaties in prison litigation.

The Slavery Convention, in contrast, was ratified without any restrictions, and was not declared non-self-executing. As far as Human Rights Watch has been able to ascertain, however, no one has ever filed suit under the Convention for prisoner-on-prisoner rape.

INTERNATIONAL MONITORING OF CONDITIONS

A number of official U.N. bodies are charged with monitoring the implementation of human rights treaties. The Human Rights Committee and the Committee against Torture monitor states' compliance with the ICCPR and the Convention against Torture, respectively.[84] The Slavery Convention, drafted decades earlier, does not contain a reference to any particular official monitoring body, but responsibility for monitoring the problem of slavery has been generally assigned to the U.N.'s Working Group on Contemporary Forms of Slavery.[85]

Both the ICCPR and the Convention against Torture require states parties to submit periodic compliance reports describing the extent to which the treaty provisions are applied and explaining any obstacles to the full implementation of the instruments. In 1994, the U.S. presented its first report on compliance with the ICCPR, and in 1999—four years after it was due—the U.S. submitted its first report on compliance with the Convention against Torture. Both reports contain detailed descriptions of the constitutional and legal structures existing for the protection of prisoners' rights, and the rules applicable in state and federal prisons, but they included little factual information on conditions and violations. Nor did either document address the question of prisoner-on-prisoner sexual abuse.[86]

The U.N. committees that review these reports do not actually visit countries to conduct factual investigations of conditions. Their assessment of compliance is therefore based on the information provided by governments, supplemented by the reports of nongovernmental groups. Although they do release a short written statement evaluating the government's progress in implementing the human rights treaty at issue, these reports appear to have little impact on human rights conditions in the United States.[87]

For the past several years, a U.N. working group has been meeting annually to hammer out a draft treaty that would establish a U.N. subcommittee authorized to make periodic and ad hoc visits to places of detention in states party to the treaty, including prisons, jails, and police lockups. Based on the information obtained during its visits, the subcommittee would make detailed recommendations to state authorities regarding necessary improvements to their detention facilities. The goal of the subcommittee would be to prevent torture and other ill-treatment. Such a body, which already exists within the European human rights system, might be able to make a practical impact in improving prison conditions in the countries it visits. U.S. membership in such a body if and when it is established—although unlikely, given the U.S. record of avoiding such scrutiny—would be of great benefit.

My name is Rodney Hulin and I work at a retirement home here in Beaumont, Texas. I am here today because of my son. He would be here himself if he could . . . . But he can't because he died in [an adult prison]. . . . [At age seventeen], my son was raped and sodomized by an inmate. The doctor found two tears in his rectum and ordered an HIV test, since up to a third of the 2,200 inmates there were HIV positive. Fearing for his safety, he requested to be placed in protective custody, but his request was denied because, as the warden put it, "Rodney's abuses didn't meet the 'emergency grievance criteria.'" For the next several months, my son was repeatedly beaten by the older inmates, forced to perform oral sex, robbed, and beaten again. Each time, his requests for protection were denied by the warden. The abuses, meanwhile, continued. On the night of January 26, 1996—seventy-five days after my son entered Clemens—Rodney attempted suicide by hanging himself in his cell. He could no longer stand to live in continual terror. It was too much for him to handle. He laid in a coma for the next four months until he died.[1]

In early 1995, Rodney Hulin, Jr., received an eight year sentence for arson. He was sixteen years old but was sentenced to serve his time in adult prison.

On November 13, 1995, Hulin was transferred to the Clemens Unit in Brazoria County, Texas. Older inmates there immediately started to threaten and harass him; within a week he was raped. With a medical examination confirming the rape, Hulin requested protective custody. "He went through all the proper channels, trying to get protection," recalled his father, who found out about the rape in a letter from his son. "Rodney was very small—probably the smallest person on the unit. He was 5'2" and weighed about 125. A first offender. I can't fathom why they wouldn't help him."[2]

Denied protective custody, Hulin faced continuing sexual abuse. He began violating disciplinary rules in order to protect himself by being placed in segregation. On January 26, while in segregation, he wrote a note saying that he was "tired of living." A friend in an adjoining cell passed the note to a guard and warned him that Hulin needed immediate attention. The guard left, not returning for another fifteen minutes. During that time, Hulin hung himself.

After Hulin's death, his parents filed suit against the Texas prison system for failing to protect their son. Among the remedies that they requested were that prison authorities "be compelled to institute programs whereby prisoners who are victims of sexual assault while incarcerated are provided with appropriate and necessary counseling and protective custody."[3] The case was settled out of court in 1998, with Texas paying a substantial settlement.[4] No prosecution of Hulin's rapists was ever attempted, although their names were known and witnesses were said to be available.

PREDATORS AND VICTIMS

Certain prisoners are targeted for sexual assault the moment they enter a penal facility: their age, looks, sexual preference, and other characteristics mark them as candidates for abuse. A clear example is that of Dee Farmer, a young preoperative transsexual with "overtly feminine characteristics" who was placed in regular housing in a maximum-security federal prison.[1] Brutally raped within two weeks of arriving, Farmer sued in federal court—later bringing the case all the way up to the U.S. Supreme Court—arguing that as a transsexual she was extremely likely to face sexual assault in prison. But a prisoner does not have to look like a woman to be vulnerable to such abuse. Rather, a broad range of factors are correlated with increased vulnerability to rape, some related to perceived femininity, some entirely unrelated.

Specifically, prisoners fitting any part of the following description are more likely to be targeted: young, small in size, physically weak, white, gay, first offender, possessing "feminine" characteristics such as long hair or a high voice; being unassertive, unaggressive, shy, intellectual, not street-smart, or "passive"; or having been convicted of a sexual offense against a minor. Prisoners with any one of these characteristics typically face an increased risk of sexual abuse, while prisoners with several overlapping characteristics are much more likely than other prisoners to be targeted for abuse.

The characteristics of prison rapists are somewhat less clear and predictable, but certain patterns can nonetheless be discerned. First, although some older inmates commit rape, the perpetrators also tend to be young, if not always as young as their victims—generally well under thirty-five years old. They are frequently larger or stronger than their victims, and are generally more assertive, physically aggressive, and more at home in the prison environment. They are "street smart"—often gang members. They have typically been convicted of more violent crimes than their victims.

The myth of the "homosexual predator" is groundless. Perpetrators of rape typically view themselves as heterosexual and, outside of the prison environment, prefer to engage in heterosexual activity. Although gay inmates are much more likely than other inmates to be victimized in prison, they are not likely to be perpetrators of sexual abuse.

> **"When I was in B pod I had 3 dude's coming to me that said they was the only thing that was keeping me from getting raped, and they wanted to jack off and look at me."**

The elements of race and ethnicity have a complex and significant bearing on the problem of prisoner-on-prisoner sexual abuse. As previously discussed, racial and ethnic distinctions are nowhere more salient than they are in prison: all social interaction is refracted through the prism of these group differences. Inter-racial sexual abuse is common only to the extent that it involves white non-Hispanic prisoners being abused by African Americans or Hispanics. In contrast, African American and Hispanic inmates are much less frequently abused by members of other racial or ethnic groups; instead, sexual abuse tends to occur only within these groups.

While all of the above factors are relevant and important, none should not viewed as controlling. In the wrong circumstances, it should be emphasized, almost any prisoner may be at risk of sexual abuse. Proper classification and monitoring of vulnerable prisoners should be one aspect of a rape prevention plan, but only one aspect: other prevention policies are equally necessary to stop sexual abuse in prison.

Age

Young or youthful-looking inmates are at particular risk of rape.[2] The expression "kid," frequently used in prison to describe the victim of a coercive sexual relationship, suggests the connection between youth and victimization. Examples such as Rodney Hulin, the seventeen-year-old Texas inmate whose case is described above, illustrate this linkage. Placed in an adult prison and repeatedly raped by older inmates, Hulin committed suicide in 1995.[3]

Human Rights Watch has had only a few direct contacts with juvenile prisoners in the course of research for this report, although it has received numerous reports about their treatment from other prisoners, in addition to hearing from some older prisoners about incidents that occurred when they were minors. In 1998, the mother of an Arkansas prisoner contacted Human Rights Watch to report that her son, a friend of his who was only sixteen, and a third prisoner were all raped in the same cellblock in April of that year.[4] Human Rights Watch wrote to the young prisoner, who was being held in an adult prison, asking about his situation. He responded:

> Sorry for taking so long to write, but I have been having a lot of trouble. I'm 16teen. I got into a fight and I got a broke bone in my arm. It don't hurt that bad. Now about the trouble I have been having. I have had 2 people try to rape me . . . . I have tryed to go to P.C. [protective custody] but they wouldn't let me.[5]

In his next letter to Human Rights Watch, R.P. explained:

> When I was in B pod I had 3 dude's coming to me that said they was the only thing that was keeping me from getting raped, and they wanted to jack off and look at me. The pod I'm in now I had 2 people come to me and put a ink pen to my neck and tell me that if I didn't let them jack off on me they were going to rape me. I told the officer but they didn't do any thing about it.[6]

R.P. never directly said that he was raped but he has complained about severe and continuing sexual harassment from adult prisoners. Prisoners in other institutions have confirmed that R.P.'s situation is typical, stating that young prisoners like R.P. are viewed as more attractive sexually and more easily abused. A Florida prisoner said:

> Mostely young youthful Boy's are raped because of their youth and tenderness, and smooth skin that in the mind of the one duing the raping he think of the smooth skin and picture a woman . . . . Prisoners even fight each other

over a youth without the young man knowing anything about it to see whom will have the Boy first as his property.[7]

An inmate in Nebraska told Human Rights Watch:

The kids I know of here are kept in the hospital part of the prison until they turn 16. Then they are placed in general population. . . . At age 16, they are just thrown to the wolves, so to speak, in population. I have not heard of one making it more than a week in population without being "laid."[8]

As described below, small size is another risk factor; small young prisoners are thus especially vulnerable to sexual abuse. A Utah inmate told Human Rights Watch:

[When I was sent to prison,] I was just barely 18 years of age, about 90 pounds. I did nine years from March 1983 to November 1991. In that 9 years I was raped several times. I never told on anyone for it, but did ask the officer for protective custody. But I was just sent to another part of the prison. Than raped again. Sent to another part of the prison. Etc.[9]

Some inmates told Human Rights Watch of hardened convicts who prey on young prisoners. One spoke of "a guy who has served over 20 years, and he is a tough guy. What he has done for years, is gets the young guys in his cell & gets them high & then chokes them unconsious & proceeds to rape them."[10] Belying the stereotype of the older predator, however, is the much more common story of the young perpetrator of sexual abuse, generally someone between twenty and thirty years old. Although very young prisoners—those under twenty—are likely to be abused by prisoners who are older than them, most inmates in their twenties who reported abuse to Human Rights Watch were not abused by inmates significantly older than they were.[11]

Size, Physical Strength, Attitude, and Propensity toward Violence

If a person is timid or shy or as prison inmates term him 'Weak,' either mentally or physically, he stands to be a victim of physical and/or sexual assault.[12]

Unsurprisingly—given that physical force, or at least the implicit threat of physical force, is a common element of rape in prison—victims of rape tend to be smaller and weaker than perpetrators. In one extreme example, an inmate who described himself as "a small person weighing only about 140 pounds" told Human Rights Watch of an attack "by a man about 6'7" and weighing approximately 280 pounds."[13] Many more inmates described being intimidated or overpowered by larger, stronger perpetrators.

Very small inmates face an especially difficult time in prison. Human Rights Watch interviewed a Texas prisoner who was only five feet tall. He said he was so vulnerable he felt like "a hunted animal" most of the time.[14] He claimed to have been sexually abused on countless occasions.

Strong, physically imposing inmates are safer from sexual abuse. An inmate's size and strength is particularly important in terms of fending off unwanted advances from cellmates, a fairly common problem. Yet size and strength alone, inmates emphasized, are never an absolute guarantee against abuse. "I don't care how big and bad you are, if you've got five dudes up against you, you're in trouble," one prisoner pointed out.[15]

"At age 16, they are just thrown to the wolves, so to speak, in population. I have not heard of one making it more than a week in population without being 'laid.'"

More important than sheer physical characteristics, in many inmates' view, is "heart"—the courage to fight and not give up even when losing—and a willingness to resort to violence when provoked. An inmate has to prove that he will stand up for himself against intimidation. A strong, aggressive attitude is just as necessary as physical strength. Inmates perceived as timid, fearful, "passive," or not aggressive are likely to be targeted for victimization, whereas inmates who have gained the respect of their fellows are likely to be safe. As one inmate explained:

> Smaller, weaker, meeker individuals are usually targets. Meeker individuals tend to "act Gay" is how it's described here and in turn invites assault through the agressors mind. A new inmate needs to come into the system ready to fight and with a strong mind.[16]

It is thus unsurprising that mentally ill or retarded prisoners, whose numbers behind bars have increased dramatically in recent years, are at particular risk of abuse.[17] An Indiana prisoner suffering from schizophrenia told Human Rights Watch that he was constantly being coerced into unwanted sex. Describing his situation, he said:

> So one day I goes to the day room going to get my medication there was a big Black guy both of them call me to the back of the day room. they were punking me out. I didn't want to fight them they made me call them daddy, made kept repeating it. . . . these things keeps happening to me. . . . these officers and these inmate they take avantige of the weak give them coffee, cigerette to make them do things for them. . . . there was a White guy that took advanteges of me in prison at another facility. . . . I don't no my rights or about the law, so I'm hit everytime I go to prison.[18]

"Smaller, weaker, meeker individuals are usually targets. . . . A new inmate needs to come into the system ready to fight and with a strong mind.

By all reports, perpetrators tend to be stronger, more physically aggressive, and more assertive than their victims. Even more importantly, they tend to be better established in the inmate hierarchy. Often they are gang members with a network of inmate allies. This is, of course, particularly true with gang rapes, but it is also true with individual acts of abuse. A less established prisoner may be intimidated into submitting to sex with a powerful inmate or gang member out of fear that, were he to refuse, a more violent gang attack would ensue.

As this might suggest, newly incarcerated first offenders are especially vulnerable to sexual abuse. Lacking allies, unfamiliar with the unwritten code of inmate rules, and likely to feel somewhat traumatized by the new and threatening environment, they are easy prey for experienced inmates. "It's a sink or swim situation," said one prisoner who was beaten and raped soon after entering prison. "I sunk."[19] He explained:

> My first mistake was not hanging out with the ignorant tough guys, and staying in my cell most of the time: they take that as a sign of weakness. I wasn't ready for the clique action. The prison was a gladiator farm back then; I kept getting into fights and finally I couldn't do it any more. I was getting beaten up every day for a month.

Describing the dangers of this initial entry period, an Arkansas prisoner told Human Rights Watch:

> When a new inmate enters an open barracks prison it triggers a sort of competition among the convicts as to who will seduce and subjugate that new arrival. Subjugation is mental, physical, financial, and sexual. Every new arrival is a potential victim. Unless the new arrival is strong, ugly, and efficient at violence, they are subject to get seduced, coerced, or raped . . . Psychosocially, emotionally, and physically the most dangerous and traumatic place I can conceive of is the open barracks prison when first viewed by a new inmate.[20]

A Minnesota prisoner gave a similar account of the reception awaiting new inmates:

> When an inmate comes in for the first time and doesnt know anyone. The clicks and gangs. Watch him like Wolves readying there attacks. They see if he spends time alone, who he eats with. Its like the Wild Kingdom. Then they start playing with him, checking the new guy out. (They call him fresh meat.)[21]

Sexual Preference

Numerous judicial decisions, newspaper and magazine stories, and even some scholarly articles describe the threat of "predatory homosexuals" in prison and the problem of "homosexual rape."[22] Yet prisoners who self-identify as gay are much more likely than other prisoners to be *targeted* for rape, rather than being themselves the perpetrators of it.[23]

To some extent, the talk of predatory homosexual inmates simply reflects a lack of semantic clarity. Since prisoner-on-prisoner rape is by definition homosexual, in that it involves persons of the same sex, its perpetrators are unthinkingly labeled predatory homosexuals. This terminology is deceptive, however, in that it ignores the fact that the vast majority of prison rapists do not view themselves as gay. Rather, most such rapists view themselves as heterosexuals and see the victim as substituting for a woman. From this perspective the crucial point is not that they are having sex with a man; instead it is that they are the aggressor, as opposed to the victim—the person doing the penetration, as opposed to the one being penetrated. Indeed, if they see anyone as gay, it is the victim (even where the victim's clear sexual preference is for heterosexual activity).

An Illinois prisoner explained inmates' views on the question:

> The theory is that you are not gay or bisexual as long as YOU yourself do not allow another man to stick his penis into your mouth or anal passage. If you do the sticking, you can still consider yourself to be a macho man/heterosexual, according to their theory. This is a pretty universal/widespread theory.[24]

Equal and voluntary gay relationships do not fit comfortably within this dichotomy. Although outsiders may perceive male prisons as a bastion of gay sexuality, the reality is quite different. Gay relationships typical of regular society are rare in prison, and usually kept secret. Indeed, many gay inmates—even those who are openly gay outside of prison—carefully hide their sexual identities while incarcerated. They do so because inmates who are perceived as gay by other inmates face a very high risk of sexual abuse. Human Rights Watch has received reports of rape from numerous gay inmates, all of whom agree that their sexual preferences contributed to the likelihood of victimization.[25]

Some prisoners have told Human Rights Watch that inmate views on homosexuality are gradually changing, with a lessening of prejudice against gays as changing societal mores begin to permeate prison culture. Even these prisoners, however, acknowledge that gay inmates are still severely stigmatized—they just believe that their treatment has lately been improving.

Gay inmates with stereotypically "feminine" characteristics are especially vulnerable to sexual abuse. As one such inmate described:

> I have long Blond hair and I weigh about 144 lbs. I am a free-world homosexual that looks and acts like a female . . . . In 1992 I came to this Unit and was put into population. There was so many gangs and violence that I had know choice but to hook up with someone that could make them give me a little respect . . . . All open Homosexuals are preyed upon and if they don't choose up they get chosen.[26]

"Psychosocially, emotionally, and physically the most dangerous and traumatic place I can conceive of is the open barracks prison when first viewed by a new inmate."

Unsurprisingly, transsexual prisoners like Dee Farmer, whose case went to the Supreme Court, face unrelenting sexual harassment unless another inmate is protecting them. Such inmates nearly always have an inmate "husband," someone powerful enough in the inmate hierarchy to keep other inmates away.

Race and Ethnicity

Past studies have documented the prevalence of black on white sexual aggression in prison.[27] These findings are further confirmed by Human Rights Watch's own research. Overall, our correspondence and interviews with white, black, and Hispanic inmates convince us that white inmates are disproportionately targeted for abuse.[28] Although many whites reported being raped by white inmates, black on white abuse appears to be more common. To a much lesser extent, non-Hispanic whites also reported being victimized by Hispanic inmates.

Other than sexual abuse of white inmates by African Americans, and, less frequently, Hispanics, interracial and interethnic sexual abuse appears to be much less common than sexual abuse committed by persons of one race or ethnicity against members of that same group. In other words, African Americans typically face sexual abuse at the hands of other African Americans, and Hispanics at the hands of other Hispanics. Some inmates told Human Rights Watch that this pattern reflected an inmate rule, one that was strictly enforced: "only a black can turn out [rape] a black, and only a chicano can turn out a chicano."[29] Breaking this rule by sexually abusing someone of another race or ethnicity, with the exception of a white inmate, could lead to racial or ethnic unrest, as other members of the victim's group would retaliate against the perpetrator's group. A Texas inmate explained, for example: "The Mexicans—indeed all latinos, nobody outside their race can 'check' one without permission from the town that, that person is from. If a black dude were to check a mexican w/out such permission & the mexican stays down & fights back, a riot will take place."[30]

> **"All open Homosexuals are preyed upon and if they don't choose up they get chosen."**

The causes of black on white sexual abuse in prison have been much analyzed. Some commentators have attributed it to the norms of a violent black subculture, the result of social conditioning that encourages aggressiveness and the use of force.[31] Others have viewed it as a form of revenge for white dominance of blacks in outside society.[32] Viewing rape as a hate crime rather than one primarily motivated by sexual urges, they believe that sexually abused white inmates are essentially convenient surrogates for whites generally. Elaborating on this theory, one commentator surmised that "[i]n raping a white inmate, the black aggressor may in some measure be assaulting the white guard on the catwalk."[33]

Some inmates, both black and white, told Human Rights Watch that whites were generally perceived as weaker and thus more vulnerable to sexual abuse. An African American prisoner, describing the situation of incarcerated whites, said:

When individuals come to prison, they know that the first thing that they will have to do is fight. Now there are individuals that are from a certain race that the majority of them are not physically equip to fight. So they are the majority that are force to engage in sexual acts.[34]

Another African American inmate, while generally agreeing with the idea of whites as easy victims, gave a more politically-oriented explanation for the problem of black on white sexual abuse:

Before I continue, let me explain that I consider myself to be speaking from mainly a black perspective. The reason I say that is not to be racist, but to emphasize that on the main, blacks, whites, hispanics, etc. . . . have a different outlook on prison rape from a convict viewpoint. Most [blacks] feel that the legal system is fundamentally racist and officers are the most visible symbol of a corrupt institution & with good reason . . . . [B]lacks know whites often associate crime with black people. They see themselves as being used as scapegoats . . . . So is it any wonder that when a white man comes to prison, that blacks see him as a target. Stereotypes are prevalent amongst blacks also that cause bad thinking. The belief that all or most white men are effete or gay is very prevalent, & that whites are cowards who have to have 5 or 6 more to take down one dude . . . . Whites are prey and even a punk will be supported if he beats up a white dude.

Criminal History

Prior studies have found that the crimes for which victims of rape are incarcerated are generally less serious and less violent than those for which the perpetrators of rape are incarcerated.[35] Although findings by Human Rights Watch on this issue are tentative—especially because many victims of sexual abuse have no idea what crime their rapists was convicted of—they tend to support this argument. A few of the victims who provided information to us were convicted of serious, violent crimes such as murder, but a striking proportion of them were nonviolent felons, many of them convicted of crimes such as burglary, drug offenses, passing bad checks, car theft, etc. Of the minority of victims who were aware of the criminal history of the perpetrator of abuse, many reported serious and violent crimes. This general pattern is consistent, of course, with the idea that perpetrators of rape tend to be more violent people than victims, both inside and outside of prison.

With one exception, no specific crime seems to be associated with either perpetrators or victims. The exception is sexual abuse of a minor. Although the vast majority of victims of prison rape are incarcerated for other crimes, it is apparent that inmates convicted of sex crimes against minors, if their crimes become known to other inmates, are much more apt to be targeted for sexual abuse in prison. A number of inmates convicted of such offenses reported being sexually assaulted by other prisoners; all stated that the nature of their crime inspired the assault or increased its likelihood. "It took about seven months before my crime became known," one such prisoner explained. "Then everyone came down on me. They beat me with mop handles and broom sticks. They shoved a mop handle up my ass and left me like that."[36]

This man was transferred to another institution but other inmates who knew of his crime were transferred with him. Some three weeks after the transfer, his cellmate woke him up at 2:30 a.m. and raped him, bashing him in the back of the head with a combination lock. "The guy told me, 'I will teach you what a baby raper is.'"

Explaining the targeting of prisoners convicted of sexually abusing minors, another inmate said:

> Inmates confined for sexual offenses, especially those against juvenile victims, are at the bottom of the pecking order and consequentially most often victimized. Because of their crime, the general population justifies using their weakness by labling rape "just punishment" for their crime. Sexual offenders are the number one target group for prisoner rape.[37]

"The officers here 1. Ignored my complaints. 2. Asked me if I was his lover. 3. Did nothing. He became more difficult to deal with and started to threaten me. Finally one day he attacked me."

Relationship between Victim and Perpetrator

Most sexual abuse in prison is not between total strangers: the victim and at least one of the perpetrators usually have some prior awareness of each other, however cursory. In some instances, victims have described a long period of harassment that escalates in stages, from leering to sexually aggressive comments to threats, culminating in a physical assault. A Texas inmate described such a scenario to Human Rights Watch:

> [My cellmate] was younger, stronger than I and larger. He introduced himself as a bi-sexual. And was for two weeks "touchie-feelie." I had to screem/yell at him to stop. The officers here 1. Ignored my complaints. 2. Asked me if I was his lover. 3. Did nothing. He became more difficult to deal with and started to threaten me. Finally one day he attacked me.[38]

In other instances, the progression is much more rapid: an inmate who makes an ugly comment at lunch may commit rape in the evening.

Of the various forms of sexual abuse, it is violent or forcible rapes, or rapes under threat of violence, that are most likely to involve strangers or inmates with a very slight acquaintanceship. More subtly coercive sexual relationships, in contrast, take time to develop. The perpetrator may initially appear to be a friend, even an apparent protector, but will take advantage of his acquaintance with the victim to intimidate and coerce him into sexual contact.

One relationship that presents a clear danger of sexual abuse, both of the overtly violent and of the coercive sorts, is that of cellmates. With two-man cells becoming more common in American prisons, due to overcrowding and space constraints, inmates are often thrown into intimate living situations with persons whom, according to the factors described above, present them with a high risk of sexual abuse. Prison officials, preoccupied with other priorities, pay inadequate attention to the question of prisoners' compatibility when assigning cell spaces. While they may take care to avoid housing members of different gangs together, or inmates known to be enemies, their attention usually stops there. Prisoners are frequently double-celled with much larger, stronger, tougher inmates, even with prisoners who have a known history of sexual abuse. Unsurprisingly, a large number of inmates report having been raped by their cellmates.

The alarming frequency of such reports indicates to Human Rights Watch that prison officials should take considerably more care in matching cellmates, and that, as a general rule, double-celling should be avoided.

Case Histories of L.O. and P.E.

L.O.

Patient was referred from the Clemens Unit to Jester IV Crisis Management following 2 episodes of cutting his arm with reported intent to kill himself. Patient claimed it was due to a rape 2 months ago while on the Ferguson Unit. He reported he could not stop thinking about the assault . . . . Testing generally supports a clinical depression with psychological damage consistent with a post traumatic process.[1]

I observed that there were maybe (5) inmates of European descent out of about 150 inmates housed on cell block M. The remaining cell block population was comprised of African-Americans and Hispanics . . . . Daily, I was called "punk ass white boy", and was told "you are going to ride (pay for protection) white boy". . . . On May 10, 1995, inmate S.E., who is an African-American, was placed in my assigned cell . . . . Shortly afterwards, inmate S.E. made numerous offensive derogatory comments against individuals of European descent, and threatened to brutally assault me unless I surrendered my sleeping bunk . . . . Inmate S.E. stated that he would kill me if I called for help, or attempted to resist him in any manner . . . . I was then raped/sexually assaulted by inmate S.E.[2]

At age twenty-two, L.O. received a six-year sentence for possession of cocaine. In April 1995, he was sent to a notoriously dangerous prison in Texas.

L.O. was one of a handful of white prisoners on the prison wing to which he was assigned, and he was immediately subject to racial harassment, threats, and violent assaults. Fearful for his life, he later told Human Rights

Watch that he purposely broke prison disciplinary rules in order to be placed on special cell restrictions, which left him locked in his cell twenty-three hours a day and therefore more protected. In May, however, another inmate, S.R., was assigned to share his cell. S.R., who was African American, told L.O. that he was a member of the Crips and displayed identifying tattoos. He immediately began to threaten L.O., demanding that L.O. give up his personal belongings and that he submit to sex. While S.R. was in the shower, L.O. alerted a guard to his situation, stating that he was afraid for his safety and did not want to be housed with S.R. The guard dismissed his fears.

For three days, S.R. threatened L.O., and L.O. repeatedly informed guards of his fears for his safety. On the third night, S.R. again demanded that L.O. submit to sex. When L.O. refused, S.R. yanked him from the top bunk where he had been resting. L.O. fell to the floor and S.R. began punching and kicking him. After a struggle, L.O. was knocked unconscious. When he came to, S.R. was holding a shank (homemade knife) to his throat. S.R. warned L.O. that he would die if he yelled. He then anally raped L.O.

Early the next morning, when guards were delivering the breakfast trays, L.O., who was visibly injured, demanded that he be taken from the cell and brought to the prison infirmary. For an entire day, the guards ignored his plea. L.O. was not examined by prison medical staff until 9:00 a.m. the following morning.

L.O. was transferred to another prison but still felt extremely insecure and unsafe. Two months later, he attempted suicide by cutting his wrists. He was transferred to the prison psychiatric unit for treatment, where he stayed for the remainder of his sentence.

In August 1996, L.O. filed a complaint with the local district attorney, asking that his rape be investigated and the perpetrator—whose name he provided—be criminally prosecuted. No such prosecution was ever instituted, and L.O.'s follow up letters received no response. He was released to a half-way house in 1997, and has since left the prison system.

P.E.

P.E. is a young heterosexual male, as he emphasizes, "attracted to females *only.*" While incarcerated in Florida, P.E. said, he submitted to unwanted sex with another inmate, not because he violently attacked, but because he felt tricked into it. He wrote Human Rights Watch:

> This letter is about rape but not as defined by law, "the forceful taking," it is more towards "psychological manipulation." It happened to me . . . . I made the excellent victim. I'm white, 27, non-violent, loner, who receives little help from the outside ie family, and low self-esteem. Other inmates saw me as a target. I'm young, good-looking, have some feminine mannerisms and naive. Some wanted to be my "friend" to "look out for me." But they just wanted to use me. One inmate would stake claim to you by becoming your "friend" hanging out with you all the time. In reality, he was saying "don't touch he's mine." Its a gradually process that you become dependent on this person whether its financial, physical or emotional. But sooner or later there comes a time when he wants a return in his investment, a sexual return . . . . You don't want to ruin your "friendship" by saying no to something you don't want to do because then you don't get the "support" financial or emotional from your friend. So you do what he wants, I did, and that's how you get hooked.[3]

"Its a gradually process that you become dependent on this person whether its financial, physical or emotional. But sooner or later there comes a time when he wants a return in his investment, a sexual return."

P.E. entered Florida prison in mid-1997, scared, unsure of himself, and unfamiliar with prison ways. Soon after he was assigned to a housing unit, an older prison befriended him: offering P.E. food, cigarettes, and other items, and "talking to me in a friendly way." P.E. felt protected and safe in the company of the other inmate. As time went on, the friendship shifted toward sex. The other inmate began by masturbating himself in P.E.'s presence, later wanting P.E. to fellate him. P.E. was bewildered and uncomfortable, but he did not feel able to refuse. The relationship lasted about six months before P.E. could muster the courage to break it off. Since then, he has had to fight off several advances from other inmates who have "heard rumors," spread by the first inmate, "that I am a homosexual."

RAPE SCENARIOS

A gang of inmates violently attacks a lone prisoner in the shower, sticking a knife to his throat and ripping his clothes off. "Don't make a sound or you're dead," they warn him. Then they rape him, one after another.

This is what people outside of prison tend to picture when they think of prisoner-on-prisoner rape. The basic scenario is not inaccurate, Human Rights Watch has found; it occurs in prisons around the country. Rape in prison can be almost unimaginably vicious and brutal. Gang assaults are not uncommon, and victims may be left beaten, bloody and, in the most extreme cases, dead.

Yet overtly violent rapes are only the most visible and dramatic form of sexual abuse behind bars. Many victims of prison rape have never had a knife to their throat. They may have never been explicitly threatened. But they have nonetheless engaged in sexual acts against their will, believing that they had no choice.

These coercive forms of sexual abuse are much more common than violent gang rapes and, for prison authorities, much easier to ignore. Although Human Rights Watch received many reports of forcible sexual attacks, we also heard numerous accounts of abuse based on more subtle forms of coercion and intimidation. Prisoners, including those who had been forcibly raped, all agree that the threat of violence, or even just the implicit threat of violence, is a more common factor in sexual abuse than is actual violence. As one explained:

> From my point of view, rape takes place every day. A prisoner that is engaging in sexual acts, not by force, is still a victim of rape because I know that

deep inside this prisoner do not want to do the things that he is doing but he thinks that it is the only way that he can survive.[1]

In attempting to delineate some of the more common scenarios of prison sexual abuse, the following chapter describes both overtly violent forms of abuse and forms in which the violence is submerged or hidden. Key to many of the latter situations are what prisoners term "manipulation techniques" or "mind games": tricks used by predatory inmates to trap those they consider vulnerable.

In a letter to Human Rights Watch, a Florida prisoner set out a rough typology of the various forms of prisoner-on-prisoner sexual abuse. He explained:

Let me say I believe there are different levels or kinds of rape in prison. First, there is what I will refer to as "Bodily Force Rape" for lack of a better term. This is the kind of assault where one or more individuals attack another individual and by beating and subduing him force sex either anal or oral on him.

Second there is what I'll call Rape By Threat. An example of this would be, when an individual tells a weaker individual that in order to avoid being assulted by the individual who's speaking he must submit to his demand for sex.

Third and by far the most common is what I'll call using a persons fears of his situation to convince him to submit to sex . . . . Among inmates there is a debate wheather this is in fact rape at all. In my opinion it is in fact rape. Let me give you an example of what happens and you decide.

Example: A new inmate arrives. He has no funds for the things he needs such as soap, junk food, and drugs (there are a great deal of drugs in prisons). Someone befriends him and tells him if he needs anything come to him. The new arrival is some times aware, but most times not, that what he is receiving has a 100% interest rate that is compounded weekly. When the N.A. is in deep enough the "friend" will tell him he can cover some of his debt by submitting to sex. This has been the "friend's" objective from the begining. To manuver the N.A. into a corner where he's vulnerable. Is this rape? I think it is.[2]

"Let me say I believe there are different levels or kinds of rape in prison."

To answer this prisoner's question—can apparently consensual sex be deemed rape—and, if so, under what circumstances is it rape—it is necessary to explore the peculiar dynamics of incarceration.

Consent and Coercion in Prison

[A]ll choices and relationships are so constrained and limited in the unfree world of the prison that what is normally meant by such terms as "free" or "voluntary" does not apply.

James Gilligan, M.D., former director of mental health
of the Massachusetts prison system[3]

The existence of freely given consent or, conversely, the absence of coercion, is a critical factor in distinguishing sexual abuse from mere sex.[4] But in the context of imprisonment, much more so than in the outside world, the concepts of consent and coercion are extremely slippery. Prisons and jails are inherently coercive environments. Inmates enjoy little autonomy and little possibility of free choice, making it difficult to ascertain whether an inmate's consent to anything is freely given.[5] Distinguishing coerced sex from consensual sex can be especially difficult.

Human Rights Watch has previously addressed the issue of inmates' consent to sex in the specific case of women inmates' sexual relations with correctional officers. In light of officers' enormous authority over inmates—a power imbalance that eviscerates traditional notions of consent—we concluded that custodial sexual contact should be deemed a criminal act even in the absence of overt or implied coercion.[6]

Prisoner-on-prisoner sexual contact might first appear to pose very different questions than custodial sexual contact as, formally at least, prisoners are not supposed to be able to exercise power over each other. The reality, however, is that in most prisons, even those where correctional authorities make a reasonable effort to maintain control of their charges, an inmate hierarchy exists by which certain prisoners enjoy a great deal of power over their fellows and other prisoners are exposed to exploitation and abuse. This power imbalance is of course much more marked in prisons where the authorities have ceded effective control to the inmate population, an all too common occurrence. Indeed, where "the inmates run the prison"—a phrase Human Rights Watch heard on several occasions—some of the most abusive relationships take place with little or no need for threats or other overtly coercive acts. For some prisoners, the atmosphere of fear and intimidation is so overwhelming that they acquiesce in their sexual exploitation without putting up any obvious resistance. J.D., incarcerated in Colorado, explained how this happened to him:

". . . by far the most common is what I'll call using a persons fears of his situation to convince him to submit to sex . . . ."

> I came to prison in April, 1991. I'd never been to prison before. I basically feared for my life . . . . Eventually, I ended up with a roommate who took advantage of my situation. He made me feel "protected" somewhat. But, at the same time, he let me know he could quite capably beat me up, if he wanted. One night, after we were all locked down for the night, he told me he could help me overcome my sexual inhibitions, if I would let him. He told me he was bisexual. I knew he was quite sexually active, so to speak, as he had female pornography in the room as well as masturbating frequently to it. But, I was surprised he would come on to me. However, I felt very much in danger if I did not give in to him. I was very scared. I ended up letting him penetrate me anally. After this, I would feign sleep at night when he'd come in. But, there were several more times he forced me to perform sexually.[7]

Viewed from outside, the sexual relationship between J.D. and his cellmate would likely have appeared consensual. Indeed, in instances where the victim makes little apparent effort to escape the abuse, both prisoners and prison authorities often fall into the trap of viewing nonconsensual sexual activity as consensual, ignoring the larger context in which the activity takes place.[8] Consent, however, assumes the existence of choice. As will be described in more detail below, where prisoners feel unprotected and know in advance that their escape routes are closed, a narrow focus on consent is misguided. In other words, the relevant inquiry in evaluating sexual activity in prison is not simply "did the inmate consent to sex?" but also "did the inmate have the power to refuse unwanted sex?"

It is important to note, moreover, that it is these apparently "consensual" sexual acts that are least likely ever to come to the attention of correctional authorities. J.D., like most inmates in his position, never told the authorities about his situation.

Violent or Forcible Assaults

Inmate victims of rape have told Human Rights Watch of sexual assaults that ended in concussions, broken bones, deep wounds, and other serious injuries. A small number of inmates, such as Randy Payne, have been killed during sexually-motivated attacks.

Payne, a twenty-three year old white inmate who had been sentenced to fifteen years for having sex with a minor, was attacked by a group of about twenty other inmates within a week of arriving at a maximum-security Texas prison in August 1994. The inmates had demanded sex and money, but Payne had refused. He was beaten for almost two hours; guards later said they had not noticed anything until they found his bloody body in the dayroom. He died of head injuries a few days later.[9]

Another Texas inmate, showing deep scars on his head, neck, and chest, told Human Right Watch that the prisoner who inflicted the wounds had raped him eight separate times from July through November 1995. The first time M.R. was raped—"which felt like having a tree limb shoved up into me"—he told the prison chaplain about it, and the chaplain had him write out a statement for the facility's Internal Affairs department. The Internal Affairs investigator brought both the victim and the perpetrator into a room together and asked them what had happened. Although M.R. was terrified to speak of the incident in front of the other inmate, he told his story, while the perpetrator claimed the sex was consensual. After both of them had spoken, the investigator told them that "lovers' quarrels" were not of interest to Internal Affairs, sending them both back to their cells. "The guy shoved me into his house and raped me again," M.R. later said. "It was a lot more violent this time."[10]

M.R. spent several months trying to escape the rapist. He filed grievances over the first couple of rapes that were returned saying the sexual assaults never occurred. Once a guard stumbled upon a rape in progress; he took

M.R. out of the rapist's cell, but the incident was never investigated. M.R. was transferred to another wing but the rapist managed to sneak over there, banging on the bars to get M.R.'s attention. "He told me he loved me. He said if he couldn't have me nobody could." M.R., who is heterosexual, tried to tell the other prisoner that he had no interest in sex with any man, but the other prisoner dismissed this.

On December 31, the rapist again showed up on M.R.'s wing, threatening to kill M.R. with a combination lock, which he showed M.R. "I was in the dayroom. I remember eating a piece of cornbread and the next thing I knew I woke up in the hospital," M.R. recalled.[11] M.R. suffered a broken neck, jaw, left collarbone, and finger; a dislocated left shoulder; two major concussions and lacerations to his scalp that caused bleeding on the brain. A room full of prisoners witnessed the rapist nearly kill M.R. and, after he was done beating him, rape him in the middle of the dayroom. The rapist hit M.R. so hard with the lock that when M.R. regained consciousness he could read the word "Master"—the lockmaker—on his temple. Four years later, a Human Rights Watch researcher could still see the round impression of the lock on the right side of his forehead. The rapist was never criminally prosecuted, despite M.R.'s efforts to press charges. From what M.R. heard from other inmates, the rapist only received fifteen days' segregation as punishment for the near murder.

Extreme violence as an element of rape is even more common with gang assaults—assaults involving more than one perpetrator. A number of inmates told Human Rights Watch of being badly beaten during such assaults, especially in instances where the victim initially resisted the attack. A Georgia prisoner related, for example: "Two violent inmates with a record of violence threatened to sexually assault me and take my store goods. I tried to fight back, which resulted in my jaw being broke in 3 places."[12]

Other prisoners described assaults involving, in many instances, more than two perpetrators, and sometimes even up to six or eight of them. The perpetrators typically take turns holding the victim down on the bed or on the floor, or holding a weapon to him, while the others sexually assault him. Sometimes violence is not used, as it is easy enough for several prisoners to overpower a single victim simply by holding him in place. Violent language and degrading insults are common, as well as threats to kill the victim if he tells the authorities.

Forcible sexual assaults can occur in almost any area where inmates are found, but the most common place for such assaults to take place seems to be inmates' sleeping areas: either group dormitories or cells. Showers, bathrooms, and other areas offering a degree of privacy are also used. "It happens anywhere there's a little nook or cranny," explained a prisoner who was violently raped by three inmates in a washroom.[13]

Coerced Sexual Abuse

At night the guards locked themselves in a cage and slept while inmates sexually and physically assaulted others. . . . I at times was asked for sexual favors in order to maintain my security. I was never forced into sex physically, but mentally I wasn't capable of saying no, as I feared for my life.[14]

[T]he acceptance of a cigarette may have a hidden price attached.[15]

D.A., a young Texas inmate, was dozing off in his bed not long after being transferred to a new prison. "The next thing I know, there's someone in my cell," D.A. told a Human Rights Watch representative two years later. "He gave me an ultimatum: he said you're going to let me fuck you, or my homeboys will stab you."[16] D.A., who believed the aggressor was a member of the Crips gang, submitted to anal sex. His story is typical of many known to Human Rights Watch—rapes committed not through violence but through the threat of violence.

"I felt very much in danger if I did not give in to him. I was very scared. I ended up letting him penetrate me anally."

In many instances, moreover, the threat of violence is never even articulated by the perpetrator of sexual abuse, although it is likely to be implicit in his interaction with the victim. Instead of overt threats, manipulation is used. The victim's acute awareness of his own vulnerability is exploited by the perpetrator, who coerces the victim into unwanted yet unforced sexual contact.

A number of prisoners described typical coercion scenarios in detail to Human Rights Watch. The following are a couple of representative descriptions:

- [One technique to force a prisoner into sex is that] one of the bad guys will set up a power play. This is accomplished by him having two or three of his friends stop down on the prisoner of his choice in a strong manner as if to fight or beat up this prisoner. This usually puts the choosen prisoner in great fear of those type guys. The prisoner that set up this will be close by when this goes down. His roll is to step in just before the act gets physical. He defends the choosen prisoner by taking on the would be offenders. This works to gain the respect and trust of the choosen prisoner. After this encounter the choosen prisoner is encouraged to hang out with his new friend. This is repeated once or twice more to convence the choosen one of the sincere loyalties of the prisoner that set all this up. . . . They become very close, the choosen one feels compelled to show his thanks by giving at first monetary favors to his protector and it progress to the point where this guy that set up the attacks on him will not accept just the money. He starts to insist on the choosen one to give him sexual favors . . . . The fear of him, the choosen one, is that if he do not have this one Protector the rest of the guys will be back after him. After all it is better to have one person that you give sexual favors than it would be to have to be forced to do the act by two or more prisoners at the same time.[17]

- What is more prevalent at TCIP . . . is best called "coercion." I suppose you have an idea what these engagements entail. The victim is usually tricked into owing a favor. Here this is usually drugs, with the perpetrator seeming to be, to the victim, a really swell fellow and all. Soon, however, the victim is asked to repay all those joints or licks of dope—right away. Of course he has no drugs or money, and the only alternative is sexual favors. Once a prisoner is "turned-out," it's pretty much a done deal. I guess a good many victims just want to do their time and not risk any trouble, so they submit. . . . The coercion-type abuses continue because of their covert nature. From the way such attacks manifest, it can seem to others, administrators and prisoners, that the victims are just homosexual to begin with. Why else would they allow such a thing to happen, people might ask.[18]

These descriptions illustrate the two basic scenarios—both of which involve debt—repeated again and again by inmates. The first is that an inmate acts as a protector to a vulnerable prisoner, scaring off (or pretending to scare off) other predators. Sometimes the protector begins by doing this for free, asking nothing in return, but eventually he will ask to be rewarded sexually. If the victim refuses, prisoners have explained, then the protector himself will threaten the victim overtly, but such overt threats are frequently unnecessary. When the victim is convinced that rape is inevitable, he will often accede under little direct pressure, hoping simply to lessen the physical violence of the act.

"I was in the dayroom. I remember eating a piece of cornbread and the next thing I knew I woke up in the hospital."

The second basic scenario is for the perpetrator to provide food, drugs, or other desirable items to a potential victim, allowing the victim to build up a debt. At some point, the perpetrator insists that the debt be repaid via sexual favors. Again, if the victim hesitates, the perpetrator may make it terrifyingly clear to him that refusal is not an option, but this last step is often unnecessary.

Constant sexual harassment—sexualized comments, whistling, groping—is often another part of the process by which the victim is pressured into submitting to unwanted sex. G.H., who entered prison when he was seventeen and was almost immediately coerced into sexual contact, said that while he was being processed through the initial orientation phase, still in shock over being incarcerated, "inmates would whistle at me and tell me Im a convicts dream 'girl' come true."[19] L.B., a small, slim first offender convicted of burglary, remembered entering a new prison in 1996: "as soon as I walked on the wing, the catcalls started."[20] Describing the effect of such harassment on the victim, another prisoner said, "the dominant party [will] first let the intended victim know that he wants to have sex with him, then begin to wear the victim down by constantly leering at him in ways that let the victim know what's on his mind. Psychologically the victim eventually begins to believe he is a homosexual and no longer resists."[21]

Seasoned inmates are usually familiar with tactics such as these, and are more skilled at managing them. As G.H. exemplifies, it is new, incoming inmates who are most vulnerable. As one prisoner put it: "Most of prison is a mind game. People get taken advantage of when they're green and don't know what to expect."[22]

Continuing Sexual Abuse

You will be lebled as a bisexual, or homosexual, pretty boy, gay, little girl, queen. Once there has been penetration or forced oral sex, the jacket is on his back, as being a punk, sissy, queer, etc.[23]

Once subject to sexual abuse, whether violently or through coercion, a prisoner may easily become trapped into a sexually subordinate role. Prisoners refer to the initial rape as "turning out" the victim, and the suggestion of transformation is telling. Through the act of rape, the victim is redefined as an object of sexual abuse. He has been proven to be weak, vulnerable, "female," in the eyes of other inmates. Regaining his "manhood"—and the respect of other prisoners—can be nearly impossible.

In a cruel twist, the fact of victimization may be viewed as justifying itself, given the common inmate belief that a real man would never submit to rape. According to one extreme variant of this view, the rapist merely recognizes and acts upon the victim's "latent homosexual tendencies." As one Texas inmate put it, many inmates are convinced that:

> "He gave me an ultimatum: he said you're going to let me fuck you, or my homeboys will stab you."

[D]udes that are turned out were like that in the first place & just wanted an excuse to come out of the closet . . . . [P]unks were born like that and it doesn't matter because if it did they'd fight and/or resist.[24]

Even prisoners who do not share this view often believe that, once the rape has taken place, the victim becomes a homosexual. Inmates speak of other raped prisoners as being "converted to women" or "made into homosexuals," as if one's sexuality might be irretrievably altered by the fact of rape.[25] That some victims of rape appear to accept the role imposed on them—by failing to report the abuse or even by adopting stereotypically feminine attributes—strengthens prisoners' adherence to this view.

Stigmatized as a "punk" or "turn out," the victim of rape will almost inevitably be the target of continuing sexual exploitation, both from the initial perpetrator and, unless the perpetrator "protects" him, from other inmates as well. "Once someone is violated sexually and there is no consequences on the perpetrators, that person who was violated then becomes a mark or marked," an Indiana prisoner told Human Rights Watch. "That means he's fair game."[26] His victimization is likely to be public knowledge, and his reputation will follow him to other housing areas, if he is moved, and even to other prisons. As another inmate explained: "Word travels so Fast in prison. The Convict grape vine is <u>Large.</u> You cant run or hide."[27]

With other prisoners being moved around the prison system, and inmates communicating via other means as well, transfer to a new prison unit is no guarantee of escaping one's reputation. It may, however, provide a respite from abuse—and, in some cases, a new start—especially if the new unit is less volatile and violent than the previous one. W.M. is a Texas prisoner who was raped soon after entering prison and became a "turn out," sexually exploited by a long series of inmates. Finally, after years of abuse, he "went renegade," as he put it. Transferred to a new prison unit, he saw it as an opportunity to make a break with the past. Heavier, stronger, and far more street smart than he was when he entered prison, he physically attacked any inmate who approached him sexually.

Explaining how he succeeded in escaping further abuse, W.M. said:

> You asked if I thought someone who is raped is necessarily going to be targeted for more abuse. The answer is an emphatic yes. Anyone who's had the pipe laid to them is going to be tried constantly throughout his stay in prison. I've got scars where I've been stabbed & cut up, I'll show you when I see you. There is a price you pay when you break away and any prison boy/gal knows it. The trick [to successfully avoiding continuing sexual abuse] is to stay low-key after you succeed & deny, deny, deny, if it's ever brought up and if there is any question or any doubt in anyone's mind, you do your best to kill the person that brought it up. Blood clears a lot of questions from peoples' heads.

But the years before W.M. made his break are more representative of the options typically open to victims of rape. After being raped by his cellmate, he was forced to "be with someone": a protector who kept other inmates away. When that person was transferred to different unit, W.M. was passed on to another man. "I usually spent about three or four months with each one. I was with one guy for ten months."[28] Inmates told Human Rights

Watch that such an outcome is considered normal: "The result of 'turning out' a kid is that the kid usually finds a 'dad'—an older, strong inmate to take care of him and to protect him from any future attacks."[29] Notably, a similar phenomenon of "protective pairing" has been documented in the case of women abducted and sexually abused during armed conflict.[30]

Numerous victims told Human Rights Watch similar stories of becoming the "kid" or the "wife" of their rapist. Some, in even worse predicaments, were forced to sexually service an entire gang for a period of time.

Just as with the initial acts of coerced sex described above, this type of continuing sexual abuse is likely to be viewed as consensual by others, including prison staff. When sexual contact is no longer violent, it may be thought that the inmate is consenting to it. Yet even if a prisoner initially fights back against his attackers, he will at some point resign himself to his situation and stop fighting it. "Rarely does somebody resist after the 5th or 6th time," explained W.M. "That's why they say its by choice not force most of the time. That's a lie though, because mental force is just as effective if not more."[31]

The only escape from abuse, except for the small minority of inmates who succeed in rehabilitating their reputation, is release from prison or transfer to a protective custody or safekeeping unit—areas designed to be havens for vulnerable inmates. Yet as will be discussed in chapter VIII, it can be very difficult to convince prison authorities to authorize such a transfer. Moreover, protective custody units tend to be extremely restrictive, even punitive, in their conditions.

"You will be lebled as a bisexual, or homosexual, pretty boy, gay, little girl, queen."

Even more worrisome, the very fact of trying to escape to protective custody by reporting sexual abuse puts an inmate at greater risk. As is explained at greater length below, the general stigma against "snitching"—reporting other inmates' wrongdoing—discourages victims from informing prison officials of their abuse. In cases of prisoner-on-prisoner rape, the perpetrators often reinforce the tacit prohibition on snitching by specifically threatening violent retaliation if the victim says a word to officials about what happened to him.

Slavery

*A convicted felon is one whom the law in its humanity punishes by confine-
ment in the penitentiary instead of death . . . . For the time being, during
his term of service in the penitentiary, he is a slave of penal servitude to the
State.*

———————

Virginia Supreme Court in *Ruffin v. Commonwealth, 62 Va. 790, 796* (1871).

*[A]n offender should not and must not, be sentenced to a term of enslave-
ment by gangs, rape and abuse by predatory inmates.*

———————

Federal district court opinion in *Ruiz v. Texas* (1999).

*[An inmate] claimed me as his property and I didnt dispute it. I became obe-
dient, telling myself at least I was surviving . . . . He publicly humiliated and
degraded me, making sure all the inmates and gaurds knew that I was a
queen and his property. Within a week he was pimping me out to other
inmates at $3.00 a man. This state of existence continued for two months
until he sold me for $25.00 to another black male who purchased me to be
his wife.*

———————

Michigan inmate, October 4, 1996.

Prisoners unable to escape a situation of sexual abuse may find
themselves becoming another inmate's "property." The word is
commonly used in prison to refer to sexually subordinate inmates, and it
is no exaggeration. Victims of prison rape, in the most extreme cases, are
literally the slaves of the perpetrators. Forced to satisfy another man's sexual appetites whenever he demands, they may also be responsible for
washing his clothes, cooking his food, massaging his back, cleaning his cell,
and myriad other chores. They are frequently "rented out" for sex, sold, or
even auctioned off to other inmates, replicating the financial aspects of
traditional slavery. Their most basic choices, like how to dress and whom
to talk to, may be controlled by the person who "owns" them. They may
even be renamed as women.[22] Like all forms of slavery, these situations are

among the most degrading and dehumanizing experiences a person can undergo.

J.D., a white inmate in Texas who admits that he "cannot fight real good," told Human Rights Watch that he was violently raped by his cellmate, a heavy, muscular man, in 1993. "From that day on," he said, "I was classified as a homosexual and was sold from one inmate to the next."[33] Although he informed prison staff that he had been raped and was transferred to another part of the prison, the white inmates in his new housing area immediately "sold" him to a black inmate known as Blue Top. Blue Top used J.D. sexually, while also "renting" his sexual services to other black inmates. Besides being forced to perform "all types of sexual acts," J.D. had to defer to Blue Top in every other way. Under Blue Top's dominion, no task was too menial or too degrading for J.D. to perform. After two and a half months of this abuse, J.D. was finally transferred to safekeeping.

Another Texas inmate explained the financial dimension that is evident in J.D.'s treatment. According to him, "when they do turn out a guy they actually own them, every penny they get it goes to there man. You can buy a kid for 20 or 30 dollars on most wings!! They sell them like cattle."[34] A third Texas inmate made a similar analogy: "It would amaze you (as it did me) to see human beings bought & sold like shoes."[35]

The testimony of another Texas inmate, describing the rules imposed on him by the prisoner who became his "man," suggests the extent to which these victimized inmates are forced to obey their abusers, sexually and otherwise:

> "You will clean the house," he said, have my clothes clean and when Im ready to get my "freak" no arguments or there will be a punishment! I will, he said, let my homeboys have you or Ill just sale you off. Do we have an understanding? With fear, misery, and confusion inside me ... I said yes.[36]

Six Texas inmates, separately and independently, gave Human Rights Watch firsthand accounts of being forced into this type of sexual slavery, having even been "sold" or "rented" out to other inmates. Numerous other Texas prisoners confirmed that the practice of sexual slavery, including the buying and selling of inmates, is commonplace in the system's more dangerous prison units. Although Texas, judging from the information received by Human Rights Watch, has the worst record in this respect, we also collected personal testimonies from inmates in Illinois, Michigan, California and Arkansas who have survived situations of sexual slavery.

Prisoners elsewhere frequently spoke of the phenomenon, suggesting that it is not limited to the states mentioned above. An Indiana prisoner, for example, told Human Rights Watch:

> most time when a young boy is turned out by a gang, the sole purpose of that is first to fuck the boy especially young boys, once they finish with the boy they are sold to another prisoner for profit, it's big business selling boys in prisons and gang members control this business.[37]

When slavery and involuntary servitude were officially abolished in the United States by the Thirteenth Amendment to the U.S. constitution, an exception was made for "a punishment for crime whereof the party shall have been duly convicted."[38] At that time, prisoners were considered the "slaves of the state," outside the purview of judicially-enforced constitutional protections. More than a hundred years later, prisoners' legal status has improved. Yet, a different, though equally horrifying, form of slavery continues in U.S. prisons, and the fundamental rights of the victims of these abuses continue to be ignored.

"Once someone is violated sexually and there is no consequences on the perpetrators, that person who was violated then becomes a mark or marked."

Sex, Violence and Power

Rape in prison is rarely a sexual act, but one of violence, politics, and an acting out of power roles.

———————

Journalist and prisoner Wilbert Rideau, in "The Sexual Jungle"[39]

Of course rape is a crime of hatred. I'm ugly as a mud fence, why would W.R. want to have sex with me?

———————

A Texas inmate, October 8, 1998.

Locked in an all male society, lacking other sexual outlets, prisoners might be assumed to commit rape as a means of sexual release. Yet the cruelty and degradation so intimately connected to rape in prison undermines this facile explanation, suggesting that inmates' real motivations for committing rape are more complicated. Theorists of rape, whose research has mostly focused on women victims, have posited that rape is as much a crime of violence as it is one of sex.[40] Prisoners' views and experiences, as conveyed to Human Rights Watch, tend to confirm this notion.

The question of whether prisoner-on-prisoner rape is primarily a crime of violence or of sex is not an academic one, since knowledge of rape's causes is obviously of benefit in crafting effective prevention strategies. Were the causes of rape found to be rooted in sexual deprivation per se, then conjugal visits, for example, might be recommended as the primary means of attacking the problem.[41]

But prison experts, academic commentators, and prisoners themselves generally concur that sexual deprivation is not the main source of the phenomenon.[42] Instead, in the prison context, where power and hierarchy are key, rape is an expression of power. It unequivocally establishes the aggressor's dominance, affirming his masculinity, strength, and control at the expense of the victim's.

People in prison are deprived of sex, but perhaps even more fundamentally they are deprived of almost all choice in or power over their lives. The most basic decisions affecting them—what to eat, when to get up, where and with whom to live—are outside of their control. As Louisiana prisoner and writer Wilbert Rideau has pointed out, "The psychological pain involved in such an existence creates an urgent and terrible need for reinforcement of [the prisoner's] sense of manhood and personal worth."[43] One means of doing so is by establishing absolute power over another prisoner via rape.

Numerous prisoners confirmed this portrayal of rape as a means of expressing power in a situation of powerlessness. Explained a Virginia inmate: "In my view the perpetrator of rape is an angry man. He lacks power and decides to steal it from others through assault." Interestingly, this same inmate drew a correlation between the imposition of a more oppressive prison regime, in which officials treat prisoners unfairly, and the likelihood of a sexual assault. He explained that he had noticed that "the more oppressive the system the higher the incidents of assaultive behavior in general . . . . Fair and objective treatment seems to create a less-assaultive environment."[44] Indeed, if prisoners' quest for dominance over others is to some extent a consequence of their

> **"You asked if I thought someone who is raped is necessarily going to be targeted for more abuse. The answer is an emphatic yes."**

lack of power in every other area of life, then it stands to reason that a harsher and more arbitrary prison regime would exacerbate the tendency.

A Nebraska inmate put the matter succinctly: "Power, control, revenge, seem to top the 'reasons' for rape."[45] Others elaborated at length on the factors that contribute to the problem:

> Most cons are emotionally alienated from themselves. The peer pressure not to be seen as "weak" pertaining to any gentler emotion, is astronomically intense . . . . In prison, to gain a simple hug which is emotionally soothing without being threatening, the dominator can only accept from the dominated. [Also] a prisoner experiences profound powerlessness of self over one's life and future. One of the most basic ways to resume an illusion of empowerment of self is to establish power over another at ground zero: life and sexual gratification.[46]

In prison, as elsewhere, money is a form of power. The financial incentives for rape are another aggravating factor, particularly in prison systems in which prisoners have no means of making money except by extorting it from other prisoners or by pimping them out.

The obvious disdain prisoners share regarding "punks" and "turn-outs"—inmates subject to sexual abuse—further strengthens the view of rape as a crime of violence and power, not of sexual passion. Indeed, "punk" is a frequently used insult in prison, denoting everything that prisoners do not want to be. A Utah inmate told Human Rights Watch: "The word 'punk' in this facility is used loosely, and is a term used to down-size someone, as well as to identify an actual 'punk' meaning a kid or guy who is used and exploited sexually because he is too timid or weak to make a stand."[47] As explained above, a raped inmate is considered degraded and humiliated; rape, in other words, is a means of degradation.

"From that day on, I was classified as a homosexual and was sold from one inmate to the next."

Still, to think that there is a strict dichotomy between rape as a sexual act and rape as a violent assertion of power may be somewhat misguided. Rapists are, in the most obvious ways, sexually stimulated by what they are doing. "[N]o matter how one characterizes it, i.e., 'control'; 'violence'; 'rage' etc.," suggested a Colorado inmate, "it is sexuality."[48] The fact that the victim of rape is injured and degraded may itself be a source of sexual arousal to the rapist. Daniel Lockwood, an expert on prison rape, has posited that sexual aggression in prison can be traced to men's sexist attitudes toward women, which, in prison, translate into a bias against men placed in female roles.[49] The fact that stereotypically feminine characteristics are so despised in male prisoners may reflect a more general contempt of women, not just men who are considered to be like women. Although misogyny would appear to be an unlikely cause of male-on-male rape, it may be an ingredient in the volatile mix that results in sexual abuse in prison.

Case Histories of S.H. and M.R.

S.H.

I was "rented out" for sexual favors, and a lot of the guys who rented me are not rapists, or assaulted as children, or any other stereotypical model. They just wanted some sexual satisfaction, even though they knew I was not deriving pleasure from it, and was there only because I was forced to . . . . I was with the Valluco (Valley) crowd, so I was only passed around to them for free. D. Town Hispanics had to pay. They were charged $3 for a blow-job, $5 for anal sex . . . . I am not effeminate, nor am I even homosexual. [1]

With two prior nonviolent felonies, S.H. received a seventy-five year sentence for burglary in 1994. He was twenty-four years old.

S.H. was sent to a minimum-security wing of a rural Texas prison. Having been incarcerated before, he was fairly confident he could manage the situation. Nearly immediately, however, he misunderstood a guard's order and received a minor disciplinary ticket, resulting in his transfer to the "North Side" of the facility, a more dangerous area.

S.H. is white, and whites were a small minority where he was sent. Among the nearly 190 inmates on a wing, less than twenty were white. In Texas prisons, then as now, racial tensions on the cell blocks were extreme. Whom prisoners socialized with, whom they would defend in a fight, whom they would victimize—even where prisoners sat—was primarily determined by race. All of the dayroom benches, for example, were "assigned" by race, the bulk of them going to black inmates. Whites, as the numerical minority, were seen as easy targets for extortion and sexual exploitation.

A large proportion of white inmates were forced by other inmates to "ride," that is, to pay protection: either money or sex or both. White inmates who refused to ride, and who would therefore fight to protect themselves, were known as "woods." In his first letter to Human Rights Watch, S.H. explained the choices facing an incoming inmate such as himself:

> A White guy comes onto the block. He stands there, someone will usually direct him to the back wall of the dayroom. If he's lucky, one of the woods will go talk to him, let him know that if he fights, they'll back him up after the first couple, then he wont have any problems. This is called "checking." If he is scared (who's not) and doesnt want to fight, he has to "get a man."[2]

At 5'11" and 150 pounds, S.H. has a medium build, but is admittedly "not a great fighter."[3] Nonetheless when he arrived on the North Side he was determined to stand up for himself. Soon after his transfer there, he had to fight two Hispanic prisoners, one after the other. Although the two inmates beat him, S.H. proved himself sufficiently that the "woods"—the whites who did not pay protection—accepted him among their group. He was allowed to sit at the "wood bench," a privilege extended only to white inmates who passed the "checking" stage.

After a few weeks, however, S.H. had a falling out with P.E., the leader of the woods, an Aryan Circle gang member. At the same time, a shortage of bench space led the Hispanic inmates, who were feeling crowded by the whites, to challenge the whites to give them more space. The Hispanic inmates proposed to "recheck" all of the white inmate—to fight the whites again—until they gained more bench space. P.E., as the leader of the white inmates, came up with a different solution. On March 31, P.E. "sacrificed" S.H. to the Hispanics:

> He told me and two others that we were banished from the group and could no longer sit on the bench. When I returned to the wing, four or five Hispanic guys surrounded me. I said, "OK, I'll ride." I knew I didn't have a chance. I tried to get out that night by telling the sergeant; he told me "be a man, go take care of your business."[4]

A few days later, on April 6, S.H. filed an "emergency" grievance requesting that he be placed in solitary confinement. Soon after, he told a classification counselor that he was considered the "property" of a Hispanic gang, and a few days later the counselor sent a sergeant into the wing to investigate. S.H. told the sergeant what was happening and the sergeant responded that he was lying, then called him a "wimp" for not fighting the gang. The sergeant wanted to call out one of the Hispanic inmates to question him about S.H.'s allegations, an action that S.H. opposed, as he felt it would put his life in danger by branding him as a snitch. The sergeant said that this was the way he conducted investigations, and if S.H. disagreed with his methods, he could ask for the investigation to be dropped. Feeling he had no choice, S.H. dropped the investigation. His written request stated that he was withdrawing his protection request because the Hispanic inmate in question would "know exactly who told what and *I*, not any guard, will be the one subjected to physical abuse over it."[5]

As a prisoner who was riding, S.H. was "controlled" by a Hispanic prisoner known as Batuco, a member of the Vallucos. S.H. was indigent so Batuco made S.H. do his housework: clean his cell, wash his clothes, etc. S.H. also had to make deliveries for Batuco: to break prison rules by sneaking over to other wings and bringing packages to other inmates. The second time he had to make a delivery, he was sent over to the cell of a large Hispanic prisoner who greeted him with the words: "You know what you're here for." When S.H. said no, the inmate forced him down on the bunk and anally raped him.

"Afterwards, I was numb from shock . . . . I stayed in my cell for twenty-four hours, I was so upset," S.H. later remembered.[6] He was too ashamed, too shocked, and too scared to report the rape and try to obtain a medical examination. Batuco let a week go by and then started forcing S.H. into giving him oral sex. He threatened to stab S.H. if S.H. reported it.

Near the end of April, the prison held a reclassification hearing. S.H. claims that when he told the presiding officer that he was being forced to ride, the officer responded, "'People like you

"After plaintiff vehemently protested that he was being truthful, [the sergeant] made comments that plaintiff 'must be gay' for 'letting them make you suck dick.'"

make me sick. You rob and steal and then come down here whining, expecting us to protect you. Be a man, for Crissakes.'"[7] His request for safekeeping status was denied.

In the meantime, Batuco was making S.H. service the rest of the Vallucos, some five or six other guys, and even "renting" him out to other Hispanics on occasion. Even though Batuco was in charge of S.H., he and S.H. argued frequently. Batuco wanted S.H. to "play like I was a woman (shave my body hair, etc. . . .)," but S.H. refused, and was beaten for it.[8] Other Hispanic inmates accused Batuco of not being able to control S.H. So Batuco, under pressure from his friends, "sold" S.H. to S.H.'s cellmate for $10. "$10 was really cheap," S.H. explained. "But he wanted to get rid of me. It usually cost $30 to get out of a ride."[9]

S.H.'s cellmate promised him that the debt would not entail any sex. Instead, S.H. washed his cellmate's clothes, as well as the clothes of other prisoners, in order to pay his cellmate back the $10. A few weeks later, however, his cellmate demanded sex from S.H. S.H. had an African American friend, Oz, who was a member of the Nation of Islam, which frowned upon sexual abuse. Oz stood up for S.H. and paid his cellmate some of the money he was owed.

At every opportunity, S.H. was requesting transfer to a safer environment, in particular, the safekeeping wing. A few days before a classification hearing on one of these requests, S.H. gave a classification counselor a list containing the names of people who had sexually abused him. At the hearing, on June 23, S.H. described his situation in detail. Nonetheless, safekeeping status was denied him: a factor cited in the denial was the absence of physical proof of assault.

In August, S.H. was transferred to another wing where he "rode" with a Hispanic inmate from Houston, named Sanchez. Sanchez forced him to submit to anal sex almost immediately. In general, he exercised a high degree of control over S.H. As S.H. described it:

> I'd ask Sanchez if I could go sit with Becker, a friend of mine who was riding with the blacks. You know when you ride with someone, they control whatever you do, even who you talk to. You have to ask before you can go talk to someone. If you're riding, in essence, you're owned.[10]

That same month, one of S.H.'s friends wrote S.H.'s mother and informed her that her son was being raped. Out of shame and embarrassment, S.H. had not spoken to her of that part of his situation, although he had told her of his desperate need for protection. S.H.'s mother had already written to the warden asking that her son be placed on safekeeping; this time she wrote explaining that her son had been raped. She received a letter in mid-August from the warden that declared, in a blatant misstatement:

> We have no reports of your son being raped . . . . Your son has not reported any incident to security, or to medical staff. I am sorry you received inadequate information to cause you to worry about your son.[11]

During that same period S.H. told another guard about his situation, providing him with the names of several other prisoners who he said would corroborate his account of sexual abuse.[12] A few days later, a sergeant visited S.H., purportedly to investigate the allegations. As S.H. described it in a lawsuit filed later:

> [The sergeant] refused to interview the inmate witnesses and told plaintiff that he was lying about being sexually abused. After plaintiff vehemently protested that he was being truthful, [the sergeant] made comments that plaintiff "must be gay" for "letting them make you suck dick."[13]

In October, Sanchez transferred out to minimum custody. Sanchez's cell mate, called Clutch, inherited S.H. from Sanchez. Within two days, Clutch made S.H. give oral sex to a gang leader named Kilo. On January 1, 1995, Clutch forced S.H. to submit to anal sex. S.H. reported the assault and in the middle of the night was taken from his cell and brought to the infirmary, where a rape kit was administered. Yet, because he had not been physically beaten and there were no tears in his anus, the rape kit showed "no objective evidence of sexual assault."

At that point, in January 1995, S.H. was finally placed in safekeeping, where the atmosphere was much less violent and racially-charged; the sexual abuse stopped. He had been victimized for over nine months.

Throughout this period of constant sexual abuse S.H. had filed numerous grievances with the prison authorities, desperately seeking removal to a safer, more controlled environment. His file for 1994 shows grievances dated April 5 (denied May 24), June 22 (denied July 11, appealed July 14, denied August 18, appealed August 20, denied September 8), August 29 (denied September 20, appealed September 28, denied November 18, appealed November 23, denied December 14), September 26 (denied October 25, appealed October 29, denied November 22, appealed December 6, denied December 20), and November 4 (denied December 6, appealed December 14, denied January 25, 1995, appealed January 29, denied March 27). He had also told numerous guards and prison psychologists what was happening to him, as well as members of prison classification committees.

S.H.'s grievances directly and unambiguously explained his problems. His June 22 grievance stated plainly: "I have been, and am repeatedly being sexually abused. I have written detailed statements telling Who, What, When, Where, How of the situations. No one has taken any type of action."[14] The warden's denial, a textbook example of bureaucratic obfuscation, stated: "In most cases, this procedure provides you with fifteen days before a grievance must be filed in this office. This time period should provide you with ample time to seek and attempt informal resolution to your issue .... No further action will be taken at this level."[15] Appealing the denial of the grievance to the deputy director of with the state prison system, S.H. begged: "I only want to be safe from sexual abuse. Please help me!" This plea too was ignored.

Once in safekeeping, S.H. spoke with prison investigators, including Internal Affairs staff, about bring criminal charges against Clutch. He twice wrote the Henderson County district attorney, in March and May 1995, demanding that rape charges be instituted. No charges were ever brought.

Throughout 1994 and 1995, S.H. sent letters to lawyers and legal service organization attempting to find a pro bono (volunteer) lawyer to intercede on his behalf. Acting as his own legal counsel, he finally filed suit in federal court in July 1996. His handwritten complaint contained a ninety-two paragraph fact section, setting out dates, names, and incidents in precise detail. He later filed five affidavits with the court in which other prisoners corroborated his claims.[16]

The federal district court hearing the case first ruled that all of S.H.'s claims relating to events prior to July 12, 1994, were barred by a two-year statute of limitations. As for incidents after that date, the court dismissed the case in May 1997, placing stress on the fact that in April 1994 S.H. had requested that the initial investigation be dropped. (As described above, that request was the result of S.H.'s very real fear that the sergeant's investigative techniques put his life in danger.) S.H. fought the dismissal of his case at every step, requesting the district court to reconsider its judgment, and then appealing the court's decision. In mid 1999, the U.S. Court of Appeals for the Fifth Circuit denied S.H.'s appeal. Its brief, unpublished opinion, which failed to deal with the substance of any of S.H.'s claims, wholly upheld the district court's decision. In a letter to Human Rights Watch describing the appellate ruling, S.H. said: "I can't convey to you how upset I am over this. It would be a lot different if I lost at trial . . . . I am devastated."[17]

Looking through S.H.'s files—the countless grievances, letters, affidavits, legal briefs and other materials, only some of which have been described here—one wonders what more a prisoner could possibly do, within the system, to save himself from sexual abuse.

M.R.

Since I've been in prison I have endured more misery than most people could handle . . . . [A]ll open homosexuals are preyed upon and if they don't choose up they get chosen.[18]

M.R., a gay white inmate, entered the Arkansas prison system in early 1992, at age twenty-one. He has, in his words, "feminine characteristics," including long blond hair, that mean that in the prison environment he is "considered to be female."[19]

M.R. was placed in the general prison population when he arrived at Cummins Unit in 1992. Faced with the gangs and violence of the unit, he knew he had to find someone to protect him. Under pressure, he chose someone to "hook up" with. The relationship only lasted a few days, however, since M.R. was considered such an attractive target that his new guardian did not feel able to protect both of them.

According to M.R., "a Black guy paid an officer 2 cartons of 'Kools' to write me up so I could be moved to his block with him."[20] M.R. claims that such guard involvement is not unusual. In prison, among both guards and inmates, "money will buy anything and I do mean anything."[21] Almost immediately, the other prisoner sexually assaulted M.R., anally raping him in his cell. M.R. escaped the abuse by requesting protective custody.

Because of a severe shortage of space in the protective custody block, however, M.R. was bounced back into general population several times. Although he was transferred into other prisons, each place he went he faced harassment and sexual abuse.

In March 1995, over his strong objections, he was transferred from a protective custody block at Cummins Unit into the general prison population. As he had expected, he immediately became the target of harassment by other prisoners. One inmate in particular appeared to be after him, repeatedly threatening him with violence. Toward the end of the month M.R. had a classification hearing on his request to return to protective custody. The hearing officers demanded that he tell them exactly who was threatening him, with the warden at the hearing reportedly telling him: "'how do you expect us to investigate this matter if you don't tell us some names?'" M.R. was afraid to give any names, fearing that members of the committee would interview the inmates, and that the other inmates would know that he snitched. Despite his fear, he did name the inmates involved. Nonetheless, he was denied protective custody.

> "Out of fear for my life, I submitted to sucking his dick, being fucked in my ass, and performing other duties as a woman, such as making his bed. In all reality, I was his slave."

Back in general population, M.R. "was forced to live with and face these same inmates (who the Classification Committee interviewed) who all called [him] a 'snitch' and threatened [him] with bodily harm."[22] Other prisoners told him bluntly, "'you snitched on the wrong motherfuckers.'"[23] The next month, the prisoner who had previously threatened him took action. As M.R. described it:

> I had no choice but to submit to being Inmate B.'s prison wife. Out of fear for my life, I submitted to sucking his dick, being fucked in my ass, and performing other duties as a woman, such as making his bed. In all reality, I was his slave, as the Officials of the Arkansas Department of Corrections under the 'color of law' did absolutely nothing.[24]

After a week of this, M.R. managed to get transferred to another cellblock, but there other prisoners continued to harass him. A month later, he was transferred back into the same cellblock with inmate B; the sexual abuse resumed. On June 3:

> I was at Inmate B.'s bed and he forced me to kiss him and suck his dick. While doing this, he had his hand on my head with his fingers entwined in my hair forcing my head up and down and trying to choke me with his dick. The entire time Inmate B. was telling me "suck it bitch." At this time, CO-1 M. observed this through the outside window of the barracks. He observed this until Inmate B. ejected sperm in my mouth, then he walked in the barracks and told us both to go to the Captain's Office.

Both M.R. and inmate B. were given disciplinary violations for a "sex offense," with M.R. receiving fifteen days' punitive isolation and the loss of privileges. He was later assigned back to protective custody.

BODY AND SOUL
The Physical and Psychological
Injury of Prison Rape

[Plaintiff L.T. is] a skinny, white, passive, non-violent, short timer, who is blind in his right eye. . . . On 1-25-97, at aproximately 2:00 A.M., plaintiff went into the bathroom of seven (7) barracks and inmate C.Williams followed after. Plaintiff used the urinal and as he turned, inmate Williams pulled a shank (glass knife) from a book and threatened to poke plaintiffs other eye out and kill him if he did not let Williams fuck the plaintiff. Williams then told plaintiff to go to the rear corner of the bathroom, pulled a small bottle of lotion from his pocket and made plaintiff rub it on his penis. Williams then put the shank to plaintiffs throat and said "turn around and pull those pants down," which plaintiff did for fear of his life if he did not. Williams then raped (penile penetration to anus) the plaintiff with the shank at plaintiffs' throat, pressing it and saying "shut up bitch" when plaintiff began to moan and wanting to scream from the pain. After climaxing and wiping himself off, Williams said "If you ever tell anyone, I or one of my gang members will kill you, in here or in the world." . . . . Plaintiff suffered great physical pain, although short lived, and continues to suffer severe emotional and psychological mental anguish as a result of being raped . . . . Plaintiff has taken, and was just re-prescribed, anti-depressant medications which do not seem to help. Plaintiff believes this incident alone . . . has caused a nervous disorder, his inability to concentrate and a worsened memory, and the lack of energy or desire to do the simplest of things, inexpressable humiliation, raging anger, etc. etc.; all of which plaintiff does not see any drugs, counseling or monetary relief from the defendants being able to cure. [1]

L.T.'s experience of rape was violent, painful, and humiliating. The rape itself was physically agonizing, the resulting rectal soreness lasted several days, and L.T.'s intense fear of contracting HIV persisted for months. But worst of all, for him, was the devastating psychological impact of the attack. Racked by continuing nightmares, depression, and thoughts of suicide, L.T. believed that the rape had irretrievably damaged his psyche. Formerly a friendly person, he found himself retreating from social contact, becoming angry, suspicious, and reclusive. Despite the mental trauma he suffered, he received no counseling while incarcerated, nor did he succeed in obtaining legal assistance in his subsequent court challenge to the abuse. Without having secured psychological treatment or any measure of accountability for the violent injustice he had endured, L.T. was paroled from prison in late 1998. His case is all too typical.

Some inmates contract HIV as a result of prison rape; for them, the consequences of the assault may be deadly. Other inmates are killed or seriously injured during the violent physical attacks that sometimes accompany rape. But all inmates who are raped suffer psychological harm.

Although invisible, the psychological effects of prison rape are serious and enduring: they raise important questions regarding the failure of prison authorities to take effective measures to prevent such abuse. The physical brutality of rape is deplorable. Nonetheless, the physical impact of such abuse is often less devastating, and far less permanent, than its psychological impact. Indeed, many instances of non-consensual sex occur through coercion, threats or deception: they may not leave physical marks, but deep and permanent psychological injury.

Physical Effects and the Threat of HIV Transmission

The physical effects of a sexual assault obviously vary according to its circumstances: whether, for example, the incident involved a violent attack, whether there was anal penetration, and whether a lubricant was used. As described in chapter V, a forcible rape that occurs as part of a larger physical assault may be extremely violent. Prisoners with whom Human Rights Watch is in contact have suffered rape-related injuries ranging from broken bones to lost teeth to concussions to bloody gashes requiring dozens of stitches. A few, like former Texas inmate Randy Payne, were killed during sexual assaults.

Another Texas inmate who tried on several occasions to fight off sexual assaults told Human Rights Watch that he could map out on his body the consequences of resisting his abusers:

> To give you an idea what I mean . . . I now have scar's where I've been gutted, under the right side of my chest below my heart, where my neck was cut open and under my left arm. That's not the many minor cuts and wound's I can't include in this letter because of lack of time & space.[2]

The medical records of several other prisoners with whom Human Rights Watch has been in contact portray a similar picture of physical savagery. And, in itself, forced anal penetration may cause intense pain, abrasions, soreness, bleeding, even, in some cases, tearing of the anus or transmission of the HIV virus.

THE THREAT OF HIV TRANSMISSION

Transmission of HIV, the virus which causes AIDS, is a serious threat to victims of prison rape. In 1994, an Illinois inmate, Michael Blucker, claimed that he contracted HIV from being repeatedly raped at the Menard Correctional Center. He tested HIV-negative after being sent to Menard in May 1993, but was HIV-positive when tested again the following April. Blucker filed suit against the Illinois Department of Correction, prompting Rep. Cal Skinner, Jr., an Illinois state representative, to introduce legislation to protect prisoners against rape.[3] As Representative Skinner warned, victims of prison rape face the possibility of an "unadjudicated death sentence," subverting the intent of the criminal justice system.

Several other prisoners with whom Human Rights Watch is in contact state that they have contracted HIV through forced sexual intercourse in prison. K.S., a prisoner in Arkansas, was repeatedly raped between January and December 1991 by more than twenty different inmates, one of whom, he believes, transmitted the HIV virus to him. K.S. had tested negative for HIV upon entry to the prison system, but in September 1991 he tested positive. During the relevant time period, K.S. made numerous requests for assistance to prison officials, describing the sexual abuse and asking for protection.

K.S. brought suit in federal court against the prison officials who failed to protect him.[4] At trial, the warden testified that it was the prisoners' own responsibility to fight off sexual abuse—that prisoners had to let the others "understand that [they]'re not going to put up with that."[5] Despite ample evidence that K.S. had been left to fend for himself against numerous stronger inmates, the jury decided in favor of one official while the court ruled in favor of two others as a matter of law. The court's decision was later reversed on appeal,[6] and as of this writing K.S.'s lawsuit is still pending. K.S. remains incarcerated and is being treated for HIV. As for his attackers, K.S. reports, two "got punitive isolation time. The rest are still raping other inmates."[7]

The threat of HIV transmission is particularly acute given the high prevalence of the virus among prisoners. In 1997, an estimated 8,900 prisoners were infected with HIV and another 8,900 had AIDS.[8] AIDS is currently the second leading cause of death among prison inmates.[9] Between 1991 and 1995 approximately one in three inmate deaths was attributable to AIDS-related causes, compared to one in ten deaths outside the prison setting. Exacerbating the danger of HIV transmission is the lack of preventative measures, with little attempt made to educate prisoners about HIV/AIDS and few risk reduction devices available (such as condoms, clean needles, and bleach).[10]

Psychological Impact

Rape's effects on the victim's psyche are serious and enduring.[11] Inmates like L.T., whether they fall victim to violent sexual attacks or to more subtle forms of sexual abuse, leave the prison system in a state of extreme psychological stress, a condition identified as rape trauma syndrome. Given that many people in such condition leave prison every year, it is important to consider the larger consequences of prison rape. Serious questions arise as to how the trauma of sexual abuse resolves itself when inmates are released into society.

Victims of prison rape commonly report nightmares, deep depression, shame, loss of self-esteem, self-hatred, and considering or attempting suicide. Some of them also describe a marked increase in anger and a tendency toward violence.

SHAME AND THE "LOSS OF MANHOOD"

The shame I experienced can't be described.

_____

A prisoner in Illinois.[12]

Victims of rape are likely to blame themselves for their predicament, leading to intense feelings of shame. As described previously, situations of unwanted sexual contact in prison run the gamut from violent gang rapes to subtle forms of psychological coercion. Even where extreme violence is used, the victim often worries, deep down, that he did not put up enough resistance. Indeed, there is some sense, under the unwritten code of inmate beliefs, that a real man "would die before giving up his anal virginity."[13] By the very fact of surviving the experience, therefore, a prisoner may worry he deserved it: that he has, at the very least, been proven to be "a punk, 'pussy,' or coward by not preventing it."[14] Although this view is not universally held—many prisoners recognize that it is the perpetrator alone who bears responsibility for their victimization—it is still widespread among inmates.

Obviously, victims of incidents of coerced sex that did not involve overt violence are even more likely to feel complicit in their own abuse. Many of them report thinking obsessively about how they could have avoided the situation, what they did wrong. They speak of profound feelings of shame and embarrassment over how they could have "allowed" the abuse to happen to them. In a letter to Human Rights Watch, a Colorado inmate whose fear enabled his cellmate to maneuver him into unwanted sexual contact, admitted, "If the truth be known, it shames me to even talk of this."[15] His feelings are typical.

In what is perhaps an unconscious effort to shield themselves from responsibility for prison abuses, correctional authorities seem to encourage such attitudes, frequently "blaming the victim" themselves. Unless a prisoner is visibly injured from a sexual assault, guards often intimate that the sex was consensual: that the prisoner actually invited it. Raped inmates frequently say that they are treated scornfully by guards who do not bother to hide the fact that they despise prisoners who are so "weak" as to be victimized. "Stand up for yourself and be a man," is a common refrain. Gay prisoners, particularly those with stereotypically feminine characteristics or mannerisms, report that guards are especially likely to ignore their claims of sexual abuse. Some guards, in fact, appear not to even recognize that gay inmates have the right to refuse other inmates' sexual advances, viewing homosexuality as a sort of open invitation to sex. As one prisoner, who is not actually gay, remembered: "I had an officer tell me that 'faggots like to suck dick, so why was I complaining.'"[16]

The tendency to misread victimization as proof of homosexuality appears to be common to guards and prisoners alike. In addition to feelings of fear, depression, and self-hatred, many prisoners have expressed a more specific anxiety about the loss of gender identity, fearing that their "manhood" has been damaged or eroded. As one sexually abused prisoner confessed: "I feel that maybe some women might look at me as less than a man. My pride feels beaten to a pulp."[17]

M.R., a Texas inmate who was nearly killed by his rapist, described this reaction, which he saw as unavoidable: "Men are supposed to be strong enough to keep themselves from being raped. So when it does happen it leaves us feeling as though our manhood has been stripped from us and that we are now less than what we once were."[18]

That which is "less than a man" for these prisoners is, to be specific, a homosexual man, albeit a homosexual defined according to the idiosyncratic rules that govern in the prison context. As described previously, the meaningful distinction in prison is not between men who engage in sex with men, and those who engage in sex with women; instead it is between what are deemed the "active" and "passive" participants in sex. Homophobia is rampant in prisons, but rather than targeting all men who have sexual contact with other men, it is focused against those who play the "woman's role" in sex: specifically, men who are anally penetrated, who perform fellatio on other prisoners, or who masturbate them.

> "I feel that maybe some women might look at me as less than a man. My pride feels beaten to a pulp."

Once a prisoner has been forced into such a role, he may easily be trapped in it. The fact of submitting to rape—even violent, forcible rape—redefines him as "a punk, sissy, queer." Other inmates will view him as such, withholding from him the respect due a "man." Having fallen to the bottom of the inmate hierarchy, he will be treated as though he naturally belongs there.

The belief that rape damages one's innermost self is strong among inmates. Indeed, for the perpetrators of rape, this belief provides a compelling reason to commit the act: rape appears to be the most powerful way to injure and degrade its victims. But what comes of the victims' conviction that they have been fundamentally damaged? Human Rights Watch's research suggests that at least some minority of prisoners who endure sexual abuse will turn violence on themselves or others.

DEPRESSION, ANXIETY AND DESPAIR

I go through nightmares of being raped and sexually assaulted. I can't stop thinking about it. I feel everyone is looking at me in a sexual way.

———————

A prisoner in Texas[19]

Psychiatrists have identified "rape trauma syndrome"—a variant of post-traumatic stress disorder (PTSD) characterized by depression, severe anxiety, and despair—as being a common result of rape.[20] In their correspondence and conversations with Human Rights Watch, victims of prison rape frequently alluded to these symptoms, stating they felt depressed, paranoid, unhappy, fatigued, and worried. Feelings of worthlessness and self-hatred were often expressed. Exacerbating the psychological stress of their situation, many victims of prison rape feel that they remain vulnerable to continuing abuse, even believing themselves trapped in a struggle to survive. The fear of becoming infected with the AIDS virus also preoccupies victims. "Catching <u>Aids</u> and <u>Hiv</u> is a major concern for everyone," an Arkansas inmate emphasized. "There is no cure."[21]

Rape trauma syndrome was first diagnosed outside of the prison setting, looking at women victims, and most research on it has continued to focus on non-incarcerated women. Experts have distinguished three stages in the aftermath of rape, corresponding to its short-, intermediate- and long-term impact. While not all rape survivors exhibit these symptoms in the order described, the typology provides a useful general outline. The short-term reaction to rape is characterized by a range of traumatic symptoms, including nightmares and other forms of sleep disturbance, intense fear, worry, suspicion, major depression, and impairment in social functioning. In the second stage, victims often experience depression and self-hatred, as well as social and sexual dysfunction. The long-term effects of rape, which may surface a year or more after the assault, often involve destructive or self-destructive behavior; common symptoms are anger, hypervigilance to danger, sexual dysfunction and a diminished capacity to enjoy life.[22]

According to one study, only 10 percent of rape victims do not show any disruption of their behavior following the assault. Some 55 percent of victims display moderately affected behavior, while the lives of another 35 percent are severely impaired.

SUICIDE

Suicide attempts are a not uncommon response to rape, particularly among prisoners who feel unprotected and vulnerable to continuing abuse. Nineteen inmates who corresponded with Human Rights Watch, including eight interviewed in person, reported that they attempted suicide as a result of rape in prison, and many more reported considering suicide.[23] Indeed, some inmates tried to kill themselves more than once. The following account is typical:

> I have been getting sexually assaulted at [Prison X] by two inmates. I tried to commit suicide in hopes of releaving the misery of it. . . . I was made to perform oral sex on the two inmates for exchange of protection from other inmates. . . . I reported the action of the inmates to the Unit authority but did not get any help so that is when I slashed both my wrists in hope of dying.[24]

Another prisoner told Human Rights Watch:

> I did nine years from March 1983 to November 1991. In that 9 years I was raped several times . . . . I came back to prison in 1993. In 1994 I was raped again. I attempted suicide. . . . The doctors here in the prison say "quote" major depression multiple neurotic symptoms, marked by excessive fear, unrelenting worry and debilitating anxiety. Antisocial suicidal ideation, self-degradation, paranoia and hopelessness are characteristic, "unquote."[25]

The case of Rodney Hulin, Jr., a seventeen-year-old Texas prisoner, is sadly illustrative of the problem. Hulin was repeatedly raped over a two-month period by older inmates. In January 1996, just after he wrote to his father saying he was tired of prison life and tired of living, he attempted suicide by hanging himself in his cell. Although the attempt was discovered before Hulin was dead, he was left in a coma and died four months later.

In general, suicide rates in prisons and jails are well above those in the outside community. Suicide ranks third as a cause of death in prison (after natural causes and AIDS), while it is the leading cause of death in jails.[26] From 1984 to 1993, the rate of prison suicide was more than 50 percent higher than the national average outside of prison.[27] Notably, "victimization" and "conflicts within the [prison] facility" are two of the main problems that experts have identified in specifying the stressful factors that result in inmate suicide.[28]

These figures are much more striking when one considers the practical difficulty of committing suicide in prison. Unlike in the outside world, where an individual can easily isolate himself from other people for hours or days at a time, in prison a person is rarely out of earshot of others, or even out of their sight. Indeed, in today's prisons, many inmates are double-celled or live in crowded dormitories, unlikely places for a suicide attempt to pass unnoticed.

> **"I was made to perform oral sex on the two inmates for exchange of protection from other inmates. . . . I reported the action of the inmates to the Unit authority but did not get any help so that is when I slashed both my wrists in hope of dying."**

Although drugs are dispensed in prison, they are more closely regulated than outside of the prison setting. Most prison suicide attempts, even those in which the inmate is determined to kill himself, are likely to be unsuccessful. Human Rights Watch was unable to obtain comparative statistics on attempted suicides, but would suspect that, in comparing prison numbers with numbers outside of prison, the rates are even more disproportionate than those involving accomplished suicides.

ANGER AND THE CYCLE OF VIOLENCE

[I]n 1991 I was raped by the Arizona "Aryan Brotherhood" a prison gang. I didnt tell the guards, I was scared & alone. The guards knew about it,

because they told me they are going to move me, & so they did, but to a worst prison. Where I got into it with more "ABs". . . . . I am a 26 year old White Boy who don't have anybody, but a lot of anger! . . . . Back to a little more about my Rape. The guys didnt get caught in the Act somebody told the guards and they asked me if I was alright. Then moved me . . . . I wanted to go back to the yard and kill them that did it![29]

In the aftermath of rape, prisoners often harbor intense feelings of anger—anger directed first at the perpetrators of abuse, but also at prison authorities who failed to react appropriately to protect them, and even at society as a whole. Some prisoners have confessed to taking violent revenge on their abusers, inspired both by anger and by a desire to escape further abuse. The best and sometimes the only way to avoid the repetition of sexual abuse, many prisoners assert, is to strike back violently. Simply put, to prove that one is not a victim, one must take on the characteristics of a perpetrator. Since violence, in the prison setting, is almost a synonym for strength and virility, a readiness to use violence confirms one's "manhood."

A Texas inmate explained the dynamic in the following way:

It's fixed where if you're raped, the only way you [can stop the abuse is if] you rape someone else. Yes I know that's fully screwed, but that's how your head is twisted. After it's over you may be disgusted with yourself, but you realize you're not powerless and that you can deliver as well as receive pain. Then it's up to you to decide whether you enjoy it or not. Most do, I don't.[30]

Summing up the situation in a phrase, he emphasized: "People start to treat you right once you become deadly."

Beyond encouraging violent behavior from its victims, prison rape also evokes violence from those prisoners with no direct exposure to it. Many inmates, including those who are relatively non-violent by nature, resort to violence as a protective shield against rape, to prove that they are not to be bullied. Studies have found that even the vague, indeterminate possibility of rape is a powerful impetus for prison violence.[31]

In a letter to Human Rights Watch, one prisoner even cited fear of rape as being among the causes of rape itself, sketching an oddly circular picture of the phenomenon. He said: "One reason [for prison rapes] is the insecure, weak inmate preying on another weaker inmate, to make an impression of toughness or ruthlessness that he hopes will discourage other inmates from doing the same thing to him."[32]

Numerous prisoners have described to Human Rights Watch the aggressive postures that they have adopted as a safeguard against rape. By reacting violently to the slightest show of disrespect, inmates believe that they can avoid the slippery slope that leads to rape. A quick resort to violence is, in their view, necessary to prove that they are ready and equipped to protect themselves.

"When I came out of prison, I remember thinking that others knew I had been raped just by looking at me."

In the prison context, even the most trivial incident can be perceived as a critical test of an inmate's "manhood." Violence may ensue at the slightest provocation. The following incident—in which, as this inmate put it, he had to prove to everyone that he was "not going to be anyone's punk"—is typical:

> one night 4 weeks into my prison stay i was tested by a very big north amerikkkan prisoner. he attempted to lay a bully game down on me by taking my seat in the lounge room. which led to me resorting back to my street warfare attack which was my only choice to set a solid example that i am not to be played with. The end result was he being put in the hospital, broke jaw/nose, an me having a broke wrist an a battery case.[33]

Besides reacting violently to other inmates' perceived aggressiveness, prisoners in fear of being raped frequently resort to preemptive violence in order to escape to a lock-up unit where they will be protected from attack. Desperate for a transfer to safer surroundings, such inmates purposely act out violently before corrections staff. As one described:

> I was sexually assaulted by 4 inmates (black). I went to staff. I was shipped to another unit. I refused to go to my housing assignment due to I was being put back into a life threatening condition. So I started to threaten the first black inmate I came into contact with. I was put in prehearing detention.

That's September 15, 1995. I started possessing a weapon and threatening black inmates. That was the only way staff would keep me locked up in a single cell.[34]

Interestingly, even though violent behavior in prison constitutes a disciplinary infraction and can, in serious cases, result in criminal prosecution and more prison time, corrections officials frequently urge inmates to employ violence to defend themselves from attack. Past studies have found that prison staff counsel prisoners to respond to the threat of sexual assault by fighting the aggressor.[35] Inmates have often reported to Human Rights Watch that guards warn them, "no one is going to babysit you"—letting them know that they have to "act like a man," that is, to react violently to aggressive sexual overtures.

Another contributing factor to violence may be the acute shame that victims commonly experience. Indeed, psychiatrist and prison expert James Gilligan, describing a theory of violence, argues that shame is the primary underlying cause of the problem.[36] Driven by shame, men murder, rape, and punish others. In describing prisons as fertile territory for the shame-violence relationship, Gilligan's observations are consistent with prisoners' reports of their experiences. As one Vermont inmate told Human Rights Watch, "When I came out of prison, I remember thinking that others knew I had been raped just by looking at me. My behavior changed to such cold heartedness that I resented anyone who found reason to smile, to laugh, and to be happy."[37] This man later committed rape after release from prison in what he said was a kind of revenge on the world. K.J., another inmate with whom Human Rights Watch is in contact, similarly believes that it was the trauma of being raped while in jail—unrelieved by any psychological counseling—that led him to later commit rape himself. "I was just locked in shame," he said, explaining the downward spiral that culminated in his rape of two women. "It seemed like rape was written all over my face."[38]

> "I was just locked in shame. It seemed like rape was written all over my face."

The anger, shame and violence sparked by prison rape—though it may originate in the correctional setting—is unlikely to remain locked in prison upon the inmate's release. As one prisoner emphasized, reflecting upon correctional officials' failure to prevent several rapes in his institution:

[The guards here believe that] the tougher, colder, and more cruel and inhuman a place is, the less chance a person will return. This is not true. The more negative experiences a person goes through, the more he turns into a violent, cruel, mean, heartless individual, <u>I know this to be a fact.</u>[39]

The brutal murder of James Byrd, Jr., in Jasper, Texas, spurred renewed consideration of the impact on society of incarcerating so many of its citizens in places of violent sexual abuse. Byrd, a disabled African American, was killed by three white men, two of whom had been released from Texas prison the previous year. While in prison, the two men acquired a deep hatred of blacks. They joined a white prison gang and covered themselves with racist tattoos. Reflecting on the sexual violence and racial conflicts that plague prisons in Texas, some commentators viewed the two men—and the horrific crime they committed—as the creations of the prison system. In an article subtitled "Did the Texas penal system kill James Byrd?" writer Michael Berryhill noted that the two men's racism "seemed intimately tied to their sexual fears," and that they "seemed obsessed with asserting their masculinity and repudiating homosexuality."[40] He concluded that the hatred evidenced in the Jasper killing was the predictable result of conditions in the state's prisons.

Prison reformers have a clear stake in asserting that prison abuses have a deleterious impact on the world outside of prisons, the logic being that even if the public cares not a whit for the suffering of inmate victims everyone agrees on the desirability of preventing abuses against victims out in society. Unsurprisingly, many reformers have asserted that stopping sexual abuse against prisoners is imperative for pragmatic as well as humanitarian reasons. According to this view, rape not only injures the victim's dignity and sense of self, it threatens to perpetuate a cycle of sexual violence.

You take a guy who's been raped in prison and he is going to be filled with a tremendous amount of rage . . . . Now eventually he is going to get out. Most people do. And all the studies show that today's victim is tomorrow's predator. So by refusing to deal with this in an intelligent way, you are genuinely sentencing society to an epidemic of future rapes.[41]

The claim that prison rape begets further crimes is not universally accepted. Daniel Lockwood, a criminologist who has written extensively on the topic of prison sexual violence, disputes the notion that victims of abuse, embittered by the experience, vent their hostility on the public when released from prison.[42] He states there is "little reliable data" to support such claims, deriding the idea as a "damaging myth."

Evidently, no longitudinal studies have been conducted to specifically document the subsequent criminal history of victims of prison rape, and further empirical research would be of value. Nonetheless, it is clear that the effects of victimization are profound, and that, left to fester, the psychological injury of rape leads some inmates to inflict violence on themselves and others.

Inadequate Treatment

In disregard of the Supreme Court's 1978 ruling that prisoners have the right to adequate medical care for their "serious" medical needs, many prisoners receive inadequate health care, particularly mental health care. While most prison rape survivors in contact with Human Rights Watch say that they were provided medical treatment for any physical injuries received during the assault, only a minority said that they received the necessary psychological counseling. Yet, by all accounts, rape trauma syndrome is a serious and potentially devastating psychological disorder, demanding careful and sympathetic treatment. Indeed, one appellate court has affirmed that a prison's failure to make adequate psychological counseling available to rape victims violates the U.S. Constitution's prohibition on cruel and unusual punishment.[43]

P.N.

I Am The Inmate Above And Being Duly Sworn deposes and says:

On 06-12-93 I reported that I was having problems out of my work squad with General Populations Inmates and it was going back to my Living Quarters. I was excluded from U.C.C. [classification committee] and denied my Safekeeping due to insufficient evidence . . . . [On another unit] I was being forced to do sexual favors. Ive tried to tell the Infirmary. They didn't want to hear it. On 02-20-95 I was physically assaulted by several I/M which I identified to Sgt. [M]. Then I refused to be placed back on the wing which I was placed on transit, awaiting transfer to another unit. I was transferred on 3-16-95 and en route to the Huntsville Unit once off bus on Unit I was assaulted severly. Once again badly . . . . Upon arrival to Beto One Unit the Warden seen [the bruises on] my face and my body and seen that I was an admitted homosexual and placed me on Safekeeping once again . . . . Then on 10-31-95 I was placed back on Beto One on close custody general population. I had to start catching houses to pay for protection (or) I was gonna be hurt, beat up, or killed. I was forced to catch houses and sex forced on me. So on 11-07-95 I executed a request for protection and on 11-17-95 I was intervieded by Lt. [F] and I told him I was being forced to perform sexual acts, etc. Nothing was done then . . . . I then was moved to another wing once again after attempt of suicide . . . . My neighbor was acting as my cellie and forcing me to do sexual acts. Then a bunch of Mexicans got word I was on T Wing and sent their homeboy to hurt me while I was on T Wing. He at first sent me a letter through SSI threatening me and I told Lt. [F] the same night and the I/M was pulled out by Lt. [F]. And threatened. And the I/M told me I was dead when he could catch me. So I wrote grievance 12-29-95 and attached the threatening letter to it and was denied ANY relief whatsoever. So the guy who was fucking me every night placed shanks in my house and told me to tell the police they were there to get away from the block before I get killed. So I did this but in court pleaded not guilty was found guilty of a weapon and placed in seg even aftr the person who put them there admitted he done it on tape.[1]

FACTS

1) Major J.E. Cook recommended the removal of my safekeep status 08-31-94 haveing full knowledge of my enemies in general population and the fact of me being a homosexual and the past assaults from my fellow I/M in my work squad 35 Hoe.

. . .

10.) On 02-16-95 I reported to security that I was being forced to preform sexual act's against my will. Which I was found positive with gonnarea on 02-16-95.

11.) On 02-21-95 I executed another step one grievance stateing that I got assaulted which positively identified as A.C. [Aryan Circle] gang members. I was placed on the transit status after refusing housing in fear of my safety and being sexually assaulted again.

. . .

WHEREFORE, Plaintiff request this HONARBLE COURT to grant the following relief:

A) Issue a declaratory Judgment that the defendants violated the UNITED STATES CONSTITUTION . . .[2]

A skinny, bespectacled man, P.N. weighed 135 pounds when interviewed by Human Rights Watch in October 1998, well above the 120 pounds he weighed when he first entered prison in 1987 at age nineteen. At that time, having violated the electronic monitoring restrictions imposed on him after he was placed on probation for burglary, P.N. was sent to a Texan prison unit that was notorious for its gang violence.

P.N. is gay, and acutely aware of the dangers that provokes in Texas prisons. "Homosexuality is a *sin* in Texas," he emphasized to a Human Rights Watch representative. "In prison it's a curse. If you're gay you really catch hell."[3] Both guards and inmates are homophobic, he believes. In 1987, on his first day in prison, P.N. was hit in the face by a Hispanic inmate named

Teardrop. The next day a group of inmates stole all of his personal belongings. "At that time I was still in the closet a bit, but they saw me as weak," he said. "These black guys told me I was going to ride and pay protection. Within a month, this guy was forcing me to have sex."

P.N.'s time in prison has been marked by continual sexual pressuring, threats, and attacks. Once he had a "husband" who, he says, "took care of me," protecting him from other inmates. During another period, when he was unprotected and subject to constant threats, he cut himself up with a knife and was placed in a medical facility for a few months. At one point he had serious problems with members of the Aryan Circle, a white racist prison gang. Members of the gang wanted him to be a "patch carrier": to have his buttocks emblazoned with a tattoo advertising that he belonged to them. They too promised to protect P.N., but he would have had to "service" dozens of gang members.

P.N. is an admittedly disruptive prisoner who has had numerous disciplinary problems. On several occasions, he claims, he has purposely been caught with a weapon in order to be placed in disciplinary segregation and thereby escape threatened harm from other inmates. He has been violently assaulted several times.

In 1995, when P.N. was in the prison medical facility for self-inflicted injuries, he filed suit against the Texas prison authorities. The gravamen of his claim was that the authorities were well aware of his vulnerability to sexual assault but had failed to protect him from other prisoners. Supporting his claim were numerous grievances he had filed warning officials that he was at risk of serious harm. His case survived defendants' efforts to throw it out on a summary judgment motion, and it went to trial, but in July 1997 a jury ruled for the defendants.

L.T.

I got a cellie . . . . and he said that he would protect me from [inmates who had threatened me] but I had to pay, if I didnt he would let them get me plus he would. He told his homeboy about what was going on and he's homeboy said he was going to protect me also but I had to pay . . . . August 1, when the officer [C] open the door I walked out and told him I need to speak with rank that it was very important . . . . I told him what my cellie wanted me to do. So he left me there and got rank . . . . Sgt. [D] ask me what was going on, I told him and told him that my life was in danger. He said for me to return to my cell and stand up and fight, because this was prison; if I didnt he would get a team and drag my ass back to my house. When I refused, he told [C] to put me in the holding cage. I walked to the cage on my own and went in. Sgt. [D] came back and told me to put the handcuffs on. When I told him I couldnt, he opened the cage door and told me to put the cuffs on. There with him was [C], [F], [M]. I told him if he was gonna force me that they needed to get the camera first. [C] put the handcuffs in my face and said that he was gonna get the camera after he fucked me up. He kept telling me to put the cuffs on, but I refused, because of the risk. So [D] told the officers to grab me. They grabbed me. Stunned me to the floor and began punching me in my head and kicking me in my ribs. They put the handcuffs on and by that time I looked up and a officer had a camera. Sgt. [D] ask me if I would get up on my own. I did. They took me to medical and brought me back to my cell. When they put me back in my cell, I was crying for what they done. My cellie's homeboy that said he would protect me he came over to my cell when they ran rec. My cellie was gone. He ask me what happen and what was I crying for. He ask me how I was going to pay him. I told him when I went to the store I would pay him. But he said I want to fuck. I told him that I didnt do that. He said you remember what the deal we made. So I said but I dont do that kind of stuff. So he kept saying he aint gonna take long. So he had me have anal sex with him. After that, my cellie came back from rec, he found out what his homeboy did and told me he wanted to do the same. He also made me have anal sex. The next day the same officers were working and I was scared to tell them because of what they did before . . . . My cellie told me that at last chow his homeboy wanted me to come over and stay all night in his cell. So I waited until last chow. I went an ate, when I came back there was a officer walking with all the inmates. So I let all the inmates go in and stop the officer and told him the problem . . . . He took me to see Lt [T]. I told her what was going on, and needed to be locked up. She told me the only way that I could get locked up was if I refused housing and I would receive a case. I said I didnt care, I just needed her help. She sent me to lock up (pre-hearing detention). There I was given 15 days solitary . . . . I was pulled out and seen by Mrs. [A], Capt. [R], and Major [I]. I told my complaint and Mrs. [A] said that I was never raped that I just gave it up. Capt. [R] said that close custody was no risk, that I was well protected. I asked him how so, when I was raped plus inmates get stabbed each day. I wasnt answered. They tried to make it look as if I was asking for a transfer and not protective custody. I was denied help and sent back to my cell . . . . I took 18 pills trying to overdose. I was sent to medical and put back in my cell. From then on I began geting cases everyday to stay in solitary. Finally they got tired of me geting cases and refusing housing and placed me in segregation.[4]

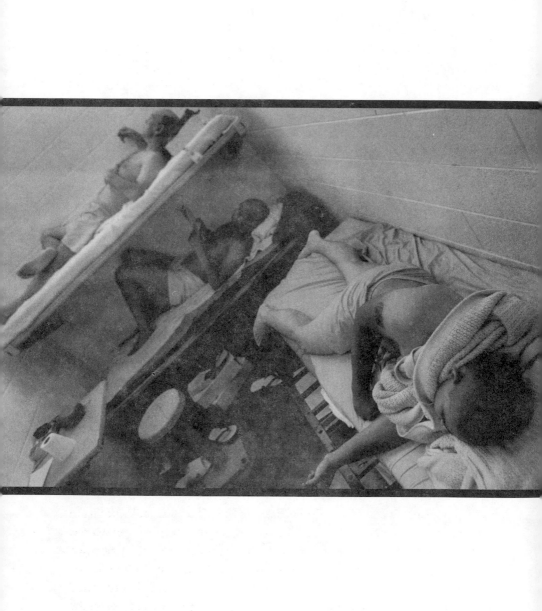

ANOMALY OR EPIDEMIC
The Incidence of Prisoner-on-Prisoner Rape

No conclusive national data exist regarding the prevalence of prisoner-on-prisoner rape and other sexual abuse in the United States.[1] *Terror in the Prisons,* the first book on rape in prison—one aimed at a popular rather than an academic audience—predicted in 1974 that "ten million" of the forty-six million Americans who are arrested at some point in their lives would be raped in prison.[2] Filled with gripping anecdotal accounts of prisoner-on-prisoner sexual abuse, the book offered no explanation as to how it arrived at this astonishingly high figure.

Few other commentators have even ventured to speculate on the national incidence of rape in prison, although some, extrapolating from small-scale studies, have come up with vague estimates as to its prevalence, suggesting that rape is "a rare event," that it "may be a staggering problem," or even that it is "virtually universal."[3] The obvious inconsistency of these estimates says much about the lack of reliable national data on the issue, as well as evidencing researchers' varying definitions of rape and other sexual abuse.

Unsurprisingly, when corrections officials are asked about the prevalence of rape in their prisons, they claim it is an exceptional occurrence rather than a systemic problem. Prison officials in New Mexico, for example, responding to our 1997 request for information regarding "the 'problem' of male inmate-on-inmate rape and sexual abuse" (the internal quotation marks are theirs), said that they had "no recorded incidents over the past few years."[4] The Nebraska Department of Correctional Services informed Human Rights Watch that such incidents were "minimal."[5] Only Texas, Ohio, Florida, Illinois, and the Federal Bureau of Prisons said that they had more than fifty reported incidents in a given year, numbers which, given the large size of their prison systems, still translate into extremely low rates of victimization.[6]

Yet a recent academic study of an entire state prison system found an extremely high rate of sexual abuse, including forced oral and anal intercourse. In 1996, the year before Nebraska correctional officials told Human Rights Watch that prisoner-on-prison sexual abuse was uncommon, Professor Cindy Struckman-Johnson and her colleagues published the results of a survey of state prison inmates there. They concluded that 22 percent of male inmates had been pressured or forced to have sexual contact against their will while incarcerated.[7] Of these, over 50 percent had submitted to forced anal sex at least once.[8] Extrapolating these findings to the national level would give a total of over 140,000 inmates who have been anally raped.[9]

The following chapter does not offer a definitive answer as to the national incidence of prisoner-on-prisoner rape and other sexual abuse. It does, however, explain why Human Rights Watch considers the problem to be *much* more pervasive than correctional authorities acknowledge. Comparing the numbers collected by correctional authorities and academic experts, this chapter explains the factors leading to drastic underestimates of the frequency of prisoner-on-prisoner rape and other sexual abuse. It also examines the disparities in academic findings on the topic, which vary according to the different situations studied, the differing methodologies utilized, and the inconsistent definitions of rape and sexual abuse employed.

Chronic Underreporting

None of the types of prison rape described [what he calls "confidence rape," "extortion rape," "strong arm rape," etc.] are rare. If anything they are rarely reported. To give you an idea of how frequent rape is in prison, if victims would report every time they were raped in prison I would say that in the prison that I am in (which is a medium minimum security prison) there would be a reported incident every day.

Pennsylvania inmate.

Only a small minority of victims of rape or other sexual abuse in prison ever report it to the authorities. Indeed, many victims—

cowed into silence by shame, embarrassment and fear—do not even tell their family or friends of the experience.

The terrible stigma attached to falling victim to rape in prison, discussed above, discourages the reporting of abuse. Deeply ashamed of themselves, many inmates are reluctant to admit what has happened to them, particularly in situations in which they did not put up obvious physical resistance. Rather than wanting others to know of their victimization, their first and perhaps strongest instinct is to hide it. "I was too embarrassed to tell the [corrections officers] what had happened," explained a Kansas inmate. "The government acts as if a 'man' is supposed to come right out and boldly say 'I've been raped.' You know that if it is degrading for a woman, how much more for a man."[10] Some prisoners informed Human Rights Watch that they have told no one else, not even their family, of the abuse. "[Y]ou are the first person I've told in all of these years," said one, describing a rape that took place in 1981.[11]

> "The government acts as if a 'man' is supposed to come right out and boldly say 'I've been raped.' You know that if it is degrading for a woman, how much more for a man."

Prisoners' natural reticence regarding rape is strongly reinforced by their fear of facing retaliation if they "snitch." As is well known, there is a strongly-felt prohibition among inmates against reporting another inmate's wrong-doing to the authorities. "Snitches" or "rats"—those who inform on other inmates—are considered the lowest members of the inmate hierarchy. "These people become victims of [assault] because of their acts in telling on other people," one inmate emphasized to Human Rights Watch.[12] In the case of rape, the tacit rule against snitching is frequently bolstered by specific threats from the perpetrators, who swear to the victim that they will kill him if he informs on them.[13]

Prisoners who failed to report their victimization explained these considerations to Human Rights Watch. In a typical account, a Colorado prisoner said:

> I never went to the authorities, as I was too fearful of the consequences from any other inmate. I already had enough problems, so didn't want to add to

them by taking on the prison identity as a "rat" or "snitch." I already feared for my life. I didn't want to make it worse.[14]

It should be emphasized, moreover, that prisoners' failure to report abuses is directly related to the prison authorities' inadequate response to reports of abuse. If prisoners could be certain that they would be protected from retaliation by the perpetrator of abuse, then they would obviously be much more likely to inform the authorities. But rather than keeping the victimized inmate safe from retaliation, prison authorities often leave them vulnerable to continued abuse. As is described at length below, Human Rights Watch has learned of numerous cases in which the victimized inmate was not removed from the housing area in which he was victimized, even with the perpetrator remaining there. In other cases, victimized inmates are transferred to another housing area or prison, but still face retaliation. As a Texas prisoner explained:

> [T]he first time I was raped, I did the right thing. I went to an officer, told him what happened, got the rectal check, the whole works. Results? I get shipped to [another prison]. Six months later, same dude that raped me is out of seg and on the same wing as I am. I have to deal with 2 jackets now: snitch & punk. I . . . had to think real fast to stay alive. This was my first 2 years in the system. After that I knew better.[15]

A Utah prisoner had a nearly identical story to tell:

> The first time [I was raped] I told on my attackers. All [the authorities] did was moved me from one facility to another. And I saw my attacker again not too long after I tolded on him. Then I paid for it. Because I tolded on him, he got even with me. So after that, I would not, did not tell again.[16]

Past academic research has confirmed the prevalence of underreporting. The 1996 Nebraska study found that only 29 percent of victimized inmates had informed prison officials of the abuses they suffered.[17] Similarly, a 1988 survey of correctional officers in Texas found that 73 percent of respondents believed that inmates do not report rape to officials.[18] A groundbreaking 1968 study of Philadelphia penal institutions found that of an estimated

2,000 rapes that occurred, only ninety-six had been reported to prison authorities.[19]

Low Numbers Reported
by State Correctional Authorities

When questioned on the topic, state prison officials report that rape is an infinitely rare occurrence. Human Rights Watch conducted a three-year survey of state departments of correction, as well as the Federal Bureau of Prisons, asking, among other things, about reported incidents of male inmate-on-inmate rape and sexual abuse.[20] Of the forty-seven corrections departments that responded to at least one of our requests for information, only twenty-three were even able to provide such statistics, with others suggesting that inmate-on-inmate sexual abuse was so infrequent that it was unnecessary to maintain separate data on the topic. The response of Hawaiian prison officials was typical:

> While there have been isolated cases [of inmate-on-inmate sexual abuse] over the years, this behavior is not a major problem in our system. Due to the small number of cases, we do not have any statistics compiled on this subject.[21]

New Hampshire officials, similarly, told us:

> Because of the very small number of allegations of rape and the even smaller number of substantiated cases, the N.H. Department of Corrections does not maintain statistical data regarding this issue . . . . In conversation with [an officer in the Investigations Office] regarding your inquiry, he said that there are 'one or two allegations a year in our men's prison of rape.' He further stated that 'of 10 allegations, perhaps one actually was a rape.'[22]

Even California—which, with a population of over 150,000 inmates, is the largest corrections department in the United States—was unable to provide Human Rights Watch with data on the topic until 1999. Although the department had a separate data analysis unit charged with maintaining all types of information on state prisoners, it did not keep statistics on inmate-on-inmate rape or sexual abuse. Instead, all such cases were compiled within the general category of inmate-on-inmate battery.[23] Only in response to Human Rights Watch's 1999 letter were they able to provide particularized data on the topic, presumably due to recent changes in record-keeping policies. The Federal Bureau of Prisons, on the other hand, was able to provide such information in 1996 and 1997, but in subsequent years reported that it did not maintain such statistics.[24]

Many other corrections departments told Human Rights Watch that they heard of only a handful of rape or sexual assault cases annually. Colorado, Kansas, Kentucky, Missouri, New Jersey, Oregon, Pennsylvania, South Dakota, and Wisconsin, for example, all mentioned fewer than ten reported cases annually in the years for which they provided information.[25] Arizona, Arkansas, California, Michigan, New York, North Carolina, and Virginia identified between ten and fifty reported cases annually in the years for which they provided information, although Virginia noted that roughly half of its reported cases were, upon investigation, determined to be unfounded.[26]

Only Florida, Illinois, Ohio, Texas, and the Federal Bureau of Prisons acknowledged having received more than fifty allegations of rape or other sexual abuse in any year for which they provided information.[27] In Ohio, however, of the fifty-five reported cases in 1999, only eight were subsequently "confirmed as sexual assault." The remainder "were deemed to have been either consensual sex acts or simply fabrications by the alleged victim."[28] At any rate, since these five prison systems are among the largest in the country (ranking fifth, seventh, sixth, second, and third in size, respectively), the number of allegations of sexual victimization are still remarkably low.

By far the highest rate and highest absolute number of *alleged* inmate-on-inmate sexual assaults, according to the numbers provided by correctional departments, belong to Texas. With 237 allegations of sexual assault in 1999 (over double the number of allegations registered in 1998), compared to an inmate population of 146,574, Texas had one allegation of sexual assault for every 618 prisoners.[29]

High Numbers Estimated by Correctional Officers

The extremely low numbers of rapes reported by prison officials contrast with the much higher prevalence found in academic surveys of inmate victimization. But even more surprisingly, these low numbers stand in stark contrast to estimates made by correctional officers on the subject. Although only a few studies have been conducted to assess guards' beliefs regarding inmates' sexual victimization, they have uniformly found a high rate of inmate-on-inmate sexual abuse.

A corrections department internal survey of guards in a southern state (provided to Human Rights Watch on the condition that the state not be identified) found that line officers—those charged with the direct supervision of inmates—estimated that roughly one-fifth of all prisoners were being coerced into participation in inmate-on-inmate sex. Interestingly, higher-ranking officials—those at the supervisory level—tended to give lower estimates of the frequency of abuse, while inmates themselves gave much higher estimates: the two groups cited victimization rates of roughly one-eighth and one-third, respectively. Although the author of the survey was careful to note that it was not conducted in accordance with scientific standards, and thus its findings may not be perfectly reliable, the basic conclusions are still striking. Even taking only the lowest of the three estimates of coerced sexual activity—and even framing that one conservatively—more than one in ten inmates in the prisons surveyed was subject to sexual abuse.

Similarly, a 1988 study of line officers in the Texas prison system found that only 9 percent of officers believed that rape in prison was a "rare" occurrence, while 87 percent thought that it was not rare.[30] These findings are even more notable when one considers that the question was limited to instance of "rape"—not sexual abuse in general—a term that many people conceive of narrowly (typically believing that rape only occurs where force is used).

Finally, the 1996 Nebraska study found that prison staff in three men's prisons estimated that in all some 16 percent of male inmates were being pressured or forced into sexual contact.[31] The rates were slightly lower that those estimated by inmates in the same facilities.

Findings of Empirical Studies

A number of empirical studies have been conducted to measure the frequency of inmate-on-inmate sexual abuse, although only two such studies date from the past decade. Their findings as to the prevalence of sexual abuse—and rape in particular—have varied. Yet even those reporting a lower prevalence still differ, by at least an order of magnitude, from the numbers cited by corrections authorities, indicating that much needs to be done to sensitize the authorities to the problem. Several studies, moreover, have found shockingly high rates of sexual abuse.

The primary empirical studies of sexual abuse in men's penal facilities are: 1) a 1968 study of Philadelphia penal facilities; 2) a 1980 study of several New York state prisons; 3) a 1982 study of a medium-security California prison; 4) a 1982 study of several federal prisons; 5) a 1989 study of an Ohio prison; 6) a 1995 study of a medium-security Delaware prison; 7) the above-mentioned 1996 study of Nebraska state prisons, and 8) a 2000 study of seven prisons in four midwestern states.[32]

The first empirical study of the issue, sparked by reports that Philadelphia pretrial detainees were being raped even in vans on the way to court, was conducted in 1968 by a local district attorney. After interviewing thousands of inmates and hundreds of correctional officers, as well as examining institutional records, he found that sexual assaults were "epidemic" in the Philadelphia system. "[V]irtually every slightly-built young man committed by the court is sexually approached within a day or two after his admission to prison," the author said. "Many of these young men are repeatedly raped by gangs of prisoners."[33] In all, he found that slightly over 3 percent of inmates—an estimated 2,000 men—had been sexually assaulted during the twenty-six-month period examined. Although he was careful to exclude instances of consensual homosexual contact from his findings, he also acknowledged that some instances of apparently consensual sex might in fact have a coercive basis, due to the "fear-charged atmosphere" of the penal system.

The New York study, conducted by criminologist Daniel Lockwood, was the second major effort to assess the prevalence of prisoner-on-prisoner sexual abuse. It too found that sexual targeting—typically accompanied by violence—was frequent, though actual rape much less common. According to Lockwood's data, based on interviews with eighty-nine randomly selected inmates, 28 percent had been the targets of sexual aggression at some point, but only one inmate had been raped.[34]

The 1982 study of a medium-security men's prison in California found that a startling 14 percent of prisoners had been forced into anal or oral sex. Based on data from anonymous questionnaires distributed to a random sampling of 200 members of the inmate population—or some 10 percent of the total inmates—the study emphasized that "sexual exploitation in prison is an actuality."[35] Indeed, asserted the authors, life behind bars is, for many inmates, "a criminal act itself."

Three subsequent empirical studies had mixed findings as to the prevalence of prisoner-on-prisoner rape and other sexual abuse. The federal prisons study, published in 1983, found that only one of 330 inmates had been forcibly sodomized while in federal prison while two others had been forced to "perform a sex act" (presumably fellatio or some other act besides sodomy). Twenty-nine percent of inmates did, however, state that they had been propositioned for sex while in their institution, and 11 percent had been "targets of sexual aggression." The authors defined sexual aggression narrowly, only considering acts that involved physical violence. Similarly, the Ohio and Delaware studies looked only at "rape" (which many people, inmates in particular, interpret as requiring the use of physical force), finding few incidents: none of the 137 inmates surveyed in Ohio had been victims of rape, and only one of 101 inmates surveyed in Delaware.[36] Five additional Delaware inmates did, however, say that they had been subject to an attempted rape; 4 percent of the inmates surveyed reported that they had witnessed at least one rape within the previous year, and 21.8 percent said that had witnessed at least one attempted rape.

The 1996 Nebraska study, discussed above, found an extremely high rate of sexual abuse, including forced or coerced oral and anal intercourse; it concluded that 22 percent of male had been sexually pressured or abused since being incarcerated. Notably, the authors focused on "unwanted" sexual contact—covering a much broader range of sexual activity than that simply involving physical force. And, in December 2000, the *Prison Journal* published the results of a similar study of inmates in seven men's prison facilities in four mid-western states. The results showed that 21 percent of the inmates had experienced at least one episode of pressured or forced sexual contact since being incarcerated, and at least 7 percent had been raped in their facility.[37]

It is obvious that precise conclusions as to the national prevalence of prisoner-on-prisoner sexual abuse cannot be drawn from the above studies.[38] Yet a closer examination of the studies reveals that their differing findings are not so much in contradiction with one another as they are simply measuring different types of behavior. Many of the studies that found lower rates of abuse either expressly counted only incidents involving the use of physical force, or did so by implication by leaving the term "rape" undefined.

The Delaware study, for example, which provided the inmates surveyed with a definition of rape, described it as "oral or anal sex that is forced on somebody." Consensual sex, also defined, was specified to be "oral or anal sex that is agreed on before the act takes place." Yet, as described in chapter V of this report, a narrow focus on incidents involving the actual use of force is likely to result in a serious underestimate of the prevalence of sexual abuse. Indeed, the authors of the Delaware study recognize this problem, stating that "the consensual sex reported by our respondents may instead be situations of sexual exploitation."[39] Nonetheless, their findings are expressed without any consideration of this important nuance: the study simply concludes that "the preponderance of [sexual contact in prison] is consensual sex rather than rape."[40]

Differing methodologies—inmate interviews vs. anonymous surveys, etc.—may also account for much of the inconsistency in the findings, yet there is another important factor as well. Human Rights Watch's research, which has been national in scale, has convinced us that there are significant differences in victimization rates among prison systems, and from prison to prison within a given jurisdiction. To some extent, these differences reflect variations in inmate populations. There are, for example, generally more violent inmates in maximum security facilities, and thus relatively more sexual abuse. But, as many inmates themselves have pointed out, an even more important factor is the level of official attention to or tolerance of the problem. "Where I am now," explained an Arizona prisoner, "the warden doesn't put up with it. When they notice someone being exploited, the situation is investigated and more than likely the victimizer is punished."[41] This prisoner compared the relative calm of his present facility to the "out of control" environment of other facilities where he had been housed. Unfortunately, from what Human Rights Watch has seen, the staff vigilance found at this prisoner's facility is far too rare.

The question of how prison officials handle the problem of prisoner-on-prisoner sexual abuse—whether they recognize it, what steps they take to prevent it, and how they respond to incidents of it—is a crucial one. The following chapter will explain the deficiencies of the authorities' approach to the problem in detail, but the short answer is that in every area they do far too little.

B.L.

I was young and yes i was weak. My weight was only 120 lbs, the first few months i was raped and beat up many times, i would always Fight back, i wanted my attackers to know i was not a Willing Subject for their evilness. I went to the Guards for help and was told there was nothing that could be done, that i would have to stand up like a Man and Take Care of my own troubles.[1]

Prisoners targeted for rape are faced with the difficult decision of how best to cope with the problem: whether to report it to prison officials or to handle it on their own. Although reporting the problem is, from the perspective of an orderly prison system, clearly the appropriate course of action, few prisoners have found it to be an effective one. Indeed, many inmates relate that guards and other correctional staff fail to take any protective measures in response to their calls for help, instead advising them to fight their attacker. Some prisoners do end up taking this tack and, for the lucky ones, it works. Yet B.L.'s story is a cautionary one for prisoners who choose to take action against their rapists.

An unwanted child from a family of poor white Southerners, B.L. bounced from caretaker to caretaker while he was growing up, spending a stint in the Kentucky Children's Home and several reform schools, and receiving only a sixth grade education. As a teenager, he was a chronic runaway and heavily addicted to sniffing glue. At age seventeen, he was sent to Tennessee State Prison for robbery. In 1977, when B.L. was twenty-six years old, he was sent to Florida State Prison for armed robbery and murder, the latter charge stemming from the accidental death of a robbery victim, who choked to death on a gag.

At that time Florida State Prison (FSP), a maximum security institution, was extremely dangerous. B.L. was quiet, scared, and physically weak, characteristics that—in the violent prison setting—guaranteed that he would be targeted for abuse. As one of his fellow prisoners later explained:

> B. was a quiet guy. He never messed with anyone else. Because B. was paranoid and worried all the time, he was easy prey for the other inmates. I knew that B. was raped at least two or three times by different guys.[2]

During the second half of 1978, B.L. caught the attention of S.M., a white gang member who had recently been transferred to FSP from another facility. A few years previously, S.M. had been found guilty of murdering another inmate: S.M. and several other inmates were reported to have sexually assaulted their victim and then stabbed him to death. At FSP, S.M. ran a prison gang that preyed up weaker inmates; B.L. was soon targeted. S.M. directed a steady stream of abuse and threats toward B.L., including threats of rape. A prisoner who knew both inmates described the situation:

> S.M.'s theft ring included his "enforcers," who would threaten anyone with physical harm if they did not turn over their valuables to S.M. If anyone resisted, they would be beaten, raped and then labeled a homosexual . . . . When S.M. came out of lock up he was moved to "K" wing where B.L. was housed . . . . S.M. began to put lots of pressure on B.L., demanding that he give S.M. money. It was easy to see how afraid B.L. was.[3]

Finally, two days before Thanksgiving, S.M. forcibly sodomized B.L. while some of S.M.'s friends held B.L. down. According to B.L., S.M. "told me if I went to the Guards I would be Killed"—therefore B.L. did not report the attack.[4] On Thanksgiving day, S.M. returned to B.L.'s cell with two other inmates, robbed him, and threatened to rape him again. B.L. then brought a homemade knife to the dining hall at lunchtime that day and stabbed S.M. three times in the back. S.M. died of his injuries, and B.L. was convicted of first degree murder.

A 1980 report by the Corrections Committee of the Florida House of Representatives, documenting the dire state of the prison system at that time of the incident—and singling out FSP for criticism—describes why an inmate might, in desperation, attack his rapist. Based on extensive documentary research and numerous interviews, including with nine Florida correctional officers, the report concludes bluntly that the prison system "seems to condone certain forced homosexual acts."[5] As it explains:

> Brutality in the form of physical attacks, many homosexual, is commonplace in some of Florida's prisons. Many [attacks] go unreported or ignored by Department employees who have knowledge of them .... [L]ittle is done to protect [rape] victims who report such assaults from further abuse. And clearly, the victim fears retaliation and may remain silent. He soon learns that his choice is to fight or be enslaved in homosexual bondage .... This is even more likely to seem his only choice after he realizes that in some instances even the correctional employees charged with protecting his welfare are not above victimizing, harassing or assaulting inmates. Desperation becomes a fact of everyday life within many of Florida's prisons .... Florida State Prison is such a miasm of unmet needs and human misery that it is difficult to formulate specific recommendations which are not so sweeping as to appear irresponsible.[6]

The testimony of correctional officers in the 1980 report is particularly informative. One officer, when asked what would happen to a young inmate newly arrived to a prison, explained that the inmate had "almost zero" chance of escaping rape, "unless he's willing to stick somebody with a knife and fortunate enough to have one."[7]

B.L.'s prosecution illustrates the pitfalls of this officer's implicit advice. The jury in the trial for S.M.'s murder recommended that B.L. be sentenced to life in prison, yet the trial judge, whose own wife was murdered when he was a young prosecutor, overrode the jury's recommendation and sentenced B.L. to death. After nearly twenty years of appeals and executive clemency proceedings, leading to a judicial ruling that the state had failed to consider relevant evidence at trial, B.L.'s death sentence was commuted in 1996 to life in prison.

DELIBERATE INDIFFERENCE
State Authorities' Response to Prisoner-on Prisoner Sexual Abuse

Rape occurs in U.S. prisons because correctional officials, to a surprising extent, do little to stop it from occurring. While some inmates with whom Human Rights Watch is in contact have described relatively secure institutions—where inmates are closely monitored, where steps are taken to prevent inmate-on-inmate abuses, and where such abuses are punished if they occur—many others report a decidedly laissez faire approach to the problem. In too many institutions, prevention measures are meager and effective punishment of abuses is rare.

It might be assumed that victims of prison rape would find a degree of solace in securing accountability for the abuses committed against them. Unfortunately, our justice system offers scant relief to sexually abused prisoners. Few local prosecutors are concerned with prosecuting crimes committed against inmates, preferring to leave internal prison problems to the discretion of the prison authorities; similarly, prison officials themselves rarely push for the prosecution of prisoner-on-prisoner abuses. As a result, perpetrators of prison rape almost never face criminal charges.

Internal disciplinary mechanisms, the putative substitute for criminal prosecution, also tend to function poorly in those cases in which the victim reports the crime. In nearly every instance Human Rights Watch has encountered, the authorities have imposed light disciplinary sanctions against the perpetrator—perhaps thirty days in disciplinary segregation—if that. Often rapists are simply transferred to another facility, or are not moved at all. Their victims, in contrast, may end up spending the rest of their prison terms in protective custody units whose conditions are often similar to those in disciplinary segregation: twenty-three hours per day in a cell, restricted privileges, and no educational or vocational opportunities.

Disappointingly, the federal courts have not played a significant role in curtailing prisoner-on-prisoner sexual abuse. Of course, the paucity of lawyers willing to litigate such cases means that only a small minority of rape cases reach the courts. Filed by inmates acting as their own counsel, such cases rarely survive the early stages of litigation; the cases that do survive rarely result in a favorable judgment. While there have been a few generous damages awards in cases involving prisoner-on-prisoner rape, they are the very rare exceptions to the rule.

In sum, the failure to prevent and punish rape results implicates more than one government body. The primary responsibility in this area, however, is borne by prison authorities. Rape prevention requires careful classification methods, inmate and staff orientation and training, staff vigilance, serious investigation of all rape allegations, and prosecution of those allegations found to be justified. At bottom, it requires a willingness to take the issue seriously, to be attentive to the possibility of victimization, and to consider the victim's interests. Without these basic steps, the problem will not go away. Rape is not an inevitable consequence of prison life, but it certainly is a predictable one if little is done to prevent and punish it.

Failure to Recognize and Address the Problem— and the Perverse Incentives Created by Legal Standards

Regrettably [rape] is a problem of which we are happier not knowing the true dimensions. Overcrowding and the "anything goes" morality sure haven't helped.

High-level state corrections official who spoke on condition of anonymity.[1]

The sharp disparities between correctional authorities' reports of the prevalence of rape and the findings of empirical studies, described in the previous chapter, signal a fundamental obstacle to prevention efforts: correctional authorities' failure to acknowledge that a problem exists. Nearly half of all state jurisdictions do not even collect statistics regarding the incidence of rape (a telling indicator of their lack of seriousness in addressing the issue); those that do collect such data report that it is an infinitely rare event. Yet, as previously stated, empirical surveys of inmates and correctional staff disclose much higher rates of rape and sexual assault. Since the causes of underreporting are well known to prisoners and prison administrators alike, a low frequency of reported cases is no reason for correctional authorities to turn a blind eye to the problem.

Unfortunately, Human Rights Watch's survey of the prevention practices of state and federal correctional departments revealed that few departments take specific affirmative steps to address the problem of prisoner-on-prisoner rape.[2] Nearly all of the departments who responded to our request for information had not instituted any type of sexual abuse prevention program and only a very few—such as Arkansas, Illinois, Massachusetts, North Carolina, New Hampshire, and Virginia—stated that correctional officers receive specialized training in recognizing, preventing, and responding to inmate-on-inmate sexual assault.[3] Similarly, not many departments had drafted specific protocols to guide staff response to incidents of assault.[4] Nor, according to a recent survey, do many departments' internal disciplinary policies explicitly prohibit sexual harassment among male inmates.[5]

Until very recently, the same was true for the problem of custodial sexual abuse of women inmates.[6] Even now, much remains to be done to address the problem effectively, but important steps in that direction have been taken. The National Institute of Corrections (NIC), for example, provides specialized training to corrections staff on the issue, and a number of states have promulgated specific written policies to guide staff handling of cases of abuse.

High profile class action law suits helped spur correctional authorities to take the problem of custodial sexual abuse seriously. Normally, the threat of litigation creates an important incentive for state authorities to come to grips with certain problems. Notably, the state of Arkansas—one of the only states that was able to provide Human Rights Watch with a concrete description of the training and orientation measures that it takes with regard to the problem—included a discussion of litigation and staff liability for prisoner-on-prisoner sexual abuse at the very beginning of its training curriculum on the subject.[7]

Yet, unfortunately, the legal rules that the courts have developed relating to prisoner on prisoner sexual abuse create perverse incentives for authorities to ignore the problem. Under the "deliberate indifference" standard that is applicable to legal challenges to prison officials' failure to protect prisoners from inter-prisoner abuses such as rape, the prisoner must prove to the court that the defendants had *actual knowledge* of a substantial risk to him, and that they disregarded that risk. As the courts have emphasized, it is not enough for the prison to prove that "the risk was obvious and a reasonable prison official would have noticed it."[8] Instead, if a prison official lacked knowledge of the risk—no matter how obvious it was to anyone else—he cannot be held liable.

The incentive this legal rule creates for correctional officials to remain unaware of problems is regrettable. Indeed, in many lawsuits involving prisoner-on-prisoner rape, the main thrust of prison officials' defense is that they were unaware that the defendant was in danger. More generally, officials in such cases often argue that rape in their facilities is a "rarity"—"not a serious risk."[9] They certainly have no incentive, under the existing legal standards, to try to ascertain the true dimensions of the problem.

The North Carolina Pilot Program

An encouraging exception to the overall absence of particularized attention to prisoner-on-prisoner sexual abuse can be found in North Carolina. In 1997, the legislature passed a law establishing a pilot program on sexual assault prevention in the prisons.[10] Covering only three units of the state prison system, the program is otherwise a laudable attempt at addressing the problem of inmate-on-inmate sexual abuse. It provides that the orientation given inmates will include information on the reducing the risk of sexual assault and that counseling on the topic will be provided to any prisoner requesting it. It also requires that the correctional authorities collect data on incidents of sexual aggression and develop and implement employee training on the topic.

The program's rules on classification and housing are particularly valuable. They provide that all prisoners must be evaluated and classified as to their risk of being either the victim or perpetrator of sexually assaultive behavior. These classifications are to be taken into account when making housing assignments. In particular, inmates deemed vulnerable to assault are barred from being housed in the same cell or in small dormitories with inmates rated as potential perpetrators.

Lack of Prisoner Orientation

I have been to 4 Ohio prisons and at no time was I ever warned about the danger of sexual assault. No one ever told me of ways to protect myself. And to this day I've never heard of a procedure for reporting rape. This is never talked about.

—————

An Ohio inmate.[11]

Prisoners almost uniformly related to Human Rights Watch that on entering prison they received no formal orientation regarding how they might avoid rape or what steps they should take if they were subject to or threatened with rape. As described in chapter IV, prisoners who are unfamiliar with the ins and outs of prison life tend to be more vulnerable to rape. Not knowing the tricks and ruses that lead to sexual abuse, they have no idea when they are being set up for victimization. A detailed and realistic prisoner orientation program—one that explains common exploitation scenarios as well as describing how to obtain official protection—could be effective in strengthening prisoners' abilities to react appropriately to sexual targeting.

A few states, whose example should be followed more widely, have in fact established orientation programs relating to the issue. The Virginia Department of Corrections, for example, told Human Rights Watch that all inmates receive orientation on how to avoid sexual aggression upon entry the prison system. The inmate handbook, which is provided to all prisoners, also includes a short section on "How to Avoid Homosexual Intimidation."[12] It gives advice such as "don't get into debt," and "don't solicit or accept favors, property or drugs." Arkansas has a similar orientation program; it too includes such warnings.[13]

The Illinois Department of Corrections said that it had a similar orientation program, and it forwarded Human Rights Watch excerpts discussing sexual assault from inmate handbooks distributed in several facilities. One excerpt was particularly useful in that it included a detailed description of the procedure by which the facility handled claims of sexual assault.[14] North Carolina, while it did not provide a copy of the course materials, also told Human Rights Watch that incoming inmates were advised "about the risks of sexual assault and what steps they may take to prevent such assault and seek assistance from staff."[15]

Improper Classification and Negligent Double-Celling

Among the goals of prisoner classification policies is to separate dangerous prisoners from those whom they are likely to victimize. At one extreme are "supermax," or administrative segregation units, where prisoners with a history of violence or indiscipline are held; at the other are protective custody units where the most vulnerable inmates are held.[16] Yet even between these extremes, the existence of various security levels (e.g., minimum, medium, maximum or close custody), and the range of categorization alternatives within these levels, are supposed to allow prison authorities flexibility in arranging inmates' housing and work assignments so as to minimize inter-prisoner violence and victimization.

In the overcrowded prisons of today, however, the practical demands of simply finding available space for inmates have to a large extent overwhelmed classification ideals. Inmates frequently find themselves placed among others whose background, criminal history, and other characteristics make them an obvious threat.

In the worst cases, prisoners are actually placed in the same cell with inmates who are likely to victimize them—sometimes even with inmates who have a demonstrated proclivity for sexually abusing others. The case of Eddie Dillard, a California prisoner who served time at Corcoran State Prison in 1993, is an especially chilling example of this problem. Dillard, a young first-timer who had kicked a female correctional officer, was transferred to the cell of Wayne Robertson, a prisoner known by all as the "Booty Bandit."[17] The skinny Dillard was no match for Robertson, a huge, muscular man serving a life sentence for murder. Not only was Robertson nearly twice Dillard's weight, but he had earned his nickname through his habit of violently raping other prisoners.

Before the end of the day, the inevitable occurred: Robertson beat Dillard into submission and sodomized him. For the next two days, Dillard was raped repeatedly, until finally his cell door was opened and he ran out, refusing to return. A correctional officer who worked on the unit later told the *Los Angeles Times*: "Everyone knew about Robertson. He had raped inmates before and he's raped inmates since."[18] Indeed, according to documents submitted at a California legislative hearing on abuses at Corcoran, Robertson had committed more than a dozen rapes inside Corcoran and other prisons.[19] By placing Dillard in a cell with Robertson, the guards were setting him up for punishment.

Whether as a purposeful act or through mere negligence prisoners are all too often placed together with cellmates who rape them. A Connecticut prisoner told Human Rights Watch how he too was raped by a cellmate with a history of perpetrating rape:

> [I] was sent to the orientation block to be cellmate with another prisoner already occupying a double cell. I did not know at the time that I was to share a double cell with him, that he was a known rapist in the prison . . . . I must point out that only a month and a half prior, he was accused of raping another man. On my fourth day of sharing the cell, I was ambushed and viciously raped by him. After being raped, I remained in shock and paralized in thought for two days until I was able to muster the courage to report it, this, the most dreadful and horrifying experience of my life.[20]

The pressures of overcrowding facing so many prisons today means that double-celling is much more common than in the past—often with two men being placed in a cell designed for single occupancy—while little care is taken to select compatible cellmates. Numerous prisoners told Human Rights Watch of being celled together with men who were much larger and stronger than them, had a history of violence, were racially antagonistic, openly threatening, or otherwise clearly incompatible. In such circumstances, rape is no surprise.

Understaffing and the Failure to Prevent

The greatest preventive measure [against rape] is posting staff, monitoring areas that are high risk for assault. The reality however, is that funding for prison administration doesn't provide for adequate patrolling . . . . Prisoners are pretty much left on their own.

———————

A Virginia inmate.[21]

You know, when you look at the low numbers of staff around—who really owns these prison?

———————

High-level state prison administrator who prefers to remain anonymous.[22]

Another casualty of the enormous growth of the country's prison population is adequate staffing and supervision of inmates. The consequences with regard to rape are obvious. Rape occurs most easily when there is no prison staff around to see or hear it. Particularly at night, prisoners have told Human Rights Watch, they are often left alone and unsupervised in their housing areas. Several inmates have reported to Human Rights Watch that they yelled for help when they were attacked, to no avail. Although correctional staff are generally supposed to make rounds at fifteen minute intervals, they do not always follow this schedule. Moreover, they often walk by prisoners' cells without making an effort to see what is happening within them.

Texas, one of the largest prison systems in the country—and one in which rape is widespread—is known to be seriously understaffed. It is short an estimated 2,500 guards, what a high official in the prison guards' union characterizes as a staffing crisis.[23] Prison attrition statistics reportedly show that about one in five guards quit over the course of 2000.

Paradoxically, lower numbers of correctional staff can lead to more ineffective monitoring by existing staff. Instead of redoubling their efforts to make up for their insufficient numbers, they are more likely to remain as much as possible outside of prisoners' living areas, because fewer staff makes close monitoring more dangerous to those employees who do make the rounds of housing units. Being at a disadvantage, they also have a stronger incentive to pacify—rather than challenge—the more dangerous prisoners who may be exploiting others.

Poor design, especially common in older prisons, exacerbates the problem of understaffing. Blind spots and other areas that are difficult to monitor offer inmates unsupervised places in which to commit abuses. Explained one Florida inmate: "Rapes occur because the lack of observation make it possible. Prisons have too few guards and too many blind spots."[24]

Inadequate Response to Complaints of Rape

An absolutely central problem with regard to sexual abuse in prison, emphasized by inmate after inmate, is the inadequate—and, in many instances, callous and irresponsible—response of correctional staff to complaints of rape. When an inmate informs an officer that he has been threatened with rape or, even worse, actually assaulted, it is crucial that his complaint be met with a rapid and effective response. Most obviously, he should be brought somewhere where his safety is protected and where he can explain his complaint in a confidential manner. If the rape has already occurred, he should be taken for whatever medical care may be needed and—a step that is crucial for any potential criminal prosecution—physical evidence of rape can be collected.

But from the reports Human Rights Watch has received, such a response is uncommon. Typical of inmate accounts is this one, from an inmate who was compelled to identify his rapist in front of numerous others and then returned back to the same unit:

> Lt. B.W. had me identify the assailant in front of approximately "20" other inmates . . . which immediately put my safty & life in danger as a "snitch" for telling on the other inmate who sexually assaulted me . . . . the Prison officials trying to Place Me Back in Population after I identified the assailant in front of 20 inmates clearly placed my life in danger Because of the "snitch" concept.[25]

Such actions demonstrate to prisoners, in a very effective way, that it is unwise to report rape.

A blatant display of disbelief is another improper response that numerous inmates have described. One prisoner, who claimed to have been raped several times, said that officers refused to take his complaints serious, telling him, "no way—you're not that good of a catch."[26] Frequently, correctional staff intimate that any sexual contact that may have occurred was consensual. A Texas inmate said that after he reported that he had been raped: "I was pulled out and seen by Mrs. P, Capt. R, and Major H. I told my complaint and Mrs. P said that I was never raped that I just gave it up."[27] Significantly, consensual sex is a rules violation in all prison systems, leaving the complaining inmate with the possibility of facing disciplinary sanctions.

Staff allegations of consensual sex are frequently combined with allegations that the complaining prisoner is gay, the implication being that gay inmates invite sex. A Florida inmate told Human Rights Watch: "I have been sexually assaulted twice since being incarcerated. Both times the staff refused to do anything except to lock me up and make accusations that I'm homosexual."[28]

A Texas inmate who was raped by numerous other prisoners over a long period of time experienced similar treatment by correctional staff when he tried to obtain their assistance:

> Defendant J.M, a security officer with the rank of sargeant, came to investigate the series of latest allegations. Defendant J.M. refused to interview the inmate witnesses and told plaintiff that he was lying about being sexually abused. After plaintiff vehemently protested that he was being truthful, defendant J.M. made comments that plaintiff "must be gay" for "letting them make you suck dick."[29]

As these accounts suggest, gay inmates, or those perceived as gay, often face great difficulties in securing relief from abuse. Unless they show obvious physical injury, their complaints tend to be ignored and their requests for protection denied. Prison officials are particularly likely to assume consent in sexual acts involving a gay inmate.[30] Although homosexuality is generally regarded as a factor supporting an inmate's claim to protective custody, many guards appear to believe that gay inmates are immune from rape—that when a gay inmate has sex with another man it is somehow by definition consensual. Moreover, some gay prisoners have told Human

Rights Watch that the guards themselves make homophobic comments, further encouraging sexual harassment from other inmates.

Another common guard response is that the inmate should defend himself using physical force, or even retaliate violently against the aggressors. "Be a man," guards urge. "Stand up and fight."[31] The suggestion is often meant well—violent retaliation may, in fact, be quite effective against sexual abuse—but the advice

"I told my complaint and Mrs. P said that I was never raped that I just gave it up."

nonetheless represents an abdication of responsibility. It is correctional staff who are responsible for protecting prisoners from violence, not prisoners themselves. Indeed, the use of force by inmates, even in self-defense, is a disciplinary offense.

Some correctional officers do respond to reports of sexual abuse, typically by moving the inmate to a place of safety, often to a holding cell or what is called the "transit" area of the prison. Sometimes a medical examination is conducted and sometimes an investigation into the incident is opened. The problem is that these steps rarely lead to adequate measures being taken against the perpetrator of abuse. Rather than internal disciplinary proceedings or external criminal prosecution, the solution is typically found in isolating the two parties. Either the rapist or, more commonly, the complaining inmate may be transferred to another prison. Serious investigation of abuses is all too rare. The basic procedures followed when a crime is committed outside of prison—involving collection of physical evidence, interviews with witnesses, interrogation of suspects—are much less likely to be employed when the crime involves inmates.

Failure to Prosecute

I have yet to hear of an inmate being charged in court with sexual assault of an inmate. Have you? If just one was found guilty, got more time, things would change.

———————

A Nebraska prisoner.[32]

As of this time I have almost 14 years in prison and have never heard of a prison rape case being prosecuted in court . . . . I'm quite sure if a man committed a rape in prison and got 5 or 10 years time, prison rape would decline.

———————

An Ohio prisoner.[33]

Human Rights Watch surveyed both correctional departments and prisoners themselves regarding whether rapists faced criminal prosecution. The response—or more accurately, lack of response—was instructive. Although corrections authorities generally stated that they referred all or some cases for prosecution by outside authorities, they had little information regarding the results of such referrals.[34] Prisoners were much more blunt: they uniformly agreed that criminal prosecution of rapists never occurs.

Judging solely by the direct accounts of rape we have received, criminal prosecution of prisoner-on-prisoner rape is extremely rare. Of the well over 100 rapes reported to Human Rights Watch, not a single one led to the criminal prosecution of the perpetrators. Even the most violent rapes, and those in which the victim pushed strongly for outside intervention, were ignored by the criminal justice system. Unlike rape in the outside community, rape in prison is a crime the perpetrator can commit without fear of spending additional time in prison.

The following letter, from an official with the Minnesota Department of Corrections, suggests just how rare such prosecutions are. Questioned in 1997 as to specific instances in which prisoners had been prosecuted for raping other prisoners, he cited a case that occurred twelve years previously:

> You also asked if I was aware of any cases in which perpetrators of inmate-on-inmate sexual assault have been criminally prosecuted. I spoke with staff

in our Office of Special Investigations and they informed me of one such case in September 1985. An inmate was charged and pled guilty to criminal sexual conduct in the third degree. He received a sentence of 1 year and 1 day to be served consecutively to his original incarceration offense.[35]

Although this response clearly indicates that rape prosecutions are rare in Minnesota, it is worth noting that almost all other state corrections department did not bring up *any* cases in which a perpetrator of rape in prison was prosecuted for the crime. Several said that they simply did not follow the progress of such cases.[36] The Missouri correctional authorities told Human Rights Watch in mid-1998 that three cases in the category "Forcible Sexual Misconduct" were submitted for prosecution in 1996, two of which had been refused by the prosecutor and one of which was still pending. They noted, in addition, that there were no criminal convictions stemming from inmate-on-inmate rape or sexual abuse during the past two years.

The case of M.R., the Texas inmate whose case was described in chapter V, is a particularly egregious example of the failure to criminally prosecute rape in prison. Not only was M.R. raped repeatedly, the last time in full view of other inmates, but he was nearly killed by the rapist, receiving a severe concussion, broken bones, and scalp lacerations. Desperate to see the man prosecuted, M.R. wrote both the local district attorney and sheriff explaining his strong desire to press charges. He even filed a grievance against the Texas correctional authorities requesting their help in securing the criminal prosecution of the rapist. None of his efforts made a difference: the prosecution was never instituted.

Why are criminal prosecutions of inmate-on-inmate rape so rare? First, it is obvious that the severe underreporting of cases of abuse means that only a small minority of rapes are known to prison authorities, let alone to anyone outside the prison. Second, the failure of prison authorities to react appropriately to complaints of sexual abuse—including collecting physical evidence of rape—and to properly investigate such complaints means that the necessary fact-finding to support a criminal prosecution is lacking. Since local police do not patrol prisons, they rely on correctional authorities to gather the proof of crime. But another crucial problem is the low priority that local prosecutors place on prosecuting prison abuses. Although local prosecutors are nominally responsible for prosecuting criminal acts that occur in prisons, they are unlikely to consider prisoners part of their real constituency. Prisoners have no political power of their own, and impunity for abuses against prisoners does not directly threaten the public outside of prison. Since many state prosecutors are elected officials, these factors may be decisive in leading them to ignore prison abuses.

Internal Administrative Penalties

M.R., the Texas prisoner who was nearly killed by his rapist, received another shock when he found out that the man was punished for the attack by spending a total of fifteen days in disciplinary segregation. Judging by the reports received by Human Rights Watch, however, the punishment meted out against M.R.'s rapist is only unusual in that it was meted out at all, not in that it was lenient. Since it is rare for prison authorities to conduct the investigation necessary to make a finding of rape, perpetrators of rape facing disciplinary proceedings are usually charged with a lesser offense such as disorderly conduct. The following account is typical:

> [While I was in a temporary cell], officers allowed another inmate who was not assigned to my cell to enter and stay in my cell for two days with me. This was two days of living hell in which he raped and abused my body. He threatened to kill me if I let officials know. However, I began kicking the cell door anyway after the second day and officials came to my aid. I informed officials of what had transpired the previous two days, but it was logged that I merely "alleged" that I had been sexually assaulted and raped. The inmate was charged only with the disciplinary offense of threatening me, he got away with the sexual assaults—a much more serious offense—unpunished.[37]

Perpetrators may spend a week or two, or even a month, in "the hole," rarely longer. Needless to say, when they return to the general prison population they may be primed for revenge.

The Failure of Mechanisms of Legal Redress

[L]awyers are, and with reason, terribly skeptical about the merits of pris-
oners' civil rights suits, most of which are indeed hoked up and frivolous.

Chief Judge Richard Posner, U.S. Court of Appeals for the Seventh Circuit.[38]

Prisons are necessarily dangerous places; they house society's most antiso-
cial and violent people in close proximity with one another. Regrettably,
"[s]ome level of brutality and sexual aggression among [prisoners] is
inevitable no matter what the guards do . . . unless all prisoners are locked
in their cells 24 hours a day and sedated."

Justice Clarence Thomas, U.S. Supreme Court[39]

L ike the public, many federal judges appear to view prisoners' legal
claims with an extremely cynical eye. Either they disbelieve prisoners' complaints of abuse, preferring to focus their concern on the constraints under which correctional authorities operate, or they seem resigned
to tolerating prison violence and exploitation. Not all federal judges are so
insensitive to prison abuses—indeed, a few worthy efforts have been made
to put a stop to prisoner-on-prisoner sexual abuse, including the rulings in
LaMarca v. Turner and *Redmond v. County of San Diego*—but it is fair to say
that the courts have not proven to be an effective champion of the sexually
abused inmate.[40]

As described in chapter III, prisoners seeking recourse for violations of
their constitutional rights can file a civil action in federal court. Especially
since the passage of the Prison Litigation Reform Act (PLRA), however, the
obstacles to such cases are daunting.

Despite the paucity of lawyers willing to litigate such cases, some inmates
do nonetheless file suit against the prison authorities in the aftermath of
rape. They typically assert that the authorities' failure to take steps to protect them from abuse violates the prohibition on "cruel and usual punishments" contained in the Eighth Amendment to the U.S. Constitution. All
too often, such cases are dismissed in the early stages of litigation, with some
judges going out of their way to excuse the actions of prison officials.

The reasoning behind the decision in *Chandler v. Jones,* although the court's comments were more candid than most, is typical. In dismissing the case, which involved an inmate who was sexually pressured and harassed after being transferred to a dangerous housing unit, the court explained that "sexual harassment of inmates in prisons would appear to be a fact of life."[41] Even while acknowledging the widespread nature of the problem, courts have been extremely reluctant to hold prison officials responsible for it. Their caution may, to some extent, reflect their belief that crucial policy and budgetary decisions affecting prison conditions are made elsewhere, and that guards and other officials should not be blamed for the predictable abuses that result.[42] By such reasoning, however, the courts have ensured near-complete impunity for prisoner-on-prisoner sexual abuse. This tendency is strongly reinforced by the requirement in such cases that prison officials have "actual knowledge" of the problem, allowing courts to dismiss even those cases in which the risk of rape would be obvious to any reasonable person in the official's position.

Finally, the rare case that does survive to reach a jury typically finds the inmate plaintiff before an unreceptive audience. Consider, for example, the case of *Butler v. Dowd,* in which the jury found that three young inmates had been brutally raped due to prison officials' deliberate indifference, but only awarded the plaintiffs the sum of one dollar each in nominal damages.[43] Or *James v. Tilghman,* in which the jury found that the inmate plaintiff had been raped due to the defendants' negligence, but awarded him nothing— neither compensatory nor punitive damages.[44] In many other cases, moreover, juries have found in favor of the defendants despite compelling evidence to the contrary. Even the well known case of *Farmer v. Brennan,* in which the transsexual victim of prisoner-on-prisoner rape prevailed before the U.S. Supreme Court, resulted in an unfavorable decision on remand to the district court.

W.H.

When Human Rights Watch interviewed W.H., a young African American inmate with thick glasses, he was held in one of the Texas prison system's administrative segregation units. With prisoners locked twenty-three hours per day in their cells under an ultra-high security regime, the ad-seg unit is designed for the "worst of the worst": those whose violent temperaments and uncontrollable behavior make them unfit for normal prison life. W.H., a first offender incarcerated for burglary, hardly fit this model; his small size (5'4" and 126 pounds) and softspoken demeanor made the ad-seg classification even more puzzling.

Yet W.II. admitted that he was facing criminal charges for assault on a public servant: in early 1997, in another prison, he had kicked a female administrative technician. The circumstances of the crime explain much about his current situation and past troubles.

W.H. told Human Rights Watch that he was violently raped by several prisoners, including his cellmate, over a five-week period in late 1996. The rapes occurred not long after he was transferred out of a safekeeping wing where he had been held since his entry into the Texas prison system two years previously. Gang members living in the wing he was placed on began to threaten him soon after his arrival there, telling him, "you gonna ride."[1] Within two weeks, W.H.'s situation fell apart. As W.H. described in a grievance: "Gang members from the Rollin Sixty Crips has since the 10th day of Nov 1996 untill the 13th day of Nov 1996 forced them selves upon me to perform homeosexual acts with them . . ."[2] On November 13, the gang members badly beat W.H.; he was then temporarily moved to another wing.

Later that month, at a classification hearing to decide where W.H. would be housed, W.H. described the assaults and his fear for his life. The classification committee nonetheless decided to place him with the same prisoners who had previously beaten and sexually assaulted him. On his way back to the cellblock, W.H. told Human Rights Watch, he climbed a barred gate to escape being locked back in with inmates who he believed were preparing to victimize him. The warden decided to transfer him to another wing, but W.H. refused this housing assignment as well. Because of this disciplinary infraction, he received fifteen days' punitive segregation. On his release from segregation, W.H. again refused to accept assignment back to regular housing, but the sergeant reportedly told him that if he would not go to his cell voluntarily he would be dragged there. He agreed to go.

On December 6, his first day back in the cellblock, W.H. filed an emergency grievance. It concluded with the plea: "I request that I be placed in a place where I will be protected from the crule and unusal punishment that will be subject if I am left in the presense of these and other members of the Rollin Sixty Crips."

The first rape occurred that evening, W.H. told Human Rights Watch. Less than an hour after he was placed in his cell, a gang member—a larger, stronger prisoner—was moved in with him. "The dude was crazy. He talked about killing, tried to scare me," related W.H.[3] The unit was on lockdown status, with prisoners supposed to be locked in their cells, but they had a method of getting in and out of cells by sticking paper in the lock before the cell door closed. At about 3:00 p.m., two prisoners entered W.H.'s cell and, together with W.H.'s new cellmate, anally raped W.H.

"Gang members from the Rollin Sixty Crips has since the 10th day of Nov 1996 untill the 13th day of Nov 1996 forced them selves upon me to perform homeosexual acts with them . . . "

At dinner, W.H. surreptitiously reported what had happened to him to an officer, but the officer took no action. "He didn't care," said W.H. "They're lazy; they don't want to deal with the paperwork."

That night, at about 1 a.m., W.H. was raped again, this time by his cellmate and an inmate from the adjoining cell. Both prisoners belonged to the Rolling Sixty Crips.

The next day, W.H. said, his cellmate raped him again. About ten minutes after the rape, a couple of correctional officers came by on their rounds to check the locks for paper. When they opened the door to W.H.'s cell, he pushed his way out. The officers knocked him to the ground and then brought him to detention, where he reported that he had been raped.

W.H. was brought to the prison infirmary to be examined. After looking at him the nurses had him sent to an outside hospital where medical tests were done. When Human Rights Watch interviewed him, nearly two years after the rapes, W.H. said he had never received the results of those tests.

The next day, a woman officer from the Internal Affairs Department (IAD) interviewed him. W.H. signed an affidavit describing the incidents that she kept; he told Human Rights Watch that he never received a copy of it. The officer asked if he wanted to file criminal charges against the perpetrators and he said yes. But he claims that no one from IAD ever contacted him again and as far as he knows charges were never filed.

W.H. was kept in segregation until his January 2, 1997 classification hearing. There he was denied safekeeping. At first, W.H. claims, the classification committee suggested that he be placed in administrative segregation, where he would be held in a one-man cell. "They could tell that was what I wanted," said W.H. "So the warden scratched out ad-seg and wrote in close custody general population. I flipped out."[4] That was when W.H. kicked the administrative technician, he told Human Rights Watch—knowing that this violent act would guarantee that he was kept locked up in segregation.

For W.H., breaking prison rules has become a habit. When Human Rights Watch interviewed him, he had spent over a year and a half in segregation. "I catch [disciplinary] cases purposely. I've been caught with contraband like extra sheets. I don't want to leave this unit. I'm going to do all my time here."[5] After the experiences that he has had in prison, safety is everything for W.H.; restrictive conditions are to be greatly desired. Unfortunately for him, confinement in administrative segregation carries with it a loss of good time credits. When W.H. is released, he will have served nearly every day of his seven year sentence for burglary, having accrued none of the time reductions due normal inmates.

Excerpts from Prisoners' Letters

I had no choice but to submit to being Inmate B's prison wife. Out of fear for my life, I submitted to sucking his dick, being fucked in my ass, and performing other duties as a woman, such as making his bed. In all reality, I was his slave, as the Officials of the Arkansas Department of Corrections under the 'color of law' did absolutely nothing.

M.P., Arkansas, pro se federal civil rights complaint filed 8/2/96

Most of the prisoners who rape are spending from 5 to life. And are part of a gang. They pick a loner smaller weaker individual. And make that person into a homosexual then sell him to other inmates or gangs. Anywhere from a pack of cigarettes to 2 cartons . . . . No one cares about you or anyone else. If they show kindness or are trying to be helpful, it is only because they want something. And if there offering you protection you can guarantee that there going to seek sexual favors. . . . When an inmate comes in for the first time and doesnt know anyone. The clicks and gangs. Watch him like Wolves readying there attacks. They see if he spends time alone, who he eats with. Its like the Wild Kingdom. Then they start playing with him, checking the new guy out. (They call him fresh meat.)

J.G., Minnesota, 8/8/96

I've been sentenced for a D.U.I. offense. My 3rd one. When I first came to prison, I had no idea what to expect. Certainly none of this. I'm a tall white male, who unfortunately has a small amount of feminine characteristics. And very shy. These characteristics have got me raped so many times I have no more feelings physically. I have been raped by up to 5 black men and two white men at a time. I've had knifes at my head and throat. I had fought and been beat so hard that I didn't ever think I'd see straight again. One time when I refused to enter a cell, I was brutally attacked by staff and taken to segragation though I had only wanted to prevent the same and worse by not locking up with my cell mate. There is no supervision after lockdown. I was given a conduct report. I explained to the hearing officer what the issue was. He told me that off the record, He suggests I find a man I would/could willingly have sex with to prevent these things from happening. I've requested protective custody only to be denied. It is not available here. He also said there was no where to run to, and it would be best for me to accept things . . . . I probably have AIDS now. I have great difficulty raising food to my mouth from shaking after nightmares or thinking to hard on all this. . . . I've laid down without physical fight to be sodomized. To prevent so much damage in struggles, ripping and tearing. Though in not fighting, it caused my heart and spirit to be raped as well. Something I don't know if I'll ever forgive myself for.

———————

A.H., Indiana, 8/30/96

If a person is timid or shy or as prison inmates term him "Weak," either mentally or physically, he stands to be a victim of physical and/or sexual assault.

———————

R.B., Colorado, 9/1/96

I am giving you a breif description of the incient's i have suffered from while I've been in this institution. To begin with on Aug 1, 1996 Approx: 12:30 pm i was housed in E building i went to the officials on duty about a problem i was having with two (2) inmate's but it was disreguard. Than around and about Aug 16, 1996 i was sexual assaulted by the same two (2) inmate's. I was then taking to the medical department in cristeanna hospital for treatment. It's a big Rumor that one inmate has Aid's.

———————

T.A., Delaware, 9/2/96

Inmates confined for sexual offenses, especially those against juvenile victims, are at the bottom of the pecking order and consequentially most often victimized. Because of their crime, the general population justifies using their weakness by labling rape "just punishment" for their crime. Sexual offenders are the number one target group for prisoner rape. Inmates who come to prison at an early age are the second target group. Being younger, more physically attractive, and less likely to be infected with H.I.V., this group "needs to learn not to come back to prison a second time." Obviously this is a poor justification for rape, but in the prison social structure any excuse will do.

L.V., Arkansas, 9/3/96

I hate to say this but if you weren't racist when you came to prison more than likely you will be when you leave. In Texas prisons *race* is the main issue and until people wake up and realize that nothing will change!

T.B., Texas, 9/3/96

I was raped in prison from Feb 1991 through Nov 1991. From that it left me HIV positive.

K.S., Arkansas, 9/4/96

I have been sexually assaulted twice since being incarcerated. Both times the staff refused to do anything except to lock me up and make accusations that I'm homosexual and that if I pursue legal action they'd ship me and both times they did.

J.G., Florida, 9/4/96

What is more prevalent at TCIP (which, by the way, is a medium security, rural institution) is best called "coercion." I suppose you have an idea what these engagements entail. The victim is usually tricked into owing a favor. Here this is usually drugs, with the perpetrator seeming to be, to the victim, a really swell fellow and all. Soon, however, the victim is asked to repay all those joints or licks of dope—right away. Of course he has no drugs or money, and the only alternative is sexual favors. Once a prisoner is "turned-out," it's pretty much a done deal. I guess a good many victims just want to do their time and not risk any trouble, so they submit.... The coercion-type abuses continue because of their covert nature. From the way such attacks manifest, it can seem to others, administrators and prisoners, that the victims are just homosexual to begin with. Why else would they allow such a thing to happen, people might ask.

J.S., Tennessee, 9/5/96

I was young and yes i was weak. My weight was only 120 lbs, the first few months i was raped and beat up many times, i would always Fight back, i wanted my attackers to know i was not a Willing Subject for their evilness. I went to the Guards for help and was told there was nothing that could be done, that i would have to stand up like a Man and Take Care of my own troubles.

B.L., Florida, 9/5/96

Some prison rapists are so ignorant or delusional, they imagine the rape victim to be the homosexual—because he's doing the taking, not dishing it out (*he's* gay! *he's* performing a homosexual act!)

J.J., California, 9/6/96

The rapes seem to be for two main reasons. 1. They hurt, someone must pay. 2. Being deprived of consensual sex, and self-centered, any hole will do. Power, control, revenge, seem to top the "reasons" for rape. The person assaulted is either seen as weaker, or gang banged if seen as stuck up kind of person. You know, refuses to swear, actually admits he is guilty, is seeking help etc. . . . I have yet to hear of an inmate being charged in court with sexual assault of an inmate. Have you? If just one was found guilty, got more time, things would change.

———————

D.A., Nebraska, 9/6/96

On January 27, 1993, I was forcefully raped! I was held down while at least 3 black inmates had anal intercourse using my rectum as their sexual pleasure release! From that day on, I was classified as a homosexual and was sold from one inmate to the next. I was sold for a $2.25 bag of coffee! . . . Blacks tend to rape the white inmates and force themselves on weaker inmates! I am one of the weaker inmates!

———————

J.D., Texas, 9/6/96

Most guys raped are guys for there first time locked up, between the ages 18–30 that looks young, not strong, looks lonely, scared. Guys watch these things.

———————

M.F., Ohio, 9/6/96

A lot of guys don't say enything about what happens to them, because they got to live there. What if they told, what could happen to them . . . I know you think they should tell what happens to them. But until you put yourself in there shoes you don't know what you do. Some prisons are hard. Fights, killings, ect. everyday. One thing guys don't like is guys who tell on others. What are your chances if you told on someone?

———————

M.F., Ohio, 9/6/96

I'm in protective custody have been since Feb of 95. My rape is known thru out the system as everyone know the person who did it likes to brag so its unsafe for me to be in population as now I'm a snitch, homo and my safety would be in jeopardy.

———————

R.G., Delaware, 9/6/96

When a man gets raped nobody gives a damn. Even the officers laugh about it. I bet he's going to be walking with a limp ha ha ha. I've heard them.

———————

J.G., Minnesota, 9/7/96

Most often the victom who reports a rape is again victimized by officials who write this inmate victom a disciplinary report of propaganda; officials do this in order to avoid law suits resulting from the rapes.

———————

E.R., Iowa, 9/9/96

When a man finally gets his victim, he protects him from everyone else, buys him anything, the victim washes his clothes, his cell, etc. In return, the entire prison knows that this guy has a "BITCH" or "girl." This gives power to the aggressors ego. In here, the egos multiply a lot more than in society.

Now I've seen this happen many many times. The response from the guards is "the strong survive," "who cares," or they join in on the teasing, tourmenting, etc.

———————

R.L., New York, 9/9/96

I've seen inmates attacked by two or three men at a time and forced to the floor, while two or three hold him down, the fourth man slaps vaseline on his rectum and rapes him. I knew two men who hung themselves after this.

———————

R.L., New York, 9/9/96

The more time a man has, the more respect he gets, the more he is feared, the more the guards ignore his misbehavior and let him do what he wants, including rape! The mentality of a lot of guards is that it's only a convicted felon screwing another, so who cares?

———————————

R.L., New York, 9/9/96

The DOC covers their actions under the guise of security and the state court wears blinders.

———————————

J.G., Florida, 9/9/96

I didn't want to tell on the inmates who raped me because I didn't want to be killed. If I had told on the inmates, They would have gotten me in another part of the Prison. Even Protective Custody Facility.

———————————

R.H., Utah, 9/10/96

Why prison sexual assault occurs: Part of it is revenge against what the non-white prisoners call, "The White Man," meaning authority and the justice system. A common comment is, "ya'll may run it out there, but this is our world!" More of it I think is the assaulters own insecurities and them trying to gain some respect in their peer group by showing that they "are a man." This subculture is concerned with appearances, and the more imposing an appearance, the more respect you command. Some of the guys I rode with didnt want any sex or $. They just wanted the status of having a "Kid." Naturally, I liked them best.

———————————

S.H., Texas, 9/10/96

I was "rented out" for sexual favors, and a lot of the guys who rented me are *not* rapists, or assaulted as children, or any other stereotypical model. They just wanted some sexual satisfaction, even though they knew I was *not* deriving pleasure from it, and was there only because I was forced to. . . . I was with the Valluco (Valley) crowd, so I was only passed around to them for free. D. Town Hispanics had to pay. They were charged $3 for a blow-job, $5 for anal sex.

S.H., Texas, 9/10/96

I had an officer tell me that "faggots like to suck dick, so why was I complaining." You and I realize that non-consensual sex is rape, regardless—a leap in thinking not possible for prison officials.

S.H., Texas, 9/10/96

Defendant J.M, a security officer with the rank of sargeant, came to investigate the series of latest allegations. Defendant J.M. refused to interview the inmate witnesses and told plaintiff that he was lying about being sexually abused. After plaintiff vehemently protested that he was being truthful, defendant J.M. made comments that plaintiff "must be gay" for "letting them make you suck dick."

S.H., Texas, 9/10/96 (legal papers)

[When I was sent to prison,] I was just barely 18 years of age, about 90 pounds. I did nine years from March 1983 to November 1991. In that 9 years I was raped several times. I never told on anyone for it, but did ask the officer for protective custody. But I was just sent to another part of the prison. Than raped again. Sent to another part of the prison. Etc. This went on for 9 years. I didn't want to tell on the inmates who raped me because I didn't want to be killed. . . . I came back to prison in 1993. In 1994 I was raped again. I attempted suicide. . . . The doctors here in the prison say "quote" major depression multiple neurotic symptoms, marked by excessive fear, unrelenting worry and debilitating anxiety. Antisocial suicidal ideation, self-degradation, paranoia and hopelessness are characteristic, "unquote."

———————

R.H., Utah, 9/10/96

[With coercive sex], one inmate will sidle up to another inmate and try to play on the inmate's emotions, as well as befriend him; this inmate usually being a "first-timer" who is quiet and reserved and without any established friends yet . . . . Eventually the weaker inmate is compelled to perform masturbation on the domineering inmate, or—at first—to pose nude before the domineering inmate while he masturbates. . . . Once the weaker inmate is hooked, the domineering inmate will share the details of his conquest with his buddies and then the weaker inmate finds himself dealing with more and more inmates vying for his services. By this time, the weaker inmate has had his self-esteem so lowered that he no longer cares and becomes a sexual substitute for whomever needs him.

———————

P.S., Texas, 9/10/96

I found out how people earn respect in here, you have to beat someone or shank them.

———————

J.G., Minnesota, 9/12/96

It's either rape or be raped and the racial tension doesn't help any.

———————

W.M., Texas, 9/13/96

Officers can't do anything unless an inmate say's something. If an inmate does, not only is that a sure sign of weakness, but a weak snitch to boot. Not worthy of living.

———————

W.M., Texas, 9/13/96

[You have to fight to be safe.] To give you an idea what I mean . . . I now have scar's where I've been gutted, under the right side of my chest below my heart, where my neck was cut open and under my left arm. That's not the many minor cuts and wound's can't include in this letter because of lack of times & space. People start to treat you right once you become deadly.

———————

W.M., Texas, 9/13/96

It's fixed where if you're raped, the only way you [can escape being a punk is if] you rape someone else. Yes I know that's fully screwed, but that's how your head is twisted. After it's over you may be disgusted with yourself, but you realize you're not powerless and that you can deliver as well as receive pain. Then it's up to you to decide whether you enjoy it or not. Most do, I don't. It's sick and depraved. It's also depressing when one of these boy's (another name for turn out), come up to you for protection because they know you won't hurt them as much because you've been through it & they don't have the nuts to break out themselves even when you tell them how.

———————

W.M., Texas, 9/13/96

My celly tried to rape me with a knife for a weapon, we fought and I got the knife and stabbed him to fight him off, I was charged with attempted murder and felonious assault and taken to trial, found guilty and received 12 to 15 years. The system feels that justice was done.

———————

L.L., Ohio, 9/14/96

What is needed in prison is one man cells, one man showers and for the officials to prosecute attackers instead of just locking them up in the hole.

————————

L.L., Ohio, 9/14/96

While serving my sentence at a former institution, I was severely beaten and
gang raped, both orally and anally, by six black inmates . . . . It started by
inmate [A] coming by my cell and waking me up at approximately 4:00 a.m.
He said he wanted to come in and watch television with me. I said, "No, I'm
trying to sleep." He said he's going to the booth and get my door open. I saw
him go to the booth and told the booth officer to open my cell door . . . My
cell door was not authorized to be opened.

By this time, I had turned on my overhead light and heard inmate [A] say
to [the officer], "Open #222, so I can get his laundry." I didn't think nothing
of it because we've had no prior problems before. I did think it was odd
though. So he came in and sat on my bed . . . . About 5 to 10 minutes after
that, inmate [B], [C], and [D] came into my cell. Then inmate [D] said, "We
want some ass." I said, "I don't think so, I don't play that shit." When he said
this, I said to myself, "Oh no! I'm in trouble!" I looked toward the door for
an escape route finding it blocked, I went into myself to prepare for the
worst.

Inmate [D] then said, "Either give it to Jesus or give it up." . . . .

It was at this time that the floor officer came by on the bottom tier (I was
on the top tier), doing or supposedly doing, his rounds. He noticed the
inmates in my cell and asked if everything was all right. Too terrified to
answer, I just nodded. [The officer] never came to the top tier during his
round. I was then directed back to my bed. Inmate [B] then stood in front
of me and pulled out his penis and forced it into my mouth. Inmate [C]
then turn his turn. Pulling me to my feet, he then took my boxers off, bent
me over and forced his penis inside. Inmate [D] laid on the bed, took my
head and forced himself inside my mouth [All four of them, plus one more]
took turns anally and orally raping me at the same time. All of them repeatedly did this.

Somewhere in the middle of this, inmate [F] entered . . . . [D]uring the
rape, I believe it was him that said "suck this dick you white bitch.". . . .

[One said:] "If you snitch on us, we'll kill you!!" The other said, "And if you do and you get transferred, you'll still die." At that time, I really believed them, and I still think this today.

———————

R.D., Virginia, 9/16/96

I remember after he left, the sun was rising, I was standing there in total shock. My body and my mind was numb. I didn't know what to do, so I just sat down on the commode and let what they ejaculated in me come out. After everything was out, I cleaned myself again. As I got up, I noticed the water in the commode was red. I washed myself again, put on all my clothes, got under the covers. The fear went on a rampage in my mind, shutting down my whole system. For the rest of the day I was like this. I do remember wanting to kill them or either myself . . . . I cannot fully state to you now the actual feelings of guilt or shame I felt at the time. In retrospect, I feel now that there was more I could have done and my mindset now is one of tremendous speculation. But, it all comes down to feelings of being inadequate in the defense of myself.

———————

R.D., Virginia, 9/16/96

I am a first-time non-violent offender, and committed a white-collar offense . . . . In September, 1994, during the week of Labor Day, I was accosted and raped in the shower . . . . While the entire incident did not last more than a few minutes, it seemed like an eternity. I was certain that I had indeed been sentenced to Hell. I was left badly bruised and crying, with a pretty hopeless outlook on the whole situation. There was no guard to be found, and so I was left to fend for myself.

———————

R.S., West Virginia, 9/16/96

Prison rapes occur for a number of reasons. One such reason is the insecure, weak inmate preying on another weaker inmate, to make an impression of toughness or ruthlessness that he hopes will discourage other inmates from doing the same thing to him . . . . The main reason why sexual assaults occur is because prison officials and staff promote them. It's their method of sacrificing the weak inmates to achieve and maintain control of the stronger aggressive or violent inmates.

W.F., Missouri, 9/21/96

[I] was sent to the orientation block to be cellmate with another prisoner already occupying a double cell. I did not know at the time that I was to share a double cell with him, that he was a known rapist in the prison . . . . I must point out that only a month and a half prior, he was accused of raping another man. On my fourth day of sharing the cell, I was ambushed and viciously raped by him. After being raped, I remained in shock and paralized in thought for two days until I was able to muster the courage to report it, this, the most dreadful and horrifying experience of my life.

B.J., Connecticut, 9/23/96

I have long Blond hair and I weigh about 144 lbs. I am a free world homo sexual that looks and acts like a female . . . . In 1992 I came to this Unit and was put into population. There was so many gangs and violence that I had know choice but to hook up with someone that could make them give me a little respect. Well after a few days I guess he figured it was more problems than it was worth and decided to give in, "to them." A Black guy paid an officer two cartons of "Kools" to write me up so I could be moved to his block with him. Well they did just that. Money will buy anything here and I mean anything . . . . All open Homosexuals are preyed upon and if they don't choose up they get chosen.

M.P., Arkansas, 9/24/96

When a new inmate enters an open barracks prison it triggers a sort of competition among the convicts as to who will seduce and subjugate that new arrival. Subjugation is mental, physical, financial, and sexual. Every new arrival is a potential victim. Unless the new arrival is strong, ugly, and efficient at violence, they are subject to get seduced, coerced, or raped ... Psychosocially, emotionally, and physically the most dangerous and traumatic place I can conceive of is the open barracks prison when first viewed by a new inmate.

L.V., Arkansas, 9/25/96

I was too embarrassed to tell the [corrections officers] what had happened [that I had been raped] .... The government acts as if a "man" is supposed to come right out and boldly say "I've been raped." You know that if it is degrading for a woman, how much more for a man.

R.B., Kansas, 9/28/96

The guys who perform/promote these assaults are the "tough-guy" sorts... . [T]hese guys commit these attacks for power & control, <u>not</u> for the sex— although they are highly interested in sex. For many (most?) of these guys, it's a "badge of honor" for them, when they can abuse a "child molester" (especially sexually) and run them into p.c. (protective custody). . . . Self-esteem is a valuable commodity, in this environment, since a pronounced lack of it is a common factor among criminals. . . . By "stealing power" from others, these individuals are able to feel superior—which boosts their self-esteem.

M.S., Nevada, 9/28/96

Prison officials seem to prefer the "slap on the wrist" in-house disciplinary approach over referring criminal charges against the perpetrators [of rape]. When pressed, they generally claim that this practice is to "protect the victim" (from an ugly court scene), but I believe it's to protect the prison from having to admit the problem exists.

M.S., Nevada, 9/28/96

When I was sentenced I didn't hear the part of sentencing that stated, "you are hereby sentenced to six years of hard labor to the Texas Dept. of Criminal Justice. While there, you will be beaten daily, savagely raped, and tortured, mentally, to the point of contemplating suicide."

L.O., Texas, 9/29/96

Young men and male of small frame structure is being beaten and raped as well as gay inmates by inmates of bigger size and gang members.

R.G., California, 10/1/96

My abuse started in the county jail where I was raped by four inmates . . . . When I was sent to prison I informed them that I have been raped by gang member and was on medication. . . . Still I was being asked for sex and tolded that I would have to given over myself one way or another; at this point (looking back on the matter) I can see that I was going through a brake down mentally. Anyway that night I've made of my mind that I was taking my life for it seem as if that was the only way out of that Hell. So the sleeping medication that they was giving me, I save for 8 days which came to 800 MG and I took them. I was taken to the medical center where I stayed for 18 days. Every so often 5 or 6 Doctors would come into that room and look at me talking to their self. They would ask me how I feel and say no more. This one Doctor tolded me that they was going to put me back on the same yard. I told him if they do, I would take my life. He than said that he don't give a dam. I just hung my head low and cryed.

R.G., California, 10/1/96

There is no safety for gays, young men, first timers and men of small built. The most rapes that happen are with the prison gangs. Young men and first timer's believe that they must join prison gangs for fear of safty of their lives. . . . It seem that young men and gays and first timmers are used as sacrificial lamb. The reason is to use these men as a way to keep the gangs and killers from turning on the system which created prison the Hell that it is. These young men, these gays, these first timers are turning into everything their abusers are.

R.G., California, 10/1/96

On 10-12-93 I inmate was assined to the Frenche Robertson Unit in Abilene Texas and sense I have been on the unit I have been bete up on and sexually assaulted. It all started a week after I got to the unit. I was confronted by inmate [F] and at that time inmate [J] come up and sed that I am going to do him a faver or I will not walk out of my cell block and that was on 10-19-93. And by the time 1994 came around I had been bete up sevrule times and had been raped 2 times by the two inmates. One 5-26-94 I got assallted by a unnown inmate and have been sexually abuesd by a number of unnown inmates seens I have been on this unit. I have told the unit werdon and a number of the officers on the unit and have not got the proper proteshone that I need and the unit classification have denide me transfer to a safe keeping unit a number of times.

D.M., Texas, 10/1/96

I was dehumanzied by the lack of empathy prison officials have towards victims of sexual assault, potential victims, inmates safety in general. Inmates are looked at and treated as subhuman across the board. If an incident can be covered it will be. If it can be ignored it will be.

K.J., Georgia, 10/2/96

Upon my arrival to prison, my being small, white, some what feminine and niave to the Big City and prison ways, made me appear as an easy mark as a victim. A victim for extortion, robbery and/or sexual assault. I survived the attacks only because I fought several times. The fighting led the preditors to believe that I wasn't an easy mark and there was easier prey to attack.

I wish my tale ended there but it doesn't. After witnessing bigger stronger guys who had also fought back, be brutally attacked by more than one inmate and sexually assaulted, I was over-come with fear. The constant fear of being jumped by three or four guys and brutally beaten until I willingly let them sexually assault me, or was forced to endure a sexual assault, was too much for me. Wondering if I was next dominated my waking hours. I began to think of ways to escape the preditors. I chose to manipulate the psychiatric department into transferring me to a prison psychiatric hospital.

I thought that I had escaped the threat of rape, but I was wrong. Another patient there in the same dorm as me said he liked me and wanted to have sex with me. It was everywhere and escape seemed utterly hopeless. I was tired of living in fear and gave in to his demands. I let him use me and my body as if I were a real woman for his personal sexual gratification. Both oral and anal sex repeatedly for hours.

I was returned to the same prison I had fled from. Within 30 days I escaped from prison, the fear of being humiliated and treated as a sexual slave was too much and greater than the fear of being shot or prosecuted. . . . . My lawyer said that I had the best duress defense he'd ever seen.

After beating the DOC's attempt to prosecute me for escape, they enacted their vengeance. Having just turned 19 years old, they transferred me to Jackson prison. "The World's Largest Walled Prison" known for its stabbings and sexual attacks on young white males. The memory I have of my arrival is yells, mating calls and whistling at me as I walked to my cell at 2:30 am.

When in one 24 hr. period I received over a hundred notes asking who was my man, or threatening me, and more verbal threats, I attempted suicide by cutting my wrist; the only escape I could envision. When that failed the next man to approach me found me hopeless and depressed and I simply no longer cared about what happened to me. He claimed me as his property and I didnt dispute it. I became obedient, telling myself at least I was surviving. . . . He publicly humiliated and degraded me, making sure all the inmates and gaurds knew that I was a queen and his property. Within a week he was pimping me out to other inmates at $3.00 a man. This state of existence continued for two months until he sold me for $25.00 to another black male who purchased me to be his wife. It was another thirty days before an attorney was able to force the DOC to transfer me to another prison.

Word quickly spread of my activities at Jackson. That was the setting for the rest of my five yr. sentence. Though I was lucky, the rest was spent with only two men, and not hundreds of men.

E.S., Mississippi, 10/4/96

Often the victim will be tied up on a bed, face down and sold until the debt is finished or until the novelty is gone.

C.M., Illinois, 10/8/96

I really don't think that male on male rape is primarily a sexual thing. It is probably more of a power thing by which one person can maintain absolute control over another, or use the other to settle some financial responsibility.

C.M., Illinois, 10/8/96

As I told you in my last letter I was sexually assulted when I was let out of adminstrative segregation July 17/96 and it got around pretty quick that I was a "turnout" they all knew. But the dude I was riding with he protected me as long as I did sexual favors for him. But he left. So no one was there to stop this inmate from falling in my house.

When he gets there he first demands money I have none so he takes my radio and headphones. He sends them to his house see he's out of place he is not supposed to be in my cell but I cant tell for fear of the other inmates. So I just stay on my bunk. Oh and we are on lock down so we only shower 3 times a week. He came in my cell Friday so he wont have a chance to go back to his cell until Monday so I just try and stay away from him.

On Saturday about 10 or 11 AM he tells me that he wants a blow job or he wants to have sex with me. Now I dont know why but I refused I said please dont so he hits me 3 times in my face and upper body I come down off the top bunk to try and defend my self but before I have a chance he pulls out a knife on me! When I reach for his wrist to try and get the knife I get cut but not to bad. But I do manage to get the knife away from him. I dont remember cutting him as many times as he was cut. But I took his own knife and I defended my self. He was cut a few times got a bunch of stitches: I then layed the weapon on the ground he picked it up and threw it out of the cell. I then started yelling for the Guards.

Now even though I was in my cell and he wasn't supposed to be there he was out of place even though I was cut and he admitted possion of the weapon and even though he admitted that he came in my cell to do me harm I was still given a major case "which fucks off chance of parole for me for a long time." I was still put in solitary for segregation for 15 days. Now on 10/8/96 I was put in administrative segregation for assult with a weapon I dont even know when I'll get out plus they might file a free world charge on me so that I get more time. I tryed to tell them it was self defence and that I need protective custody but they wouldnt listen. I dont know what I'll do if Im charged cause I'll have to plea bargin I'd be to scared to take it to trial for fear of losing. Those people dont care about what happens in here and if I lose I'd get more time than if I plea bargined and alls I can do is hope for the best.

T.B., Texas, 10/8/96

I didn't know how the prison system work, so this inmate come up to the A & O unit and gives me three packs of cigarettes, I didn't know where they came from, or why they was given to me, I took the cigarettes, two weeks later I was placed in population, and here come this big old guy name [M, telling me that I belong to him because he had bought me, and had the same guy there who had brought me the cigarettes to verify it.

C.D., Indiana, 10/8/96

I know you don't want to hear this but it is prison officials, jail officials that causes men to be fucked in prison.... [P]rison officials approve of men getting fucked in prison and to attack it at the prisoners level, you are fighting a losing battle, start with prison officials, people in authority, they are the one that causes people to get fucked against their will.

———————

C.D., Indiana, 10/8/96

I have seen or heard of rapes on a weekly basis at the least. Mostly it is a daily occurrence. Rapes are a *very* common occurrence due to the fact of coercion being "played" on ignorant first timers. Once someone is violated sexually and there is no consequences on the perpetrators, that person who was violated then becomes a mark or marked. That means he's fair game.

———————

M.B., Indiana, 10/10/96

As I go back to the time I was attacked, I was only about 145 lbs, white, blue eyed and smoothed skin. I was about 5' 10" and very disliking of crowds. It was about 1 pm or 1:30 pm before showers. 2 black males (gang related) ran into my cell, one very large and the other more my size. I was hit, and put face down on the mattress. A knee in my back and a pillow case under my chin (like a horse bridle), being weaker made me vulnerable to be taken advantage of (note: this paragraph is not detailed action for action but only a brief take). Being scared I was too much in a trance to go to the unranked officers because many at the time were promoters of the non-survival of the weak.... I feel that maybe some women might look at me as less than a man. My pride feels beaten to a pulp.

———————

E.R., Texas, 10/10/96.

Someone with a slower mental process or lower I.Q. usually gets tricked into sexual devastation in some decivious way and the officers look the other way or leave, as Texas stays understaffed for that reason so an officer can just walk off and never see a thing.

_____

R.B., Texas, 10/13/96

At least 90% of assaults are not even reported to staff. Occasionally the victim is a person who could fight off one inmate but there is a bet between groups or gangs to make him a "bitch," and the bettor will get a few of his home boys and go assault him.

_____

R.B., Texas, 10/13/96

Smaller, weaker, meeker individuals are usually targets. Meeker individuals tend to "act Gay" is how it's described here and in turn invites assault through the agressors mind. A new inmate needs to come into the system ready to fight and with a strong mind. He will be approached by a bigger guy who will let him know he's going to "fight, fuck or pay protection." . . . . He will offer the new comer wire (for a radio antena) coffee or something so the new comer will come back and the subject will come up every time the new comer comes around and before long the new comer wants to know what the deal is. They go to a job or fall off in a cell agree to be easy, keep it between them, just do each other, ect. When the dude get's the new comer it's over and the dude will tell the new comer he'll take care of him or he'll tell everybody he's just a little bitch . . . . Should the new comer seek assistance of staff, staff just laughs at him, the physic department just says what do you want me to do. It's a no win situation and frustration often leads them to keep up the practice.

_____

R.B., Texas, 10/13/96

Another game is to get an inmate indebted to an inmate give them a week to have your money when they don't it automatically doubles. Then the next week you take it out in trade. Even if the new comer has someone out there that will send the money, by the time they write and the money is sent and posted it's too late anyway. This way some will fight some will feel obligated. [The games] are endless but ever so real.

————————

R.B., Texas, 10/13/96

I have been on 3 units on one of the units I have been on, you heard of rapes just about daily on the other 2 though maybe you heard of rape once a month maybe. The units with the younger offenders seem to carry by far the higher rates of sexual assaults.

————————

R.B., Texas, 10/13/96

Texas does not pay inmates. Some inmates sell there bodies just for basics like toothpaste, soap, shampoo, tooth brush, deoderant, things others take for granted.

————————

R.B., Texas, 10/13/96

On the younger units I would say you have a rape at least weekly. From the people I have known in my 10 years I would say about 50% have been forced to hook up with someone not necessarily for protection but due to survival having necessities or attention.

————————

R.B., Texas, 10/13/96

I would say the bigger prisons allow more rape because of understaffing and the prisons with the younger offenders, not necessarily maximum security.

————————

R.B., Texas, 10/13/96

Even after the gang rape I endured, I was still poorly classified and two violent inmates with a record of violence threatened to sexually assault me and take my store goods. I tried to fight back, which resulted in my jaw being broke in 3 places.

K.J., Georgia, 10/13/96

The man who is responsible for my rape has a history of this type of behaviour. He usually preys on young white kids. His method of approach is lending smokes and drugs to get them in debt and then asks to be repaid. When the person can't pay he offers to let them have sex, and when they say no, he rapes them. I don't know why I was a victim I owed him nothing neither did I associate with him. Did I turn him on? I porbably did, since I was 23 years old at that . . . as they say in prison—*a sweet pretty young thing.* My rape is known throughout the prison system as everyone knows the person who did it and likes to brag about it, so its unsafe for me to be in population as now I am a snitch, a homo and my safety is in jeapordy.

R.G., Delaware, 10/17/96

Another type of coerced sex is for the dominant party to first let the intended victim know that he wants to have sex with him, then begin to wear the victim down by constantly leering at him in ways that let the victim know what's on his mind. Psychologically the victim eventually begins to believe he is a homosexual and no longer resists. It's similar to how a sexual abuse victim, afterward, begins to believe there is something wrong with them that caused the abuse to happen, which causes them to accept part of the responsibility for their abuse.

P.S., Texas, 10/17/96

Being raped in prison is degrading and humiliating. It tags you as belonging to the inmate who raped you. One must never talk openly about being raped for fear of being severely beaten or killed.

———————

M.G., Oklahoma, 10/19/96

When a person come to prison, if they see fear in their face, or anywhere, they will be easy prey.

———————

M.O., Illinois, 10/20/96

While I was being uncuffed at the rec door by Officer W. he made the comment that faggots are sickening and disgusting. . . . Inmates see this type of behavior as approval to beat, rape and extort gay men in prison because of the anomosity and hateful attitudes displayed by the state.

———————

A.H., Indiana, 10/27/96 (offender grievance, denied 10/30/96, with response that "Officer W. states that he at no time mentioned the word fagget")

On 10-21-96 Officer G. came to get me from rec. . . . He had the leash wrapped around my waist, then yanked on it spinning me around. Telling me "move fag." I asked him what the hell was his problem. He shoved me and then yanked on the leash several times in the course of escorting me to my cell. Then pulled out the mace as though he were to spray me. He continued calling me a faggot dick sucker throughout this process. Officer M. witnessed this. . . . I have suffered from a lot of abuse in this prison including my rape to this kind of abuse from staff. I am sick of this treatment.

———————

A.H., Indiana, 10/21/96 (grievance filed, denied with response: "WRONG FORM")

Older men who have been in here for a long time like Young men because they are more healthy, better looking, and more inexperienced. The older men like the "power" they have over their victims. A Younger man is scared, nervous, shy, etc. He doesn't know what to do, so he freezes, get's very quiet, and allows himself to be victimized.

R.L., New York, 10/21/96

The guards just turn their backs. Their mentality is the tougher, colder, and more cruel and inhuman a place is, the less chance a person will return. This is not true. The more negative experiences a person goes through, the more he turns into a violent, cruel, mean, heartless individual, <u>I know this to be a fact.</u>

R.L., New York, 10/21/96

Transexuals and homosexuals are for the most part viewed as weak. One step up from rapist on the social ladder. Usually considered the property of another inmate.

In prison, male on male sexual relations are viewed differently then those of free-society. The aggressive person (male role) isn't considered a homosexual, or bisexual. He's thought of as heterosexual. Only the passive (female role) is considered homosexual or bisexual.

E.S., Mississippi, 10/21/96

To begin let me tell you a little about myself. I am 32 yrs of age, I'm an American of African decent. I'm currently serving a 5-yr sentence for trafficking in stolen property .... I feel I should also add because it has bearing on some of the observations I'll share with you, I'm gay and have been since I was aware of my sexuality ....

Let me say I believe there are different levels or kinds of rape in prison. First, there is what I will refer to as "Bodily Force Rape" for lack of a better term. This is the kind of assault where one or more individuals attack another individual and by beating and subduing him force sex either anal or oral on him.

Second there is what I'll call Rape By Threat. An example of this would be, when an individual tells a weaker individual that in order to avoid being assulted by the individual who's speaking he must submit to his demand for sex.

Third and by far the most common is what I'll call using a persons fears of his situation to convince him to submit to sex.

I will give you my observations on all these types of assult shortly; but first I feel I should tell you the people most at risk. And they are white males usualy slight of build and physicaly atractive, between 17–25 yrs of age. Please note although other ethnic groups such as young blacks and Hispanics have sufferd these indignities it happens to them far far less often than to young whites . . . . .

The last form of "rape," using a persons fear against him. Among inmates there is a debate wheather this is in fact rape at all. In my opinion it is in fact rape. Let me give you an example of what happens and you decide.

Example: A new inmate arrives. He has no funds for the things he needs such as soap, junk food, and drugs (there are a great deal of drugs in prisons). Someone befriends him and tells him if he needs anything come to him. The new arrival is some times aware, but most times not, that what he is receiving has a 100% interest rate that is compounded weekly. When the N.A. is in deep enough the "friend" will tell him he can cover some of his debt by submitting to sex. This has been the "friend's" objective from the begining. To manuver the N.A. into a corner where he's vulnerable. Is this rape? I think it is.

B.H., Florida, 10/22/96

I believe only a minute amount of these incidences get reported; the individules this happens to live in fear. In fear of the perpetrators, but even more signifagant, thay fear other people knowing thay've been victomized in this mannor. They suffer in silence, think thay are less than men and fearing the world and thair familys will know of thair shame.

B.H., Florida, 10/22/96

The first time [I was raped] I told on my attackers. All they did was moved me from one facility to another. And I saw my attacker again not too long after I tolded on him. Then I paid for it. Because I tolded on him, and he got even with me. So after that, I would not, did not tell again.

R.H., Utah, 10/22/96

Most of the assults are done through threat of violence. The actual assult is mainly done by one person but the victim knows if he defies that one person then 10 to 15 other people will jump on him when he goes somewhere. Most of the time the victim doesnt even fight because he's scared. The only time there is really a group of people doing the actual rape is when the victim is fighting back and then they will beat him up and hold him down and rape him, but that is rare.

T.B., Texas, 10/23/96

When they have a punk or a kid that they've turned out they treat them like trophies it makes them feel important or somebody with status! They thrive on the status they couldnt get in the free world. The punks or kids that they turnout they are like a flag to tell every one that this is mine I own this cause when they do turn out a guy they actually own them, every penny they get it goes to there man. You can buy a kid for 20 or 30 dollars on most wings!! They sell them like cattle.

T.B., Texas, 10/23/96

[Someone attempted to rape him using a knife as a weapon:] [The rapist and I] went in front of the disciplinary committee. . . . [The officer] said well what do you want I said P.C. He said no not on my unit. He said Im locking you up for assault with a weapon. They would rather lock me in seg than put me on P.C. So I recieved the same thing the rapist did, it doesnt make any sence.

T.B., Texas, 10/23/96

When I came out of prison, I remember thinking that others knew I had been raped just by looking at me. My behavior changed to such cold heartedness that I resented anyone who found reason to smile, to laugh, and to be happy.

_____

B.E., Vermont, 10/26/96 (he later committed rape himself)

During my time in prison, I have seen 19 violent rapes. I hear about rapes off and on, most are not known and not reported, cause most of them take place behind closed doors. If a vicitim is scared enough, he may never tell what happen to him, it depends on what the victim is focused on, like embarrassment, shame, escape, pain, aids, suicide, or living with a scar the rest of his life as a homosexual or bisexual, not letting go of the abuse in there minds. . . . The ones who get raped here are mostly the weaker prey, or someone who's in debt, or looking protection from someone else. Rapes happen to more younger prisoners. . . . What starts the biggest problem is when that vicitim get into it with an official, and that official because of his attitude will give out information like the inmate was a childmolester.

_____

C.K., Texas, 10/28/96

You will be lebled as a bisexual, or homosexual, pretty boy, gay, little girl, queen. Once there has been penetration or forced oral sex, the jacket is on his back, as being a punk, sissy, queer, etc.

_____

C.K., Texas, 10/28/96

One game is to have two/three guys threaten someone, and another guy come jump into it and tell them to back off. They do and the "Savior" tells the guy he'd be better off to get a ride. Lots of new guys dont know any better, but once you accept a ride, you can never be a man again. At least here on Beto. On Ferguson you can win back your manhood (provided you were never sexually assaulted) by a number of fights.

S.H., Texas, 10/28/96

Gays are targeted as are meek, mild-mannered individuals. The general assumption is that since we are gay, we don't mind being raped, The staff pretty much thinks the same thing.

P.E., Illinois, 10/28/96

The theory is that you are not gay or bisexual as long as YOU yourself do not allow another man to stick his penis into your mouth or anal passage. If you do the sticking, you can still consider yourself to be a macho man/heterosexual, according to their theory. This is a pretty universal/widespread theory.

P.E., Illinois, 10/28/96

After all it is better to have one person that you give sexual favors than it would be to have to be forced to do the act by two or more prisoners at the same time.

M.H., Florida, 10/29/96

Prisoners pay close attention to their fellow prisoners. [One technique to force a prisoner into sex is that] one of the bad guys will set up a power play. This is accomplished by him having two or three of his friends stop down on the prisoner of his choice in a strong manner as if to fight or beat up this prisoner. This usually puts the choosen prisoner in great fear of those type guys. The prisoner that set up this will be close by when this goes down. His roll is to step in just before the act gets physical. He defends the choosen prisoner by taken on the would be offenders. This works to gain the respect and trust of the choosen prisoner. After this encounter the choosen prisoner is encouraged to hang out with his new friend. This is repeated once or twice more to convence the choosen one of the sincere loyalties of the prisoner that set all this up . . . . They become very close, the choosen one feels compelled to show his thanks by giving at first monetary favors to his protector and it progress to the point where this guy that set up the attacks on him will not accept just the money. He starts to insist on the choosen one to give him sexual favors . . . . The fear of him, the choosen one, is that if he do not have this one Protector the rest of the guys will be back after him. After all it is better to have one person that you give sexual favors than it would be to have to be forced to do the act by two or more prisoners at the same time.

M.H., Florida, 10/29/96

[S]ometimes [because of the rape] I fill like I've done something wrong but yea I hate myself for it but it was kind of hard to get away from 3 other guys. Now I'm at this place and a guy from [my last prison] got transferred here and has told alot of people what happened and now its even worse they think I'm a snitch or some one comes and starts homosexual conversations with me.

F.H., Georgia, 10/29/96

The kids I know of here are kept in the hospital part of the prison until they turn 16. Then they are placed in general population. . . . At age 16, they are just thrown to the wolves, so to speak, in population. I have not heard of one making it more than a week in population without being "laid."

D.A., Nebraska, 10/31/96

I'm a gay white slender male. That is the most terrible person to be. I'm unfortunately slightly feminine, soft as inmates say.

———————

A.H., Indiana, 11/1/96

I have made it more than clear in writing and conversation to Mr. [G] for 3 weeks that I feel threaghtened and unsafe sexually. He has made it clear to me that he can not save the world. And won't do any thing til I come out here with my ass torn up with sperm in it.

———————

A.H., Indiana, (Request for Protection, signed 6/3/96, denied 6/5/96), forwarded 11/1/96

"Debt obligation" is where someone is allowed to run up a debt such as getting drugs on credit, to such a point where they can't pay it off; then the pressure (threat of violence—either to the inmate, or to his family on the streets) is applied, and it becomes a "put out, or be hurt" proposition. In Max. joints, the victim is often "used" for awhile, then "run off the yard" (chased into p.c.), or traded to another group, when the users tire of him. The process of turning someone into a punk is called "turning out."

———————

M.S., Nevada, 11/2/96

Rapes occur most often in housing units with 2 man cells, and in prisons where the inmates have less to lose if someone tells on them. Maximum security inmates often just don't "give a shit," because they have *so* little to lose; for them, rape is often a "win-win" situation, with no real down-side, since "hole time" simply means some extended privacy, and quiet time.

———————

M.S., Nevada, 11/2/96

There's also a "protection" game. This is where one guy will thump a "fish" (new arrival), and another one will step in, stop the fight, and offer to protect the fish. Usually, the aggressor and "savior" are good friends. Fish who have no means of paying the protection fees are generally talked into "turning out." Eventually, the fish winds up being passed to the aggressor, as a "peace offering."

———————

M.S., Nevada, 11/2/96

A male con maintains his sense of masculinity by forcing himself on another male, because the victim is reduced to a punk, "pussy," or coward by not preventing it.

———————

A.P., Kansas, 11/4/96

I go through nightmares of being raped and sexually assaulted. I can't stop thinking about it. I feel everyone is looking at me in a sexual way.

———————

J.D., Texas, 11/5/96

On January 27, 1993, I was what is called checked to see if I was a strong white inmate. I had to fight 4 different inmates back to back. I can not fight real good. (I have a bad left leg.) My cellie allowed this to happen. At rack time, my cellie and I fought. (He is 200 lbs and muscled. A stocky inmate that is known to fight 2 or more at one time and win.) He knocked me out and I came to while he was sexually assaulting me anally. He told me if I told anyone he would kill me. . . . I was moved to another pod, where I was sold as a piece of meat. I was sold to the highest bidder by the white inmates. I was sold to a black inmate named Blue Top. From February to the end of April I was forced to perform all types of sexual acts. I was rented out to other black inmates. I finally went to staff and refused to go back to my cell. The indangerment paperwork was filed. Classification was ran and I was put in safekeeping for 2 years. . . . I was shipped to [another unit] from Colfield unit on July 14, 1995. I was housed in closed custody where I was the only white inmate on my wing out of 48 inmates! I was in 13 fights in 14 days. I was sexually assaulted by 4 inmates (black). I went to staff. I was shipped to another unit. I refused to go to my housing assignment due to I was being put back into a life threatening condition. So I started to threaten the first black inmate I came into contact with. I was put in prehearing detention. That's September 15, 1995. I started possessing a weapon and threatening black inmates. That was the only way staff officials would keep me locked up in a single cell.

J.D., Texas, 11/5/96

In my view the perpetrator of rape is an angry man. He lacks power and decides to steal it from others through assault . . . . In my observation, the more oppressive the system the higher the incidents of assaultive behavior in general. This had been evident over the years here as we fell under the control of various wardens with a variety of concepts of how to treat prisoners (and staff). Fair and objective treatment seems to create a less-assaultive environment.

The victims I'm familiar with seem to have one thing in common, they each had some quality or trait that was interpreted by their rapists as saying, "I am vulnerable." . . . . The traits that seem to communicate "vulnerability" seem to be traits that are consistent with feminine and/or childlike qualities. These include passivity, being slight of stature, and probably most common, being young . . . . Conversely, a person who demonstrates aggressive qualities, or confidence and self assurance is not attractive to the perpetrator. One thing I hear people tell a young guy is to "get some ugly on him." That means growing facial hair, getting some tattoos, and looking unkempt.

D.G., Virginia, 11/7/96

The greatest preventive measure [against rape] is posting staff, monitoring areas that are high risk for assault. The reality however, is that funding for prison administration doesn't provide for adequate patrolling . . . . Prisoners are pretty much left on their own.

————————

D.G., Virginia, 11/7/96

Over the years it has become evident that if a man reports that he has been raped he naively sets himself up for additional victimization, this time by the prison administration. Case in point: One of the victims I know was raped at knife point by his cell partner the third night after his arrival at the prison. The next morning he stayed in bed until the rapist left, then he used the toilet, showered, and reported the rape to his counselor. She notified the watch commander and sent the victim to medical. They informed him that there was nothing they could do since the evidence was eliminateed by using the toilet and showering. The watch commander locked him up in protective custody ostensibly to keep him safe while they conducted an investigation. He stayed in there for weeks with no communication about the investigation or when it would be safe for him to return to population. He finally chose to forego further "protective custody" and return to population. He learned that except for a brief shakedown of the rapist's cell (they wanted the knife but it was hidden the first morning after) nothing else had been done. There was nothing ever said of any investigation or any results. The rapist was free all the time the victim was locked up and continued to be. This seems to be the pattern when reporting rapes except that often the victim is transferred to another prison.

————————

D.G., Virginia, 11/7/96

On maximum security wings, blacks and whites don't even sit together. The Blacks have there own benches and the Mexicans have theres and the Whites if there are enough to fight for one has theres. And if a white went to sit on a Black bench he would be jumped on ditto for blacks and Mexicans. Even in celling assignments the whites will refuse to live with a colored or a mexican because there cellie who has friends will steel there stuff or they will jump on the white dude so they refuse to live with them. And if a white dude kicks it or talks to blacks or mexicans a lot of the whites will run court on him (court means an ass whoppin). Its the same for blacks and mexicans. . . . The whites hate the Blacks and Mexicans because those two races have a lot of people in here and take advantage of us by making the small and week ones ride or turn them out, and the big ones have to fight all the time. If you come in here as a non-racial white man and you fight for your proporty more than likely when you leave you'll be a full fledge KKK member! There are a lot of racial groups here and with the way the whites get treated, they get mixed up in those groups and become haters. Prison is the best recruiting ground the white power movement has!

T.B., Texas, 11/15/96

Safe keeping is a wing where supposely inmates who are week and cant stand up for them selves are put. But its not too friendly because its easy to get on and that is where they put homo/bi/trans/sexuals. So a lot of hard core convicts want to go over and sometimes they do make it. If you ask any guard the close custody safe keeping wing is more violent than the regular one is.

T.B., Texas, 11/15/96

The prison system is just a stage of the final solution to get rid of America's so-called problem, especially the Blacks and the Latinos. I ask the question [is it] bad luck, good luck or a set up that the prison system in the U.S. is half filled with Blacks when in fact they don't even make-up half of the population of the U.S.? . . . When individuals come to prison, they know that the first thing that they will have to do is fight. Now there are individuals that are from a certain race that the majority of them are not physically equip to fight. So they are the majority that are force to engage in sexual acts.

V.H., Arkansas, 11/17/96

From my point of view, rape takes place every day. A prisoner that is engaging in sexual acts, not by force, is still a victim of rape because I know that deep inside this prisoner do not want to do the things that he is doing but he thinks that it is the only way that he can survive.

V.H., Arkansas, 11/17/96

Most guys run in a pack, and most of them run in a pack just to keep from getting fucked, especially young guys, gang affiliations plays a major role in everything in prison there are more people turn out be gang affiliations than any other, most time when a young boy is turned out by a gang, the sole purpose of that is first to fuck the boy especially young boys, once they finish with the boy they are sold to another prisoner for profit, it's big business selling boys in prisons and gang members control this business.

C.D., Indiana, 11/20/96

[S]ay for instant you come into prison, you don't have anything, and they put you next door to me, here I am sitting here in this cell, I am watching T.V. color at that, listen to music, eating popcorn or whatever, drinking coffee, pop, smoking cigarettes, and etc. You don't have anything, you don't have any money to buy it, and nobody on the outside is sending you anything, so you will eventually ask me for something, or somebody, and once you take it, your ass is out you are in debt, and if I am a dog which most prisoners are, you will never pay the debt off even if you get the money, because I am not going to let you pay it off until I get what I want, and once you give up the ass or head there is no stopping, some live with it and other cut their wrist or anything else to escape the dicks, some get lucky and hook up with a guy that takes care of them, then they only have one guy to have sex with, then they don't like it or want to do it but they can live with it, then they have to go through the thing the guy wants, like ... wearing tight jeans and etc. The prisoner one hook up with want you looking more like a woman than you do.

C.D., Indiana, 11/20/96

Once [my rape by a cell mate previously accused of sexual assault] was reported, prison officials expressed profound disdain and indifference with regard to the collection of evidence and the investigation process. It got even worse while in therapy at the prisons' mental health unit. I have been harassed [for taking legal action] and threatened by a guard that he coming to my cell to fuck me in the ass; his exact words. I am 5' 11" and weigh 150 pounds . . . . my attacker is 5' 8" and 250 pounds.

B.J., Connecticut, 11/25/96

The unwritten policy for the DOC here is to allow the gangs the opportunity to rape and extort the weaker inmates in return for not rioting and hurting the staff . . . . If you are not in a gang then you are eligible for rape.

L.E., Illinois, 12/2/96

It was in Cook County Jail, in Chicago, Jan. '75, that I first witnessed such [a rape]. It involved 4 or 5 large blacks, who held a homemade knife to the throat of a young, small & weak 17 yr-old white kid named [name withheld]. One of the main reasons I recall this incident so well is, I then traded my new $165 leather jacket to a fellow who worked in the officers' dining-room for 6 butter-knives and sharpened them, giving several friends (a loose term) each one. We retaliated about a week later, by stabbing 8 members of the gang which was involved in this and a number of other racial attacks, including several of the individuals who were involved . . . . [M]ost of the rapists never even went to "the hole," much less court . . . . There have been many rapes since then, but that sort of epitomizes most of them. The vast majority of these rapes are on young, small white kids by the black gang-bangers. And, for reasons I can't imagine, few prison officials care to attempt prosecution of these hateful rapists. It's as if there's actual encouragement of such, by athorities.

R.J., Arkansas, 12/9/96

[I]n 1991 I was raped by the Arizona "<u>Aryan Brotherhood</u>" a prison gang. I didnt tell the guards, I was scared & alone. The guards knew about it, because they told me they are going to move me, & so they did, but to a worst prison. Where I got into it with more "ABs". . . . I am a 26 year old White Boy who don't have anybody, but a lot of anger! . . . . Back to a little more about my Rape. The guys didnt get caught in the Act somebody told the guards and they asked me if I was alright. Then moved me . . . . I wanted to go back to the yard and kill them that did it!

————————

W.W., Arizona, 12/31/96

I feel so dirty and Sucidal cause I can't seem to get no help. Say if you must know all details it all started at McNoll Unit. About two or three Mexicans pushed me in to a cell and started slapping me and threatend to brutally beat me up if I didnt do what they said or if I snictched. They keep moving me to diffent pods. But as they call it here in prision these prisoners seem to have put a jacket on me that seems to follow me from prision to prision. And so what happend to me they first time has seemed to follow me from pod to pod or prision to prision . . . . So I got send to Darrington so some of they Guy's that had been at McNoll were there. And soon it spead that dude is a turn-out . . . . So then I got shipped to Hughe's unit and at that unit there were some Guy's there from McNoll and they word got out that I was a Pushover. So mam the same thing happend there Guy's would come up to me and say your going to be with me so if anyone ask you who you with say your with me.

————————

F.C., Texas, 1/6/97

Any [inmates] coerced into sex? In the interest of getting my own abuse to stop, and being extremely selfish, concerned with my own survival I can name three guys I personally coerced into sexual relations. Not with me, but with my own man to stop the abuse I was receiving from him. Selfish I know but my first concern is my own well-being. It's that kind of world in here.

————————

E.S., Mississippi, 1/15/97

I was 32 1/2 years old when the rape took place. . . . I am thin in built. My race is Native American . . . I am not a gay person . . . . I am also a very quiet and shy person. I also don't like being around people that much.

The inmate who assaulted me . . . . is a weight lifter, big built and very strong. . . .

Sometimes I fell that it was my fault and it drives me crazy to think about it . . . . I am mostly scared of what I might do when I get out of here. Very Suicidal - I just mean that I wish that I was dead at times and most of the times.

———————

C.B., Washington, 1/19/97

I do believe that there is a lot of coercion that is forced on inmates and these incidents are not turned in by the inmates who are raped or assaulted. They are afraid of retaliation from both the inmates, and the prison system.

———————

C.B., Washington, 2/11/97

The word "punk" has several meanings, it could mean a coward or a homosexual; "Queen" is a homosexual that dresses in drag and often looks like a woman; "Turn out" is also a homo that was turned into a homo, by being coerced; the word "Boy" is another way of saying my partner friend, etc. As far as crimes that don't fit it, usually are rapist, molesters, there looked upon with disdain and often find it rather hard to survive, once it's clearly established that they wasn't falsely accused, this has been a big problem. The relationship between a so-called Queen, and Man, are basically the same relationship between a male and a female, relations on the street. The Queens are majority practicing homos, so just picture normal male-female relations on the street, remember the whole objective is to make it as realistic as possible, that why homos try and look like women.

———————

R.B., California 2/14/97

The word "punk" in this facility is used loosely, and is a term used to down-size someone, as well as to identify an actual "punk" meaning a kid or guy who is used and exploited sexually because he is too timid or weak to make a stand . . . . A queen is an inmate acts like a woman. She wears make-up smuggled into the facility, or made by crushing up colored pencils etc. . . . To "turn-out" someone is to either get them to consent to sex, or to rape them. The result of "turning out" a kid is that the kid usually finds a "dad"—an older strong inmate to take care of him and to protect him from any future attacks. He is called a "boy." A boy is a nicer term for punk, so those terms overlap.

———————

J.O., Utah, 2/18/97

It is different here in maximum security as opposed to population in medium or minimum. The power structure here is based on strength, rep-utation, and sheer extreme violence. If your a tough convict and will poke an eye out or stab someone on the drop of a hat then you won't be bothered unless you owe drug money or something. Then the gangs will step in and its difficult to battle 10 guys at a time. The gang situation is ugly and out of hand. Mainly its the nazis and the black disciples. If you have drugs and con-nections meaning "back-up," then your pretty powerful. And the ones who sell the dope usually run with the gangs. But here in maximum, as I stated above, it comes down to raw brutality.

———————

J.O., Utah, 2/18/97

It is my observation that the most likely to be raped is the young kid new to prison who is not hip to the components of this ugly machine. The kid who just comes to prison, who is not willing to fight back is the unfortunate vic-tim of rape . . . . A lot of times when a kid is raped he is told not to "snitch" or "else." The young rape victim is brainwashed to believe that by telling he is breaking the "code of the convict", and by doing so is doing something bad. Then he is brainwashed-exploited-turned out. He becomes a punk, a boy, someones property, and becomes just another silent victim. This cycle must be broken. Rather the kid tells, or arms himself with 10 inches of steel and thrusts it into the eye of his attacker—something must be done because I don't see it changing or getting any better.

J.O., Utah, 2/18/97

To answer your questions, "lifers" are the most powerful within the prisoner hierarchy. This includes those prisoners who are serving life sentences and life without possibility of parole, as well as the older prisoners who have spent a majority of life in prison. Their power comes from respect; they are the most respected, thus are the most influencial. They have the most experience in prison life and usually don't have too much to lose as a consequence for their actions. So they are also the most feared because they are more likely to carry out certain acts.

At the bottom of the hierarchy are sex offenders. They are the least respected and the most preyed upon. It does not matter the age of their victims . . . . These people usually become victims of sexual abuses by other prisoners to experience what they put their victims through. Usually when this is done a background check is conducted to gather as many facts as possible about the crime and efforts are made to re-enact the scene as similar as possible.

Also at the bottom of the hierarchy are the "snitches" or "rats." These people become victims of [assault] because of their acts in telling on other people. . . .

A "punk" is someone who is considered weak . . . . A boy is someone who really has no place and is just used for whatever he has to offer. They are also commonly referred to as "fuck-boys," since it's usually their sex that they are used for. A "turn-out" is someone who may or may not actually be gay, but they never had a homosexual experience outside of prison. However, when they come to prison they engage in sexual activities, though usually under heavy persuasion in the beginning . . . .

In essence, "respect" is the ultimate key to survival in prison life.

S.K., Washington, 2/18/97

I got a cellie . . . . and he said that he would protect me from [inmates who had threatened me] but I had to pay, if I didnt he would let them get me plus he would. He told his homeboy about what was going on and he's homeboy said he was going to protect me also but I had to pay . . . . August 1, when the officer open the door I walked out and told him I need to speak with rank that it was very important . . . . I told him what my cellie wanted me to do. So he left me there and got rank . . . . Sgt. [P] ask me what was going on, I told him and told him that my life was in danger. He said for me to return to my cell and stand up and fight, because this was prison; if I didnt he would get a team and drag my ass back to my house. When I refused, he told [C] to put me in the holding cage. I walked to the cage on my own and went in. Sgt. [P] came back and told me to put the handcuffs on. When I told him I couldnt, he opened the cage door and told me to put the cuffs on. There with him was [C], [B], [V]. I told him if he was gonna force me that they needed to get the camera first. [P] put the handcuffs in my face and said that he was gonna get the camera after he fucked me up. He kept telling me to put the cuffs on, but I refused, because of the risk. So [P] told the officers to grab me. They grabbed me. Stunned me to the floor and began punching me in my head and kicking me in my ribs. They put the handcuffs on and by that time I looked up and a officer had a camera. Sgt. [P] ask me if I would get up on my own. I did. They took me to medical and brought me back to my cell. When they put me back in my cell, I was crying for what they done. My cellie's homeboy that said he would protect me he came over to my cell when they ran rec. My cellie was gone. He ask me what happen and what was I crying for. He ask me how I was going to pay him. I told him when I went to the store I would pay him. But he said I want to fuck. I told him that I didnt do that. He said you remember what the deal we made. So I said but I dont do that kind of stuff. So he kept saying he aint gonna take long. So he had me have anal sex with him. After that, my cellie came back from rec, he found out what his homeboy did and told me he wanted to do the same. He also made me have anal sex. The next day the same officers were working and I was scared to tell them because of what they did before . . . . My cellie told me that at last chow his homeboy wanted me to come over and stay all night in his cell. So I waited until last chow. I went an ate, when I came back there was a officer walking with all the inmates. So I let all the inmates go in

and stop the officer and told him the problem . . . . He took me to see Lt [T].
I told her what was going on, and needed to be locked up. She told me the
only way that I could get locked up was if I refused housing and I would
receive a case. I said I didnt care, I just needed her help. She sent me to lock
up (pre-hearing detention). There I was given 15 days solitary . . . . I was
pulled out and seen by Mrs. [P], Capt. [R], and Major [H]. I told my complaint and Mrs. [P] said that I was never raped that I just gave it up. Capt.
[R] said that close custody was no risk, that I was well protected. I asked him
how so, when I was raped plus inmates get stabbed each day. I wasnt
answered. They tried to make it look as if I was asking for a transfer and not
protective custody. I was denied help and sent back to my cell. . . . I took 18
pills trying to overdose. I was sent to medical and put back in my cell. From
then on I began geting cases everyday to stay in solitary. Finally they got
tired of me geting cases and refusing housing and placed me in segregation.

L.T., Texas, 2/19/97

Turn-out . . . is the term used to describe the process of getting a man who
has never had male-male sex to have sex with another man. Almost always
as a passive partner. The act of turning out usually implies that the man
enjoys the sex now or will willingly continue to have sex with other men
after the turn out. People are turned out through rape, threats, con games,
pressure, aquiring debts or romance. A man who has been "turned out" usually becomes a queen or fag and is always a catcher. There is literally thousands of mind games used to turn out, unsuspecting, naive young men.

E.S., Mississippi, 2/21/97

[Inmates low on the prison power structure include:] Any man who has, or
is having sex with another man, by helping that other man obtain a climax
through performing oral sex on him or letting the other man penetrate his
rectum. Within this catagory is a structure. A. Queen because they are open
about it and closest to being a woman. B. Fag, because they didn't become

gay in prison. C. Boy. D. Punk because he does it out of fear, for protection or as a victim.

E.S., Mississippi, 2/21/97

[T]wo things are considered when making a target for rape: 1. Appearance and sex appeal. 2. Finance. A young good looking guy who's family sends him money is the choice target for rape. In most cases the rape is only to break his spirit and make him submissive and open for financial scams. Sex becomes the control agent. There are other rapes occurring . . . . Targets are feminine guys, for sexual pleasure: proud guys . . . usually for a show of power or ego (confirming of manhood) by degrading another.

E.S., Mississippi, 2/21/97

The Mexicans—indeed all latinos, <u>nobody</u> outside their race can "check" one without permission from the town that, that person is from. If a black dude were to check a mexican w/out such permission & the mexican stays down & fights back, a riot will take place.

T.D., Texas, 3/14/97

While being checked isn't deemed a sexual attack, if one doesn't show heart & breaks weak he will become anothers property. It would amaze you (as it did me) to see human beings bought & sold like shoes. Don't get me wrong, mexicans are turned out by mexicans & blacks by blacks & then sold to other races. A person who may be only paying protection to one group could be sold to another & be turned out. All races are guilty the white race is only more victimized because there are less whites in prison.

T.D., Texas, 3/14/97

[B]ased on my experience the most common kind of rape in prisons today is the confidence rape which involves the rapist getting the confidence of the victim and then at some point turning on him and raping him. In my opinion the next in frequency would be the date rape where one inmate convinces another to double cell with him and then at some point rapes him. The next would be extortion rape followed by drugging rape and finally strong arm rape. The reason strong arm rape is the least frequent is because it is so much easier to rape an inmate using the other techniques. None of the types of prison rape described are rare. If anything they are rarely reported. Rape really is a big problem in prisons today. To give you an idea of how frequent rape is in prison, if victims would report every time they were raped in prison I would say that in the prison that I am in (which is a medium minimum security prison) there would be a reported incident every day.

V.H., Pennsylvania, 3/15/97

In my thinking much of the consensual homosexual activity in prisons today are engaged in out of one parties' fear of prison if not of his lover. Thus most prison sexual relations are unequal.

V.H., Pennsylvania, 3/15/97

There is no procedures for reporting sex abuse in here, it either happen or it dont, and "NO" I don't know of anyone who is being prosecuted for raping a guy. The only thing these guys can do is learn to fight better than the next guy. . . . [H]ere an inmate is turned out, and made to like it.

C.D., Indiana, 5/27/97

[O]ne day I was moved into a cell with this big guy that got into a lot of trouble and got into fights a lot. Well, I don't really know how to say it but I was affraid of him and when he told me he wanted sex one night I did it with him. I basically became his sex toy after that. Every night we had sex, and whatever he wanted. Oral, anal, and some disgusting stuff. This went on for a long time until I was able to get moved out of that cell.

G.M., Ohio, 5/28/97

If I had a young good looking male friend, who had money and was not a fighter, coming to prison and I had to give him a formula for survival this is what I would say to him . . . . First, and foremost do not become familiar or personal with anyone. Trust no one, guards or inmates. Keep your case, personal views and opinions, family life, history and dreams to yourself. Do not share them . . . . Secondly, do not appear feminine in appearance, speech or actions. Maintain some facial hair, short nails, short hair, etc. to keep from being even accidently mistaken as a possible victim. Third, stick to your own race group as associates, but do not be racist.

E.S., Mississippi, 6/1/97

When I was beaten and raped it was in the shower that was at the old Mansfield prison in Mansfield Ohio. . . . I have been to 4 Ohio prisons and at no time was I ever warned about the danger of sexual assault. No one ever told me of ways to protect myself. And to this day I've never heard of a procedure for reporting rape. This is never talked about . . . . I've basically found that guards and staff of the prisons don't care about your safety . . . . At the old Mansfield prison where my assault took place this type of stuff took place daily.

So no I didn't tell anyone about it. To be honest, you are the first person I've told in all these years and that is because you are not part of the prison. I was put on Protective Custody/Suicide Watch because I tried to kill myself several times and because they heard guys threaten to rape me, beat me up

G.M., Ohio, 6/27/97

I believe the reason prison rape occurs is because the administration does not care, if you rape another inmate you do a few days in the hole and the victum goes to P.C. protective custody "hole" but if he fights and hurts his attacker as I did he is prosecuted and receives more time. As of this time I have almost 14 years in prison and have never heard of a prison rape case being prosecuted in court . . . . I'm quite sure if a man committed a rape in prison and got 5 or 10 years time, prison rape would decline.

L.L., Ohio, 8/10/97

it is a lot of mental slavery involde and most of the sexual abuse and rapes never get reported because the victim is scare so the rest of their time in prison they become someone wife as they call it here. a lot of times when it is reported to Guards will over look it because they thing the inmate is just have a little problem with the one they are tied or married with. when a Report is done they lock up the inmate who did what ever he did for about 30 at the most and let him back out of the hold. they may send him to another camp. but the victim goes through a lot of pressure because of what happen and it will happen more and they get beat up or threaten with knifes so they end up submitting to them so they will not get hurt or killed.

K.R., Missouri, 9/8/97

what happen to me was because I am a Homosexual I have a Husband in the free world on the other side of the Prison fence I did not want to do anything while I am in prison. Well there was 4 black inmate and 2 white inmates that raped me the Guards did nothing because I am a Homosexual.

K.R., Missouri, 9/9/97

On March 13, 1994 I was sexually assaulted by E.W. . . . . I was 21 yrs. old at the time and a non-violent inmate . . . . The way the crime took place is that I was in the bed asleep when the floor officer left his post. When Officer W.

left his block E.W. had my door opened by the officer in the booth. He came into my room and put a knife (homemade) to my throat and told me if I moved he would kill me. He then pulled the blanket off of me and told me to fall over onto my stomach. He then pulled my undershorts down and squirted somekind of petroleum greese into my rectom. He then penetrated me and when he finished he told me if I said anything he would kill me. He then left my room and his partner R.S. came in and found me crying. He told me to shut up before he hit me and gave me something to cry about. At this time R.S. told me he come into my room to do the same thing but changed his mind. He told me I could either let him gun me down (look at my rear end necked while he masturbated) or it would be worse then the first time. He then told me to follow him to his room. I followed him to his room and tried to talk him out of doing this to me. At this time Sgt. D and c/o White came into the block and saw me in R.S.'s room. They took me to the Sgt.'s office to find out what was going on. I told them what had happened and they arranged for me to be taken to the hospital. At the hospital they done a rape kit and charges were filed against E.W. for (crimes against nature and 2nd degree sexual assault). On March 27, 1996, Mr. D.B., the D.A for [this] county arranged for a telephone call for me to call his office. At this time Mr. B. told me he had to dismiss charges against Mr. W. because he messed up on his paper work. He said that with all the evidence from the rape kit another inmate's testimony and E.W.'s prior record (in prison for 2 counts of rape plus 2 or 3 charges of rape in prison) we would have won with no problem.

J.E., North Carolina, 9/15/97

Most prisoners that have been raped are then forced by the rest of the prison population to continue to play the female role whether they prefer homosexuality or not.

J.E., North Carolina, 9/15/97

Most prisoners are in general a con artist, and prison rape can occur as part of a con game. There is a never ending stream of new people being placed in prison. In this hostile and violent enviornment one can easily see why one might look for a friend, that is a persons first mistake. Prison rapist will use this search for friendship to get to familiarize themself with a person, and then use the first chance they get to rape the person. Some will phsically force the inmate into a sex act, and some will mentally break an individual down by bombarding him with a strong prison mentality about it being okay. Some try to get an inmate in debt to where they can't pay and then make them feel they are obligated to perform the sex act as payment. There are numerous ways inmates use to so called "break a person down", and in my over 7 years in prisons I've seen some shocking incidents.

_____

J.E., North Carolina, 9/15/97

I was forced into masturbating him to his ejacolation . . . . He told me if I were to tell he would kill me . . . . [T]he emotional termoil I struggle with since that night is so sickening, hard to feel good about self. To make things worse is that the reporting officers let this sick inmate get away with what he did and made me do.

_____

K.G., Utah, 9/17/97

As far as I know NOTHING happened to [the inmate who raped me.] I don't even believe he faced disciplinary action . . . . No, I didn't get a letter from [the district attorney] on why charged [against the rapist] were dismissed. He talked to me on the telephone. He couldn't even meet me face to face to tell me. All I recall him saying is that [the rapist's] lawyer filed a motion for a fast and speedy trial and he didn't pay attention to the dates on his paper work.

_____

J.E., North Carolina, 9/30/97

A big male may approach this young scared kid with: "You fuck me, or you fuck that whole gang." . . . The young man or kid hasn't a prayer. If he fights back, and stabbs someone in his self protection, the Administration makes a freeworld case over it, and it's all to common that a kid can come down with a 5 yr sentense, and within a year or two, wind-up with life without parole. If a kid is raped, and reports it to the Administration, they severely punish the kid, and do absolutely nothing to the predators. I've seen this time after time. Usually here, a youth takes "a Man" and becomes his: "Fuck Boy." He submits at the pleasure of "His Man." The Man may prostitute him for money, drugs or what-ever. His Man forms a protection network, "Friends" to protect his territory.

———————

P.S., Alabama, 10/6/97

I came to prison in April, 1991. I'd never been to prison before. I basically feared for my life . . . . Eventually, I ended up with a roommate who took advantage of my situation. He made me feel "protected" somewhat. But, at the same time, he let me know he could quite capably beat me up, if he wanted. One night, after we were all locked down for the night, he told me he could help me overcome my sexual inhibitions, if I would let him. He told me he was bisexual. I knew he was quite sexually active, so to speak, as he had female pornography in the room as well as masturbating frequently to it. But, I was surprised he would come on to me. However, I felt very much in danger if I did *not* give in to him. I was very scared. I ended up letting him penetrate me anally. After this, I would feign sleep at night when he'd come in. But, there were several more times he forced me to perform sexually . . . . Luckily, we were separated when he asked to move in with a friend. Therefore, I had to endure no more abuse. I never went to the authorities, as I was too fearful of the consequences from any other inmate. I already had enough problems, so didn't want to add to them by taking on the prison identity as a "rat" or "snitch." I already feared for my life. I didn't want to make it worse . . . . If the truth be known, it shames me to even talk of this. I fear it places a stigma on me of being homosexual or being an "easy target" for others.

———————

J.D., Colorado, 10/12/97

one night 4 weeks into my prison stay i was tested by a very big north amerikkkan prisoner. He attempted to lay a bully game down on me by taking my seat in the lounge room. which led to me resorting back to my street warfare attack which was my only choice to set a solid example that i am not to be played with. The end result was he being put in the hospital broke jaw/nose an me having a broke wrist an a battery case.

L.Q., Indiana, 12/3/97

Keep in mind that tough and hard in the upper and middle classes is far different than that of the lower classes. For where being nice and sociable may be accepted in the upper and middle classes, it is a tabu in the lower, and especially when confined. . . . [A prisoner's problems] will be reciprocal to his youth, race, and size. . . . [When first assigned to a cell, he] will be under microscopic inspection for any weakness. Because if he smokes, the acceptance of a cigarette may have a hidden price attached.

W.M., Texas, 12/26/97

More often than not, Human Error in Classification and assignment of prisoners adds to the prison and jail sexual assaults and rapes. Not to mention the arbitrary imposition of punishment by intentional misclassification or mis-assignment [because of] spite or dislike for a prisoner.

W.M., Texas, 12/26/97

[L]atent homosexual tendencies may be seen in a timid or passive person who has been misclassified.

W.M., Texas, 12/26/97

[My cellmate] was younger, stronger than I and larger. He introduced himself as a bi-sexual. And was for two weeks "touchie-feelie." I had to screem/yell at him to stop. The officers here 1. Ignored my complaints. 2. Asked me if I was his lover. 3. Did nothing. He became more difficult to deal with and started to threaten me. Finally one day he attacked me.

————————

D.G., Texas, 1/15/98

[Here is a typical scenario you may face as a prisoner:] you are fairly young, good-looking and not emotionally hardened. You are fearful and lonely and respond to a smiling seemingly kindly face. This person knows all the blind spots and the guards' timing, even who'll look away. Suddenly you find yourself alone with a very different person and in a few minutes are utterly over-powered physically or with a blade holding you still, while you swallow his organ or are split open in your bowels. Then he goes and tells his friends and very soon you are a "candy store" for them. If you tell, a hit is put on you and sooner or later someone will collect, often someone you don't even know.

————————

D.W., Kansas, 2/23/98

Most cons are emotionally alienated from themselves. The peer pressure not to be seen as "weak" pertaining to any gentler emotion, is astronomically intense. Such a display sets one up to be the victimized very quickly. Also, the societal culture mind-set that men don't have finer emotions, has conditioned men not to display physical emotional bonding except with someone who is physically "inferior," ie., women, children, etc. In prison, to gain a simple hug which is emotionally soothing without being threatening, the dominator can only accept from the dominated. [Also] a prisoner experiences profound powerlessness of self over one's life and future. One of the most basic ways to resume an illusion of empowerment of self is to establish power over another at ground zero: life and sexual gratification.

————————

D.W., Kansas, 2/23/98

I have been getting sexually assaulted at the Unit Mark W. Stiles in Beaumont by two inmates. I tried to commit suicide in hopes of releaving the misery of it. . . . I was made to perform oral sex on the two inmates for exchange of protection from other inmates. . . . I reported the action of the inmates to the Unit authority but did not get any help so that is when I slashed both my wrists in hope of dying.

———————

D.E., Texas 5/14/98

I have aquired me a Husband to make my time easy he is a very big guy about 295 lbs and 6'3 or 4" cocoa brown he is a black man very big black man. However he's been real good to me.

———————

P.N., Texas, 5/14/98

This letter is not the easiest letter to write, in fact, it's very hard. You see, I am such a prisoner. I was raped on the Beto one unit of Texas Dept. of Criminal Justice, (TDCJ), in 1991, by 3 black inmates. I was snatched into a cell and raped by two, while the 3rd kept watch for the gaurd and held a homemade knife to my throat. They alternated for an hour . . . . No body seems to care. It is very depressing. I dont know where else to turn to. I've completely exhausted my grievance procedures. My grievance came back to me stating that my denial of protective custody was not a grievable claim. Ironic. I had just gotten almost killed yet I dont have a claim to protective custody. Ive been forced to give up my money, my self esteem, I've been raped, I've been beat up numerous times, had my ribs broken, yet I still don't have a claim to protective custody! Maybe when I am dead they will say I should have been placed into protective custody.

———————

J.W., Texas, 5/31/98

In my experience having a "boy" (meaning white man) to a negro in prison is sort of a "trophy" to his fellow black inmates. And I think the roots of the problem goes back a long time ago to when the African Americans where in the bonds of slavery. They have a favorite remark: "It ain't no fun when the rabbit's got the gun, is it?"

J.W., Texas, 5/31/98

I think [rape] also occurs because a lot of the inmates of all races are financially poor. They have no family in the free world to send them money. Even here money is a very important issue. A lot of white inmates pay money to one gang to protect them from another. It's called catching "a ride." It's also not uncommon for an inmate to be sold to another gang to avoid a gang war.

J.W., Texas, 5/31/98

I only can tell you that the inmates act aggresively to inmates who look like they are scared.

D.E., Texas, 6/2/98

On the Conally Unit I was forced to pay protection fees and I was beaten on a regular basis but was often denied medical treatment because the officers felt the smaller weaker inmates should just die or suffer because we are unable to defend ourselves. On several occasions I was masturbated on while I tried to shower and once I was beaten because I would not perform sexual favors for two black inmates . . . . [At Telford Unit] I was constantly pressured to perform sexual favors and once I was held at knife-point and was raped by an inmate named Cruz. I was ashamed and very confused. I went to the units officials for help and was treated very harshly. I was affraid to tell them I had been raped.

L.B., Texas, 6/20/98

I've seen one guy raped but the prison authorities not prosecute the rapist because they said the guy was a homosexual who was raped and because it happened in the rapist's cell. The guy raped was "out-of-place" there . . . . I think many case of sexual assault go unreported because of what we see take place of past reports. For example with the guy above, they said things like "the guy was gay, he asked for it." Bullshit. I knew the guy. Besides, noone bleeds like that who isnt forced.

J.W., Texas, 7/5/98

I would say the occurrence of a person being violently raped like I was is rare. Most often the person is coerced into submitting to sexual activity slowly. Each time it progressively gets worse in the extent to which it is taken. Before you know it you've gone from washing personal laundry to wearing lipstick.

J.W., Texas, 7/5/98

When I was on the Robertson Unit I was rape by 4-5 blacks I was in my cell and they fell in and said arc you going fight or fuck I said I going fight they gang up on me and forced me down and forced oral and anal sex and they did repeatly about 9 times they also beat me up pretty bad I was also forced by the mexicans for anal sex when I was in the dorms for protection. I didn't report none of this cause of fear of getting hurt they hurt me pretty bad when they raped me.

J.S., Texas, 9/1/98

Prison rape has left me a different person. In jail there's no help really. I have to deal with it on my own.

E.K., New Mexico, 9/10/98

Sorry for taking so long to write, but I have been having a lot of trouble. I'm 16teen. I got into a fight and I got a broke bone in my arm. It don't hurt that bad. Now about the trouble I have been having. I have had 2 people try to rape me. I have been in 8 fights' and got beat by the officers 4 times .... I have tryed to go to P.C. [protective custody] but they wouldn't let me.

_____

R.P., Arkansas, 9/14/98

Lt. B.W. had me identify the assailant in front of approximately "20" other inmates . . . which immediately put my safty & life in danger as a "snitch" for telling on the other inmate who sexually assaulted me .... Prison officials claimed Nothing happen yet they transferred the assailant who sexually assaulted Me. Showing the officials guilt. But by the Prison officials trying to Place Me <u>Back</u> in Population after I identified the assailant in front of 20 inmates clearly placed my life in danger Because of the "snitch" concept.

_____

D.A., Texas, 9/18/98

[My brother] Chris has been the victem of numerous assaults by various groups of inmates; namely, African American's, some belonging to a gang known as the "Crips." These individuals have repeatedly tried to force their extortion demands, and sexual advances upon Chris. Whenever he resists these demands/advances, he gets beaten down severely. Incidently, Chris has also served time in the California Dept of Corrections (CDC). While he was in the CDC, he was unwillingly made a member of the California Aryan Brotherhood; which is a long time rival of the Texas Aryan Brotherhood! Some of Chris' assailants are members of his rival gang in Texas (AB). Chris has suffered from several serious injuries from these assaults, involving members of the Crips and the Texas AB both (e.g., broken leg, broken nose, broken teeth, lacerations, concussions, contusions, trauma, threats, etc.) ... . Many of these attacks occurred in the presence of TDCJ-ID correctional officers, yet none of the officers would intervene on Chris' behalf.... There are many young caucasian men in TDCJ-ID, that are being victimized like

Chris. I believe that the answer, in part, is "racial segregation"! And for the officials to take such complaints . . . <u>More Seriously!</u>

S.K., Texas, 9/18/98

This letter is about rape but not as defined by law, "the forceful taking," it is more towards "psychological manipulation." It happened to me . . . . I made the excellent victim. I'm white, 27, non-violent, loner, who receives little help from the outside ie family, and low self-esteem. Other inmates saw me as a target. I'm young, good-looking, have some femine mannerisms and naive. Some wanted to be my "friend" to "look out for me." But they just wanted to use me. One inmate would stake claim to you by becoming your "friend" hanging out with you all the time. In reality, he was saying "don't touch he's mine." Its a gradually process that you become dependent on this person whether its financial, physical or emotional. But sooner or later there comes a time when he wants a return in his investment, a sexual return . . . . You don't want to ruin your "friendship" by saying no to something you don't want to do because then you don't get the "support" financial or emotional from your friend. So you do what he wants, I did, and that's how you get hooked.

P.L., Florida, 9/27/98

While I have never been raped or forced into any homosexual activity, during my first prison sentence I did encounter some subtle sexual pressure to engage in it. . . . The game goes like this - the prey is usually a new arrival into the prison who has but a relatively short time to do, who is young and naive. The predator will befried the new arrival but at the same time he will have some of his partners confronting the new arrival with intimidation and threats of sexual violence. Once the new inmate is pressured hard enough the predator will make an advance towards him with a threat if rejected that he'll be at the mercy of the predators friends unless the new arrival becomes his "boy," then he'll be protected and no one else will harrass him.

G.L., Florida, 9/28/98

The one playing the male role refuses to see himself as a homosexual he see himself as a real man with strenght. He doesn't realize he's giving into his baser desires is really a sick perverted weakness. The one who plays the female role is known as a "baby." The "real" men like to get together to brag about their conquests, compare and trade information about all of the "babies" in the prison system, or spread malicious rumors about those babies or the straight guys who spurn them.

––––––––––––

G.L., Florida, 9/28/98

I am a self-confessed homosexual . . . . I have witnessed on numerous occassions many rapes forcefully and through manipulation. I have been a victim of both on a couple of occassions. . . . Homosexual harassment in the Fl D.O.C. is common. Every day I experience some type of harassment from officers and inmates alike. Name calling, joking, Aids jokes, stereo-typed as having Aids etc. . . . Rape is widespread in F.D.O.C., however most of the sexual targeting is done through manipulation and putting fear into the weak timid young guys.

––––––––––––

D.L., Florida, 9/29/98

The two people that tryed to rape me they wher both black they were alot biger then me they wher both G.D. [Gangster Disciples, a gang] they wher from Little Rock . . . . When I was in B pod I had 3 dude's coming to me that said they was the only thing that was keeping me from getting raped, and they wanted to jack off and look at me. The pod I'm in now I had 2 people come to me and put a ink pen to my neck and tell me that if I didn't let them jack off on me they were going to rape me. I told the officer but they didn't do any thing about it.

––––––––––––

R.P., Arkansas, 10/5/98 (age 16)

Why does prison rape occur? . . . . There are a number of white "Pecker-woods" see temporary sexual fulfillment, such as blow-jobs or anal sex as temporarily acceptable. Not me. I suggest it's homosexual.

_____

B.H., Oregon, 11/2/98

As cops look the other way on tatooing, traficing and trading, consental sexual activities they begin to look the other way on other things also. They begin ignoring what they see in all aspects. If it's an assault they try to patch it over so they don't have to do the paperwork.

_____

R.B., Texas, 11/10/98

I was 17 years old and weighed 133 pounds when I first came to the TDC ID back in January of 1992. While I was going through the process to be assigned to a unit many inmates would whistle at me and tell me Im a convicts dream "girl" come true.

Other inmates would tell me "I hope you can fight" because "they" are going to "check" me and see if I would stay down fur mine and if I don't well I will be wearing cool offs or using colored pencils for make up.

Many inmates would tell me horror stories about prison and "they" would tell me I would probably go to Furgason or Beto one [units]. What those inmates were doing was putting the fear of God into me telling me Im going to get beat down probably clicked on to break me and in my young mind I know Im going to break because I don't want to go through that kind of pain or abuse.

. . . . The cellie I had [at my first unit] was asking me what am I going to do. I said what do you mean? He said are you going to fight, fuck, or bust a sixty. . . . So that night I spent there I was so scared I couldn't eat sleep or barely walk. . . . I was thinking I rather kill myself than go through all that torture and pain and misery. So the closet thing I came to was the razor I had so I broke it down and sliced my wrist. I cut my wrist 9 different times my blood just splurting out and about. But it just wasn't enough time to do what I wanted.

. . . . Well before long one day I went to the shower somehow I was all by myself and [a Mexican inmate who was a weightlifter] came in there and saw me well thats when he said "you know what time it is." I said what are you talking about. He said he wants me to give him oral sex or he'll beat me down and take me the way he wants to. I started crying because of what he was doing so I told him no so he started knocking me around and said I am going to do it. He just kept on so with shame in myself I gave him oral sex and later he forced his self upon me from the other end.

I put up with that for about a year but I was scared to tell anyone of staff because I was afraid all they would call me is a weak homosexual and not help me so I kept it to myself. . . .

[Later in another unit] I met my cellie [X]. . . a dude that became my problem. Well while I was studying him he was telling me if any one trys to make me ride let him know and he would take care of it. No sooner than he said that a big black dude they call big moe . . . came to my door. . . . . No sooner than that my cellie jumped in the conversation while Mosely was trying to get my cell door open, and [X] said that it was all good we don't need no problems. So Mosely said Oh hes with you and left. . . .

[X] said Im riding with him and if I don't like that we can fight then Ill let my homeboys have you. If you don't want to go through that then this is the deal. "You will clean the house," he said, have my clothes clean and when Im ready to get my "freak" no arguments or there will be a punishment! I will, he said, let my homeboys have you or Ill just sale you off. Do we have an understanding? With fear, misery, and confusion inside me . . . I said yes with a faint sound. Then he said one more thing. He told me if I ever run to staff for help about my situation Im in he would kill me, beat me to the bloody, or have me killed and later I found out all these dudes are the Crips. . . .

The next cellie I had which was a small but cool Mexican dude that didn't give me any problems so I was alright for that time. . . .

After four months of going through so much shame, hatred and abuse I didn't know what I should do with myself.

. . . . Well before long I ended up talking to a Sargent. Who was Sargent [D.] that work 2nd shift from 2 pm to 10 pm. When he took me into the office the first thing he said was a sarcastic sounding, "whats the problem someone makein you ride tryin to sell you to someone, and you come to tell on someone." I didn't know how to explain my situation to him very well because of what remarks he was giving me making me feel like a weak punk telling me Im not the only one here with the same problem.

––––––––––

G.H., Texas 12/1/98

Though I am 5'10" in height, I am a small person weighing only about 140 pounds. In addition, I am gay and quite obviously effeminate and my mannerisms attract other more aggressive prisoners who seek to sexually abuse my body. I am unable to adequately defend myself from muscle-bound individuals . . . . When I entered the TDCJ-ID this time on or about May 4, 1994, the mainframe classification computer recommended that I be placed back in safekeeping . . . . Despite the mainframe computer's recommendation to place me back in safekeeping, the Clemens Unit officials overrode that recommendation and placed me in the regular general population. As soon as I arrived in my housing area the aggressive prisoners came to me and tried to pressure me into giving in to their sexual demands. I was beaten three times within the first month, each time because I refused to "ride" with certain individuals, or because I wouldn't "choose a man," as they referred to it. On each occasion in which another prisoner threatened or assaulted me I immediately informed officials. Instead of realizing the problem—that I was going to be prone to assaults and sexual assaults in the future, that I was not in the appropriate classification assignment—prison officials charged me with disciplinary offenses of fighting as a result of my futile attempts to defend myself. Prison officials in the TDCJ-ID customarily charge both inmates involved in a physical altercation with disciplinary offenses, regardless of who was the culprit, and regardless of who came out the victor. On each occasion I was the one who was attacked and beaten, yet I received disciplinary offenses nevertheless . . . . Prison officials would treat me in the infirmary, bandage me up, and then release me right back to the same area(s) in which the assaults occurred. My personal property was stolen from me on several occasions and I was eventually forced to give in to inmates' desires for sex because prison officials would not protect me to prevent the assaults from recurring.

––––––––––

J.C., Texas, 12/16/98

[While I was in a temporary cell], officers allowed another inmate who was not assigned to my cell to enter and stay in my cell for two days with me. This was two days of living hell in which he raped and abused my body. He threatened to kill me if I let officials know. However, I began kicking the cell door anyway after the second day and officials came to my aid. I informed officials of what had transpired the previous two days, but it was logged that I merely "alleged" that I had been sexually assaulted and raped. The inmate was charged only with the disciplinary offense of threatening me, he got away with the sexual assaults—a much more serious offense—unpunished.

———————

J.C., Texas, 12/16/98

More recently on [another] unit, I was assaulted by a man about 6'7" and weighing approximately 280 pounds. He grabbed me by the throat and threw me a few feet to the ground. He did this because I had my shirt off in the day room while in public. It was as if he felt that a "girl" isn't supposed to have "her" shirt off in public. Yet, I told him that I was a man just like him, at which time he committed the assault. I immediately informed officials, who then ordered a physical. However, I was afterword told to return to my cell, where the individual lived a few doors down, and that nothing else would be done to protect me. I was assaulted by the same individual three days in a row, each time I informed officials of what happened and pointed him out.

———————

J.C., Texas, 12/16/98

After my several attempts up to that point in trying to get officials to protect me in situations where I was threatened, assaulted or sexually assaulted from other inmates because I am a smaller, effeminate man, I finally gave in to some black Crip gang members who pressured me to "ride" with them or else. I realized that informing officials of the threats and my fears resulting was futile, that every time it was me who got punished. So, I gave in and was forced to perform sexually for numerous members of this gang for two and a half months.

———————

J.C., Texas, 12/16/98

I have been threatend with being raped on numerous occasions. One statement was "the snitchen bitch ought to be fucked in the ass until <u>she</u> can't talk, then she'll never be able to tell again." The newly remodled showers in our wing now have no privacy midsection curtains, like they used to. Even the menial task of taking a shower has become a forum for verbal sexual threats.

C.W., Nevada, 12/24/98

I'm a victim of another prisoner targeting me & attempting to punk me out, and make me his boy. He used threats, intimidation, and violence. This went on for a few weeks, however, he never got what he was after! He did pull my pants down & touched me. He knocked me out once, but nothing happened as far as I could tell.

C.B., Minnesota, 1/23/99

Sexual assaults are common everyday occurances in prisons, a simple fact . . . . And it is a <u>violent sexual act</u> (no matter how one characterizes it, i.e., 'control'; 'violence'; 'rage' etc., it is sexuality).

J.C., Colorado, 1/31/99

A lot of the housing here is in "open bay" dorms. A guy was sleeping on the top bunk, laying on his stomach, about six or eight other guys come up to him, without waking, and carefully draped a sheet over his upper body. At that point, two of them braced their feet under his bed and pulled down on the sheet, therefore pinning him to his bed. A couple more held his legs, pulled his clothing off, and raped him, each taking turns as the others held him. As they run in packs such as that down here in the Florida system, any sign of weakness is pounced upon.

C.P., Florida, 2/18/99

Mostely young youthful Boy's are raped because of their youth and tender-ness, and smooth skin that in the mind of the one duing the raping he think of the smooth skin and picture a woman . . . . Prisoners even fight each other over a youth without the young man knowing anything about it to see whom will have the Boy first as his property.

W.W., Florida, 2/19/99

I am of slender build and not very muscular, though I am not a bean-pole either. Due to my demeanor and awkwardness (gait, inability to effectively talk as a typical prisoner, etc.) I am targeted for harassment and extortion by other prisoners. I am not homosexual and it has been my resistance to those inmates against it (when approached or threatened for sexual acts) that has brought me injury and reproach . . . . The first incident of sexual harassment and assault occurred at Union Correctional Institution in 1994 on the recreation yard . . . . The inmate had been attempting to extort me for sexual acts and assaulted me on the recreation yard after I would not yield. I was shortly after transferred to Florida State Prison for my own protection . . . . For approximately two (2) years I was in a single-man cell with open bar fronts. The verbal sexual harassment continued from those inmates around me . . . . When I confronted the administration with the true facts of what was occurring to me, I was told to use violence to solve my problem.

R.M., Florida, 2/25/99

9 times out of 10 when someone in here is raped no one knows. It is like a tree falling in the woods when no one is around . . . Why? Because if the rape victim goes to the officer and tells he's been raped all that can follow is <u>Hell</u> for the victim. And all inmates know this . . . . So if one gets raped he may either #1 pay for protection from other inmates. #2 Check in. Request pro-tection for some other reason. Very seldom will someone let it be known that he was raped . . . . Word travels so Fast in prison. The Convict grape vine is <u>Large.</u> You cant run or hide.

R.E., Florida, 3/5/99

I have not reported any incidents, either [sexual] assault or harassment. Unfortunately, it is a fact of prison life and exists in all prisons I have been to . . . . I have not sought any type of counseling and in fact am in denial that it has happened to me. I feel like I am no longer a "man", at least not recognized as one on the inside. I constantly have to watch what I do and say, so that it is not misinterpreted for something else. I can not accept "gifts" from anyone, for fear that it may have a "catch" to it. And of course the I'm your friend trust me . . . . I built a wall around me and everyone will remain on the other side a stranger. I try to stay in the officers' view at all times. And of course I have a weapon now in case I have to defend myself I would rather die than go through that horror.

———————

P.E., Florida, 3/6/99

[Why does prison rape occur?] Predatory inmates/gangs are rarely prosecuted by state and federal courts for extorting and sexually abusing inmates in prisons. . . . Gangs of black and spanish inmates are very angry at free-world white people for a variety of reasons, and this results in an attitude of vengeance towards white people in prisons. . . . Victim inmates are scared to report sexual abuse to prison officials because they fear that will be attacked by friends of the victimizer or by another racial group—even if transferred to another prison unit or placed in protective custody. [What are the characteristics of prison inmates who are sexually abused?] Mentally ill; primarily white inmates; physically small; inmates who are not emotionally or physically violent in nature (passive people); child molesters/rapists. . . . I have had to stab other inmates to prevent them from sexually abusing me. . . . I have been approached numerous times over the past 6 _ years of my incarceration. They either want sex or money.

———————

J.F., Texas, 3/22/99

Rape in the Illinois prison system is out of control. It seems that at times guards have placed me in dangerous situations on purpose. I came in the system at a young age and was raped in the first cell I was placed in. The shame that I experienced can't be described. Since then I've been attacked 3 times each resulting in rape. I'm now in a supermax prison where I'm safe, but I can't stay here for ever.

———————

A.R., Illinois, 3/28/99

When I first came into Lake Butler [prison] I was being raped by the same person everyday . . . . This is my first experience in prison so I did not know what to expect. I thought that kind of thing happens in prison, I just never thought that I would encounter the experience myself. When I went to speak to the inspector he was also trying to tell me that I was a homosexual. He was making this assumption by the way I was sitting and talking with him in his office. He was telling me that I was bring on the problem myself, in other words, he was telling me that because of the way I look.

———————

G.C., Florida, 5/13/99

[In prison], sometimes the sex act is for purely sexual purposes (gratification), other times it is a vehicle of expression of other passionate psychological dynamics (to give a sense of strength and power via sexual domination and subjugation; hatred; racism; expression of sadistic cruel tendencies, etc)—at other times (but this is rare) there occur true homosexual love affairs.

———————

J.G., Arizona, 5/24/99

When I first came to prison in 1968 (I had just turned 17 yrs. old . . .), I was approached by an older prisoner for sex; after I beat him about his head and shoulders with a pipe wrench, he never came near me again.

———————

J.G., Arizona, 5/24/99

I've known instances where a youngster will come into prison, and a sexual predator (or group of rapists) will attack and repeatedly sodomize (orally &

anally) him, and then instruct him, if he wants protection from gang rape, he must become the "bitch" for that group or one member of that group.

_____

J.G., Arizona, 5/24/99

The victim [of sexual abuse] is (the true charactoristic, irregardless of his size) <u>afraid, intimidated, afraid to fight</u>—sexual abuse is <u>violent sexuality</u>; if you want to remain free of victimization, you must resist violence by violence.

_____

J.G., Arizona, 5/24/99

I was in a cell with a White guy, they move him and put a Black guy in the cell with me. he said he was trying to help me. this how they get you. the Black read me cause I explain something about myself to him. So he goes out and tell the other guys that I was cool not in a gang nothing. So the other inmates said I was a punk a soft ass. So one day I goes to the day room going to get my medication there was a big Black guy both of them call me to the back of the day room. they were punking me out. I didn't want to fight them they made me call them daddy, made kept repeating it. . . . these things keeps happening to me. . . . these officers and these inmate they take avantige of the weak give them coffee, cigerette to make them do things for them. . . . there was a White guy that took advanteges of me in prison at another facility. . . . I don't no my rights or about the law, so I'm hit everytime I go to prison.

_____

B.S., Indiana, 6/16/99 (schizophrenic on medication)

I would estimate that 40% rape for control and recognition . . . . Whites will either submit to this new and horrible life of being a sex slave or seek protective custody but in today's prison system it is <u>extremely</u> difficult to seek protection from physical & sexual assaults, so it's kind of as though the administration condones these acts. . . . I had a neighbor who was so racist we would always go hungry because if a white man brought his food or cof fee he would throw it on them. He used to talk about his "boys" he had on the pound. White boys. He said he used to only get oral sex from them because he "<u>wasn't gay</u>" (I wanted so bad to tell him if you're pitching or catching you're still playing the game) but that he used to do it because they were white and because they wouldn't fight and he loved to degrade them. He swore he would never ever do that to no black man but instead would beat that other black man into acting like "a man."

_____

K.M., Florida, 6/18/99 (Puerto Rican inmate)

How to eradicate rape? 1) A very strict & thorough classifying system that will segregate known preditors from potential victims <u>automatically</u> unless a potential victim waives his rights to extra security and unless the known preditor has shown serious signs of amending his aggressive behavorior.

2) Unrelenting and automatic criminal prosecution with maximum sentences imposed. *NO EXCEPTIONS!*

3) More security. Rapes occur because the lack of observation make it possible. Prisons have too few guards and too many blind spots . . . .

4) <u>Manditory</u> classes for known preditors <u>with</u> extra gain time upon successful completion of course . . . .

4A) Manditory training for employees on how to recognize signs of sexual victimization and how to respond to allegations of rape or threats of rape, as well as viewing video tapes of victims classes, to become more sensitive to the matter.

_____

K.M., Florida, 6/18/99

Minnesota is a milder less violent prison population than most other systems in our country. In fact the only sexual assault I've witnessed is my own. What I've witnessed, a great deal of, is manipulation & light intimidation. And of course this is typically the new-younger guys being manipulated, by guys who have typically been down for many years.

_____

C.B., Minnesota, 7/19/99

One case, individual, I'm pretty familiar with is a guy who has served over 20 years, and he is a tough guy. What he has done for years, is gets the young guys in his cell & gets them high & then chokes them unconsious & proceeds to rape them. But as I said in most cases it's manipulation & light intimidation, not forced.

C.B., Minnesota, 7/19/99

[During one six-month period], I had the orbit of my left eye fractured, and was assaulted by another prisoner with a knife, among other altercations. This was all due to my refusal for sex. My mother has been a prison guard for over 20 yrs in Florida and the other prisoners wanted to "turn me out" to homosexuality to get back at her and the department.

After 6 months of this treatment I requested to be placed in Protective Management (P.M.), and was taken before the special review board where I presented several letters written by other prisoners who were threatening me with violence if I would not "be with them" sexually. The board refused to put me on P.M. . . . . I was then placed back in administrative confienment, waiting on an open cell in population. It was then that I realized the violence would not stop. At the end of my mental and emotional endurance, I tried to kill myself with a razor. 40 stitches and 11 days later I was returned to A.M. II where I wouldn't need "protection" because I was locked in a cell 24 hours a day.

6 months later, in 1997, I was returned to population where I promptly requested P.M. once more. I was given the distinct impression that if I tried to pursue the issue I would be put back on A.M. I couldn't stand the thought of being locked away in another cell all my life, so I did the only thing I could do—I found someone to "be with." I determined I'd be better off to willingly have sex with one person, than I would be to face violence and rape by multiple people. The most tragic part to this is that the person I chose to "be with" has AIDS.

. . . . My life is in danger at F.S.P., and I want the public to know this. A place like F.S.P. could not exist, could not do such things without public support. The opposite of compassion is not hatred, it's indifference.

M.M., Florida, 7/30/99

At night the guards locked themselves in a cage and slept while inmates sexually and physically assaulted others. I made friends with the Mexican gang because I spoke Spanish. They protected me as they comprised the majority of the population. I at times was asked for sexual favors in order to maintain my security. I was never forced into sex physically, but mentally I wasn't capable of saying no, as I feared for my life.

R.L., Arizona, 8/26/99

Appendix II

Miscellaneous Documents

1. U.S. Department of Justice, Federal Bureau of Prisons,
   "Program Statement: Sexual Abuse/Assault Prevention and
   Intervention Program," Directive 5324.04 (December 31, 1997)   234

2. Excerpts from Arkansas Department of Correction, "Sexual
   Aggression in Prisons and Jails: Awareness, Prevention and
   Intervention" (undated)   252

3. Curriculum outline from the Illinois Department of Corrections,
   "Inmate Sexual Assault" (February 1, 2000)   288

4. Declaration of Plaintiff's Counsel in the case of Dillard v. Decker,
   Case No. CV F-94 5048 AWI SMS (E.D. Ca. 2000)   295

5. Sample letter from Human Rights Watch to correctional
   department regarding rape prevention and prosecution strategies.   311

6. Sampling of responses from correctional departments to
   Human Rights Watch's survey of rape prevention and
   prosecution strategies.   312

U.S. Department of Justice
Federal Bureau of Prisons

Change
Notice

DIRECTIVE AFFECTED: 5324.04
CHANGE NOTICE NUMBER: 5324.04
DATE: 12/31/97

1. <u>PURPOSE AND SCOPE</u>. To update the Program Statement pertaining to Sexual Abuse/Assault Prevention and Intervention Programs

2. <u>SUMMARY OF CHANGES</u>. This Program Statement broadens the definition of sexual abuse/assault to include instances of staff-on-inmate sexual abuse/assault and to present more detailed mental health treatment protocols for victims of sexual assault.

3. <u>ACTION</u>. File this Change Notice in front of the Program Statement Sexual Abuse/Assault Prevention and Intervention Programs.

/s/
Kathleen M. Hawk
Director

U.S. Department of Justice
Federal Bureau of Prisons

Program
Statement

OPI: CPD
NUMBER: 5324.04
DATE: 12/31/97
SUBJECT: Sexual Abuse/Assault
Prevention and
Intervention Programs

1. <u>PURPOSE AND SCOPE</u>. To provide guidelines to help prevent
sexual assaults on inmates, to address the safety and treatment
needs of inmates who have been sexually assaulted, and to
discipline and prosecute those who sexually assault inmates.

Research indicates that a small percentage of individuals express
aggression and seek to dominate others through violent sexual
behavior. Forceful and pressured sexual interactions are among
the most serious threats to inmate safety and institutional
order. Victims may suffer physical and psychological harm, and
could be infected with a life-threatening disease.

Consequently, each institution is required to have a Sexual
Abuse/Assault Prevention and Intervention Program that includes
several major elements:

   a. prevention,
   b. prompt and effective intervention to address the safety and
      treatment needs of inmate victims if an assault occurs, and
   c. investigation, discipline, and prosecution of assailant(s).

2. <u>PROGRAM OBJECTIVES</u>. The expected results of this program
are:

   a. Effective procedures to prevent sexually assaultive
behavior will be operative in each Bureau institution.

   b. The medical, psychological, safety, and social needs of
victims of Sexual Abuse/Assault will be promptly and effectively
met.

PS 5324.04
12/31/97
Page 2

c. All allegations of Sexual Abuse/Assault will be promptly and effectively reported and investigated.

d. Assailants, once identified, will be controlled, disciplined, and/or prosecuted.

3. DIRECTIVES AFFECTED

a. Directive Rescinded

PS 5324.02   Sexual Assault Prevention and Intervention Programs, Inmates (2/2/95)

b. Directives Referenced

PS 1210.17   Office of Internal Affairs (8/4/97)
PS 1330.13   Administrative Remedy Program (12/22/95)
PS 1351.04   Release of Information (12/5/96)
PS 1380.05   Special Investigative Supervisors Manual (8/1/95)
PS 3420.08   Standards of Employee Conduct (3/7/96)
PS 3906.16   Employee Development Manual (3/21/97)
PS 5180.04   Central Inmate Monitoring System (8/16/96)
PS 5270.07   Discipline and Special Housing Units (12/29/87)
PS 5290.10   Intake Screening (8/11/97)
PS 5310.12   Psychology Services Manual (8/13/93)
PS 5500.09   Correctional Services Manual (10/27/97)
PS 6000.05   Health Services Manual (9/15/96)

4. STANDARDS REFERENCED

a. American Correctional Association 3rd Edition Standards for Adult Correctional Institutions: 3-4268, 3-4380-1, 3-4386

b. American Correctional Association 3rd Edition Standards for Adult Local Detention Facilities: 3-ALDF-3E-08, 3-ALDF-4B-02-1, 3-ALDF-4F-03

c. American Correctional Association 2nd Edition Standards for Administration of Correctional Agencies: 2-CO-3C-01, 2-CO-4F-01

d. American Correctional Association Standards for Adult Correctional Boot Camp Programs: 1-ABC-3D-06, 1-ABC-5A-01-1, 1-ABC-4F-07

PS 5324.04
12/31/97
Page 3

5. <u>DEFINITION</u>. For the purposes of this Program Statement, the following definitions apply:

a. <u>Inmate-on-Inmate Sexual Abuse/Assault</u>. One or more inmates engaging in, or attempting to engage in a sexual act with another inmate or the use of threats, intimidation, inappropriate touching, or other actions and/or communications by one or more inmates aimed at coercing and/or pressuring another inmate to engage in a sexual act. Sexual acts or contacts between inmates, even when no objections are raised, are prohibited acts.

b. <u>Staff-on-Inmate Sexual Abuse/Assault</u>. Engaging in, or attempting to engage in a sexual act with any inmate or the intentional touching of an inmate's genitalia, anus, groin, breast, inner thigh, or buttocks with the intent to abuse, humiliate, harass, degrade, arouse, or gratify the sexual desire of any person. Sexual acts or contacts between an inmate and a staff member, even when no objections are raised, are always illegal.

6. <u>PROGRAM COORDINATION</u>. Preventing sexual abuse/assault, intervening when sexual assaults do occur, investigating allegations of sexual assault, and disciplining/prosecuting perpetrators of sexual abuse/assault involves the coordinated efforts of several institution departments (e.g., Correctional Services, Psychology Services, Health Services, Legal, Unit Management, Religious Services, etc.). Each Warden shall assign one staff member, ordinarily an Associate Warden, overall responsibility for ensuring that all elements of this Program Statement are met in a coordinated, interdisciplinary fashion. Specific program elements include:

a. educating and training staff and inmates,
b. safeguarding, assessing, treating, and managing sexually assaulted inmates, and

c. investigating, disciplining, and/or prosecuting perpetrators of sexual assault.

7. <u>PREVENTION</u>. All staff and inmates are responsible for being alert to signs of potential situations in which sexual assaults might occur.

a. <u>Screening and Classification</u>. All inmates entering the Bureau are screened consistent with applicable Health Services, Psychology Services, and Case Management policy. When an inmate

PS 5324.04
12/31/97
Page 4

reports having been a victim of sexual abuse/assault and expresses a willingness to participate in treatment, staff shall refer the inmate to Psychology Services. Psychology Services staff shall assess the inmate's need for treatment and discuss available treatment options when appropriate. The results of this discussion should be documented in the Psychology Data System (PDS).

Preventing sexual abuse/assault also suggests that staff should attempt to identify sexually assaultive inmates. In fact, care must be taken to identify and document any history of sexually assaultive behavior. Accordingly, during intake screening procedures, staff shall review available documentation (e.g., judgment and commitment orders, criminal records, presentence investigation reports, Central file data, etc.) for any indication that an inmate has a history of sexually aggressive behavior. Staff shall refer any inmate with a history of sexually abusive behavior to Psychology Services staff for an assessment and possible treatment. The results of this assessment along with any treatment recommendations and the inmate's motivation to participate in treatment should be documented in the PDS.

   b.   Staff Training. All staff shall be trained to:

      (1)   recognize the physical, behavioral, and emotional signs of sexual assault;
      (2)   understand the identification and referral process when an alleged sexual assault occurs; and
      (3)   have a basic understanding of sexual assault prevention and response techniques.

For new employees, a discussion of sexual abuse/assault prevention and intervention shall be part of Introduction to Correctional Techniques training and should include a review of the Bureau's sexual abuse/assault policy and staff responsibilities to prevent and report sexual assaults. For existing staff, more extensive information about the program shall be included as a part of Annual Refresher Training. The Chief Executive Officer shall designate one staff member each year to conduct this training session.

In addition to Annual Refresher Training, specialized training should be made available to staff who are likely to be most involved in the treatment or management of sexually assaulted

PS 5324.04
12/31/97
Page 5

inmates (e.g., Health Services staff, Psychology Services staff, unit management staff, lieutenants, etc.). This specialized training may be offered by Bureau employees or consultants from the community who are especially knowledgeable regarding issues pertaining to sexual abuse/assault and may be included as part of larger training programs offered to these disciplines at the Management Specialty Training Center in Aurora, Colorado or other designated locations.

c.   Inmate Education. As part of the institution's Admission and Orientation Program, a staff member the Warden designates shall include a brief, candid presentation about the Sexual Abuse/Assault Prevention and Intervention Program, including:

(1)   how inmates can protect themselves from becoming victims while incarcerated,

(2)   treatment options available to victims of sexual assault, and

(3)   methods of reporting incidents of sexual abuse/assault (including a discussion of filing an administrative remedy directly to the Regional Office when the issue is considered sensitive in accordance with the Program Statement on the Administrative Remedy Program.)

This presentation shall also include information on services and programs (counseling, sex offender treatment) for sexually assaultive or aggressive inmates. Each inmate shall also receive an information pamphlet summarizing key elements of this presentation.

Where inmates do not participate in the formal A&O program (e.g., WITSEC cases or high security/high profile cases placed in SHU), the Warden shall designate a staff member to insure that the information pamphlet on the Sexual Abuse/Assault Prevention and Intervention program is appropriately disseminated.

8.   PROMPT AND EFFECTIVE INTERVENTION. Staff sensitivity toward inmates who are victims of sexual abuse/assault is critical. Staff shall take seriously all statements from inmates that they have been victims of sexual assaults and respond supportively and non-judgmentally (see the Sexual Abuse/Assault Crisis Intervention Protocol (Attachment A)). Any inmate who alleges that he or she has been sexually assaulted shall be offered immediate protection from the assailant and will be referred for

a medical examination as well as a clinical assessment of the potential for suicide or other related symptomatology.

   a. Referral. Using Attachment A as a guide, staff shall provide services to victims and shall conduct investigations of sexual abuse/assault incidents. Information concerning the identity of an inmate victim reporting a sexual assault, and the facts of the report itself, shall be limited to those who have a need to know in order to make decisions concerning the inmate-victim's welfare and for law enforcement/investigative purposes.

When a staff member(s) is alleged to be the perpetrator of inmate sexual abuse/assault, the Warden shall be advised immediately. The Warden shall refer the incident directly to the Office of Internal Affairs (OIA) and OIA, in turn, shall refer the matter to the Office of Inspector General (OIG). The Warden may also refer the matter to the FBI (or other appropriate law enforcement agency). The timely reporting of all incidents and allegations is of paramount importance.

When an inmate(s) is alleged to be the perpetrator, it is the Special Investigative Supervisor's (SIS) responsibility to ensure that the incident is promptly referred to the appropriate law enforcement agency having jurisdiction. For other circumstances (e.g., sexual abuse/assault while on writ or in a CCC), appropriate law enforcement officials should be contacted.

   (1) Normal Business Hours. During normal business hours, staff shall promptly advise the Operations Lieutenant of any inmate who has been, or claims to have been, sexually assaulted. The Operations Lieutenant or designee shall immediately provide for the inmate's physical safety and ensure that the inmate is promptly referred to appropriate Health Services and Psychology Services staff for examination and treatment. The Operations Lieutenant shall also ensure that the SIS, Captain, Associate Warden, and Warden are notified.

   (2) Non-business Hours. During the evening and night shifts, when the potential for sexual assaults is greater, staff shall immediately notify the Operations Lieutenant, who shall notify the SIS, Health Services staff, the Duty Officer, and the Chief Psychologist or on-call Psychologist. Correctional Services staff shall immediately provide for the physical safety (e.g., separating the assailant from the victim) of the inmate who reports being sexually assaulted. Health Services and Psychology Services staff shall promptly inform the Duty Officer

PS 5324.04
12/31/97
Page 7

of their initial findings and treatment recommendations.

(3) <u>Medical Report of Injury</u>. When an assault is reported, Health Services staff shall encourage the inmate to complete an Inmate Injury Assessment and Follow-up form (BP-S362) as required by the Health Services Manual.

b. <u>Services</u>. At a minimum, the following services should be available to all inmates who claim to be the victim of a sexual abuse/assault during their incarceration. These services should be provided in an environment that meets both the inmate's safety and therapeutic needs.

(1) <u>Medical</u>. Examination, documentation, and treatment of injuries arising from an alleged sexual assault, including testing for HIV and other Sexually Transmitted Diseases (STD).

(2) <u>Mental Health Services</u>. Crisis intervention, assessment of treatment needs, documentation of evaluation and treatment needs, psychiatric referral, and/or other treatment options including referral to community mental health resources in his or her release area.

(3) <u>Social</u>. Family support and/or peer support should be provided, when available and appropriate. Unit and Psychology services staff should be sensitive to family concerns if the inmate-victim notifies relatives or friends of the assault.

(4) <u>Protective</u>. Staff consultation and/or action to prevent further assaults should be considered (e.g. closer supervision, protective custody, transfer, etc.)

c. <u>Responsibilities</u>. All staff are responsible for immediately referring cases of sexual abuse/assault when they become aware of them to the appropriate medical, psychological, and correctional staff. All staff are also expected to handle allegations of sexual abuse/assault sensitively and non-judgmentally. Additionally, staff in specific institution departments have more defined roles:

(1) <u>Unit Team staff</u>, particularly the Unit Manager, Case Manager, Correctional Officer, and Counselor, shall

PS 5324.04
12/31/97
Page 8

closely monitor and supervise any inmate who has been sexually assaulted. This may include additional team meetings, application of Central Inmate Monitoring policies, and the careful review of security and housing assignments.

Additionally, unit staff are to refer inmates who have committed sexual assaults to Psychology Services staff for an evaluation and possible treatment (which may be impacted in part by pending disciplinary or legal actions). Refusal to participate in treatment, when it is determined to be necessary, must be documented by Psychology Services staff and placed in the medical section of the Inmate Central File.

(2) <u>Psychology Services staff</u> shall offer appropriate care, which may include mental health evaluation and counseling, support services, and follow-up care/tracking. Competency issues of the victim may need to be addressed.

(3) <u>Chaplaincy staff</u> shall offer support and pastoral care, when requested by the victim.

(4) <u>Correctional Services and Legal staff</u> shall coordinate such matters as evidence and witness testimony collection and corroboration and consultation on administrative and disciplinary issues.

9. <u>INVESTIGATION AND PROSECUTION</u>. If an inmate alleges sexual assault, a sensitive and coordinated response is necessary.

a. Appropriate referrals shall be made to OIA, OIG, and the FBI.

b. Appropriate staff shall preserve the crime scene and collect information/evidence in coordination with the referral agency and consistent with evidence gathering/processing procedures outlined in the Special Investigative Supervisor's Manual.

c. Based on such factors as availability of in-house expertise and general security considerations, the Warden may use either a staff physician (see the Health Services Manual, Sexual Assault) or a contracted clinical care service to examine the victim. The results of the physical examination and all collected physical

PS 5324.04
12/31/97
Page 9

evidence are to be provided to SIS staff. Appropriate infectious disease testing, as determined by Health Services staff, may be necessary. Part of the investigative process may also include an examination of and collection of physical evidence from the suspected assailant(s).

10. TRANSFER OF INMATES TO HOSPITALS/OTHER INSTITUTIONS

     a. In institutions where Health Services staff are not trained or certificated in sexual assault evidence gathering, the inmate should either be examined at the institution by trained health care professionals from the local community or be transported to a local community facility that is equipped (in accordance with local laws) to evaluate and treat sexual assault victims (see Attachment A, Medical Transfers for Examination and Treatment).

     b. If necessary to sustain life and/or stabilize vital functions, Health Services staff shall make emergency referrals to an appropriate community or Bureau medical center for inmates seriously injured as a result of a sexual assault.

11. TRACKING SEXUAL ASSAULTS. The major purpose of the Bureau's Sexual Abuse/Assault Prevention and Intervention Program is to protect inmates in Bureau custody. Monitoring and evaluation are essential to assess both sexual assault levels and agency effectiveness in reducing sexually abusive behavior. Accordingly, the SIS must maintain two types of files.

     a. General files which includes data on:

          (1) the victim(s) and assailant(s) of a sexual assault,
          (2) crime characteristics, and
          (3) formal and/or informal action(s) taken.

     b. Investigative files which are opened following any allegation of sexual assault which include copies of:

          (1) all reports,
          (2) medical forms,
          (3) supporting memos and videotapes, and
          (4) any other evidentiary materials pertaining to the allegation.

The SIS shall maintain these files chronologically in a secure location. Each SIS shall maintain a current listing of the names of sexual assault victims and assailants along with the dates and locations of all sexual assault incidents occurring within the institution on his or her computerized incident index system.

The SIS shall give inmate sexual assault assailant(s) and victim(s) involved in a Bureau sexual assault incident a specific STG SENTRY assignment. Access to this SENTRY assignment shall be limited to those staff who are involved in the treatment of the victim or the investigation of the incident. The STG SENTRY assignment will allow administrative, treatment, and SIS staff the ability to track inmates across the system who have been involved in a sexual assault either as a victim or as an assailant.

Based on STG SENTRY data, the Intelligence Section, Correctional Programs Division, Central Office shall report annually the number of sexual assaults occurring within the Bureau.

12. <u>INSTITUTION SUPPLEMENT</u>. Each institution shall publish an Institution Supplement within 90 days from the effective date of this Program Statement. Since the risk and likelihood of sexual abuse/assault vary greatly by the mission and security level of each institution, staffing resources fluctuate across institutions, and the availability of specialized, community-based services (e.g., rape crisis/trauma units within medical centers, clinics, and hospitals) differ among communities, the Institution Supplement shall reflect the unique characteristics of each institution, and specify how each institution shall comply with this Program Statement.

Each Institutional Supplement shall be submitted to the appropriate Regional Office for review and approval. Regional reviewers from Correctional Services, Correctional Programs, Psychology Services, Health Services, and the Regional Counsel shall ensure that each institution:

a. specifies procedures for offering immediate protection to any inmate who alleges that he or she has been sexually assaulted;

b. specifies local response procedures (including referral procedures to appropriate law enforcement agencies) to be followed when a sexual assault occurs;

c. establishes procedures to involve outside agencies in sexual abuse/assault prevention and intervention programs, if such resources are available;

PS 5324.04
12/31/97
Page 11

d.   designates specific staff (e.g., psychologist, Associate Warden, appropriate medical staff, etc.) to be responsible for staff training activities;

e.   specifies how the safety needs of the victim will be protected over time;

f.   specifies which Associate Warden is responsible for insuring that staff are appropriately trained and respond in a coordinated fashion when an inmate reports an incident of sexual abuse/assault;

g.   designates a specific staff member to be responsible for inmate education regarding issues pertaining to sexual assault; and

h.   specifies how medical staff will be trained or certified in procedures for examining and treating victims of sexual assault in institutions where medical staff will be assigned these activities.

/s/
Kathleen M. Hawk
Director

PS 5324.04
12/31/97
Attachment A, Page 1

SEXUAL ABUSE/ASSAULT CRISIS INTERVENTION PROTOCOL

This protocol is intended to serve as a guideline for staff in the management of sexual assaults. Some procedures may not be applicable or feasible for implementation at a particular institution. In most circumstances, these procedures should be followed as closely as possible.

I. VICTIM IDENTIFICATION (all staff)

A. The following are primary ways staff learn that a sexual assault has occurred during confinement:

    1. Staff discover an assault in progress.
    2. Victim reports an assault to a staff member.
    3. An assault is reported to staff by another inmate, or is the subject of inmate rumors.
    4. Medical Evidence.

    While some victims will be clearly identified, most will probably not come forward directly with information about the event. In some circumstances, staff may hear of an inmate being threatened with sexual abuse/assault or rumored to be a victim. Some victims may be identified through unexplained injuries, changes in physical behavior due to injuries, or abrupt personality changes such as withdrawal or suicidal behavior.

B. The following guidelines may help staff in responding appropriately to a suspected victim:

    1. If it is suspected that the inmate was sexually assaulted, the inmate should be advised of the importance of getting help to deal with the assault, that he/she may be evaluated medically for sexually transmitted diseases and other injuries, and that trained staff are available to assist.

    2. Staff should review the background of a suspected victim, and the circumstances surrounding the incident, without jeopardizing the inmate's safety, identity, and privacy.

    3. If staff discover an assault in progress, the suspected victim should be removed from the immediate area for care and for interviewing by appropriate staff.

PS 5324.04
12/31/97
Attachment A, Page 2

4. If the suspected victim is fearful of being labeled an informer, the inmate should be advised that the identity of the assailant(s) is (are) not needed to receive assistance.

5. The staff member who first identifies that an assault may have occurred should refer the matter to the institution's Operations Lieutenant or SIS.

II. PROCEDURES FOR STAFF INTERVENTION AND INVESTIGATION

The following procedures may apply for reported or known victims of sexual assault. If the inmate was threatened with sexual assault or was assaulted on an earlier occasion, some steps may not be necessary.

A. Early Intervention Techniques (all staff)

1. It is important that all contact with a sexual assault victim be sensitive, supportive, and non-judgmental.
2. It is not necessary to make a judgment about whether or not a sexual assault occurred.
3. Identify the inmate victim(s) and remove them from the immediate area;
4. Alert medical staff immediately and escort the victim to the Health Services Unit for a medical evaluation as soon as possible. If necessary, medical staff shall refer the victim to a local emergency facility.
5. Appropriate staff shall coordinate other services to do follow-up (e.g, housing, suicide assessment).
6. To facilitate evidence collection, the victim should not shower, wash, drink, eat, defecate or change any clothing until examined.
7. A brief statement about the assault should be obtained from the inmate. (The victim may be in shock, and unable to give much detail. It is important to be understanding and responsive. Opportunities to secure more details will occur later.)

PS 5324.04
12/31/97
Attachment A, Page 3

8. Following medical evaluation/treatment, the victim may need to be reassigned to protective custody or to another secure area of the facility. Ensure that the alleged assailant(s) is not located in the area.

B. **Collect Evidence from Victim - (Correctional Services-SIS staff)**

1. Be sure to use HIV infection precautions and procedures. Contact medical staff to determine how to preserve medical indications of sexual assault. In the crime scene area, look for the presence of semen that can be used as evidence. For example, blankets and sheets should be collected.
2. Use standard evidence collection procedures (photographs, etc.) identified in the SIS Manual.

C. **Collect Evidence from Assailant - (Correctional Services-Health Services staff)**

1. Identify the assailant if possible and isolate the assailant, whenever possible, pending further investigation.
2. Use standard evidence gathering procedures identified in the SIS Manual.
3. Report the incident to the appropriate law enforcement agency.
4. If institution medical staff attempt to examine the alleged assailant, findings should be documented both photographically and in writing. A written summary of all medical evidence and findings should be completed and maintained in the inmate's medical record. Copies of this written summary should also be provided to the SIS and appropriate law enforcement officials.

III. **MEDICAL ASSESSMENT OF VICTIM - (Health Services staff)**

A. If trained medical staff are available in the institution, render treatment locally whenever feasible.

B. If the alleged victim is examined in the institution (see the Health Services Manual, Sexual Assault) to determine the extent of injuries, all findings should be documented both photographically and in writing. An original Inmate Injury Assessment and Follow-up form (BP-S362) should be filed in the inmate's medical record. A copy of BP-S362 should be

PS 5324.04
12/31/97
Attachment A, Page 4

provided to the SIS or appropriate law enforcement official.

C. If deemed necessary by the examining physician, follow
    established procedures for use of outside medical
    consultants or for an escorted trip to an outside medical
    facility.

D. Notify staff at the community medical facility and alert
    them to the inmate's condition.

E. When necessary, conduct STD and HIV testing.

F. Refer the inmate for crisis counseling as appropriate.

**IV. MEDICAL TRANSFERS FOR EXAMINATION AND TREATMENT -
       (Correctional and Health Services staff)**

A. If determined appropriate by the institution physician and
    if approved by the Warden or designee, the inmate may be
    examined by medical personnel from the community. A
    contractual arrangement may be developed with a rape crisis
    center or other medical service if available in the
    community and should be utilized to enhance institution
    medical services as deemed appropriate by institution
    medical staff and the Warden. The contract should provide
    for clinical examination, for assessing physical injuries,
    and for the collection of any physical evidence of sexual
    assault. It should also allow for contract medical
    personnel to come into the institution and for the escorting
    of inmates to the contract facility (e.g., crisis care
    center, medical clinic, hospital, etc.).

B. Escorting staff should treat the victim in a supportive and
    non-judgmental way.

C. Information about the assault is confidential, and should be
    given only to those directly involved in the investigation
    and/or treatment of the victim.

PS 5324.04
12/31/97
Attachment A, Page 5

V.   **MENTAL HEALTH SERVICES** - (**Psychology Services**)

A.   Psychology Services or other mental health staff shall be
      notified immediately after the initial report of an
      allegation of sexual abuse/assault of an inmate.

B.   Any alleged victim(s) shall be seen, within 24 hours
      following such notification, by a mental health clinician to
      provide crisis intervention and to assess any immediate and
      subsequent treatment needs.

C.   The findings of this initial crisis/evaluation session shall
      be summarized in a written format within one week of the
      initial session and, once completed, shall be placed in the
      appropriate treatment record, with a copy provided to the
      Clinical Director and other staff responsible for oversight
      of sexual abuse/assault prevention and intervention
      procedures.

D.   Additional psychological or psychiatric treatment, as well
      as continued assessment of mental health status and
      treatment needs, shall be provided as needed and only with
      the victim's full consent and collaboration. Decisions
      regarding the need for continued treatment and/or assessment
      shall be made by qualified clinicians according to
      established professional standards, and shall be made with
      an awareness that victim(s) of sexual abuse/assault commonly
      experience both immediate and delayed psychiatric and/or
      emotional symptoms.

      If the victim(s) choose to continue to pursue treatment, the
      clinician will either provide appropriate treatment or
      facilitate referral of the victim(s) to the appropriate
      treatment option(s) including individual therapy, group
      therapy, further psychological assessment, assignment to a
      mental health case load and/or facility, referral to a
      psychiatrist, and/or other treatment options. Pending
      referral, mental health services shall continue unabated.
      If the victim(s) chooses to decline further treatment
      services, he or she shall be asked to sign a statement to
      that effect.

PS 5324.04
12/31/97
Attachment A, Page 6

E. All treatment and evaluation sessions shall be properly documented and placed in the appropriate treatment record to ensure continuity of care within, between, or outside Bureau facilities.

F. Should the victim(s) be released from custody during the course of treatment, the victim(s) will be advised of community mental health resources in his/her area.

VI. MONITORING AND FOLLOW-UP - (Psychology and Health Services staff)

A. Arrange with the unit team and Correctional Services to place the inmate in appropriate housing.

B. Monitor the physical and mental health of the victim and coordinate the continuation of necessary services.

C. Dispense medication, provide routine examinations and STD and HIV follow-up.

D. Conduct post-crisis counseling and arrange for psychiatric care if necessary.

E. Psychology staff should watch for reaction stages and provide support as needed during critical stages.

F. Determine the risk of keeping the victim at the same facility where the incident occurred.

VII. RELEASE PREPARATION AND CONTINUING CARE - (Psychology and Unit Management staff)

A. Psychology staff shall ordinarily determine the need for aftercare and transitional treatment services, and notify the Case Manager of their recommendations.

B. The willingness of the victim to participate in treatment in the community should be determined.

C. For those cases that will use continuing care services, efforts to facilitate them should begin about 12 months prior to their release.

D. If CCC services are used, mental health counseling and other transitional services that facilitate the victim's healthy

LETTER FROM THE DIRECTOR

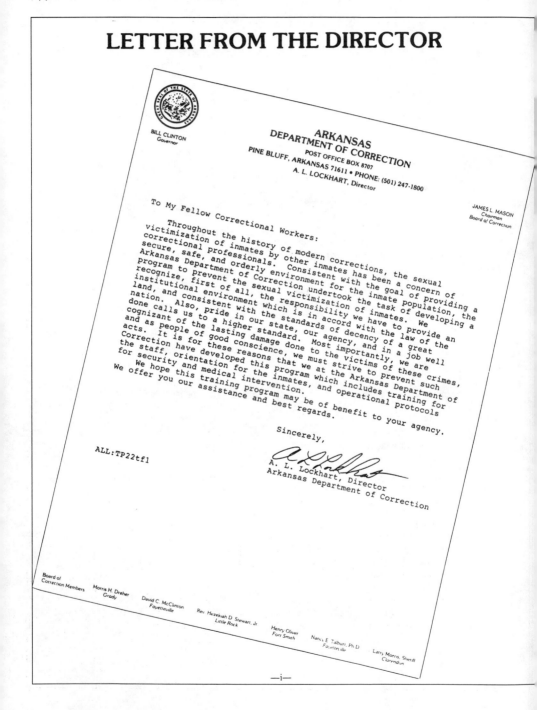

BILL CLINTON
Governor

ARKANSAS
DEPARTMENT OF CORRECTION
POST OFFICE BOX 8707
PINE BLUFF, ARKANSAS 71611 • PHONE: (501) 247-1800
A. L. LOCKHART, Director

JAMES L. MASON
Chairman
Board of Correction

To My Fellow Correctional Workers:

Throughout the history of modern corrections, the sexual victimization of inmates by other inmates has been a concern of correctional professionals. Consistent with the goal of providing a secure, safe, and orderly environment for the inmate population, the Arkansas Department of Correction undertook the task of developing a program to prevent the sexual victimization of inmates. We recognize, first of all, the responsibility we have to provide an institutional environment which is in accord with the law of the land, and consistent with the standards of decency of a great nation. Also, pride in our state, our agency, and in a job well done calls us to a higher standard. Most importantly, we are cognizant of the lasting damage done to the victims of these crimes, and as people of good conscience, we must strive to prevent such acts. It is for these reasons that we at the Arkansas Department of Correction have developed this program which includes training for the staff, orientation for the inmates, and operational protocols for security and medical intervention.

We hope this training program may be of benefit to your agency. We offer you our assistance and best regards.

Sincerely,

A. L. Lockhart
A. L. Lockhart, Director
Arkansas Department of Correction

ALL:TP22tfl

—i—

COURSE DESCRIPTION

COURSE DESCRIPTION:

SEXUAL AGGRESSION: AWARENESS, PREVENTION AND INTERVENTION PROGRAM

The above-named course is an eight (8) hour course designed to train correctional personnel to recognize and prevent potential sexual abuse among the inmate population and to intervene quickly and efficiently in instances of suspected, actual, or on-going abuse.

ACKNOWLEDGMENTS

Program Coordinator — TOM PITTS, Internal Affairs Investigator, Arkansas Department of Correction; B.A., University of Arkansas at Pine Bluff

SPECIAL THANKS — to DR. DANIEL LOCKWOOD His scholarly writings were invaluable in the production of this program. We would like to take this opportunity to recognize his contribution to the body of knowledge and express our personal appreciation for his work.

CONSULTANTS
(listed in alphabetical order)

LISA CALHOUN (forensics) — Forensics Serologist, Arkansas State Crime Lab, and Chairperson, Governor's Task Force on Rape; B.S., University of Arkansas at Fayetteville

YVONNE HATHCOCK (editorial) — Graphic Arts Supervisor, Arkansas Correctional Industries; M.A., Arkansas State University

TED KNIGHT (sociologist) — Chairperson, Department of Social and Behavioral Sciences, University of Arkansas at Pine Bluff; Ph.D., Oklahoma State University

GERALDINE F. NAGY (management) — Private Practice; Ph.D., Kansas State University

MAX J. MOBLEY (psychologist) — Assistant Director of Treatment Services, Arkansas Department of Correction; Ph.D., University of Arkansas at Fayetteville

MARY L. PARKER (criminology) — Professor of Criminal Justice and Graduate Program Coordinator, University of Arkansas at Little Rock; M.A., Northeast Louisiana University

Persons desiring further technical assistance may contact Tom Pitts,
Arkansas Department of Correction, P.O. Box 8707, Pine Bluff, Arkansas 71611.

For information concerning reprints, contact Arkansas Correctional Industries, P.O. Box 8707, Pine Bluff, Arkansas 71611.

—ii—

COURSE OUTLINE

SECTION I:

DYNAMICS OF SEXUAL AGGRESSION IN A CORRECTIONAL ENVIRONMENT.

  A. Administrative problems resulting from sexual aggression.

  B. Legal responsibilities and potential liability of correctional personnel.

  C. Societal attitudes toward rape in general and in the correctional environment in particular.

  D. Exploring the myths surrounding sexual expression among inmates and sexual abuse in particular, within the correctional environment.

  E. Factual assessment of the range and scope of sexual abuse in the correctional environment.

SECTION II.

POTENTIAL TARGETS AND PATTERNS OF VICTIMIZATION.

  A. Target Profile.

    1. Age
    2. Ethnicity
    3. Physical Appearance
    4. Commitment Offense
    5. Sexual Orientation
    6. Prior Commitment
    7. Regional Background

  B. Special Class Targets.

    1. Homosexuals
    2. Sex Offenders
    3. Mentally Disturbed or Retarded

  C. Target Response to Aggression

    1. Violence
    2. Verbal
    3. Avoidance: Formal and Informal
    4. Submission to Sexual Demands

  D. Target Reaction to Attacks.

    1. Rape Trauma Syndrome
    2. Suicide
    3. Escape
    4. Aggressive Behavior

SECTION III:

AGGRESSORS AND METHODS OF OPERATION.

A. Aggressor Profile.

1. Age
2. Ethnicity
3. Physical Appearance
4. Commitment Offense
5. Sexual Orientation
6. Prior Commitments
7. Regional Background

B. Aggressor Tactics.

1. Gorilla
2. Player
3. Gang Member

C. Recognition of Aggressor Activity.

D. Profile of an Attack.

1. Review Incident

SECTION IV:

PREVENTION AND INTERVENTION.

A. Prevention.

1. Direct observation of inmates by security and treatment personnel.
2. Special classification for known or potential targets.
3. Special classification for known aggressors.
4. Inmate orientation aimed at sexual abuse prevention.

B. Intervention.

1. Sexual Aggression Security Protocol.
2. Evidentiary and Medical Examination.

INTRODUCTION

An examination of sexual victimization in prison should be prefaced with a discussion of the prevalent social attitudes toward rape as a crime in the free world, for the causal social factors underlying the rape of men in prison are very similar to those associated with the rape of women. Some criminologists assert that the rape of imprisoned males represents, to a large extent, a microcosm of the rape of females in the outside world.[1] It is a distorted, deviant image, but in many ways alarmingly similar to the outside world; most specifically that segment from which the majority of the inmate population is drawn. The pattern of sexual victimization in society as a whole is reproduced in the prison culture in a clearly recognizable form. Section I will explore the relationship between the two, and also examine issues of particular importance to correctional personnel.

PERFORMANCE OBJECTIVES:

A. <u>Section I:</u> By the end of this session participants will be able to:

1. Discuss the misconception of rape of women in the free world as a crime for sexual fulfillment.

2. Discuss the theory of prison rape as an act of violence.

3. Explain the importance of preventing sexual harrassment.

4. Identify 7 guidelines for correctional officers which may help them avoid legal liability for the failure to protect inmates from sexual victimization.

5. Identify 7 problems in the institution which are caused or aggravated by the incidence of sexual harrassment/assault.

A. MANAGEMENT PROBLEMS

Regardless of your position, whether you are a new recruit or a warden, you manage inmates. That makes you a manager, and as a manager you will encounter problems as a result of sexual aggressive behavior on the part of some inmates. Avoiding these problems make your job safer and easier. The following are some specific areas of concern for correctional managers.

1. **VIOLENCE:** This includes everything from simple assault to murder. According to Lockwood, 51% of known incidents involved violence.[2] An earlier study by Toch stated that 25% of inmate aggression in the California state system had homosexual roots.[3] Another study revealed that homosexual activity was the leading motive for inmate homicides in American prisons.[4]

2. **ESCAPES:** Pressure from aggressors have been linked to several escapes and escape attempts.[5] Fear of sexual assault could no doubt be a powerful motivating force for many men to try an escape.

3. **SUICIDES:** According to Lockwood, 38% of all targets of sexual aggression have made a suicidal gesture while in prison.[6] Likewise, the shame associated with being an actual victim has been linked to attempted and successful suicides.

4. **INCREASED TENSION AMONG INMATE POPULATION:** Most inmates are not involved in homosexual activity. The convict code prevents them from coming to the defense of the victim, but they cannot help but feel involved. This is especially true if the target and aggressor are of different race. Also, other inmates who witness the incidents may perceive themselves as potential targets and develop a strike-first philosophy. There is also competition among aggressors which creates tension.

5. **REQUIREMENT FOR SPECIAL HOUSING OF TARGETS:** These special units require a higher level of security, meaning more expense to an already underfunded system and more work for an over-burdened staff.

6. **INCREASED MEDICAL COST:** The stress the target experiences very often results in stress-related medical problems or psychological disorders requiring extensive treatment, during and after incarceration.[7] Also, the possibility of serious sexually-transmitted disease requires extensive testing and treatment.

7. **DANGER TO STAFF:** Any circumstance which produces the type of volatile emotions that sexual aggression does would constitute a threat to the security staff. The California Department of Corrections classifies this as one of the most dangerous encounters for an officer.[8] Either of the participants could react violently toward an officer—the aggressor, in an attempt to prevent detention, or the victim from revenge. An officer may also be attacked by a target who wants to be removed from the area but does not want to ask for protection. Attacking the officer serves a two-fold purpose; it gets him locked up where the aggressor can't get at him, and it contributes to his reputation for being "tough", which makes him a less attractive target.

B. STAFF LIABILITY

There is no question that a Department of Correction has a legal responsibility to protect the inmates committed to its care from sexual aggression.[9] Protection from sexual victimization by other inmates is an absolute requirement madated by numerous court decisions, as well as state and federal law. Courts are increasingly finding in favor of victims of prison rape, holding the correctional staff as well as the institution liable for monetary damages.[10]

A South Dakota inmate collected a total of $37,046.00 after his rape.[11] The state court held that the South Dakota Department of Correction had shown a "reckless disregard of his right to be free from violent attacks from fellow inmates." This is by no means an isolated case. Successful suits have been brought by inmates against the states of Maryland, Missouri, Arizona, New York, Wisconsin, California, and several others. Cash awards have ranged from $2,000.00 to $1,000,000.00![12] Virtually every geographical region is represented here, demonstrating that the problem of sexual abuse in prisons is not a local problem. And, that courts in various jurisdictions, and at different levels, are determined to punish any system or person who allows an immate to be sexually abused.

The problem was considered so serious by one Delaware State Senator that he proposed legislation (SB 113) which would establish prison sentences for prison guards and health care workers who permit the sexual molestation of inmates or patients![13]

The correctional officer can best protect himself from expensive legal action by following these suggestions:

1. Know and enforce the rules regarding the sexual conduct of inmates. Most Correctional Systems have rules which, when followed, will prevent most sexual aggression.

2. Maintain a professional bearing at all times. Don't laugh or joke about homosexual activity or sexual abuse with or around inmates.

3. Don't use female names, pronouns or prison slang when referring to an inmate.

4. Make it clear that homosexual behavior is **not** acceptable, and is in fact a violation of departmental policy and state law.

5. Treat any suggestion or allegation of sexual abuse as serious. Follow established procedures to protect the target.

6. Never recommend that an inmate use force to repel sexual advances. To do so makes **you** responsible for his actions. Also, it indicates very poor management to suggest that the inmate must protect himself.

7. Recognize that this is a very sensitive and important issue.

C. SOCIAL ATTITUDES TOWARD RAPE

Attitudes toward rape vary widely in our society. We seem to swing from one extreme to the other on the subject. Some label the offender as a pervert and want him castrated; a punishment particularly harsh by comparison with actual sentences most often imposed by law. On the other hand, it is commonly believed that women will often use a cry of rape to get even with a man for some real or imagined wrong. While true in some cases, this is not as common as is suggested by some. Many blame women for dressing in a provocative manner designed to tease men and lead them on; therefore, they are responsible for making themselves victims. It is also suggested that women invite rape by frequenting disreputable establishments, or traveling into dark and deserted areas. Closely associated with this viewpoint is the supposition that the rapist is a sexually deprived man; just a lonely misfit without any other outlet for his sexual desires.

As much as these two positions are opposed they are founded on a common misconception; i.e., rape is a crime that is committed for sexual fulfillment. Informed individuals reject this for they are aware that rape is a crime of violence where sex is used as a weapon to humiliate and gain a sense of power and control over the victim.[14] This statement is of course a condensation of a very complex psychological process, but it is essentially correct. Perhaps the best manner in which to prove this theory is to disprove the earlier stated societal attitudes toward rape.

Dr. A. Nicholas Groth, director of the sex offender program at the Connecticut Correctional Institution at Sommers, states that 34% of the offender population experienced a sexual dysfunction during the attack. This ranged from a complete inability to achieve an erection, to difficulty in ejaculating.[15] Indeed, this study and others have shown that in many cases of rape there is no ejaculation even when penetration is made and long periods of time are spent. This and other similar data support the position that rape is a crime committed to fulfill needs which are not basically sexual in origin. If, therefore, this is an accurate interpretation of the causal factors for rape, then castration would be an ineffective means of preventing continued sexually aggressive behavior for in many cases the rapist is essentially castrated already. In addition, castration would not necessarily prevent the offender from carrying out his crime, but would mean only that it would be necessary to accomplish the desired control and sense of power in another manner. Perhaps by using an instrument (a common practice) in place of the penis. It might be argued that mandatory castration, because of the severity of the punishment, would deter other would-be rapists. There is no empirical basis for this assumption, of course, for such a sanction almost certainly would not pass an Eighth Amendment challenge in our present court system. Additionally, one need but become familiar with the type of activity engaged in by many rapists such as forced anal then oral intercourse (this and similar type behavior is not uncommon during a rape). This is clearly an attempt to demean and humiliate the victim that goes beyond any recognizable sexual need.

The other common social myth concerning rape is that women invite rape by their style of dress. Or they expose themselves to danger by traveling dark alley ways or frequenting sleazy bars. A mere cursory examination of the facts quickly disproves these erroneous assumptions. First of all, most rapes occur in the home of the victim, (45% in the state of Arkansas),[16] not in some bar or dark alley. The majority of the remainder take place in the victim's automobile, place of employment, or the residence of a friend or family member. Furthermore, 59% of all rapes are committed in Arkansas by an assailant known to the victim.[17] This figure is most likely higher than reported, for the victim may be reluctant to divulge the name of the attacker out of fear of reprisal, or shame. A more disturbing fact yet is that 14% of all rapes in Arkansas are committed by one family member against another.[18]

To debunk the other rape myth — that is that the rapist has no outlet for his sexual tension but rape — one need not rely on crime statistics or psychological theory. First of all, it is evident that the type of activity involved in most rapes goes beyond a desire for just sexual release. Also, how reasonable is it to assert that anyone must rape in light of the liberal attitude most people have about engaging in intercourse today. Likewise, prostitution is always a viable option. Prostitutes are available in a wide variety of types and price ranges, from a few dollars to several hundred. Moreover, if a man is willing to pay enough, or will compromise on appearance or age, he may indulge virtually any sexual desire he wishes

If, however, more formal means of persuasion are needed, it should be considered that a study by Burgess and Groth demonstrates that at least one-third of all convicted rapists were married and living with their wives at the time they committed the offense. Many others had live-in girl friends.[19]

There is an abundance of additional information, both empirical and intuitive, available which supports the above stated facts.

Rape of women in the free world and the rape of offenders in correctional institutions are crimes of violence! Both involve the use of sex as a weapon to humiliate and gain power and control over the victim.[20] Unfortunately, there are many myths regarding victims of rape that cloud our preception of the problem. These myths result in emotional superstitions that are rarely directed towards other victims of physical violence. The purpose of this session is to challenge those myths. It is our hope that by putting these myths to rest correctional professionals, such as yourself, will take a more objective and non-judgmental approach to victims of sexual harrassment/assault within the institution.

By exploring some of the common myths regarding the rape of women in the free world, we can draw some parellels between these myths and similar myths regarding victims of sexual assault within correctional institutions.

What are some myths regarding rape in the free world?

1. The offender is a sexual pervert.
2. Women use a cry of rape to get even with a man for some real or imagined wrong.
3. Women provoke rape by dressing in a provocative manner, by teasing the man, or by leading him on. Women are, therefore, responsible for making themselves victims.
4. Women invite rape by frequenting disreputable establishments, or traveling into dark and deserted areas.
5. A healthy adult woman cannot be forcibly raped unless she cooperates.
6. The rapist is a sexual deprived man; just a lonely misfit without any other outlet for his natural desires.

All of these myths are destructive. They either lead to ineffective and emotional solutions (e.g., mandatory castration) or further victimize the victim — "It's her own fault," or "She must have welcomed the assault since she didn't fight."

Furthermore, all of these myths are based on a common misconception — that is, rape is a crime that is committed for sexual fulfillment. Let's examine this misconception further.

Evidence that disproves the idea of rape as a crime for sexual fulfillment comes from a variety of sources. One study, conducted by Dr. A. Nicholas Groth, director of the Correctional Institute at Sommers, offers particularly convincing evidence. Dr. Groth reported that 34% of the offender population studied experienced a sexual dysfunction during the attack.[21] The reported sexual dysfunctions range from complete inability to achieve an errection to difficulty in ejaculating. Indeed, in many cases there was no ejaculation even when there was penetration for long periods of time.

The notion that rape is a crime committed to fulfill needs which are not basically sexual in orgin is supported by other evidence. For example, the type of activity involved in many rapes (e.g., forced anal then oral intercourse) goes beyond a desire for just sexual release. The more likely explanation is that these activities are an attempt to demean and humiliate the victim.

Also, it's unlikely that most rapist commit their crimes because of lack of normal sexual outlets. A study by Burgess and Groth reported that at least one-third of all convicted rapists studied were married and living with their wives at the time they committed the offense.[22] Many others had live-in girlfriends. This, added to the availability of prostitutes and the liberal attitudes many people hve about engaging in sexual intercourse today, makes it very difficult to conclude that these men acted out of sexual deprivation.

Finally, many of the myths discussed earlier are simply not supported by the facts. A mere cursory examination of the statitics disproves the idea that women invite rape by traveling dark alleyways or frequenting sleazy bars. Most rapes occur in the homes of the victims (45% in the state of Arkansas), not in some bar or dark alley.[23]   The majority of the remainder takes place in the victim's automobile, place of employment, or residence of a friend or family member. Furthermore, 50% of all rapes committed in Arkansas are by an assailant known to the victim.[24]   This figure is most likely higher than reported, for the victim may be reluctant to divulge the name of the attacker out of fear of reprisal, or shame. A more distrubing fact yet is that 14% of all rapes in Arkansas are committed by one family member against another.[25]

Rape is a misunderstood crime. The underlying motivtion for the rapist is not sexual fulfillment but violence and power.

D. RAPE IN PRISON

If public sentiment toward rape in the free world is so out of line with reality, one can only surmise how askew the attitude is toward rape in prison.

It is not an uncommon attitude to consider rape a normal aspect of prison life. There is a tacit acceptance that rape is part of the prison experience, and in fact should serve as a deterrent to crime. This is of course a ludicrous position for only certain inmates are in danger of being raped; primarily those who are young, and/or non-violent offenders. A six-foot-tall, 200-pound, armed robber/murderer has little to worry about as far as being a rape victim in prison. It is, rather, the young thief or drug dealer who is most at risk. If then we seek to present the possibility of rape as a deterrent to crime, it appears we are targeting the wrong group. Would it not be better to arrange to have the violent offenders deterred?

Actually we do much the same thing to the inmate rape victim in prison that we often do to the victim in the free world — that is, place the blame on the victim, and not on the rapist.[26] Consider that the prison victim is often accused of being a closet homosexual (whereas the female victim is accused of being promiscuous) who cooperates and only yells rape if the act is discovered. While this is surely true in some cases, all prison rapes cannot be dismissed in this manner, as they all too often are. This misconception is fueled by the widely-held perception among the public, and many who work in corrections, that homosexual activity is the accepted norm in prison.[27] Accurate figures of between 35% to 40% have been reported by independent researchers for adult correctional facilities, with slightly higher rates for youth institutions.[28] The Federal Bureau of Prisons reports a rate of 28%. These are far below estimates based solely on guess and myth. (It should be noted that the figure is substantially lower in the federal system due primarily to the higher average age of the inmate population.) At first glance, the figure quoted above of 35% to 40% does appear high until it is compared to the general male population which has a rate of 20% to 25% reporting an experience that could be termed homosexual.[29]

The primary difference between the two groups is that for the male in the public there is a greater probability that the experience took place during adolescence. While for the inmate there is more of a likelihood (50%) that the homosexual act was an adult experience. Therefore, the rate of homosexual activity among prison inmates would only reach about 25% of the population if adolescent experiences are discounted. This is, of course, an average figure and would be higher or lower depending on the region from which the population sample is primarily drawn; i.e., urban versus rural. Among both groups, free world and prison, about 3% of the sample described themselves as homosexual or bisexual.[30] Another study put this figure for the inmate population at about 10%.[31] If we accept this and adjust the figures accordingly, the disparity between the two groups is diminished further. That is, if the actual rate of homosexuals in prison is more than three times that of the free world, then the incidence of situational or experimental homosexuality is just about the same for both groups.

It is apparent that homosexual activity does indeed take place in prison, but it certainly is not as pronounced as is generally believed. One researcher suggests that there is comparatively very little sexual activity of any kind in prison. It is suggested that the reason is that prison environment is not conducive to sexual arousal and the inmate's libido will adjust accordingly.[32]

Another similarity between the treatment accorded prison rape victims and free world rape victims is the proposition that rape in prison is due to sexual deprivation. The information supplied above concerning the numbers of inmates involved in consentual homosexuality should dispel this argument. Additionally, it should be noted that prostitution is a thriving institution inside prison as well. It may, therefore, be reasonably inferred that if all that is desired is sexual release, there is an abundant supply of willing partners; 3% to 10% are admitted homosexuals, while at least another 15% to 20% are occasional participants. In fact, the man in prison has much the same type of outlets for sexual release as the man on the outside. He can masturbate, form a long-term relationship, have casual sex, or hire a prostitute.

Just as the level of homosexual activity is exaggerated, so also is the numbers of rapes alleged to happen in prison. This heightened awareness of prison rape is due in a large part to films, t.v. programs, and other popular fiction.[33] The attitude of Hollywood script writers appears to be that rape is a NORMAL facet of prison life, accepted by inmate and correctional staff alike. In many of these dramas the rape issue is dealt with in a comic manner. One notable example would be the Richard Pryor-Gene Wilder film, "Stir Crazy." In this movie the two principal characters spend several minutes attempting to demonstrate their aggressiveness in order to avoid the inevitable sexual assault. The end result is a very funny scene. There is little doubt, however, that any film producer would dare handle the pending rape of a woman in such a comic manner, for to do so would bring charges of extreme insensitivity to the victims of rape. This willingness of film producers to treat inmate rapes as a comic situation is perhaps the clearest indicator of all as to what the actual attitude toward rape in prison is — it's a joke.

The actual incidence of reported rapes in American prisons appears to be from 1% to 3% of the total population.[34] This figure cannot be accurately adjusted for under-reporting because empirical data of sufficient quantity is not available.[35] Some experts suggest that only one-half of prison rapes are reported. Others suggest that the actual figure is only one in five reported, which approaches the under-reporting rate suggested by some experts for women in the free world. The above-stated absence of empirical information notwithstanding, most people will intuitively agree that the under-reporting rate of rape for men is certainly higher than it is for women. But the possibility of sexual assault in prison still remains far below the almost certainty ascribed to it by many.

There are some factors which suggest that indeed the incidence of prison rape could be as low as the 1% to 3% figures quoted above. We know that the victims' fear of retaliation prevents the reporting of many assaults. But balancing this is the lack of privacy and close security of most institutions. In addition, because of the serious nature of the offense and the desire on the part of correctional officials to avoid legal liability, the inmate who informs on another inmate(s) involved in a rape could reasonably expect some type of reward from the system. This policy of rewarding an inmate for information, although normally covert and unofficial, is a common practice in corrections nationwide.

Since the more obvious explanation for prison rape, sexual deprivation, is for the most part invalid, other avenues of inquiry must be examined. The theory which seems most plausible is the proposition that prison rape is supported by subculture norms and, in fact, reflects the subculture value placed on aggression and violence. Wolfgang and Ferracuti in *The Subculture of Violence* (1967),[36] suggest that a violent subculture in our society exists with its own set of values and norms. Norm adoption in this deviant society is the same as for society at large; a psychological process of establishing one's membership by demonstrating those attributes deemed desirable by the culture. In the case of the subculture in question, the norms are markedly different from generally accepted social norms. The attributes most valued are violence, dominance through physical aggression, and a rejection of legitimate authority. Just as other cultures offer rewards and sanctions for certain behavior, so also does the subculture in question reward and censure its members. The rewards in question are a dark simile of the prestige and social stature accorded to those who succeed within the confines of legitimate social convention. Many of the rewards available to the general poulation as a whole, such as stability of relationships and moderate financial security, would actually have negative prestige for this group. A man who prospers because he works hard and saves his money would be regarded as weak in this subculture. By comparison, the man who takes what another has worked for establishes himself as strong, which equates to success.

Amir (1971) first applied this theory of a violent subculture to rape, showing a similarity of rapists to other violent offenders.[37] His work suggests that rape is regarded as a further indice of success among the subculture group. Even in circumstances where several attackers subdue a lone victim,[38] it is still accorded high positive prestige for among this group aggression is closely related to sexuality. It might reasonably be argued that predominantly accepted social norms are not substantially different as regards the connection between sex and aggression. This is a valid point with a very significant variation, however. Whereas, the subculture member demonstrates his masculinity by being directly sexually aggressive, the cultural norm for most of society is that displays of physical prowess such as participation in contact sports, is sufficient to establish one as sexually desirable. The actual goal is to validate one's masculinity. Other activities which carry high positive prestige in contemporary male society also serve as means by which masculine validation can be achieved. Examples would range from having an occupation with high prestige such as a doctor or rock star, or those vocations which possess a possibility of danger and excitement, such as a policeman or fighter pilot. For the most part, these positions are not easily attainable goals for those commonly exposed to the subculture environment due to social conditions. Only the very talented or dedicated are able to break away. Since there is little access to economic or educatioal indices of status, and few if any responsible male identity figures are available, the lower class male turns to violence to prove his masculinity to himself, and primarily other males.[39]   Moreover, differential association tends to perpetuate the subculture values. Wolfgang and Ferracuti support this position by stating that " . . . aggression is an outcome of learned responses and social conditions and contributing to criminality." And further, subculture participants, " . . . learn values supporting and undergo experiences motivating aggression."[40]

If the attitudes toward rape in the free world are so out of line with reality, one can only begin to surmise how disorted those attitudes are towards rape in prison. Some common beliefs about rape in prison are:

1.   Rape is a normal aspect of prison life.
2.   Rape acts as a deterrent to crime.
3.   The victim is a closet homosexual who cooperates and only yells rape if the act is discovered.
4.   Rape in prison is due to sexual deprivation.

1.   Rape is a normal aspect of prison life: Rape in prison is not as common as people have been led to believe. This heightened awareness of prison rape is due, in large part, to films, T.V. programs, and other popular fiction.[41]   The attitude of Hollywood script writers appears to be that rape is a normal facet of prison life, accepted by inmate and correctional staff alike. In many of these dramas the rape issue is dealt with in a comic manner. One notable example would be "Stir Crazy" which starred Richard Pryor and Gene Wilder. In this movie, the two principal characters spend several minutes attempting to demonstrate their aggressiveness in order to avoid the inevitable sexual assault. The end result is a very funny scene. This willingness of film producers to treat inmate rape as a comic situation is perhaps the clearest indicator of all as to what the actual attitude toward rape in prison is — it's a joke.

The percentage of **reported** rapes relative to the total prison population in America is from ½% to 3%.[42]   The accuracy of these figures for estimating the **actual** percentage of rapes is questionable, however, because of the lack of empirical data of sufficient quantity to determine the rate of under-reporting.[43]   Some experts suggest that only one-half of prison rapes are reported. Others suggest that the actual figure is only one in five reported, which approaches the under-reporting rate suggested by some experts for women in the free world. The above-stated absence of empirical information notwithstanding, most people will intuitively agree that the under-reporting rate of rape for men in prison is certainly higher than it is for women. Nevertheless, the possibility of sexual assault in prison still remains far below the almost certainly ascribed to it by many.

2.   Rape is a deterrent to crime. Those who rape as a common part of prison life, often argue that it serves as a deterrent to crime. This is, of course, a ludicrous position for only certain inmates are in danger of being raped; primarily those who are young, and have committed non-violent offenses such as theft of drug dealing. A six foot-tall, 200-pound offender, convicted of armed robbery/murder is unlikely to be raped in prison. Thus, if rape is a deterrent to crime, it appears to be targeting the young group. Wouldn't it be better to arrange to have violent offenders deterred?

3.   Inmate rape victims are closet homosexuals who cooperate and only yell rape it the act is discovered. While this is surely true is some cases, most prison rapes cannot be dismissed in this manner. Again, this is an example of blaming the victim.[44]

This misconception that most inmate rape victims are homosexual is fueled by the widely-held perception among the public, and many who work in corrections, that homosexual activity is the accepted norm in prison.[45] While homosexual activity certainly does take place in prison, it is not as pronounced as generally believed. Independent researchers have estimated the incidence of homosexual activity to be between 35% to 40% of the inmate population in adult correctional facilities, with slightly higher rates for youth institutions.[46] The Federal Bureau of Prisons reports a rate of 28%. (Homosexual activity is probably lower in the federal system due primarily to the higher average age of the inmate population.)

The figures above appear high until one compares them to figures on the general male population. Studies of males in the general population indicate that 20% to 25% report an experience that could be termed homosexual.[47] The primary difference between the two groups is that for males in the general public there is a greater probability that the experience took place during adolescence. In contrast, for prison inmates there is a greater probability that the homosexual act was an adult experience (50%). Therefore, the rate of homosexual activity among prison inmates would only reach about 25% of the population if adolescent experiences are discounted. This is, of course, an average figure and would be higher or lower depending on the region from which the population sample is primarily drawn; i.e., urban vs. rural. Among both groups, free world and prison, about 3% of the sample described themselves as homosexual or bisexual.[48] Another study put this figure for the inmate population at about 10%.[49] If we accept this and adjust the figures accordingly, the disparity between the two groups is diminished further. That is, if the actual rate of true homosexuality in prison is more than three times that of the free world, then the incidence of situational or experimental homosexuality is just about the same for both groups.

It is apparent that homosexual activity does indeed take place in prison, but it certainly is not as pronounced as is generally believed. One researcher suggests that there is comparatively very little sexual activity of any kind in prison. It is suggested that the reason is that prison environment is not conducive to sexual arousal and the inmate's libido will adjust accordingly.[50]

4.   **Rape in prison is due to sexual deprivation.** The prison environment does deprive the offenders of female sexual companions. However, just as male sexual relationships with women need not result in rape, consensual sexual relations are possible for inmates and prostitution is common inside prison. Overall, it can be reasonably argued that any male in prison has much the same type of outlets for sexual release as the man on the outside — he can masturbate, form a long-term relationship, have casual sex, or hire a prostitute.

Prison Rape as an Act of Violence: Since the most common explanation for prison rape, sexual deprivation, is for the most part invalid, other possibilities must be examined. The theory which seems most plausible is that prison rape is supported by subculture norms which value aggression and violence. Wolfgang and Ferracuti in *The Sub-Culture of Violence* (1967)[51]   suggest that a violent subculture in our society exists with its own set of values and norms. Norm adoption in this deviant society is the same as for society at large; members establish themselves as part of the culture by demonstrating those attributes deemed desirable by the culture. In the case of the violent subculture the attributes most valued are violence, dominance through physical aggression, and a rejection of legitimate authority. Many of the rewards available to the general society actually have negative prestige for this group. A man who prospers because he workd hard and saves his money would be regarded as weak. By comparison, the man who takes what another has worked for establishes himself as strong, which equates to success.

Amir (1971) first applied this theory of a violent subculture to rape, showing a similiarity of rapists to other violent offenders.[52] His work suggests that rape is regarded as a mark of success among the subculture group. Furthermore, sexual aggressiveness, even in circumstances where several attackers subdue a lone victim,[53] is considered a sign of masculinity.

Although aggression is seen as a valued masculine trait in the general population, this subculture takes it to an extreme. Whereas, the subculture member demonstrates his masculinity by being overly sexually aggressive, the culture norm for most of society is that displays of physical prowess, such as participation in contact sports, is sufficient to establish oneself as exually desirable. Other activities, such as high perstige occupations or vocations which possess a possibility of danger and excitement, also serve as a means for masculine validation. Due to social conditions these positions are not easily attainable for those commonly exposed to the subculture environment. Thus, the subculture male may be unable to achieve masculine identification and pride through avenues other than sex.[54] Sex, therefore, becomes the expression of aggression and the victimization of others. Moreover, differential association tends to perpetuate the subculture values. Wolfgang and Ferracuti support this position by stating that ". . . aggression is an outcome of learned responses and social conditions and contributing to criminality." And further, subculture participants, ". . . learn values supporting and undergo experiences motivating aggression."[55]

It is no place in this subculture more evident, and dominant, than prison. To a great extent, the inmate population of American prisons is made up of men from the social strata that includes this subculture of violence. They carry into prison with them the value system discussed above, and in the rarefied prison environment the need to demonstrate masculinity by displays of violence becomes intensified. The sexual domination of another is a very important facet of the subculture system. It is perhaps even more so in the prison environment with it's extreme emphasis on masculinity and aggression.

In conclusion, rape in prison is not primarily motivated by the frustration of sexual needs. Sex in prison occurs for the same reasons it occurs in the community; to hurt, to humiliate, to dominate, to control, and to degrade. It is a way of establishing power because it identifies who is in control and who is controlled.

E. SEXUAL AGGRESSION

In corrections our concerns must not be limited to only rape. The much broader area of sexual aggression must be considered. This is important if, for no other reason than, it appears that sexual aggressive episodes in prison are progressive; i.e., the incidents often are initially verbally abusive and increase in intensity to physically abusive, culminating in a sexual attack.

According to Lockwood, 28% of all inmates entering the correctional setting will be the victim of some form of sexual aggression.[56] When we narrow our sample to include only those in the prime target group, the percentage of those abused jumps to 71%.[57] Aggression runs the gamut from a polite request for sex to brutal forced sodomy. As stated earlier, few inmates are actually raped. However, many, if not most, of a certain group of inmates, are harassed, which is the primary form of abuse.

You might question how a polite request for sex constitutes abuse, but place yourself in the position of the target for a moment. You have entered prison with the same misconception about inmate rape as the general public — that is virtually **all** young first offenders are raped. A larger, older, obviously experienced inmate comes over to you, compliments you on your appearance and asks if you would allow him to have anal and/or oral intercourse with you. He assures you that he has good personal hygiene, and will be very gentle. He offers in return to protect you and provide you with items such as cigarettes, drugs or commissary items. How do you feel? Angry? Threatened? Frightened? Humiliated?

To be propositioned by another man is so psychologically devastating to the average male in our culture that it cannot be done in a non-offensive manner. The reaction would be even more acute when a man is asked to play the passive or feminine role. This is the real key to target reaction. A request for sex from a man questions the masculinity of the target. The implication is that the target is not perceived as a man **sexually** and therefore is not a true man. Under these circumstances the only reasonable reaction for the target is a negative one. And, even if the aggressor(s) continues to frame the request in a non-threatening manner, the target cannot accept it as anything but a threat for it threatens his very identity.

We recognize now that women have the right to be protected in the work place from the unwanted advances of co-workers. In fact, several successful lawsuits have been brought by women who allege that a male supervisor or co-worker repeatedly asked for a date or attempted to involve them in a relationship. The behavior on the part of the man in these cases is considered harassment because it is unwanted. The same theory applies to the inmate. Any unwanted advance constitutes harassment, and the courts have demonstrated a willingness to punish those correctional personnel who do not protect the inmate from such treatment.[58]

Very often the harassment, although still only verbal, is more aggressive in nature. These statements are usually vulgar or are prison slang. Even the target who is not initiated into the prison culture understands these taunts are threats. The aggressors watch the target closely, for his reaction to the provocative remarks will determine if he is a suitable target and if so the tactics to use. These episodes may go beyond just talk and include touching or grabbing of the buttocks, genitals, etc. These incidents take place in cells, common areas, showers, recreation rooms or yards; basically, any place security personnel are not present.

The next form of abuse is overt threats of violence. (The aggressor may act alone but usually with one or more others.) A weapon may be displayed in an attempt to further intimidate the target. More often, the disparity in size between the target and aggressor or the presence of more than one aggressor is sufficient, so a weapon is not needed. This will lessen the risk of punishment for the aggressor in the event of discovery. The target may be slapped or shoved around in an attempt to convince him the threats are serious. The aggressors will avoid, if possible, leaving marks or bruises which would substantiate the allegations of abuse.

In a very small percentage of cases there is an attempted or actual rape. The force used may be threts or a weapon. The victim may be knocked down, held, and; or, be forced to perform felatio literally with a knife to his throat. These incidents can include one or several attackers. The actual physical injury to the victim could be very little or extensive. Just as with the rape of a woman in the free world, the physical damage resulting from the attack may not exceed that experienced during consensual intercourse. This makes rape hard to prove from an evidentiary standpoint. Weaker inmates may be forced to serve as virtual sex slaves by strong, more aggressive inmates because they are aware that the chance of proving they were raped is slight. Most often it is their word against several others. And, since they cannot prove the rape by the evidence , they expose themselves to a certain danger of retaliation for snitching.

INTRODUCTION

Recognition of potential targets may be the most effective method of preventing sexual victimization available to correctional personnel. Once an inmate has been identified as a probable target, measures can be taken to lessen the likelihood of his being victimized. It is, therefore, very important that correctional personnel be able to identify probable victims.

Any officer who has spent even the minimum amount of time at a unit can recognize most potential targets. This section does not, therefore, impart new knowledge to the experienced officer, but rather helps him/her to formalize existing experiences into a usable outline. The following information profiles the prime target for sexual abuse.

PERFORMANCE OBJECTIVES

B.   Section II: By the end of this session participants will be able to:

1.   List and discuss the 7 attributes of inmates who are targets of sexual harrassment/assault in the prison setting.

2.   Describe the 3 special classes of inmates that are targets of sexual harrassment/assault in the prison setting.

3.   Identify the 4 most common reactions of targets to sexual aggression.

4.   Describe the three stages of the "Rape Trauma Syndrome."

D.   TARGET REACTION TO ATTACK

Target reaction to an attack can be a viable diagnostic tool. Unfortunately, it may be too late, after reaction has manifested, to stop initial abuse, but subsequent abuse can be prevented. And, abuse of future targets may be prevented by identifying aggressors. The following is a list of behavior patterns indicative of an attack:

1. **RAPE TRAUMA SYNDROME:**   Leading experts, Donald J. Cotton and A. Nicholas Groth, state that the reaction of a male in prison to sexual victimization is for the most part identical to the bio-physcho-social impact of sexual assault on a female in the community.[87]

   The following information is quoted from the Arkansas Law Enforcement Training Academy Rape Investigation Course Manual,[88]   with deletions and additions applicable to this program.

   The Rape Trauma Syndrome was developed by two Drs. Burgess and Holstrom. It gives a title to the list of usual symptoms and reactions of rape victims. (There is no typical victim just like there is no usual rapist.) But after researching thousands of rape victims, they found some common factors found.[89]

Impact Stage

This is the immediate reaction right after the attack. Reactions may be expressed or controlled and may be one or all of the following:

   Shock: Automatic pilot comes on and person starts responding as they normally do. If this response does not work, crisis sets in.
   Denial: Refusing or avoiding talking or thinking about the incident. Wants to forget it. This is usually a short-lived but immediate defense (especially if this is their usual coping pattern). Most authorities misinterpret this reaction—they expect hysteria.
   Rationalization: Involves much talking and repeating the same things over and over — often may be void of emotion. Just a verbal processing of thoughts "what ifs and why did I's, etc," These are non-rational cognitive responses.

Acute Stage

This stage may last 4-6 weeks after the attack and occurs when the usual coping behavior has not worked and a stage of disorganization sets in—crisis. The symptoms manifest themselves as:

   Physical: Fatigue, soreness, pain, etc. Some are real and some are psychosomatic. It is important to determine the difference although both are real to the victim and are common.

Sleep pattern disturbances are common. The victim usually has trouble sleeping or fitful nights when they wake and cannot go back to sleep. Some will have nightmares and wake up screaming, etc.

Eating pattern disturbances can include decreased appetite, nausea and vomiting, or stomach pains (real or imagined).

Symptoms specific to focus of attack could be the mouth and throat — irritation caused by oral sex; rectal pain, bleeding, swelling, etc. caused by anal sex.

   Emotional: Primary symptom found by Burgess and Holstrom was fear — fear of death, injury, multilation, etc. This fear explains the range of symptoms associated with the rape trauma syndrome —acute stress reaction. The victim feels a combination of 'thankful to be alive' and 'fear of death' which is related to a loss of control. Burgess and Holstrom also found shame, guilt, anger, etc., but it was not as common or the primary focus of a victim's reactions.

—21—

Thoughts — Cognitive: Victims will often try to suppress thoughts of attack but subconscious seldom lets you do that. Often when this approach is used, the victim suffers from flashbacks and nightmares. Most go through a rationalization process throughout the duration of syndrome — "What if . . .", "If only I had . . .", "Why did it happen to me?"

Long Term Reorganization/Recoil Stage

Gradually the victim resumes healthy coping patterns and begins a healing time — time when the real therapeutic work is done. Issues are dealt with and resolved. Previous level of functioning will hopefully be regained.

Disruption in 4 areas of life:

Physical: Muscular pain, urinary problems, gastrointestinal complaints.

Psychological: Flashback, nightmares, etc. Two types of guilt; couldn't get away — guilt at failure; used force to regain control.

Social: "Unlike the rape victim in the community who can change address, job, lifestyle, and relationships, the inmate victim is not able to make such changes to regain a sense of self-control, and the recovery process may be delayed until he is released from the institution and is able to regain a feeling of personal control once again. Even then, the recovery process may remain incomplete." (Cotton and Groth)[90]

Sexual: The victim may worry about his ability to perform sexually,[91] and just as with women, thoughts of the attack may be difficult to suppress during sexual intercourse later with a wife or girlfriend. This is further compounded by feelings of sex role confusion. One researcher has suggested that the victim may adopt a homosexual lifestyle[92] after release as a method of rationalizing his failure to prevent the attack and his subsequent victimization. It may be more acceptable to the male ego to be a homosexual than to be a victim, especially if the attacks are repeated.

2. **SUICIDAL:** As previously mentioned, the possibility of suicidal gestures is high for a target or victim. If an inmate who fits the target profile makes threats or attempts suicide, a thorough investigation should be conducted to determine if the subject has been victimized.

3. **ESCAPE:** This area was also covered earlier, but bears repeating. Correctional personnel should consider that for an inmate this may seem to be the only alternative to rape, particularly if the security staff has exhibited a callous attitude toward the issue of sexual abuse.

4. **AGGRESSIVE BEHAVIOR:** Inmates who fit the target profile and are involved in numerous fights should be considered prime candidates for victimization.[93] The fights may reflect attempts at self defense. Also, victimization produces violence in a ripple effect. Once accultured to violence by the aggressive episode, the inmate victim very often adopts the prison norm for violence. Unfortunately, he carries this new attitude of violence back to the streets when he leaves prison.

INTRODUCTION

Aggressor profiling, while a valuable tool from a standpoint of prevention, is not as valuable as target profiling for there is a very strong correlation between the target profile and subsequent victimization. We can state, with a high degree of accuracy, that an inmate who looks and acts in a certain manner will be a target. The same degree of accuracy cannot be claimed as regards aggressor profiling. Perhaps the most important benefit to be derived from the following section is a basic understanding of aggressor psycho-sexual attitudes.

PERFORMANCE OBJECTIVES:

C. Section III: By the end of this session participants will be able to:

1. List and discuss the 7 attributes of inmate aggressors.

2. Describe the 3 primary operating styles of inmate aggressors.

C. RECOGNITION OF AGGRESSOR ACTIVITY

By accurate identification of high probability aggressors, security staff can intervene early in the victimization process, before the acute stages occur and the target suffers physical or psychological injury.

a. Beware of known aggressors in the inmate population. Strong arm tactics are usually preceded by verbal harassment. Watch for the other cues as well, such as grouping of probable aggressors, friendly overtures made toward potential targets by aggressors in an attempt to lure them into a trap, and subtle intimidation in the showers, exercise yard or elsewhere.

b. Watch for con games intended to trap the target by making loans or allowing unrestricted credit. The exorbitant rate of interest charged can quickly make repayment impossible by any means other than sex.

c. Controlling gang-related activity is nearly impossible in some correctional systems. Because the gangs are often so well organized, correctional personnel must be prepared to act at once when they become aware an inmate is in danger.

d. All blatant sexual harassment, such as taunting new commitments, must not be tolerated. When correctional officers stand idle while this type activity goes on, it sends a message of tacit approval to the inmate aggressor.

D. PROFILE OF AN ATTACK

The following is a summary of an investigative report of a rape which allegedly took place at one of the units of the Arkansas Department of Correction. The names of the victim and the assailants have been changed; all other information was taken unchanged from the report.

A brief profile of each participant is provided for purposes of comparison.

RED	Age 35	Ht. 5'6"	Wt. 109
	Priors: 0	Offense: Carnal Abuse	
YELLOW	Age 33	Ht. 5'8"	Wt. 195
	Priors: 2	Offense: Burglary; Grand Larceny; Theft; Aggravated Robbery	
GREEN	Age 29	Ht. 5'10"	Wt. 162
	Priors: 2	Offense: Burglary & Robbery	
BLUE	Age 32	Ht. 5'11"	Wt. 179
	Priors: 2	Offense: Receiving Stolen Property; Resisting Arrest	
ORANGE	Age 22	Ht. 5'7"	Wt. 151
	Priors: 1	Offense: Burglary; Grand Larceny	

The alleged victim is a 35-year-old, white male. Inmate Red, received on August 3, 19___, from Blank County, was sentenced to two years for First Degree Carnal Abuse. Inmate Red, who is past his parole eligibility date, will flatten his sentence on March 12, 19___.

At 12:09 p.m. I interviewed Inmate Red. Inmate Red, in discussing the matter, was initially confused concerning the date of the alleged rape. After thinking for several moments, he positively stated that the incident occurred on the "Saturday before last". That would have been February 7, 19___. Inmate Red, in his earlier statement to the Captain, had indicated that the alleged assault took place on Friday, February 6, 19___. However, he seemed confident about the incident occurring on February 7. I, therefore, used that date in interrogating other witnesses.

Inmate Red stated that on February 7, 19___, at approximately 11:00 p.m., he was lying on his bed attempting to go to sleep. He said that Inmate Blue approached him and said, "I want you to do something for me." Inmate Red said, "No, I'm going to sleep." Inmate Blue then left. A few minutes later Inmate Green came and sat on Inmate Red's lockerbox near the head of Inmate Red's bed. Inmate Green said that he wanted Inmate Red to go to a private room and "do something" for Inmate Green. Inmate Red responded by saying, "No, I'll stay where I am and go to sleep." Inmate Green then asked several more times and Inmate Red refused in each instance. Inmate Green then began threatening Inmate Red. Inmate Red was unclear concerning exactly what was said. Inmate Red continued to refuse and Inmate Green left the area.

Inmate Red, who believed he would be safer in the day room with other people, went to the day room. Inmate Red stood in the day room for a few minutes and then went toward his bed. However, when Inmate Red started up the hall to his bunk he had to pass the "private room" on the north side of the building. Inmate Green and Inmate Blue were standing in the doorway of the private room. They blocked the hall and began threatening Inmate Red. Inmate Red then went back to the day room.

In the day room Inmate Orange also propositioned Inmate Red. Inmate Orange threatened Inmate Red when his proposition was refused. Inmate Orange continued to badger Inmate Red even when Inmate Red moved from place to place. Inmate Orange's comments were made in a low tone of voice. Inmate Red did not advise the building officer that he was having problems. After a few minutes Inmate Orange stopped sexually propositioning Inmate Red.

Inmate Red claimed that he believed the officer was uninterested in protecting him. He had no explanation for that belief. Thus when he started toward his bed and was again verbally accosted by Inmate Green, he decided to capitulate to avoid violence. He went with Inmate Green into a private room.

Once in the room, Inmate Green gave Inmate Red a can of Royal Crown hair grease to lubricate himself. Inmate Red entered the walk-in closet, pulled his underwear down, greased his rectum, and allowed Inmates Green, then Yellow, and finally Blue to sodomize him. Inmate Red then pulled his pants up and went to bed.

Inmate Red said that he did not advise staff of the problem because he was frightened and ashamed. He said he finally told staff because he feared that it would happen again.

> **NOTE:** With the aide of an unnamed informant and the use of polygraph tests, it was established that the victim's report was accurate.

This incident is fairly typical in all respects except the age of the victim. As pointed out earlier, aggressors would naturally prefer a young, attractive target, but other considerations may be more important such as size and availability.

Some of the important points to be drawn from this case are:

1. The victim's size, in relation to the aggressors', made physical resistance pointless.

2. His commitment offense made him a social outcast, negating any possible peer support.

3. The multiple aggressors were successful, when the lone aggressor failed.

4. The victim demonstrated behavior consistent with rape trauma syndrome; i.e., confusion, fear, shame, etc.

5. The victim violated the "convict code" only after he was threatened with another rape.

6. The victim took as much evasive action as possible before submitting.

The scarcity of verifiable facts in the preceding report graphically demonstrates the problems associated with proving a rape has taken place. Many times it is simply one inmate's word against several others, for there is little if any objective evidence. Even the physical evidence obtained during a medical examination may only prove there was intercourse. Other evidence is necessary to establish if it was forced or consenual.

INTRODUCTION

Prevention of sexual abuse within the institution must be a high priority task for correctional personnel. The preceding discussion of legal liability, administrative problems, and the possibility of injury to inmates or staff is ample justification for maximum efforts directed toward prevention. In addition, the nature of the offense raises the need for prevention to the level of a moral obligation for correctional personnel. The following is a summary of possible measures.

PERFORMANCE OBJECTIVES:

D.   Section IV: By the end of this session participants will be able to:

1.   Explain the importance of security measures in the prevention of sexual harrasment/assault.

2.   Identify 4 guidelines for identifying aggressor and intervening before the target suffers physical or psychological injury.

3.   Explain the procedure that must be used when an assualt is suspected.

4.   Explain the procedures which must be followed in cases of known or reported sexual assualt.

A. PREVENTION

1. **SECURITY:** The most effective method of preventing sexual abuse is the presence of security. Rapes have taken place in virtually every area of the institution. Davis reported seven assaults in transportation vans.[121] By following good sound security procedures, such as: 1. policing the assigned area regularly but at varied times; 2. being aware of new inmate assignments to the barracks, 3. determining if the new inmate fits either the aggressor or target profile, and 4. observing the interaction of new inmates with the existing population, the correctional officer can be the most effective preventive measure available.

2. **SPECIAL CLASSIFICATION OF POTENTIAL TARGETS:** Obvious or suspected targets may be protected from aggressors by being assigned to a special area of the institution.[122] Often this is a tier or barracks where all the targets, plus known homosexuals, are housed. This often presents a problem for the target. Being assigned to the "punk barracks", as it is often called, stigmatizes the inmate. Regardless what his sexual preference is, the assumption is that he is homosexual. Being labeled such is so repugnant to many men that they choose the dangers of regular population assignment rather than be regarded as homosexual and/or weak.[123] Unfortunately, being assigned to a protective area may carry unavoidable penalties, aside from the stigma of assignment, such as restricted job or vocational opportunities. In some systems this may actually hinder the inmate's chance for parole. Failure to participate in educational or vocational programs may limit the amount of good time an inmate receives, and non-participation prevents correctional personnel from accurately evaluating efforts at rehabilitation on the inmate's part. Special assignment may prevent the target from being attacked, but it certainly doesn't prevent abuse; it may actually bring an increase in the amount of verbal abuse an inmate suffers. Sadly, this abuse comes not only from the inmate population, but also from callous and nonthinking staff who refer to the protective assignment area as the "punk barracks" or the "sissy company", and who, along with the inmate population, label the men housed there as weak and homosexual.

3. **SPECIAL CLASSIFICATION OF KNOWN AGGRESSORS:** Since special classification for targets often has the net effect of punishing the target, the logical conclusion seems to be to lock up the aggressors. This, however, is difficult due to the absence of actual evidence of prohibited behavior. Many times all that exists is an unsubstantiated allegation by the target or observation by staff of behavior which fits the aggressor profile. These circumstances normally will not support administrative action for the inmate's due process rights require objective, concrete evidence before he can be deprived of any rights or privileges. However, if the suspected aggressor has a past history of sexually assaultive behavior, then administration action may be taken. This action may entail reassignment to a high visibility job and living area where the inmate can be more closely observed by staff, or transfer to another unit with fewer potential targets and a higher level of security. In most cases, the aggressor's actions are not so overt as to justify these measures and it is up to the security staff to monitor the suspected inmate's activity and be prepared to intervene.

4. **NEW COMMITMENT ORIENTATION:** Another effective measure in combating sexual aggression is orientation of new commitments. Many times new inmates become victims of sexual aggression because they misinterpret the actions of the aggressors. They don't understand that the offer of protection or of commissionary items from an older inmate is not merely a friendly gesture, but is instead payment for further sexual favors. They are unaware that the convict code supports a demand for sex as payment. When they refuse the demand, the aggressor is justified under the code to use force to collect the debt. The aggressor takes advantage of the target's naivete. If the target is prepared, however, he can avoid the debt and the subsequent obligation to pay with his body. It also helps if the new commitment is aware that the majority of inmates are not involved in homosexual activity. (Very often the target is assured that everybody does it, so you should too.) By making the new commitment aware of the dangers of sexual attack, he can protect himself by avoiding entanglements with aggressor types and also by staying clear of isolated areas where attacks may be carried out. Orientation would also be an ideal time to advise potential aggressors that homosexual acts, especially forced ones, are a violation of departmental rules, and state law. Also, these acts are considered serious violations and will be punished to the full extent allowed by departmental policy and state law. Further, it can be stressed that homosexual activity is a significant factor in the spread of sexually transmitted disease — especially A.I.D.S. (Appendix #1)

B.   INTERVENTION

Intervention in suspected or actual instances of abuse should take place at once. The longer the episodes last the more potential for violence there is. If security can intervene early in the victimization pattern, the target will be spared additional psychological or physical injury. There is also a danger that the target will react in a violent manner toward the aggressor. Correctional personnel must always be aware that, regardless whom the initial subject for violence is, they could ultimately be the one to suffer injury. These situations are highly emotionally charged and create a very dangerous climate for nmate and officer alike. The following intervention protocols are suggested:

1.   SEXUAL AGGRESSION SECURITY PROTOCOL

Sexual assault investigations require a coordinated effort involving unit security, medical personnel, local police agencies, and departmental investigative authorities. To assure that the investigation is handled in the proper manner a supervisory employee should be assigned the role of case manager. It would be his/her responsibility to assure:

1.   that the correct medical and legal procedures are adhered to.

2.   that the appropriate personnel and agencies have been notified.

3.   that all required reports and documentation are complete and in the proper format.

4.   and, produce a final report to the unit administration detailing the incident and what action has been taken.

The following procedures are to be used when an assault is suspected:

1.   Make certain not to endanger the victim during investigation. Protect his identity. Only the minimum number of required personnel should be present during the interview with the inmate.

2.   Interview the suspected victim in a safe area, away from the other inmates.

3.   Use open-ended questions which encourage the inmate to trust you such as, "You seem to be having problems. How can we help you?"

4.   If the inmate denies having any problems assure him that if he does he can talk to a security supervisor, a counselor, or medical personnel now or in the future.

5.   If the inmate confirms the suspicion of assault assure him that the security staff can protect him. Encourage him to identify the aggressor(s) but make certain he understands that he will be helped regardless. If he was raped he should be checked for injury and sexually transmitted disease. Arrange for a mental health evaluation as soon as possible, and place the inmate in a safe area.

The following procedures are to be followed in cases of known or reported sexual assault:

1.   Take immediate steps to isolate the victim from all other inmates and transport to medical services as soon as possible for evaluation and evidence collection. If the assault occurred within 48 hours of discovery, instruct the victim not to wipe, wash, or bathe at all. Do not allow him to smoke, eat, drink, or go to the bathroom prior to the examination.

2. Secure the crime scene until the proper investigative authorities arrive.

3. Obtain a brief statement of the facts from the victim if possible. A more detailed account will be taken later by appropriate authorities.

4. Have the inmate undress standing on a clean sheet placed on the floor. Include the sheet along with the inmate's clothing to be sent to the state crime lab. Any items stained with body fluids (blood, semen, etc.) must be air dried prior to packaging. All articles are to be packaged after drying in new **paper** bags only and sealed with tape. **Plastic bags may not be used under any circumstances**. Sheets, blankets, towels, or items collected are to be handled in the same manner.

5. After sealing all evidence label as follows:

Collected From: _____
            NAME   DOC #

Collected Where: _____
            BE SPECIFIC

Date: _____

Time: _____

Description of
   Items: _____

Collected By: _____
            NAME   POSITION

6. **Evidence must be handled as little as possible** by as few persons as possible.

7. Arrange mental health evaluation as soon as possible and place inmate in a safe area.

8. The Warden or his designee will notify the Director's Office according to Director Policy, Incident Notification, 8-1-85.

9. Evidence collected from known or suspected assailant(s) should be collected and handled in the exact same manner. It should **not** be examined, dried, packaged, or stored in any area where it could possibly have come into contact with samples or evidence from the alleged victim.

10. Paper bags containing evidence may be placed in a larger paper bag or box for ease of transportation. However, bags containing evidence collected from the victim must not be placed in the same container as bags containing evidence from the assailant(s). When transported the respective containers should not be placed in the same area in the transportation vehicle.

STATE OF ARKANSAS
SEXUAL ASSAULT EVIDENCE COLLECTION KIT INSTRUCTIONS
(FOR MEDICAL PERSONNEL)

This kit has been designed to assist the examining physician and nurse in the collection of evidentiary specimens from victims of sexual assault for analysis by the State Crime Laboratory. The hospital is not requested or encouraged to analyze any of the specimens/evidence collected in this kit. Any specimens required by the hospital are to be collected with hospital supplies.

Sexual assault is a legal matter for the court to decide and is not a medical diagnosis. The physician should express no conclusions, opinions or diagnosis to the victim or others, nor should this be written in the record.

☐ **STEP 1**   <u>OUTER CLOTHING AND UNDERWEAR COLLECTION</u>

> Note: 1. Wet or damp clothing should be air dried before packaging.
> 2. If patient is not wearing the clothing worn at the time of the alleged assault, collect only the items that are in direct contact with patient's genital area.
> 3. If patient has changed clothing after assault, inform officer in charge so that the clothing worn at the time of the assault may be collected by the police.
> 4. Do not cut through any existing holes, rips or stains in patient's clothing.
> 5. Do not shake out patient's clothing or microscopic evidence will be lost.
> 6. If clothing bags are required, use new paper bags (grocery-type) only.

Place a clean cloth sheet from hospital stock on floor. Instruct patient to stand in center of cloth sheet and carefully disrobe. Collect each item as removed and place in a separate Outer Clothing bag. Collect patient's underwear and place in Underwear bag. (If any foreign debris, such as dirt, leaves, fiber, hair, etc. falls onto cloth sheet, place in envelope from hospital stock.) Seal all bags and write patient's name, collector's and date on the bag.

☐ **STEP 2**   <u>ORAL SWABS</u>

> Note: Do not moisten swabs prior to sample collection.

Using both swabs simultaneously, carefully swab the buccal area and gum line. Allow both swabs to air dry. Return swabs to the ORAL SWABS envelope. Seal and fill out all information requested on envelope.

☐ **STEP 3**   <u>VAGINAL SWABS AND SMEAR</u>

> Note: Do not stain or chemically fix smear. Do not moisten swabs prior to sample collection.

Remove all components from envelope. Using two swabs simultaneously, carefully swab the vaginal vault, then put swabs used aside to air dry.

Using the two additional swabs provided, repeat the swabbing procedure. Then prepare one smear on the slides provided. Allow swabs (4) and smear (1) to air dry. Return smear to slide holder and the swabs to their original paper sleeves. Mark the sleeve containing the first two swabs collected with "DNA". Return smear and swabs to VAGINAL SWABS AND SMEAR envelope.

☐ **STEP 4**   <u>RECTAL SWABS</u>

> Note: Do not moisten swabs prior to sample collection.

Using both swabs simultaneously, carefully swab the rectal canal. Allow both swabs to air dry. Return swabs to the RECTAL SWABS envelope. Seal and fill out all information requested on envelope.

☐ **STEP 5** **PUBIC HAIR COMBINGS**

Remove paper towel and comb provided in PUBIC HAIR COMBINGS envelope. Place towel under patient's buttocks. Using comb provided, comb pubic hair in downward strokes so that any loose hairs and/or debris will fall onto paper towel. Fold towel in manner to retain both comb and any evidence present. Return to PUBIC HAIR COMBINGS envelope. Seal and fill out all information on envelope.

☐ **STEP 6** **KNOWN SALIVA SAMPLE**

> Note: The patient should not have anything to drink, eat or smoke for a minimum of 15 minutes prior to saliva sample collection.

Remove filter paper disk from SALIVA SAMPLE envelope. Do not touch inner circle. Place folded paper in patient's mouth and instruct patient to thoroughly saturate inner circle with saliva. Allow sample to air dry. Return disk to SALIVA SAMPLE envelope, seal and fill out all information requested on envelope.

☐ **STEP 7** **KNOWN BLOOD SAMPLE**

Using the blood tube provided, and following normal hospital/clinic procedures, draw specimens from patient allowing tube to fill to maximum volume. Place filled blood tube in bubble pack bag and then return to KNOWN BLOOD SAMPLE envelope. Seal and fill out all information requested on envelope.

☐ **STEP 8** **EVIDENCE SUBMISSION SHEET**

Have investigating officer fill out all information requested on form, then return form to you.

FINAL INSTRUCTIONS

1) Make sure all information requested on sample envelopes, bags and the Evidence Submission sheet has been filled out completely.

2) Insert completed evidence Submission Form (see Step 8) in envelope on bottom of kit box.

3) With the exception of the sealed and labeled Clothing bags, return all other evidence/envelopes, used or unused, to kit box.

4) Initial and affix police evidence seals where indicated on kit box.

5) Fill out all information requested on top of kit box under "For Hospital Personnel".

6) Hand sealed kit and sealed bags to investigating officer.*

*Note: If officer is not present at this time, place sealed kit and sealed bags in secure and refrigerated area, and hold for pickup by investigating officer.

CONCLUSION

Correctional personnel must never adopt the attitude that sexually aggressive behavior is acceptable for the inmate population. It is not normal or right anywhere for any person to be forced into a sexual relationship or raped. The emotional scars received often last a lifetime.

That correctional personnel have a legal responsibility to prevent sexual abuse is beyond question. More importantly, we have a moral obligation. If the call to enforce the law or professional pride and ethics are not enough to persuade one to become serious about preventing sexual victimization, then one should put oneself in the place of the victim. If we are not concerned about sexual abuse for any other reason, we should be concerned because it is wrong — the kind of wrong that cannot go unchallenged.

2. EVIDENTIARY AND MEDICAL EXAMINATION

A physical examination should be performed in all cases of sexual assualt, regardless of the length of time which may have elasped between the assault and the examination.

Some victims may ignore symptoms which would ordinarily indicate serious trauma, such as internal injuries sustained by blunt trauma or foreign objects inserted into body orifices. Also, there may be areas of tenderness which will later develop into bruises, but which are not apparent at the time of initial examination.

If the assault occured within 48 hours prior to the examination, then an evidence collection kit should be used.

This examination is to be conducted by appropriate medical personnel. Policy will vary from area to area but usually will require examination by a M.D. or R.N.

The role of security during this phase is limited but important. It is the responsibility of the security staff to assure that the victim does not inadvertently destroy evidence, and is examined as soon as possible. Also, once evidence has been collected it must be handled and transported in the proper manner.

There is no legal requirement that a security officer be present during an examination and it should be avoided. If the examination is to be conducted at a public health facility the transporting officer must decide, based on the past record of the inmate, if it is advisable to permit the inmate to be examined outside the officer's presence.

Since the medical evidentary examination is of such great importance to a successful rape investigation, security personnel should at least be familiar with the procedure. The following is a brief step by step description of an examination using a sexual assault evidence collection kit. (More detailed information may be obtained by referring to the Evidentiary and Medical Protocol, Appendix II.)

BIBLIOGRAPHY

Abarbanel, Stephanie, "Conquering The Mountain." Family Circle, May 17, 1988.

Buffum, Peter C., "Homosexuality in Prison." Washington, D.C.: U.S. Department of Justice, 1978.

California Department of Corrections, "Lesson Plan — Unusual Inmate Behavior."

Clute, Penelope D, The Legal Aspects of Prisons and Jails. Springfield, Illinois: Charles C. Thomas.

Corrections Compendium, January 1988, page 7.

Cotton, Donald J. and A. N. Groth, "Inmate Rape Prevention and Intervention." Journal of Prison and Jail Health, Vol, 2, No. 1: Human Services Press, 1982.

Groth, A. N., Men Who Rape. New York, New York: Plenum, 1979.

Groth, A. N., "Sexual Dysfunction During Rape." New England Journal of Medicine, Vol. 297, No. 4.

Groth, Nicholas A., Ann Wolbert Burgess, Lynda Lytle Holstrom, "Rape: Power, Anger, and Sexuality." American Journal of Psychiatry: Vol. 134, No. 11, American Psychiatry Association, November, 1977.

Hazelwood, Robert R., "The Behavior-Oriented Interview of Rape Victims: The Key to Profiling." FBI Law Enforcement Bulletin, U.S. Justice Department.

Hopper, C. B., "Patterns of Sexual Adjustment Among Prison Inmates." Paper presented at the annual meeting of the Popular Culture Association, Atlanta, Georgia: April 4, 1986.

Jacobs, James B., Stateville: The Penitentiary in Mass Society. Chicago, Illinois: University of Chicago Press.

Johnson, Robert and Hans Toch, The Pains of Imprisonment. Beverly Hills, California: Sage Publications, 1982.

Lockwood, Daniel, Prison Sexual Violence. New York, New York: Elsevier, 1980.

Martin v. White, 742 F.2d 469 (1984).

Moss, Scott C. and Ray E. Hosford, "Sexual Assault in Prison." Psychological Reports, 1979.

Nacci, Peter and Thomas R. Kane, "Sex and Sexual Aggression in Federal Prisons." Federal Bureau of Prisons: Vol. 1, No. 1, 1982.

POSRIP (People Organized to Stop the Rape of Imprisoned People) Bulletin. San Francisco, California, 1988.

Petersen, David M. and Charles W. Thomas, Corrections: Problems and Prospects. Englewood Cliffs, New Jersey: Prentice-Hall, 1980.

Rapeline of Russellville, "What Is Rape? How to Help and What to Do." Russellville, Arkansas, 1985.

Scacco, Anthony, Rape In Prison. Springfield, Illinois: Charles C. Thomas Co., 1975.

Staff, "The Men Who Murder." FBI Law Enforcement Bulletin, August, 1985.

Staff, "Escaping Rape." Woman's Day, August 19, 1986.

Staff, Jail Protocol for Victims of Sexual Assault. San Francisco: Department of Public Health, Sexual Trauma Services.

Van Wormer, Katherine, "Becoming Homosexual In Prison: A Socialization Process." Criminal Justice Review, Vol. 9, No. 1, Page 22-27, Atlanta, Georgia: College of Public and Urban Affairs.

Vedder, Clyde B. and Patricia G. King, Problems of Prison Homosexuality. Springfield, Illinois: Charles C. Thomas Co., 1967.

Williams, Vergil and Mary Fish, Convicts, Codes and Contraband." Cambridge, Massachusettes: Ballinger Publishing Company, 1974.

INMATE ORIENTATION PROGRAM

Orientation should be conducted as soon as possible after the new committment arrives at the institution. It is recommended that an inmate peer counselor, under the supervision of a staff member, conduct the orientation. The supplied text should be followed closely, but enough variation should be allowed to compensate for individual speaking style and special circumstance.

INTRODUCTION:

Now that you are in prison, many of you will be approached by other inmates who want you to have sex with them. It doesn't matter if you are not a homosexual; if you look or act like someone they can get over on they are going to try. You have the right to do your time without being harassed by these people. The following are some ways to help you avoid this problem.

A. Don't talk about sex. Other inmates will think you are hinting that you're interested in a sexual relationship. Also, if you wear your hair and fingernails long you will appear more feminine and could be thought to be inviting sexual advances. Likewise, casual displays of nudity may be thought as a come-on so be careful when you shower or change clothes and be as modest as circumstances allow.

B. Be alert at all times. Don't walk into a setup. Avoid places that are out of the way. Don't let yourself be talked into meeting with another inmate in some dark or hidden place by promises of drugs or booze. He probably has something other than smoking a joint on his mind and will most likely have two or three of his friends with him to hold you while they take what they want — you!

C. Don't get into debt; it's a trap. Don't ask for or accept gifts, loans, or favors. These people will try to get you into debt and then demand that you pay by providing sex for them and their friends. Everything in prison has a price. There are no gifts.

D. If someone tries to talk you into homosexual relationship, make it clear that you're not interested at all! Be firm. No matter what some inmates tell you, most inmates are not involved in homosexual acts and don't think it's o.k. to have sex with other men while you are in prison. Also, homosexual acts are a violation of DOC rules and state law.

E. If someone threatens you, talk to a correctional supervisor (Lieutenant, Captain, Major). It's their job to help you. If you don't want to talk to an officer, you can talk to the Chaplain, a doctor or nurse, your work supervisor, or one of the counselors. You don't have to name the person who threatened you to get help. You will be moved to an area where you will be safe. This is not snitching or being "weak". This is just the way to handle the problem without getting yourself into trouble.

SPECIAL NOTE: NO EMPLOYEE OF THE DEPARTMENT OF CORRECTIONS SHALL AT ANY TIME OR IN ANY MANNER ENCOURAGE AN INMATE TO USE FORCE AGAINST ANOTHER INMATE. LIKEWISE, INMATES FUNCTIONING AS PEER COUNSELORS SHALL NOT IN AMY WAY ADVISE OR SUGGEST THE USE OF FORCE BY ANY INMATE.

Appendix I/2

F. If you find yourself in a position that you feel you are going to be attacked, try to find a correctional officer fast! It will be up to you and you alone to decide what the best course for action is if you can't get away from the attacker(s). There are many things you can consider doing, such as making enough noise to attract attention, or yelling fire, but you must consider the risks and make up your own mind. The smart thing to do is keep your eyes open and avoid the traps mentioned earlier so you are never put in this position.

G. If some inmate(s) forces you to have sex, you need to be examined by the doctor. You could have hidden injuries or V.D. DOC will help you by providing medical and psychological treatment. And with your help, they will keep the sick people that raped you in prison a lot longer.

H. If you are one of the inmates who force others to have sex consider this:

1. If you are caught, criminal charges will be filed against you in the freeworld, plus the DOC will try you inside. You could lose a year's good time, your class, and get a trip to the MAX UNIT. If the freeworld court finds you guilty of rape (a serious felony) you could receive 10 to 40 years or life! Think about it. Is it worth it?

2. If you have trouble controlling your sexual urges, you can talk to a counselor or the DOC can arrange other psychological help.

3. Consider how you make a man feel when you treat him this way. Put yourself in his place for just a minute. No matter who he is, the most valuable thing a man has is his manhood, and you want to rob him of this.

4. When a man has sex with another man it is a homosexual act. You can play all the word games you want to but it won't change that fact. It doesn't matter what you call the man on bottom. If a man wants to have sex with another man he is a homosexual.

5. And finally, what about AIDS? Are you willing to risk your life? That's what you do every time you have sex with the kind of people who are in prison. They are a very high risk group for this disease, and you could catch it. You can't tell by looking if someone has AIDS. It is only in the final stages of the disease that symptons appear. A person could be infected for years before anyone except a doctor could tell. Also it only takes one sexual contact with an AIDS carrier to contract the disease.

Last Revision
02/01/2000

INMATE SEXUAL ASSAULT

PERFORMANCE OBJECTIVES

1. Understand the key aspects of the A.D. 04.01.301, Inmate Sexual Assault Prevention and Intervention.

2. Learn the Department's definition of sexual assault.

3. Be able to define with the characteristics of victims and perpetrators of sexual assault.

4. Develop prevention strategies which can be utilized to minimize episodes of sexual assault during your shift.

5. Learn specific steps to take if an inmate reports an incident of sexual assault to you.

INTRODUCTION

Research indicates that a small percentage of inmates express aggression and seek to dominate others through violent sexual behavior. Forceful and pressured sexual interactions are among the most serious threats to inmate safety and institution order. Victims may suffer physical and psychological harm and could be infected with a life-threatening disease.

DEFINITION

Sexual assault is any unwilling contact between the sex organ of one person and sex organ, mouth, or anus of another person or any intrusion of any part of the body of one person into the sex organ, mouth, or anus of another person by use of force or threat of force, including pressure, threats, or any other actions or communications by one or more persons to force another person to engage in a partial or complete sexual act.

POLICY

It is the policy of the Illinois Department of Corrections to provide a safe and secure environment for all inmates and to maintain a program for the prevention of sexual assaults. Prompt staff intervention shall be provided in the event of a suspected or actual inmate sexual assault.

Consequently, the Department has developed a Sexual Assault Prevention and Intervention Program in order to:

a. Effectively prevent sexual assaultive behavior.

b. Prompt effective reporting and intervention if an assault is suspected or occurs.

c. Prompt investigation, disciplinary action, and referral for prosecution where appropriate.

IMPORTANCE OF INTERVENTION

WHY SHOULD STAFF CARE ABOUT WHETHER YOUTHS AND INMATES ARE
SEXUALLY ASSAULTED OR PRESSURED?

Sexual assault and sexual pressure among prisoners present the institution with potential
management problems, and sexual assaults usually lead to additional, more serious episodes of
inmate-on-inmate violence.

For example, a study done in the 1980's at the United States Penitentiary in Lewisburg reported
that 5 of 8 homicides had a sexual motivation, including sexual pressure. In another study
conducted in California's Correctional System, it was found that during one calendar year, 25%
of inmate-on-inmate aggressive incidents had sexual underpinnings.

If staff do not respond appropriately to a sexual assault or alleged sexual assault, there can be
legal ramifications. For example, at an institution in Florida, a group of inmates filed a lawsuit
in Federal Court complaining that other inmates were threatening them and demanding sexual
favors. The judge ruled in favor of the inmates and fined the superintendent $178,000 to be
divided up between the inmates. The judge stated that the staff, including administrative staff,
knew that inmates in their facility were likely to be sexually assaulted within 24 hours of their
incarceration and they did not take steps to prevent this from occurring.

In another lawsuit, a transsexual inmate complained that the Federal Bureau of Prisons did not
adequately cover his risk for harm when they placed him in the general population of a major
penitentiary. While the inmate did not "win" his case, the U.S. Supreme Court did indicate in its
decision that Bureau staff may be liable if they know or believe that a harmful act is likely to
occur to a specific inmate and choose to take no action to prevent it (the concept of "deliberate
indifference").

The Department has established procedures which are designed to prevent sexual assaults.

a. All new admissions shall be screened by medical staff regarding any history of sexually
    assaultive behavior or victimization. Predators or victims shall be identified and
    referred to the Sexual Assault Prevention Program Coordinator.

b. During the classification process, the pre-sentence report, statement of facts, and other
    material in the master file shall be reviewed for any indication of assaultive behavior or
    victimization. If found, the inmate shall be identified as a predator or victim and
    referred to the Program Coordinator.

c. During intake, mental health professionals shall inquire whether the committed person
    has been a victim of sexual assault in the past. If so, he/she shall be identified as a
    victim and referred to the Program Coordinator.

d. The Program Coordinator shall make a recommendation regarding any treatment,
    counseling, or special housing needed. Priority shall be given to any court ordered
    placement in a treatment or counseling program.

Providing a safe, humane environment for committed persons is a significant part of the
Department's mission. Being aware of and taking steps to prevent sexual assaults among the

population is part of your job. This is also the right thing to do because youths and inmates are human beings and it is our ethical duty to protect them from abuse.

ASSAULTIVE/ABUSIVE BEHAVIOR

It is important that all staff be able to recognize abusive behaviors by committed persons which lead to sexual assault. This may occur over a period of time and include pressure, threats, or other actions and communications by one or more inmate/youth to force another inmate to engage in a partial or complete sexual act.

Examples of inmate/youth behavior which fit into this category might include:

    a.   Staring at another inmate/youth while he/she is dressing or showering.

    b.   Expressing a wish to or threatening to have sex with another inmate/youth.

    c.   Actually fondling another inmate/youth.

Behaviors such as these must be met with staff intervention. Protection of the potential victim and appropriate disciplinary action toward the intimidator are as important as in cases of actual assault.

CHARACTERISTICS OF SEXUAL ASSAULT VICTIM/PERPETRATOR

While some victims will be clearly identified, most will probably not come forward directly with information about the event. In some circumstances, staff may hear of an inmate being threatened with sexual assault or rumored to be a victim. Some victims may be identified through unexplained injuries, changes in physical behavior due to injuries, or abrupt personality changes such as withdrawal or suicidal behavior. The following guidelines may help a suspected victim:

Victims do not ordinarily "ask for it" or put themselves at risk on purpose. In most cases, rape has little to do with sex and much to do with control, dominance, or power over someone. Sexual acts are only a means to achieve these non-sexual ends. What better way to humiliate or control or person than by forcing such an act on them.

1.   Victims of sexual assault:

    a.   Are often younger than their aggressor.

    b.   Are often first time offenders who are unaware of prison customs.

    c.   Tend to be smaller in physical stature than their aggressor and tend to wear their hair somewhat longer than average.

    d.   Often lack "streets smarts."

    e.   There are also certain groups who are "at risk" for sexual assault or sex pressure. These include:

        • the elderly
        • the mentally retarded or mentally ill

- homosexuals (It should be noted that an inmate's sexual preference or pattern of previous sexual contacts does not preclude them from being the victim of rape or sexual pressure. In the case of homosexuals, these factors may, in fact, increase their probability of being targeted by other inmates as potential victims of sexual assault.)
- effeminate-acting males
- pedophiles (i.e., child molesters)

2. Perpetrators of sexual assault also tend to demonstrate a number of general characteristics. They:

   a. Tend to be slightly older than their victim.

   b. May have a prior history of sexual assault

   c. May have been a victim of childhood sexual and/or physical abuse.

   d. May have difficulty controlling anger.

   e. May display poor coping skills/strategies.

   f. May exhibit voyeuristic/exhibitionistic behavior.

   g. May have prior charges/convictions for stalking, voyeurism or sex crimes other than rape.

There are a number of reasons or motives for engaging in sexually assaultive behavior. Some assaults are acts of revenge or retaliation or anger toward the victim.

For some perpetrators, aggression itself becomes eroticized. These individuals find excitement and gratification in the sexual abuse and degradation of their victim.

Some perpetrators feel pressure to participate in gang rape in order to maintain status and membership with their peers. Acceptance and recognition by one's peers can become a dynamic in group rape and mutual participation in the assault can serve to strengthen and confirm the social bond among perpetrators. Sometimes gang "wanna-be's" may rape to prove their dominance over other inmates/youths and to demonstrate that they will do anything to be part of the gang.

In some cases the assailant attempts to punish the victim as a way of dealing with his own unresolved and conflicting sexual interests.

Sometimes sexual assault is used to enforce the social dominance and hierarchy in the prison. Conquering and controlling through rape proves that the perpetrator can dominate others.

The following are quotes from inmates who engaged in sexually assaultive behavior. See if you can determine their motivation for their actions they describe.

   a. Case #1 – Mike is a 22 year old, single white male. He stated that as part of a gang rivalry, he and another male got into a fight. As they were struggling, it was becoming quite sexual. Mike stated, "I grabbed his genitals. He told me to let go, but I pinned him down and pulled off his shorts, greased him with suntan oil and raped him. While I did that, I masturbated him. I know this sounds like a rationalization, but I felt that he really wanted this but had to show resistance. Afterwards, he had tears … I felt kind of funny because he was so upset. What was really exciting though, was that all during the assault I felt total control over him." (Motive – Control and Conquest/Sexual Conflict)

b. Case #2 – The inmate stated, "It wasn't for sex. I was mad. I wanted to prove who I was and what he was. I didn't have an erection. I wasn't really interested in sex. I felt powerful and hurting him made me excited. It was more to degrade him than for my sexual satisfaction." (Motive – Revenge and Retaliation/Sadism and Degradation)

c. Case #3 – Chuck, a 20 year old inmate in a county jail and his 19 year old cellmate were victims of gang rape. Chuck stated, "The two of us were in our cell, and four dudes come into our cell. They said, "We're the power here," and they started beating on us. After they had worked us over, they said they were going to give us a full initiation. They raped us several times and said, "Now you know who's the boss. If you rat on us, we'll break your legs and arms." (Motive – Status and Affiliation/Control and Conquest)

If a committed person is identified as the possible assailant, he or she shall normally be placed on investigative status.

SEXUAL ASSAULT AWARENESS, PREVENTION, INTERVENTION

Staff must be able to recognize the signs of sexual assault, and understand their responsibility in the identification and referral process when an alleged sexual assault occurs.

It is important to recognize that sexual assaults can occur in any hidden corners or out of the way places within the facility. The most common areas include places such as cells (especially at night), showers, and library.

Being aware of a sexual assault or sexual pressure is important for all staff. This information may be gained in a number of ways:

a. You might discover a sexual assault while it is in progress or personally witness an incident which includes sexual threats or pressure.

b. A victim may report that an incident has occurred.

c. Another youth/inmate may inform you that an incident has occurred.

d. Medical evidence of an incident may be discovered during a medical examination even though the inmate has reported no incident. For example, following a sexual assault incident an inmate might seek out medical attention. He might tell medical staff that he was in a fight over a gambling debt or about disrespect, but the medical evidence may indicate that he was sexually assaulted.

e. You may overhear committed persons talking about the incident.

Behaviors might indicate that a sexual assault has occurred or that the youth or inmate is upset about something.

Victims often become:

    a.   Withdrawn or isolate themselves.

    b.   Develop depression or hopelessness.

    c.   Lash out in anger or frustration.

    d.   Develop anxiety, fear, or paranoia.

    e.   Experience nightmares.

A victim may also experience concerns about sexually transmitted diseases as well as physical symptoms which may be related to various sexual acts (i.e., throat problems, stomach aches, rectal or genital pain or abrasions). Other physical symptoms like pain, tremors, nausea, loss of appetite, constipation, diarrhea, hypertension, headaches, etc. are also potential problems.

Once a victim has been identified, whether reported, discovered, or suspected, the youth or inmate shall be removed from the area and offered immediate protection. If the assault is recent, he/she shall be immediately referred/taken to health services for treatment and evidence collection or be referred to an outside medical facility. Any youth or inmate who alleges a sexual assault shall also be evaluated by mental health services to assess need for counseling services.

Any observation of sexual activity shall be treated as a possible sexual assault. Staff respond in a prompt, supportive, non-judgmental manner. The youth/inmate shall be provided counseling and supportive services, such as psychological services, chaplaincy services, correctional counselors, group therapy, etc. He/she shall be tested for sexually transmitted diseases if he or she consents to the testing.

The committed person's protective housing needs shall also be addressed. If the victim is transferred to another facility, the receiving facility shall be immediately notified of the alleged sexual assault to ensure the youth or inmate is observed and proper follow-up services are provided.

Any sexual assault shall be **immediately** reported through the chain of command as an Unusual Incident. Any staff who initially responded shall complete an Incident Report prior to leaving the facility at the end of their shift.

Once the victim's needs have been addressed, attempt to seal off "the crime scene" as soon as possible so that evidence of the incident can be collected. If you are tasked with evidence collection, be sure to use universal precautions and evidence gathering procedures.

Staff must always be sensitive to the victim's feelings. Do not interrogate them. Listen to what they have to say. Be as supportive and non-judgmental as possible. Remember, they do not have to tell you who assaulted them to receive care and protection.

All staff have some general responsibilities regarding sexual assault prevention and intervention.

    a.   Report any reasonable suspicion of sexual assault or coercion to your supervisor and/or the Program Coordinator.

    b.   Monitor your own behavior around youths and inmates. Be responsible for not perpetuating myths or stereotypes. For example, don't refer to an inmate as "she" just because the inmate displays effeminate characteristics or is a known homosexual.

    c.   Be aware that some explanations for incidents on the unit may be a cover for a sexual situation (i.e., gambling debts, fight, illness).

    d.   Be empathic. How would you feel or react if you were raped or assaulted sexually? How would you want to be treated? What if this were a member of your family (wife, daughter, son). Remember, committed persons are still human beings.

SUMMARY

Procedures are in place to insure the Chief Administrative Officer of a family takes the necessary steps to provide for the care, protection, prevention of additional assaults upon resident victims. Each facility will have an appointed Sexual Assault Prevention Program Coordinator and Alternate Program Coordinator for the facility. These are either mental health professionals and/ or individuals who serve in a supervisory capacity and have had training in intervention into sexual assault crisis issues.

The confidentiality of the youth/inmate victim for his/her own protection is to be emphasized throughout the detection, investigation, and protection phases of the incident. Training on self-protection and confidentiality of reporting sexual assault incidents is to be given to each inmate/ youth, along with the medical and crisis assistance available. Training will also be afforded concerning the crime scene preservation, evidence collection, investigation, treatment, crisis intervention and referrals for prosecution.

Remember preventing sexual assaults among committed persons is part of your job. Ignoring the issue may lead to bigger, more complex institutional problems and may increase your risk of personal legal liability.

```
 1   LAW OFFICES OF BASTIAN & DINI
     ROBERT L. BASTIAN, JR.[SBN 170121]
 2   MARINA R. DINI [SBN 169176]
     1925 Century Park East, Suite 500
 3   Los Angeles, CA 90067-2700
     Telephone (310) 789-1955
 4   Facsimile (310) 822-1989

 5   Attorneys for plaintiff
     EDDIE WEBB DILLARD
 6

 7

 8              UNITED STATES DISTRICT COURT

 9              EASTERN DISTRICT OF CALIFORNIA

10

11   EDDIE WEBB DILLARD,          )   Case No. CV F-94 5048 AWI SMS
                                  )
12              Plaintiff,        )   DECLARATION OF PLAINTIFF'S
     vs.                          )   COUNSEL ROBERT L. BASTIAN,
13                                )   JR., REGARDING HISTORY OF
                                  )   WAYNE ROBERTSON, IN
14   ROBERT ALLAN DECKER,         )   SUPPORT OF PLAINTIFF'S
     et al.,                      )   OPPOSITION TO SUMMARY
15                                )   JUDGMENT
                Defendants.       )
16   _____)   Before the Honorable
                                      Anthony w. Ishii
17
                                      Date:    3-19-01
18                                    Time:    1:30 p.m.
                                      Ctrm:    "3"
19

20       Plaintiff EDDIE WEBB DILLARD hereby submits the Declaration his

21   counsel, Robert L. Bastian, Jr., setting forth pertinent portions of the C.D.C.

22   history of Wayne Robertson in support of Plaintiff's Opposition to Summary

23   Judgment.

24   DATED:    March 5, 2001            LAW OFFICES OF
                                        BASTIAN & DINI
25

26
                                        ROBERT L. BASTIAN, JR.
27                                      Attorneys for Plaintiff
                                        EDDIE WEBB DILLARD
28
```

-1-

1   DECLARATION OF ROBERT L. BASTIAN, JR.

2

3   Robert L. Bastian, Jr. declares:

4

5   1.   Each fact set forth herein is within my personal knowledge except

6 those matters alleged on information and belief, and if called upon to testify, I

7 could and would competently swear as follows:

8

9   2.   I am partner in the Law Offices of Bastian & Dini, attorneys for

10 intervenor EDDIE WEBB DILLARD.

11

12   3.   The foregoing declaration is directly solely at organizing the pertinent

13 history of Wayne Robertson. The exhibits in support of this history will be set

14 forth separately under seal in order to protect the identity of persons that were

15 raped and/or assaulted by Robertson.

16

17   4.   What follows is an overview of my preliminary review of the records

18 of inmate Wayne Robertson within our office's possession. These records fill two

19 bankers box and number in the thousands. Having reviewed these records, it is

20 clear that our office has not received all pertinent records regarding Robertson.

21 Accordingly, what follows is only a partial summary of some pertinent

22 "highlights" regarding Mr. Robertson's career and propensity for sexual assault

23 and rape within the prison system, as reported in Robertson's files. The following

24 tracks Robertson's sentence through his stays at, *inter alia,* Old Folsom, New

25 Folsom, San Quentin, Corcoran and Pelican Bay.

26

27   5.   In the late 1970's, Robertson was arrested for rape. Ultimately, the

28 charge was reduced to unlawful sexual contact with a sixteen year old, resulting in

1   his first conviction.

2

3   6.   Robertson's second conviction was for murder wherefor he received

4   a term of life without possibility of parole. Robertson robbed a liquor store at gun

5   point. He emptied the contents of a cash register onto the floor and demanded

6   that the clerk obtain a bag and retrieve the money from the floor. Even though

7   the clerk was complying with his demands, Robertson shot him and the only

8   witness to the event execution style. *Ibid.*

9

10   7.   Robinson was received by the C.D.C. from the Los Angeles County

11   Jail in January 1981. *Ibid.*

12

13   8.   On April 26, 1983, it was reported that Robertson threatened an

14   inmate Doe 1, with a weapon while attempting to compel sexual favors. On or

15   about the same day, it was noted that Robertson had a stone in his cell that he was

16   ostensively using to sharpen weapons.

17

18   9.   On April 29, 1983, a Watch Lieutenant concluded that "Robertson's

19   [*sic*] a predator who preys on smaller weaker inmates to try and satisfy his

20   admitted unquenchable desire for sexual favors." Further, he references an

21   inmate assault that occurred by Robertson in November 1982 and that there is

22   "evidence which clearly shows Robertson was fashioning weapons to assist him in

23   his exploitation of others." *Ibid.*

24

25   10.   In the April 26, 1983 report it was noted that on a prior occasion in

26   1982, Robertson, maintaining a vaseline-covered erection, cut off an inmate Doe

27   2's underwear with a razor and attempted to forcibly rape him. The C.D.C.

28   employee preparing the report complained that Robertson was moved to SHU

1   (Security Housing Unit), but that Robertson characteristically ingratiated himself

2   with staff "with supposedly hot information" to win his release from the SHU.

3   *Ibid.*

4

5   11.   On August 7, 1984, an altercation took place between Robertson and

6   an inmate Doe 3. The classification committee determined that the matter

7   concerned a bisexual love triangle, and that inmate Doe 3 was the aggressor.

8   Accordingly, Robertson was released into the general population.

9

10   12.   On October 4, 1984, a cell mate of Robertson, inmate Doe 4, was

11   accused of planting a weapon in the cell in an effort to break the bond of a

12   purported four year homosexual relationship between the two dating back to

13   Folsom Prison (at this time, Robertson is at San Quentin). In his memorandum on

14   the subject, the program administrator noted that inmate Doe 4 "appeared to be

15   nervous and willing to `give up" inmate Robertson." The administrator believed

16   Robertson's denial of knowledge of the weapon and concluded that inmate Doe 4

17   was framing Robertson. Accordingly, Robertson was released back into the

18   general population.

19

20   13.   On November 20, 1985, a memorandum documented that several

21   inmate sources reported that Robertson was pressuring an inmate Doe 5 for sexual

22   favors. The memo noted that Robertson "is viewed as a lone predator, as

23   repeatedly demonstrated in his numerous CDC-115's. He has a reputation for

24   `turning out' young Blacks and preying on homosexuals." A memorandum dated

25   November 19, 1985, indicated that Robertson tried to choke Doe 5 out because

26   Doe 5 would not have sex with him. The guard noted red marks on Doe 5's

27   neck. The guard further noted that a subsequent search of the cell revealed a note

28   by Robertson, torn up, wherein he complained that Doe 5 was not submitting to

-4-

1 his sexual advances and that he was going to kick his ass.

2

3   14.   On February 28, 1986, Robertson received a Rule 115 violation in

4 connection with his attempted rape of inmate Doe 6.

5

6   15.   On June 28, 1986, a C.D.C. Rule 115 violation was found against

7 Robertson for his sexual aggression towards an inmate Doe 7. This inmate

8 reported to medical call with rectal pain and bleeding, accompanied by Robertson.

9 A guard, noting that Doe 7 looked fearful, correctly deduced that he was a rape

10 victim and separated the two. Referenced in the report were 3 confidential

11 chronos dated 12-19-85, 4-29-85 and 3-3-86 regarding Robertson pressuring other

12 inmates for sex, and two CDC-115's for "Fights with Cell Mates (behind sex

13 pressures)."

14

15   16.   On July 3, 1986, a sexual assault by Robertson on an inmate at San

16 Quentin is referenced.

17

18   17.   On May 19, 1987, a sexual assault by Robertson on an inmate at San

19 Quentin is referenced.

20

21   18.   On May 27, 1987, there is a chrono from a confidential source

22 indicating that Robertson was pressuring someone for sex, "another incident

23 displaying inmate Robertson's long history of predatory behavior and violence."

24   19.   On July 23, 1987, Robertson participated in a fight in the dining area

25 wherefore he was later found guilty of Inciting a Riot.

26

27   20.   On July 24, 1987, a correctional officer observed Robertson

28 assaulting an inmate Doe 8. The guard reported that he heard Robertson say,

1 "You better give up that bootie boy, before I get real mad and take it from you."

2 Additionally, he saw Robertson trying to pull the inmate's pants off.

4   21.   On September 17, 1987, Robertson reportedly raped an inmate Doe

5 9. He received a Rule 115 violation for the act of sodomy.

7   22.   On June 16, 1988, Robertson received a Rule 115 violation for

8 attempted sexual assault on an inmate Doe 10.

10   23.   On July 13, 1988, Robertson received a Rule 115 violation for

11 attempted sexual assault on an inmate Doe 11. Robertson was reportedly stabbed

12 in retaliation for this incident.

14   24.   On December 7, 1989, Robertson was transferred to Corcoran SHU

15 where he remained (except from June 29, 199889 to July 11, 1989) until

16 November 20, 1989.

18   25.   On August 3, 1988, it is reported that Robertson attempted to

19 sexually assault an inmate Doe 12 which resulted in a cell fight. The September

20 9, 1988, report regarding it makes reference to Robertson's participation in

21 another similar incident occurring on June 18, 1988.

23   26.   On January 8, 1989, the staff responded to a Robertson appeal for a

24 cell partner as follows:

26   Your deviant sexual behavior is well documented and as

27   a consequence you will not or cannot be housed with

28   another inmate. We do not have the luxury of single

1   cells in 4R because of overcrowding. Your errant
2   behavior warrants your placement in 4B1L.

3

4   27.   On August 13, 1989, Robertson received a Rule 115 violation
5 relative to a fight in his cell with inmate Doe 13.

6

7   28.   On December 12, 1989, a Rule 115 report was prepared related to an
8 inmate Doe 14's complaint that he was being pressured for sexual favors.

9

10   29.   On January 23, 1990, the following reply to a Robertson appeal is
11 entered:

12

13   A review of your Central File has clearly indicated that
14   you have on numerous occasions, pressured inmates for
15   sexual favors. No staff here at Corcoran has fictious
16   [*sic*] accused you of pressuring when pages of
17   documentation clearly establish your type of behavior.
18   Since your placement at Corcoran/SHU you have been
19   moved to 4B-1L for a more restricted housing, due to
20   your sexual behavior. On 12-13-89, you appeared
21   before U.C.C. at which time P.A. [ ] informed you that
22   the committee would not tolerate the type of behavior
23   from you. You stated "You fully understood the
24   message and there would be no more of it." Just 10 days
25   after you were released back to a regular SHU, you
26   pressured your cellie for sexual favors, which this
27   behavior from you was documented. You'll receive a
28   housing review on 1-28-90, at which time U.C.C. will

-7-

1   make their determination for your housing.

2

3   On February 6, 1990, Robertson wrote his reply demanding that the former cell

4   mate that he was accused of sexually assaulting be interviewed, that he was forced

5   to live with him against his will, but that "I have a homeboy named [Doe 15] that

6   just got clear to leave from over here that I can live with."

7

8   30   On November 3, 1990, Robertson was "counselled about covering his

9   light fixture with paper/any other material."

10

11   31.   On July 14, 1991, a "Serious Rules Violation Report" was prepared

12   regarding a July 9, 1991 incident. The reporting guard stated:

13

14   Robertson was angered by the placing of an inmate in

15   cell #36, because Robertson wanted a cellie, specifically

16   the inmate in cell #36. Due to Robertson's past

17   behavior, he is on single cell status. During the tray

18   pickup, he refused to give up the tray saying that he

19   wanted to see the Sergeant. I informed him that I would

20   pass along his request as stated, but he said the tray was

21   "his insurance."

22

23   32.   On August 11, 1991, an inmate Doe 16 refused to re-enter the cell,

24   asserting to the guards that Robertson had been "forced to commit sexual acts

25   under the threat of violence." The night before he had passed a note to guards

26   indicating that he was being raped, but no action was taken at the time.

27

28   33.   On August 12, 1991, Robertson received a Rule 115 violation related

1   to his rape of inmate Doe 17.

2

3   34.   On December 18, 1991, Robertson was placed in segregated housing

4   for assaulting inmate Eddie Webb Dillard.

5

6   35.   On September 10, 1992, Robertson received a Rule 115 violation for

7   his rape of inmate Larry Anderson. The day before in a classification review, it

8   is noted that Robertson had over 48 CDC 115's that included fighting, sexual

9   assault and rapes and that he was suspected of possessing a weapon in the

10   Anderson matter. *Ibid.*

11

12   36.   On September 28, 1992, Robertson received a Rule 115 violation for

13   an assault on an inmate Doe 18. Robertson told Doe 18 to "fight or fuck."

14

15   37.   On November 4, 1992, a 128G (information chrono) references an

16   attempted sodomy by Robertson.

17

18   38.   On November 17, 1992, Robertson filed an appeal claiming that the

19   C.D.C., by placing him on single cell status, violated his due process rights and

20   that it was a reprisal against him for using the appeal process. It was denied.

21

22   39.   On December 2, 1992, a report was prepared regarding a

23   Classification review which placed Robertson in SHU (Security Housing Unit) on

24   single cell status. It states:

25

26   Inmate Robertson indicated that he understood the

27   reasons for placement in SHU, however, was in

28   disagreement with Committee decision to place him on

single cell status. Inmate Robertson indicated that
Committee failed to consider his psychological needs and
there was some indication from him that he would
involve himself in misconduct including the setting of
cell fires in retaliation to his being placed on single cell
status.

Nonetheless, the Committee elected to maintain Robertson on single cell
status.

40.   On January 14, 1993, a classification hearing was held wherein it
was noted that Robertson has a "deviant sex history [which] includes numerous
sexual misconducts while in custody."

41.   On March 5, 1993, Dillard was placed into Robertson's cell. Over
the next 3 days, he was assaulted and raped three times. On March 8, 1993,
Dillard escaped from the cell as the cell door opened to facilitate Robertson going
to a hearing regarding a rules violation. The rules violation was that Robertson
was accused of covering his light fixture. The hearing officer found in
Robertson's favor.

42.   At the time the 6'4" Robertson was described in various testimony as
somewhere between 210 and 240 lbs. According to Robertson, he was
benchpressing over 400 lbs at the time. Dillard weighed less than 120 lbs. at the
time.

43.   On June 15, 1993, inmate Doe 19 reported that he had been raped by
Robertson. In an interview dated May 27, 1997, Doe 19 explained how

Robertson choked him out and forced himself upon Doe 19. Doe 19 further explained how he had been set up by the guards by falsely listing him as a "Blood" and thereby cell compatible with Robertson.

44. On August 18, 1993, Robertson refused to relinquish a razor blade in his cell unless he was ultimately moved to the Medical Observation Unit. According to the guard, "[a]s [Robertson] was being escorted to MOU, he was laughing and stated: I told you I'd get my move, and tomorrow I'll be back in one right (1R), and I'll have a cellie!" The guard concluded that Robertson used the pretense of inflicting self-injury to manipulate staff into moving him.

45. On August 25, 1993, Robertson received a Rule 115 violation for an assault on an inmate Doe 20.

46. On the same date, August 25, 1993, two further sexual assaults occurring in the summer of 1993 are referenced, inmates Does 21 and 22.

47. On October 27, 1993, a classification report indicates that Robertson "was reminded that the S/C (single cell status) was previously affirmed by ICC (classification committee) due to his predatory behavior towards cell-mates."

48. On February 15, 1994, a Corcoran program Sergeant (who was subsequently promoted and assigned to C.D.C. internal affairs) wrote an appeal response to Robertson, who claimed that being placed on single cell status violated his due process rights:

> This appeal is being partially granted, as you will be
> afforded to have a cell partner, if the individual is

-11-

1   willing to be housed in your assigned cell. Unit staff are

2   in agreement with such and Program Supervisory

3   Personnel must endorse the move. However, a written

4   documentation will be required, requesting yourself and

5   this person you wish to cell with.

6

7   49.   On December 12, 1994, Robertson was placed in Administrative

8   Segregation because he was a suspect in a sexual assault. Nevertheless, a

9   Corcoran Correctional Lieutenant prepared the following entry on a C.D.C.

10   128(a) (correctional counseling) form:

11

12   Inmate ROBERTSON does not require "Single Cell

13   Status" or Walk-Alone Status. No other special housing

14   considerations exist. "Inmate (Doe 23), is the suspected

15   victim in this Assault, and is to be considered an

16   enemy."

17

18   50.   On February 8, 1995, Robertson received a Rule 115 violation for

19   raping and sodomizing an inmate Doe 24.

20

21   51.   On May 1, 1995, a guard found Robertson and a cell mate, Doe 25,

22   unclothed. Robertson was quoted as saying: "We were not indulging in sodomy.

23   The other guy is my punk. He's my bitch and I'm his man."

24

25   52.   On August 9, 1995, Robertson was endorsed by a classification to

26   serve an indefinite SHU term "based on [his] persistent sexual assaults on other

27   inmates."

28

53.   On November 25, 1996, Robertson persuaded a rookie guard to put him into a cell with an ex-cell mate to purportedly discuss some missing property. Doe 26 struck Robertson as he entered the cell. Subsequently, it was noted that Robertson knew he was violating rules and that the attack was likely provoked.

54.   On January 25, 1997, Robertson was involved in an altercation with an inmate Doe 27 which was described as mutual combat.

55.   On or about November 30, 1997, Robertson cut an inmate Doe 28 with a razor after he refused to perform oral sex on Robertson.

56.   Our law firm's access to records regarding Robertson ceases in 1998.

57.   The foregoing summary has left out references to numerous other assaults which may or may not be related to efforts to force sexual favors out of inmates. However, the paperwork related to these incidents is missing from the file provided our office.

58.   Further, the foregoing account has left out numerous staff assaults, attempts to manipulate staff and failure to follow orders that, in many cases, seem to be directly related to Robertson's desire to maintain a steady flow of new cell mates.

59.   The foregoing has addressed only the institution's tolerance of Wayne Robinson's recividistically sexually assaulting and raping inmates. Our office does not have access to the files of other C.D.C. inmate rapists.

60.   Nevertheless, I am informed and believe that an inmate, Doe 28, is

1   another example of a sexual predator which the C.D.C. condoned by continually

2   returning him to double cell status. I am informed and believe that, C.D.C. Rule

3   115 violation, Log # RVRC-87-3-59, is an example of Doe 28 being found guilty

4   of raping another inmate. I am further informed and believe that, thereafter, Doe

5   28 was restored to double cell status.

6

7   61.   Additionally, it is this declarant's experience in litigating these types

8   of cases, speaking to guards and inmates, and reading related literature and case

9   law on the subject, that the incidence of violent sexual abuse caused by Robertson

10   and others is probably *under-reported*. Some of the factors contributing to this

11   conclusion: First, Robertson is, according to the records, a "shot caller" within

12   the prison and has reportedly threatened persons for snitching. Thus, Robertson

13   has both the propensity and the means for effectively intimidating prisoners into

14   silence. Second, it appears that guards are sometimes complicit in covering up his

15   rapes, the Dillard rapes being a notable example. Third, it appears that some of

16   the incidents simply have not been provided in the production of documents.

17   [One study of a Nebraska prison concluded that 22% of the male population had

18   been raped or forced into sex while incarcerated; Only 29% of that number said

19   they had reported their attacks to prison authorities. "Sexual coercion reported by

20   men and women in prison," *Journal of Sex Research*, vol. 33, no. 1, 1996, pp.

21   67-76; Mary Dallao, "Fighting prison rape: how to make your facility safer,"

22   *Corrections Today*, vol. 58, no. 7, December 1, 1996 [as cited in Parenti,

23   "Lockdown America, Police and Prisons in the Age of Crisis," (Verso 1999), p.

24   273]

25

26   62.   Nevertheless, a few generalizations can safely be made. First,

27   C.D.C. guards have been placing inmates in Robertson's cell, notwithstanding

28   Robertson's history and crystal clear propensities for violence and rape regularly

1   for almost two decades.

2

3   63.   Second, there is a strong inference that, far from an unforeseeable

4   aberration, placing known sexual predators into double cells where the predators

5   committed foreseeable sexual assaults and rapes, is -- at least until 1998 --

6   essentially a common occurrence in the C.D.C. and a way the C.D.C. conducted

7   its business. Indeed, the C.D.C. has placed Robertson in double cells in

8   circumstances where it would be utterly shocking if the ultimate result was not an

9   attempted sexual assault.

10

11   64.   Moreover, Robertson has been placed in cells where it is likely he

12 will rape his cell mate so often and so regularly that it is fair to consider it a

13 C.D.C. custom, policy and practice. Likewise, its guards, in carrying out the

14 customs, policies and practices of the C.D.C. were acting within the course and

15 scope of their employment.

16

17   65.   One inference that a person might derive from these facts is that the

18 C.D.C. is incompetent in its professed desire to promote the safety of its inmates.

19 Yet, in determining whether the C.D.C. maintains control of its facilities, it

20 should be noted that Robertson, notwithstanding numerous enemies and multiple

21 assaults, has managed to live undeterred for two decades in the C.D.C.'s various

22 facilities.

23

24   66.   Thus, an alternative and more plausible inference is that Robertson

25 has survived and thrived because the C.D.C. has used Robertson as an enforcer.

26 This is supported by another inference a person might derive from the facts stated

27 in this declaration -- that no institution could be this consistently *incompetent*. But

28 whether *incompetent* or *corrupt*, the facts suggest that placing persons such as

1 Robertson in double cells, notwithstanding his well-documented propensities, is

2 and has been how the C.D.C. conducts its business.

3

4   67.   Lamentably, the C.D.C. has elected heretofore not to defend (and,

5 thereby, under California law, indemnify the officers) on grounds that it bears no

6 responsibility for the rapes and it would be unfair to implicate the C.D.C'S budget

7 in such matters. The parties are awaiting a ruling from the Honorable Lynn C.

8 Atkinson's ruling in the matter of *Decker, et al., v. California Department of*

9 *Corrections*, Kings County Superior Court Case No. 00C2852, on defendants

10 Decker, Sanchez, Sylva and Horton-Plant's petition for a writ of mandate

11 requesting a defense.

12

13   I declare under penalty of perjury under the laws of the United States that

14 the foregoing is true and correct. Executed on this 5th day of March, 2001, in

15 Los Angeles, California.

16

17

18   ROBERT L. BASTIAN, JR., declarant

19

20

21

22

23

24

25

26

27

28

HUMAN RIGHTS WATCH
350 Fifth Ave., 34th Floor
NYC, NY 10118
Telephone: (212)290-4700
Facsimile: (212)736-1300
E-mail: marinej@hrw.org

Website: http://www.hrw.org

Darwin Weeldreyer
South Dakota Department of Corrections
3200 East Highway 34, Suite 8
Pierre, SD 57501-5070

April 10, 2000

Dear Mr. Weeldreyer:

Human Rights Watch is surveying prevention and prosecution strategies employed by state correctional authorities in addressing the problem of male inmate-on-inmate rape and sexual abuse. We request that you take the time to assist us by briefly describing your department's approach to this issue.

In particular, we would like the following information:

- Any statistics that you maintain on incidents of male inmate-on-inmate rape or other sexual abuse, including, if available, information regarding how many such incidents were reported annually between 1997 and 1999.

- Information regarding how your department normally responds to complaints of rape (for example, are rape kits administered and is an investigation initiated). We would like a copy of the Department's protocol for both responding to allegations of inmate-on-inmate rape and sexual abuse and screening inmates to prevent sexual assaults from occurring as well as training materials or course curriculum for corrections staff on rape prevention and response to incidences of sexual assault.

- Information regarding whether inmate-on-inmate rapes are normally referred out for criminal prosecution. We ask for statistics regarding the number of inmate-on-inmate rape and/or sexual abuse cases which have been referred for prosecution and the number of subsequent convictions.

- Information regarding whether victims of rape receive psychological counseling.

- Information regarding whether your department administers any type of inmate screening procedures or sexual assault prevention programs and, if so, we wish to obtain copies of materials distributed to inmates and/or corrections staff in the Department's sexual abuse prevention program.

I would appreciate your prompt attention and response. I also agree to pay any reasonable fees for copying, etc., that you may incur in responding to this request.

Thank you for your time in assisting us. I look forward to hearing from you.

Sincerely,

Joanne Mariner
Associate Counsel

BRUSSELS   HONG KONG   LONDON   LOS ANGELES   MOSCOW   NEW YORK   RIO DE JANEIRO   WASHINGTON

U.S. Department of Justice

Federal Bureau of Prisons

9

Washington, DC 20534

Ms. Joanne Mariner
Human Rights Watch
Associate Counsel
350 Fifth Avenue, 34th Floor
New York, NY 10118-3299

For Further Inquiry Contact:
Federal Bureau of Prisons
320 First Street, N.W.
Room 738, HOLC Building
Washington, D.C. 20534

Re: Request No. 97-1946

Dear Ms. Mariner:

This is in response to your June 23, 1996, Freedom of Information Act request for information regarding reported cases of inmate-on-inmate rape and sexual assaults within the Federal Bureau of Prisons (BOP) during 1997. You also requested information pertaining to the reasons that the majority of the allegations could not be confirmed, whether any of the cases were referred for criminal prosecution, and imposed disciplinary sanctions.

We have contacted the Psychology Department and were informed that during 1997, there were 66 reported cases of sexual assaults within the BOP. Ten cases were confirmed. The Bureau does not maintain any additional retrievable information prior to 1998 that is responsive to your request.

We trust that the information provided will be of assistance to you.

Sincerely,

Elizabeth M. Edson
Chief, FOIA/PA Section

U.S. Department of Justice

Federal Bureau of Prisons

ATTN: FOIA/PRIVACY OFFICE

Washington, DC 20534

Human Rights Watch
350 Fifth Ave., 34ᵗʰ Floor
NYC, NY 10118
Attn: Joanne Mariner

For Further Inquiry Contact:
Federal Bureau of Prisons
320 First Street, N.W.
Room 738, HOLC Building
Washington, DC   20534

Re: Request No. 2000-2180

Dear Ms. Mariner:

This is in further reply to your February 18, 1999, Freedom
of Information Act request for information. Specifically, you
request information about male inmate-on-mail inmate rape or
other sexual abuse.

The Bureau of Prisons (Bureau) Research Department has
advised this office that the Bureau does not maintain any
statistics regarding inmate rapes. Based on the aforementioned,
we have no information in regards to your subject matter.

Pursuant to Title 28, Code of Federal Regulations, Section
16.9, this response may be appealed to the Attorney General by
filing a written appeal within sixty days of the receipt of this
letter. The appeal should be addressed to the Co-Director,
Office of Information and Privacy, U.S. Department of Justice,
Flag Building, Suite 570, Washington, D.C. 20534. Both the
envelope and the letter of appeal itself must be clearly marked:
"Freedom of Information Act Appeal."

Sincerely,

Katherine A. Day/DH
Katherine A. Day
Chief, FOIA/PA Section

DEPARTMENT OF CORRECTIONS

REPLY TO: Denise Reynolds
Deputy Director
Division of Institutions

4500 Diplomacy Dr., Suite 207
Anchorage, AK 99508-5927

Telephone: (907) 269-7411
Fax: (907) 269-7420

December 15, 1999

Joanne Mariner, Associate Counsel
Human Rights Watch
350 Fifth Avenue, 34th Floor
New York, NY 10118-3299

Re: Prisoner-on-prisoner sexual assault

Dear Ms. Mariner:

I am responding to your letter to Commissioner Pugh. Our Department has not seen a sexual assault between prisoners in over 10 years. We, luckily, have no need to keep statistics, as this has not been a problem. However, if we notice a prisoner who demonstrates predatory or promiscuous behavior, s/he is immediately placed in segregation and moved away from general population. We also have very small prisons and jails, compared with most in this country. Our largest prison has a capacity of 486 prisoners. This allows us to be more aware of the potential for problems before they arise.

We do not have any sexual assault prevention programs for prisoners, as they have not been shown to be necessary in our prison system. If in the future this becomes a problem, we will certainly implement a prevention program.

If I can provide further information, please contact me.

Sincerely,

Denise Reynolds
Deputy Director of Institutions

cc: Margaret Pugh, Commissioner

Arizona Department of Corrections

1601 WEST JEFFERSON
PHOENIX, ARIZONA 85007
(602) 542-5536

FIFE SYMINGTON
GOVERNOR

TERRY L. STEWART
DIRECTOR

August 12, 1997

Ms. Joanne Mariner
Associate Counsel, Human Rights Watch
485 5th Avenue
New York, NY 10017

Dear Ms. Mariner:

Thank you for your inquiry on how the Arizona Department of Corrections deals with inmate-on-inmate rape and sexual abuse.

We have Criminal Investigators in each of our prisons and every allegation of inmate-on-inmate rapes and sexual abuse is investigated. If it contributes to the gathering of evidence or the victim's welfare, the victim is taken to one of our medical units for treatment and a rape kit is administered by medical staff. This evidence is then given to the investigator. When evidence supporting the allegation is found, the investigative report is referred to the County Attorney for prosecution.

During fiscal year 1997, there were 13 cases of sexual assault reported in our system. Victims of rape have psychological counseling available to them on an emergency or routine basis if they or staff request it.

The Arizona Department of Corrections have policies and procedures designed to reduce crime in our prisons, including rapes and sexual abuse. We stress the training of staff regarding these cases, however, we do not have a separate sexual assault prevention program. We enforce all the law in our prisons, including the statutes that apply to inmate-on-inmate rape and sexual abuse.

If we can provide any other information addressing these complaints, please notify us.

Sincerely,

Terry L. Stewart
Director

TLS/GP/kl

GKM GP97513

STATE OF CALIFORNIA--YOUTH AND ADULT CORRECTIONAL AGENCY PETE WILSON, *Governor*

DEPARTMENT OF CORRECTIONS
P.O. Box 942883
Sacramento, CA 94283-0001

June 18, 1997

Joanne Mariner
Associate Counsel
Human Rights Watch
485 5th Avenue
New York, NY 10017

Dear Ms. Mariner:

Your letter to Mr. Thomas M. Maddock, Interim Director, has been referred to me for review and response. In your letter you request data regarding inmate-on-inmate rape and sexual abuse. Additionally, you requested information on the Department's response to cases of inmate-on-inmate rape and sexual abuse.

I spoke to Art Chung, in the Offender Information Services Branch's Data Analysis Unit, who reported that the information you requested on cases of inmate-on-inmate rape and sexual abuse are collected, but are reported under the category of inmate-on-inmate battery. They are not distinguished from other types of battery.

In regards to the Department's response to reported cases of inmate-on-inmate rape and sexual abuse, all cases are investigated and rape kits are used by medical staff in cases of rape. Each case is reviewed by the institution investigative unit, and those cases meeting the criteria set forth by the local district attorney's office for prosecution are submitted for prosecution. The department does not have a program to provide psychological counseling to inmate rape victims nor is a sexual assault prevention program for inmates administered. An inmate may request to speak to the staff psychologist and the inmate's correctional counselor may refer him/her for a psychological evaluation at any time.

Thank you for your interest in Corrections. Should you wish the department's data on these issues, please contact Richard Welch, Offender Information Services Branch, 1515 S Street Room 450N, at (916) 445-1310.

D. Morton

STEVE CRAWFORD
Facility Captain
Institution Services Unit

cc: Richard Welch
        Art Chung
        MC 97-02396

STATE OF CALIFORNIA—YOUTH AND ADULT CORRECTIONAL AGENCY

GRAY DAVIS, *Governor*

DEPARTMENT OF CORRECTIONS
1515 S Street, 95814
P.O. Box 942883
Sacramento, CA 94283-0001

DEC 3 1 1999

Ms. Joanne Mariner
Human Rights Watch
350 Fifth Avenue, 34th Floor
New York, NY 10118-3299

Dear Ms. Mariner:

This is in response to your request for information regarding incidents involving inmate-on-inmate sexual assaults reported in 1998, and processed to date for 1999 within the California Department of Corrections. The chart below includes allegations that were reported but where the investigation may not have been completed. These allegations have not been verified to be factual. For that reason, this information should be considered preliminary and unofficial.

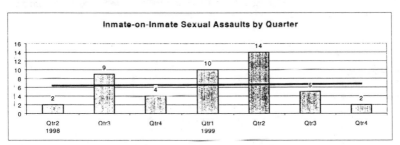

The inmate population has averaged approximately 160,000 in 1998 and 1999. In 1998, 15 inmate-on-inmate sexual assaults were reported. That number increased to 31 in 1999.

You also requested information on any sexual assault prevention program that we may have. The CDC provides orientation to inmates at our Reception Centers that includes instructions to report any sexual assaults to their correctional counselor or other staff member. The intake process each time an inmate is transferred also includes an orientation where inmates are provided a packet and view a film on this topic. Inmates who exhibit effeminate characteristics, have a history of prostitution, or received hormonal treatments are placed in specialized housing for their protection.

The CDC's inmate housing assignment process is designed to prevent this type of behavior as much as possible. Each inmate's history is evaluated as part of the initial

Ms. Joanne Mariner
Page 2

classification and in all subsequent classification reviews, which are held annually, at a minimum. If the inmate has a history of in-cell sexual abuse, assaultive behavior towards a cell partner, significant in-cell violence against a cell partner, or verification of predatory behavior towards a cell partner or dormitory partner, the inmate is considered for single cell status.

Approval of double cell assignments are based on a review of both of the inmates' central files and an evaluation of any security concerns.

Additionally, if an inmate has a history of victimization, has been identified as mentally ill, developmentally disabled, or meets the Disability Placement Program criteria, the inmate will receive special consideration when housing assignments are made to prevent their victimization.

In the event that an inmate reports a sexual assault by another inmate, the Program Lieutenant has the authority to place both inmates on segregated housing status pending an investigation and to refer the inmate to classification committee action for review of housing status within the next 10 days. All allegations of inmate sexual assault are promptly and thoroughly investigated.

If you have any questions or require additional information, please contact Margaret Howerton, Staff Services Manager, at (916) 324-2352.

For/ *Justina Mooby*

BART POWELL
Facility Captain
Institution Services Unit

STATE OF CONNECTICUT
DEPARTMENT OF CORRECTION
24 WOLCOTT HILL ROAD
WETHERSFIELD, CONNECTICUT 06109

December 13, 1999

Joanne Mariner
Associate Counsel
Human Rights Watch
350 Fifth Avenue, 34th Floor
New York, NY 10118-3299

Dear Ms. Mariner:

In response to your letter dated November 16, 1999 regarding the incidence of prisoner-on-prisoner sexual abuse, the Connecticut Department of Correction has an offender objective classification system that involves assessing an inmate's security risk level, medical and mental health needs. This assessment is primarily used for determining the appropriate medical facility, housing assignment and recommended program/treatment services. Inmates who may be assaultive or disruptive are appropriately restricted and youthful offenders or others who may need special protection during confinement are separated from adult populations or potential predators.

The University of Connecticut Health Center provides medical services to our population and has established protocols for providing appropriate, comprehensive medical/mental health care for inmates who allege forced sexual contact. Our training academy provides thorough training curriculum in all aspects of this topic, which include: prevention techniques, victim/predator profiles, Rape Trauma Syndrome (RTS), intervention techniques, and evidence protocols. Currently, the training academy is also developing an orientation program for inmates upon entering the system, that will include a video and brochure with similar information.

Our department does not maintain statistics regarding inmate on inmate rape or sexual abuse primarily because it is seldom reported and has significant low occurrence. In 1998, there were no substantiated allegations reported.

If I can be of any further assistance, please contact me at your convenience. Thank you.

Sincerely,

John J. Armstrong
Commissioner

An Equal Opportunity Employer

**FLORIDA
DEPARTMENT of
CORRECTIONS**

An Affirmative Action/Equal Opportunity Employer

2601 Blair Stone Road • Tallahassee, FL 32399-2500

Governor
LAWTON CHILES

Secretary
HARRY K. SINGLETARY, JR.

http://www.dc.state.fl.us

July 8, 1998

Ms. JoAnne Mariner
Human Rights Watch
485 5th Avenue
New York, New York 10017

Dear Ms. Mariner:

In regard to your inquiry of June 17, 1998, I submit the following information.

During 1997, the Florida Department of Corrections had a total of 93 allegations of sexual battery reported to staff.

As I previously indicated, this department handles all sexual batteries as criminal offenses. A criminal investigation is initiated following each allegation and, if evidence is obtained supporting the allegation, the case is referred to the State Attorney's office. Of the sexual batteries reported to staff in 1996 and 1997, thirty-six were referred. The following is a breakdown of the results of those referrals:

	1996	1997
Prosecution Declined	13	14
Prosecution Pending	3	4
Subject Pled Guilty (to Simple Battery)	1	0
Subject Found Guilty (of Simple Battery)	1	0
Total Referred for Prosecution	18	18

Should you need additional information, please do not hesitate to ask.

Sincerely,

Fred Schuknecht
Inspector General
FWS/MC

Quality is Contagious

FLORIDA
DEPARTMENT of
CORRECTIONS

Governor
JEB BUSH

An Affirmative Action/Equal Opportunity Employer

Secretary
MICHAEL W. MOORE

2601 Blair Stone Road • Tallahassee, FL 32399-2500

http://www.dc.state.fl.us

December 8, 1999

Ms. Joanne Mariner, Associate Counsel
Human Rights Watch
350 Fifth Avenue, 34th Floor
New York, NY 10118-3299

Dear Ms. Mariner:

Your letter of November 16, 1999, concerning sexual assault was received and forwarded to this office for response.

During calendar year 1998, the Office of the Inspector General received 89 allegations of sexual battery. Please understand that this number reflects only alleged assaults. It does not reflect the number of incidents that were actually substantiated.

From January 1, 1999 until December 7, 1999, this office received 91 allegations of sexual battery. The department is currently updating the Inmate Orientation manual. The security department has been directed to develop a module on preventing sexual assault in prison. This module will be included in the orientation once finalized.

Sincerely,

E.A. Sobach
Chief of Investigations

ES/jb

Jim Edgar
Governor

Odie Washington
Director

ILLINOIS
DEPARTMENT
OF
CORRECTIONS

1301 Concordia Court / P.O. Box 19277 / Springfield, IL 62794-9277 / Telephone: (217) 522-2666
TDD: (800) 526-0844

May 6, 1997

Ms. Joanne Mariner
Associate Counsel
Human Rights Watch
485 5th Avenue
New York, NY 10017

Dear Ms. Mariner:

Department policy provides that whenever an inmate is the victim of an alleged sexual assault, staff shall expeditiously investigate the incident, ensure that the inmate receives proper medical attention, and pursue criminal prosecution of the perpetrator(s) of this criminal act.

In Illinois, a sexual assault is defined as " any contact between the sex organ of one person and the sex organ, mouth or anus of another person, or any intrusion of any part of the body of one person or object into the sex organ or anus of another person by the use of force or threat of force."

An inmate suspected of being the victim of a sexual assault shall be examined by medical staff as an emergency patient and receive counseling. Evidence Collection (ie. Rape) Kits are available at all facilities. The investigation shall include an interview of the victim, perpetrator and other witnesses, a review of the medical findings, and where deemed necessary a polygraph examination. A final conclusion report shall be filed. If the charge is substantiated, disciplinary action shall be taken and the case shall be referred to the State's Attorney for prosecution.

Issues concerning sexual pressures from other inmates are addressed during initial orientation to the facility. Specific pressures may warrant removal from the general population and placement in protective custody units.

Over the last two year period 97 incidents of alleged sexual assault have been reported. To date a total of 12 cases have been substantiated.

Sincerely,

Odie Washington
Director

Printed on Recycled Paper

Illinois
Department of
Corrections

George H. Ryan
Governor

Donald N. Snyder Jr.
Director

1301 Concordia Court / P.O.Box 19277 / Springfield , IL. 62794-9277 / Telephone: (217) 522-2666 / TDD: (800) 526-0844

April 7, 2000

Ms. Joanne Mariner
Associate Counsel
Human Rights Watch
350 Fifth Avenue, 34th Floor
New York City, New York 10118

Dear Ms. Mariner,

The information you have requested regarding incidents of sexual assaults is as follows:

January through December 1998   130 incidents of alleged sexual assault reported
                               8 incidents were substantiated
January through December 1999   118 incidents of alleged sexual assault reported
                               12 incidents were substantiated
                               4 incidents are pending investigation

I have included the curriculum outline on Inmate Sexual Assault Prevention and Intervention. This curriculum, provided by the Department's Staff Development & Training Unit, is utilized in the training of all new employees' as well as in mandatory cycle training. I have also included examples of pages from inmate handbooks from several facilities. This topic is covered during inmate orientation and the material is representative of all Illinois Correctional Centers.

Should you have any additional questions please feel free to contact me.

Sincerely,

Donald N. Snyder, Jr.
Director

COMMONWEALTH OF KENTUCKY
Department of Corrections
Adult Institutions
State Office Building
Frankfort, Kentucky 40601
FAX (502) 564-3520

Doug Sapp
Commissioner

Tom Campbell
Deputy Commissioner

September 8, 1997

Ms. Joanne Mariner
Associate Counsel
485 Fifth Avenue
New York, New York 10017-6104

Dear Ms. Mariner:

I am in receipt of your letter regarding the problem of inmate-on-inmate rape and sexual abuse. These instances are very rare in our state and once the few cases we have are turned over to the Kentucky State Police, we do not maintain a central list of the disposition of these cases.

When a rape is reported, we immediately have the individual checked by our medical personnel, who will then treat and administer the appropriate tests. Any further treatment or counseling is handled on a case by case basis.

Finally, we believe the best prevention for any inappropriate behavior in our institutions is through good supervision and classification.

Sincerely,

Carol T. Shirley
Director of Operations

CTS/mh
xc: File

The Commonwealth of Massachusetts
Executive Office of Public Safety
Department of Correction
Health Services Division
45 Hospital Road, S Bldg., P.O. Box 317
Medfield, MA 02052-0317

Larry E. DuBois
Commissioner

Michael T. Maloney
Deputy Commissioner

Kathleen M. Dennehy
Associate Commissioner

Phone: (617) 727-8528
Fax: (617) 727-8569

July 7, 1997

Joanne Mariner, Associate Counsel
Human Rights Watch
485 Fifth Avenue
New York, N.Y.

Dear Ms. Mariner,

Commissioner Larry E. DuBois has forwarded your correspondence regarding inmate sexual abuse and rape to me for a response.

The Massachusetts Department of Correction has long maintained a policy of vigilance and responsiveness to any evidence of inmate sexual assault. Attached you will find our sexual assault policy, including an outline of procedures which are followed by the Beth Israel Hospital in Boston, where all cases are referred for follow up. All reports are independently investigated and our Central Office maintains a file of all incidents. There are no systematic statistics available, however, these can be generated by a review of files.

The affiliation with Beth Israel Hospital ensures that the inmate victim receives a comprehensive medical response as well as review of his or her mental status. Follow up recommendations are made by this hospital and accompany the inmate upon return to confinement. In addition, a periodic training is conducted by Beth Israel staff for all medical, mental health and security staff. All new correctional officers receive training in the sexual assault policy, and it is formally reviewed as part of the in-service training curriculum every two years.

I hope this has been helpful to you, please feel free to contact this office for further information, or clarification.

Sincerely,

Kathleen M. Dennehy
Associate Commissioner for Programs, Classification and Health Services

KMD/TOB/pm

cc: Larry E. DuBois, Commissioner
        Michael T. Maloney, Deputy Commissioner
        File:dennehy\sexasslt.inq

State of Minnesota
Minnesota Department of Corrections

April 12, 2000

Joanne Mariner, Associate Council
Human Rights Watch
350 Firth Ave., 34th Floor
New Your City, New York 10118

Dear Ms. Mariner:

This is in response to your letter of March 21, 2000 to regarding prevention and prosecution strategies employed by state correctional authorities in addressing the problem of male inmate-on-inmate rape and sexual abuse. In addition to answering your survey questions, I am including a copy of the Minnesota Department of Corrections Policy "Offender Alleged Sexual Assault."

I hope the information I have provided is helpful. Please contact me if you need further information or have any questions. Thank you.

Sincerely,

Terry Carlson
Adult Facilities Support Unit Director
Minnesota Department of Corrections

c: Sheryl Ramstad Hvass, Commissioner
   Erik Skon, Assistant Commissioner
   Cari Gerlicher, Director, Office of Special Investigations
   Nan Schroeder, Health Services Director

Any statistics or numbers that you maintain on incidents of male inmate-on-inmate rape or other sexual abuse, including, if available, information regarding how many such incidents were reported each year from 1997-1999. **Minnesota Dept. of Corrections Response: in 1997 –1999 we had approximately 8 allegations of male inmate-on-inmate rape/sexual abuse. In each case the allegations were unfounded.**

Information regarding how your department normally responds to complaints of rape (for example, are rape kits administered and is an investigation initiated). **Minnesota Dept. of Corrections Response: a complete investigation is conducted, a rape kits is administered and the inmate receives appropriate medical care.**

Information regarding whether inmate-on-inmate rapes are normally referred out for criminal prosecution. **Minnesota Dept. of Corrections Response: none of these cases were referred out for criminal prosecution due to insufficient evidence or withdrawal of the complaint by the inmate.**

Information regarding whether victims of rape receive psychological counseling. **Minnesota Dept. of Corrections Response: per our department policy, all offenders who allege that they have been sexually assaulted during incarceration receive psychological and medical services in addition to forensic examination. These services include treatment for sexually transmitted diseases, HIV pre- and post-counseling, and psychological support. (see attached DOC Policy 500.600 for specific information).**

Information regarding whether your department administers any type of inmate screening procedures or sexual assault prevention programs and, if so, descriptions of the components of these programs. **Minnesota Dept. of Corrections Response: At the intake center, staff conduct a mental health screening on each offender, with referrals made for further evaluation if indicated.**

Additionally, offenders are assigned a custody classification level based on an objective assessment of public risk, the safety of staff and other offenders, the security needs of the offender and the programmatic needs of the offender.

We conduct an incompatibility review of all offenders at intake and any time we need to assess whether precautions need to be taken because an offender is determined to be in physical danger from one or more identified offenders. An incompatibility review can be initiated by staff or offender.

At intake, we provide an HIV/AIDS and sexually transmitted diseases awareness and prevention program.

STATE OF MISSISSIPPI

DEPARTMENT OF CORRECTIONS

JAMES V. ANDERSON
COMMISSIONER

March 30, 2000

Ms. Joanne Mariner
Associate Counsel
Freedom Rights Watch
350 Fifth Ave., 38th Floor
NYC, NY 10118

RE: INFORMATION INVOLVING INCIDENTS
MALE INMATE ON INMATE RAPE

Dear Ms. Mariner:

Pursuant to your recent Freedom of Information Act request *6 U.S.C. Sec 552(a.),* the Mississippi
Department of Corrections is pleased to provide the following responses.

- ♦ Any statistics or numbers that you maintain on incidents of male inmate on inmate
   rape or other sexual abuse, including, if available, information regarding how many
   such incidents were reported each year from 1997-1999. **No. The Mississippi
   Department of Corrections does not maintain specific records regarding male
   inmate on inmate rape.**
- ♦ Information regarding how your department normally responds to complaints of rape
   (for example, are rape kits administered and is an investigation initiated). **The prison
   system investigates all allegations of sexual assault pursuant to state statute.**
- ♦ Information regarding whether inmate-on-inmate rapes are normally referred out for
   criminal prosecution. **Yes.**
- ♦ Information regarding whether victims of rape receive psychological counseling. **Yes.
   Counseling is provided if the victim requests it.**
- ♦ Information regarding whether your department administers any type of inmate
   screening procedures or sexual assault prevention programs and, if so, descriptions of
   the components of these programs. **No.**

If we may be of further service to you, please advise.

Sincerely,

Ken Jones

Ken Jones
Public Relations Director

723 NORTH PRESIDENT STREET • JACKSON, MISSISSIPPI 39202-3097 • PH: (601) 359-5600
FAX: (601) 359-5624

State of New Hampshire

JEANNE SHAHEEN
GOVERNOR

DEPARTMENT OF CORRECTIONS

OFFICE OF THE COMMISSIONER

105 PLEASANT ST., MAIN BLDG., 4TH FLOOR
P.O. BOX 1806
CONCORD, NH 03302-1806
(603) 271-5600
FAX (603) 271-5643

PAUL E. BRODEUR
COMMISSIONER

EDDA S. CANTOR
ASSISTANT COMMISSIONER

July 7, 1997

Ms. Joanne Mariner
Associate Counsel
Human Rights Watch
485 5th Avenue
New York, NY 100017

Dear Ms. Mariner:

This is in response to your most recent letter in which you seek
information concerning male inmate-on-inmate rape and sexual
abuse.

Because of very small number of allegations of rape and the even
smaller number of substantiated cases, the N.H. Department of
Corrections does not maintain statistical data regarding this
issue. However, any allegation of rape is immediately
investigated by our internal Office of Investigations. In
conversation with Lt. Gil Provost of that office regarding your
inquiry, he said that there are "one or two allegations a year in
our men's prison of rape." He further stated that "of 10
allegations, perhaps one actually was a rape."

If, after investigation, enough evidence is compiled to indicate
a rape did, in fact, take place the N.H. Attorney General's
Office is notified and prosecution proceeding are instituted.

Prison medical staff said that if a male rape victim were
referred to them they are equipped and trained to give the
required treatment and counseling.

All corrections officers, indeed, all employees of the N.H.
Department of Corrections must successfully complete an eight-
week Corrections Officers Academy were the issue of sexual
assault and abuse prevention are addressed.

Sincerely,

John Gifford
Information Officer

TTY/TDD: 1-800-735-2964

STATE OF NEW YORK

DEPARTMENT OF CORRECTIONAL SERVICES

THE HARRIMAN STATE CAMPUS

1220 WASHINGTON AVENUE

ALBANY, N.Y. 12226-2050

GLENN S. GOORD
COMMISSIONER

February 16, 2000

Ms. Joanne Mariner
Human Rights Watch
350 5th Avenue
34th Floor
New York, NY   10118-3299

Dear Ms. Mariner:

This is in response to your letter of January 19, 2000 requesting information on prevention and prosecution strategies in addressing the issue of male inmate-on-inmate sexual assault. The New York State Department of Correctional Services (DOCS) recognizes that any instances of sexual assault between inmates, regardless of infrequency, must be treated as a very serious matter and therefore, a number of significant steps have been taken to prevent this type of crime from happening.

Incidents of criminal behavior by inmates are entered into an electronic reporting system, and all crimes are referred to the New York State Police for investigation. Rape kits are regularly administered as part of the investigation of sexual assault, and psychological counseling is available for victims. DOCS maintains a sex crimes unit within the Office of the Inspector General which also is notified of inmate assault cases and conducts an investigation in conjunction with the Bureau of Criminal Investigation (BCI) of the New York State Police. After the investigation is completed, and if substantiated by evidence and/or the complainant's testimony, cases are referred to the county district attorney's office for prosecution. Eighteen incidents of sexual assault were reported in 1998 and 16 incidents were reported in 1999.

A program to prevent sexual assaults of male inmates begins at DOCS' intake and classification facilities. Information on every new inmate is reviewed prior to his arrival at intake centers and includes information from county jails, DOCS' inmate folders for inmates who have served prior prison incarcerations, and communications from family members and attorneys, which may facilitate the identification of inmates who appear to be prone to victimization. At-risk inmates are referred to an extended classification process that allows more time for staff to discuss pertinent issues with the inmates and to determine appropriate housing assignments. All inmates are notified of

Joanne Mariner
February 16, 2000
Page 2

the penalties for attempting to force others to engage in sexual acts and that all offenses may be referred to law enforcement agencies for prosecution through the courts.

Alternatives to general population housing are available throughout the state prison system for inmates at any time during their incarceration. All medium and maximum security prisons provide involuntary protective custody (IPC) and voluntary protective custody (VPC) housing assignments for inmates likely to be assaulted by other inmates. Also, Clinton, Eastern, Sullivan, Wende, Arthur Kill, Collins, and Oneida Correctional Facilities have specialized units to serve inmates with special needs and provide protection to potential or actual victims of sexual assault. An alternative housing assignment may be requested by an inmate or a staff member who believes the inmate may be assaulted if he remains in his current housing location.

DOCS strongly supports and encourages the prosecution of all incidents of inmate criminal behavior, including sexual assault. It is felt that the deterrent effect of an additional criminal sentence greatly diminishes the likelihood of such acts from taking place. I am interested in receiving the results of your survey of state correctional agencies concerning sexual assaults of male inmates in order to learn how other states address this issue.

If I may be of further assistance, please contact me.

Sincerely,

Glenn S. Goord
Commissioner

Ohio Department of Rehabilitation and Correction

1050 Freeway Drive North
Columbus, Ohio 43229

Bob Taft, Governor   www.drc.state.oh.us   Reginald A. Wilkinson, Director

December 30, 1999

Joanne Mariner
Associate Counsel
Human Rights Watch
350 Fifth Avenue, 34th Floor
New York NY 10118-3299

Dear Ms. Mariner:

Thank you for your letter to Director Reginald Wilkinson dated November 16, 1999 regarding information about inmate-on-inmate sexual assaults in Ohio.

Allegations of inmate-on-inmate sexual assaults are investigated internally for potential prison rule violations, as well as by the Ohio State Patrol for possible criminal prosecution. Primarily, the information we keep on inmate-on-inmate assaults is not specific to sexual incidents. We recently had an occasion to look at this issue and gathered some statistics on sexual assaults for 1999. In total, there were 55 alleged incidents among the 31 prisons in Ohio this year. Of that 55, 8 cases were subsequently confirmed as sexual assault. The remaining 47 were deemed to have been either consensual sex acts or simply fabrications by the alleged victim.

In 1998, there were a total of 429 inmate-on-inmate assaults; six of those assaults were reported as sexual assaults. Again, our records did not at that time consist of the detailed information we have gathered for 1999.

Orientation of new inmates entering Ohio's prison system does not include specific instruction relative to sexual assault. They are, however, encouraged to report any difficulties with other inmates or staff to an employee immediately.

Ohio's recent initiatives in "community justice" have put into place an avenue for inmate victims of such assaults to provide information on how the incident impacted them. Victims then have access to counseling if they so desire.

I hope that this information has been beneficial to you. Thank you again for your interest in the Ohio Department of Rehabilitation and Correction. If you have any additional questions, please do not hesitate to contact me.

Sincerely,

Rhonda Millhouse

Rhonda Millhouse
Administrative Assistant 4
Office of Prisons – North Region

cc: File

Ohio Department of Rehabilitation and Correction

1050 Freeway Drive, North
Columbus, Ohio 43229

George V. Voinovich, Governor

Reginald A. Wilkinson, Director

May 8, 1997

Joanne Mariner, Associate Counsel
Human Rights Watch
485 5th Avenue
New York, NY 10017

Dear Ms. Mariner,

Your letter to Director Wilkinson regarding inmate-on-inmate rape and sexual abuse within the Department of Rehabilitation and Correction was forwarded to my office. In response, I can offer you the following information.

As of January 1, 1997 our department began tracking all reported inmate-on-inmate rape and sexual abuse. Since this time there has been one reported case of rape. Staff are to complete the inmate-on inmate assault report and forward this to the Bureau of Research for statistics gathering.

All inmates who report sexual abuse are evaluated by the medical staff and a rape kit is administered. The case is referred to the Ohio State Highway Patrol for further investigation. If findings of the investigation support the inmates allegations then the case is presented to the County Prosecutor for possible prosecution of the individual.

At this time the department does not have a sexual assault prevention program. However, any inmate who is found to have sexually abused is offered mental health counseling.

If you have further questions or concerns, please feel free to contact this office.

Sincerely,

Norm F. Hills
North Region Director

Ohio Quality Corrections . . .
. . . Quality Services through Partnership

Q|S
t|P

JAMES L. SAFFLE
DIRECTOR

FRANK KEATING
GOVERNOR

STATE OF OKLAHOMA
OKLAHOMA DEPARTMENT OF CORRECTIONS

December 13, 1999

Ms. Joanne Mariner
Associate Counsel
350 Fifth Avenue, 34th Floor
New York, NY 10118-3299

Dear Ms. Mariner:

I am in receipt of your request for information regarding the incidence of prisoner-on-prisoner sexual abuse in United States correctional facilities.

The Oklahoma Department of Corrections does not maintain annual statistics on prisoner-on-prisoner rape and/or sexual assault. Sexual assaults and rapes, however, are both subject to investigation according to the department's disciplinary process and felony prosecution by the district attorney. Each facility maintains this specific data.

During the reception and assessment process inmates are provided with an intensive orientation that includes the following:

- A list of staff persons to contact concerning any issue.
- Access to medical services, including full-time psychiatrist staff.
- Information on contacting staff using the "Request to Staff" form.
- Inmate grievance process.

Policy related to the orientation process and inmate security may be accessed via our web site www.doc.state.ok.us reference the icon "Policies and Procedure." OP-060201 Initial Assessment and Reception of Inmates and OP-060106 Special Inmate Management are related to your request.

Please feel free to contact me if any additional information is required concerning this issue.

Sincerely,

James L. Saffle

3400 MARTIN LUTHER KING AVENUE • P.O. BOX 11400 • OKLAHOMA CITY, OKLAHOMA 73136-0400
OFFICE: (405) 425-2500 • FAX: (405) 425-2064 • www.doc.state.ok.us/

 recycled paper

COMMONWEALTH OF PENNSYLVANIA
DEPARTMENT OF CORRECTIONS
P. O. BOX 598
CAMP HILL, PENNSYLVANIA 17001-0598

OFFICE OF THE
SECRETARY OF CORRECTIONS

March 2, 2000

Joanne Mariner
Associate Counsel
Human Rights Watch
350 Fifth Avenue, 34th Floor
New York, NY 10118-3299

Dear Ms. Mariner:

This letter is provided in response to your correspondence to me in which you requested information regarding statistics on prisoner-on-prisoner rape and/or other sexual assaults during 1998 and 1999.

In August 1997, the Department implemented a misconduct tracking system that allows for the collection, analysis, tracking and dissemination of misconduct data. From August 1997 to December 1999, there were five misconduct charges issued for rape. In order for criminal charges to be filed for rape, the inmate who is raped is required to press charges, by the same process that occurs in the community. If the raped inmate declines to press charges, then no criminal investigation can be conducted. If the inmate does press charges, then the Pennsylvania State Police are responsible for conducting the investigation. Therefore, it is the responsibility of the inmate to pursue these charges being filed.

In addition to the Department's misconduct tracking system, the Bureau of Health Care Services instituted, in December 1999, a process which is followed by each of the institution medical departments, of tracking and reporting to the Bureau of Health Care Services, the inmate medical complaints for which there is medical evidence of sexual activity. This data, in combination with the data gathered through the misconduct tracking system, helps ensure that an accurate reflection of prisoner-on-prisoner sexual assaultive activity is being tracked.

You inquired as to whether the Department administers a sexual assault prevention program. Our prisons are safer places today than they were five years ago. Inmate on staff assaults declined by 32% from 1995 to 1999. Inmate-on-inmate assaults declined by 26% from 1995 to 1999. Serious misconducts declined by 28% from 1995 to 1999. Given the significant reduction in assaults and serious misconducts, as well as only 5 incidents of rape over a 2½-year period, the Department has elected not to administer a sexual assault prevention program.

It is my commitment, as the Secretary of Corrections, to maintain a safe and secure correctional system. I believe that our population of 36,544 inmates is managed in a safe and secure manner as reflected through the data I've shared with you, and as a result of sound Departmental policy and procedures. If you have additional questions regarding the information that I have provided, please feel free to contact me.

Sincerely,

Martin F. Horn
Secretary of Corrections

MFH/CM/em
cc: File (Mariner.MFH.CM.3.2.00)

GREAT FACES. GREAT PLACES.

DEPARTMENT OF CORRECTIONS

CENTRAL OFFICE

115 East Dakota Avenue
Pierre, SD 57501-3216
Phone: (605) 773-3478
Fax: (605) 773-3194

June 9, 1997

Joanne Mariner, Associate Counsel
Human Rights Watch
485 5th Avenue
New York, NY 10017

Dear Ms. Mariner:

I am writing in response to your letter I received on April 25, 1997 regarding the South Dakota Department of Corrections Policy on inmate on inmate rape and sexual abuse. Currently, South Dakota does not have a written policy on inmate on inmate rape and sexual abuse.

Offenders committed to the South Dakota Department of Corrections are advised at the time of admission of prohibited acts. Included in the list of prohibited acts are: threatening another with bodily harm, assaulting another including sexual assault, and engaging in consensual sexual contact and/or unnatural acts. Any offender caught performing one of the prohibited acts will result in internal sanctions against the offender, and all cases of major rule violations are referred to the South Dakota Division of Criminal Investigation.

We do maintain statistics on the number of reported incidents of inmate on inmate rape and sexual abuse. We have had only two reported cases. In the first case, the inmate's reports were investigated by the Division of Criminal Investigation and the reports were all found out to be cases of consensual sex acts. In the second case, the inmate has numerous bite marks all over his body and was taken to the local hospital for treatment. At the hospital, a rape kit was administered and the case is still under investigation.

If you need any additional information and I can be of help, please don't hesitate to give me a call at (605) 773-3478 or write to the South Dakota Department of Corrections.

Sincerely,

Patricia Warkenthien
Policy Assistant

DEPARTMENT OF CORRECTION
PLANNING AND RESEARCH SECTION
4TH FLOOR RACHEL JACKSON BLDG.
320 SIXTH AVENUE NORTH
NASHVILLE, TENNESSEE 37243-0465
PHONE: (615) 741-6918
FAX: (615) 741-9883

July 17, 1997

Ms. Joanna Mariner
Associate Counsel
Human Rights Watch
485 5th Avenue
New York, NY 10017

Ms. Mariner:

Your request for information was forwarded to this office for response.

Psychological counseling would be provided on a case by case basis in the event of inmate-inmate rape. The offender/victim would have the last say as to whether or not they wanted such counseling. The Tennessee Department of Correction does not have a formalized sexual assault program, but does have plans to develop a policy that addresses inmate rape. Rape kits are done at the local hospital rather than in-house.

With respect to statistics, this office also is charged with monitoring and reporting incidents. Overall, while there are many incidents of sexual misconduct, there are few if any cases of reported rape within the incident reporting process. The General Counsel also has recollection of very few to no cases which have been referred for prosecution.

I am sorry if I can be of no further assistance. If you have any questions or need additional information, please do not hesitate to contact me at your convenience.

Sincerely,

Gary A. Lukowski, Ph.D.
Assistant to the Commissioner
Planning and Research

GAL

glukowski@mail.state.tn.us

TEXAS DEPARTMENT OF CRIMINAL JUSTICE

P.O. Box 99 • Huntsville, Texas 77342-0099

Wayne Scott
Executive Director

May 19, 1997

Ms. Joanne Mariner
Associate Counsel
Human Rights Watch
485 5th Avenue
New York, NY 10017

Dear Ms. Mariner:

In response to your survey, I have outlined our agency's approach regarding sexual assault among offenders. Our practice is to assist and treat the sexual assault victims, then diligently collect evidence that can lead to their predator's prosecution. We do not administer a sexual assault prevention program.

Once an offender reports having been raped, the immediate response is to direct him to the medical clinic. There he is examined by a doctor who administers a rape kit, if the incident occurred within 12 hours. A referral is then made to psychiatric services to offer the victim therapeutic counseling.

Meanwhile, the Classification Department is notified of the reported rape, and they issue a request to security for an investigation. Facts of the incident are collected, including the time and location of the incident, the name of the attacker(s), and names of witnesses. If confirmation exists to presume a rape did occur, the victim is segregated from the other population. The investigative report is reviewed by the Classification staff. Based on whether or not the allegations are considered founded, the department makes a recommendation for the victim's transfer to another unit and/or placement in safekeeping housing, or has the claimant returned to his housing assignment to resume regular activities.

In conjunction, the Internal Affairs Department is also notified. Departmental staff interview the victim and review evidence and reports to determine the validity of the case. If the elements of the case are vague or deficient, the process stops. Otherwise, the victim is given the choice of pressing charges against his assailant. If he doesn't, the case is null and void. If he chooses to press charges, Internal Affairs oversees the case on the unit level. Once all the evidence is collected, including DNA and/or blood tests, the case is given to the District Attorney or the Special Prosecutor's Office. The evidence is presented to a grand jury who determines whether the case will be heard in court. In addition to the possibility of criminal charges against him, the sex offender is also subject to unit disciplinary action.

Over the past four years, an average of 110 offender sexual assault cases have been investigated annually. Since 1984, Internal Affairs has investigated a total of 519 cases of this nature. Four cases have resulted in prosecution, with the guilty party receiving an additional prison sentence.

I hope this information is helpful to you in conducting your survey.

Sincerely,

Debby Miller
Executive Services

TEXAS DEPARTMENT OF CRIMINAL JUSTICE

Wayne Scott
Executive Director

P.O. Box 99 • Huntsville, Texas 77342-0099

June 29, 1998

Ms. Joanne Mariner
Associate Counsel
Human Rights Watch
485 5th Avenue
New York, NY 10017

Dear Ms. Mariner:

Per your request, I have provided the number of reported cases of inmate-on-inmate rape and sexual assaults within our system. In the year 1997, approximately 123 offender sexual assault cases were reported. From January 1 to June 1, 1998, 59 cases have been reported. Since our Internal Affairs Division is not always notified by the prosecuting attorneys as to the outcome of these cases, we do not have the precise number of cases that are prosecuted and result in an additional prison sentences.

Regarding your request for names of perpetrators, dates, places and sentences, we ask that you contact Norma Rasbeary in our Internal Affairs Division directly. You may send correspondence to the Internal Affairs Division at P. O. Box 4003, Huntsville, Texas 77342, or contact the office by phone at 409-294-6735.

I hope this information is helpful to you in completing your study.

Sincerely,

Debby Miller
Executive Services

TOTALS BY CALENDAR YEAR

	1991	1992	1993	1994	1995	1996	1997	1998	1999	2000
OFFENDER ASSAULTS	301	366	555	652	1,449	1,388	1,499	1,510	1,704	418
STAFF ASSAULTS	261	365	357	311	739	918	1,442	1,674	2,044	605
ALLEGED SEXUAL ASSAULTS	N/A	35	75	84	131	84	87	89	237	62
DISTURBANCE	47	71	143	107	222	211	187	175	178	36
HOMICIDE***	3	1	3	6	6	5	10	6	7	1
NATURAL DEATHS	116	159	199	274	349	342	272	320	375	116
ACCIDENTAL DEATHS	2	3	2	5	5	3	3	5	5	0
EXECUTIONS	5	12	17	14	19	3	37	20	35	12
SUICIDES***	11	5	16	14	20	20	19	21	22	9
ATTEMPTED SUICIDES	96	118	217	318	392	524	628	607	619	130
SELF-MUTILATION	75	107	225	402	540	574	682	678	637	153
ESCAPES BY INCIDENT	7	5	10	13	18	17	14	13	5	1
ESCAPES BY PERSON	13	10	13	17	24	22	16	16	6	1
ATTEMPTED ESCAPES	18	24	19	33	29	34	38	23	27	7
EMPLOYEE ARREST	140	189	229	350	529	548	562	598	560	153
TOTAL INCIDENTS (reported per year)	1,604	2,038	3,005	3,527	7,215	8,295	10,614	11,767	14,669	3,718
POPULATION**	49,764	52,228	62,855	84,355	107,587	130,413	135,895	143,085	146,574	149,790
MAJOR USE OF FORCE	5,957	6,378	7,190	7,069	10,107	7,806	7,140	8,051	8,106	1,808

*2000 STATISTICAL INFORMATION THROUGH March 31, 2000. STATISTICAL INFORMATION KEPT BY CALENDAR YEAR.

**1991-1999 POPULATION IS YEARLY AVERAGE POPULATION.

***1997 HOMICIDE & SUICIDE TOTALS UPDATED AUGUST, 1998 TO REFLECT FINAL RULING.

BEGINNING WITH 2000, POPULATION REPRESENTS CALENDAR-YEAR-TO-DATE AVERAGE.

THE EMERGENCY ACTION CENTER WAS ESTABLISHED IN LATE 1984. RECORDS FOR STATISTICAL INFORMATION PRIOR TO 1991

AVAILABLE ON REQUEST.

(REV.04/05/2000)

COMMONWEALTH *of* VIRGINIA

Department of Corrections

RON ANGELONE
DIRECTOR

P. O. BOX 26963
RICHMOND, VIRGINIA 23261
(804) 674-3000

May 27, 1997

Ms. Joanne Mariner, Associate Counsel
Human Rights Watch
485 5th Avenue
New York, New York 10017

Dear Ms. Mariner:

Thank you for your letter of April 20th, which requests
information regarding the Virginia Department of Corrections'
approach to inmate-on-inmate rape and sexual abuse.

We do indeed keep statistics on allegations of nonconsensual
sexual activity. The following numbers indicate investigations
in recent years by the Department's Internal Affairs Unit:

Year	# Investigations	# Founded
1993	17	5
1994	12	4
1995	11	6
1996	22	9

The Department takes allegations of sexual activity very
seriously. All criminal investigations conducted by the
Inspector General's Office, whether founded or unfounded, are
referred to the appropriate Commonwealth's Attorney for review
and prosecutorial consideration. In addition, the Department
utilizes its inmate disciplinary procedure to impose sanctions
on the perpetrator. All victims of nonconsensual sex have
access to psychological counseling and receive necessary medical
treatment.

The Department also takes several preventive measures regarding
nonconsensual sexual activity. First, the Department provides a
reception/orientation course to all inmates on how to avoid
sexual situations. Second, we have developed specialized
training segments for our corrections officers so that they may

pinpoint potentially dangerous situations and intervene. Third, the Department utilizes protective custody housing for inmates who want protection, and administrative segregation for predators and other inmates who are suspected of engaging in disruptive behavior. Fourth, we have the ability to transfer inmates to other prisons in order to separate enemies; every institution has a classification committee which continuously reviews an inmate's situation and assesses his placement needs. Fifth, the Department is improving the design and architecture of our prisons to allow better observation and fewer blind spots within the prison. And finally, we have significantly limited personal property items inside prisons with which inmates use to barter.

I trust this description provides you with an idea of how the Department prevents and responds to incidents of sexual activity. Please feel free to contact me if you would like more specific information.

Sincerely yours,

Ron Angelone

RA/am

PREFACE

1. Letter from A.H. to Human Rights Watch, August 30, 1996. In this excerpt, as in other excerpts from prisoners' letters included in this report, the author's idiosyncracies of spelling and grammar have been retained. In addition, prisoners' names and other identifying facts have been withheld to protect their privacy.

2. See Human Rights Watch, *All Too Familiar: Sexual Abuse of Women in U.S. State Prisons* (New York: Human Rights Watch, 1996); Human Rights Watch, "United States—Nowhere to Hide: Retaliation Against Women in Michigan State Prisons," *A Human Rights Watch Short Report*, vol. 10, no. 2, September 1998.

3. There is little published research on the topic of female prisoner-on-prisoner sexual abuse. A 1996 study that covered both men and women prisoners found a much lower rate of coerced sex among women than men. See Cindy Struckman-Johnson et al., "Sexual Coercion Reported by Men and Women in Prison," *Journal of Sex Research*, vol. 33, no. 1 (1996), p. 75. The most recent published examination of the topic describes instances of sexual abuse inflicted on or witnessed by a woman who spent five years in prison. It finds that sexual pressuring and harassment among women prisoners to be more common than actual sexual assault. See Leanne Fiftal Alarid, "Sexual Assault and Coercion among Incarcerated Women Prisoners: Excerpts from Prison Letters," *The Prison Journal*, vol. 80, no. 4 (2000), p. 391.

4. Prisons, which generally hold prisoners after their conviction, are operated by state and federal authorities; jails, which generally hold prisoners who are awaiting trial or who have received sentences of less than one year, are operated by local (county and city) authorities. For a more comprehensive description of the structure of incarceration in the United States, see the Background chapter.

5. See Alan J. Davis, "Sexual Assaults in the Philadelphia Prison System and Sheriff's Vans," *Transaction*, vol. 6, no. 2 (December 1968), pp. 8–16 (concluding that some 3 percent of men who "passed through" the Philadelphia jails were sexually assaulted); Wilbert Rideau, "The Sexual Jungle," in Wilbert Rideau and Ron Wikberg, eds, *Life Sentences: Rage and Survival Behind Bars* (New York: Times Books, 1992), pp. 90–91; see also Robert A. Martin, "Gang-Rape in D.C. Jail," in Pamela Portwood et al., eds., *Rebirth of Power: Overcoming the Effects of Sexual Abuse Through the Experiences of*

Others (Racine, Wisconsin: Mother Courage Press, 1987); *Gregory v. Shelby*, 220 F. 3d 433 (6th Cir. 2000) (jail inmate who died as a result of injuries sustained during violent sexual abuse by another inmate). But see Daniel Lockwood, *Prison Sexual Violence* (New York: Elsevier, 1980), p. 25, who found much less sexual aggression among inmates in New York jails than in state prisons.

6. See Clemens Bartollas, Stuart J. Miller, and Simon Dinitz, "The 'Booty Bandit': A Social Role in a Juvenile Institution," *Journal of Homosexuality*, vol. 1, no. 2 (1974), p. 203.

7. "Memorandum in Support of the United States' Motion for a Preliminary Injunction Regarding Conditions of Confinement at the Jena Juvenile Justice Center," *United States v. Louisiana*, Civil No. 98–947-B-1, filed March 30, 2000.

8. A Kenyan human rights group, for example, included the following description in its report on prisons in that country:

> [O]ne respondent reported an incident in which nine male juveniles were so badly sodomised by adult prisoners that their rectums protruded. . . . Similarly it was reported that first offenders in Machakos prison are preyed upon by older inmates who will even resort to rape if the younger inmates refuse to submit. Other young inmates engage in homosexual relations with older inmates in exchange for protection from the attentions of other prisoners.

Kenya Human Rights Commission, *A Death Sentence: Prison Conditions in Kenya* (Nairobi: Kenya Human Rights Commission, 1996), pp. 76–77. See also Moscow Center for Prison Reform, *In Search of a Solution: Crime Criminal Policy and Prison Facilities in the Former Soviet Union* (Moscow: Human Rights Publishers, 1996), p. 12; Observatoire international des prisons, *Le guide du prisonnier* (Paris: Les Editions Ouvrières, 1996), p. 139.

The most comprehensive analyses we have found of prisoner-on-prisoner rape outside of the United States are included in Daniel Welzer-Lang et al., *Sexualités et violences en prison* (Lyon: Aleas Editeur, 1996) (French prisons), and David Heilpern, *Fear or Favour—Sexual Assault on Young Prisoners* (New South Wales: Southern Cross University Press, 1998) (concluding that one in four male prisoners aged 18–25 is sexually assaulted in prisons in New South Wales, Australia). Surprisingly, a recent British study of inmate victimization made no reference to the issue. See Ian O'Donnell and Kimmett Edgar, *Bullying in Prisons* (Oxford: Centre for Criminological Research, University of Oxford, 1998).

Previous Human Rights Watch prison reports touching on the problem of rape include: Human Rights Watch, *Behind Bars in Brazil* (New York: Human Rights Watch, 1998), pp. 117–18; Human Rights Watch/Americas (now the Americas Division of Human Rights Watch), *Punishment Before Trial: Prison Conditions in Venezuela* (New York: Human Rights Watch, 1997), pp. 54–55; Africa Watch (now the Africa Division of Human Rights Watch), *Prison Conditions in South Africa* (New York: Human Rights Watch, 1994), p. 46; Helsinki Watch (now the Europe and Central Asia Division of Human Rights Watch), *Prison Conditions in Czechoslovakia* (New York: Human Rights Watch, 1989), pp. 31–33.

9. See, for example, Heilpern, *Fear or Favour* (finding that gay prisoners are disproportionately subject to rape).

CASE HISTORIES OF S.M. AND C.R.

1. Human Rights Watch interview, Texas, March 1999.
2. Deposition of S.M., *Ruiz v. Scott*, Civil Action No. H-78–987, January 20, 1999.
3. Human Rights Watch interview, Texas, March 1999.
4. S.M. said he had some problems with cellmates who threatened him, but was never raped during this period.
5. Human Rights Watch interview, Texas, March 1999.
6. Deposition of S.M., *Ruiz v. Scott*, Civil Action No. H-78–987, January 20, 1999, p. 40.
7. Human Rights Watch interview, Texas, March 1999.
8. Ibid.
9. Ibid.
10. Deposition of S.M., *Ruiz v. Scott*, Civil Action No. H-78–987, January 20, 1999, pp. 83–84.
11. Human Rights Watch interview, Texas, March 1999.
12. Ibid.
13. Letter to Human Rights Watch, October 30, 1996.
14. Human Rights Watch interview, Texas, October 1998.
15. Ibid.
16. Ibid. "Camp" is prison slang for prison; "boss" is slang for correctional officer; "ho" is slang for prostitute (whore).
17. Memorandum Opinion and Order of Dismissal, *R. v. Scott*, Civil Action filed July 23, 1996, p. 6.
18. Ibid.
19. Ibid.

CHAPTER II. BACKGROUND

1. Kathleen Maguire and Ann L. Pastore, eds, Bureau of Justice Statistics, U.S. Department of Justice, *Sourcebook of Criminal Justice Statistics 1998* (Washington, D.C.: USGPO, 1999), pp. 481, 497.
2. See "Nation's Prison Population Climbs to Over 2 Million," Reuters, August 10, 2000. According to the Justice Policy Institute, an estimated 1,983,084 adults were behind bars on December 31, 1999, a figure expected to rise to 2,073,969 by the end of the year 2000. Justice Policy Institute, "The Punishing Decade: Prison and Jail Estimates at the Millennium," 1999. This figure does not include the additional 100,000 juveniles that were in detention. See Maguire and Pastore, *Sourcebook*, p. 479.
3. As far as is known, China has the second largest inmate population, with an official

figure of 1.6 million prisoners. While this number is likely to be a serious underestimate, it should be noted that China's resident population is many times that of the United States, and therefore its rate of incarceration is much lower. The only countries whose incarceration rates compare to the U.S. rate are Rwanda, where the 1994 genocide and subsequent incarceration of some 130,000 suspects have resulted in an incarceration rate of roughly 1,000 to 2,000 prisoners per 100,000 residents; Russia, with a rate of roughly 740 per 100,000; Kazakhstan, with a rate of roughly 500 per 100,000, and Belarus, with a rate of roughly 600 per 100,000. Statistics on file at Human Rights Watch; see also André Kuhn, "Incarceration Rates Across the World," *Overcrowded Times,* vol. 10, no. 2 (April 1999), p. 1.

4. U.S. Department of State, Initial Report of the United States of America to the Committee Against Torture (Part I. General Information), October 15, 1999 (hereinafter DOS, Torture Report).

5. "Three strikes, you're out" laws (the phrase is borrowed from baseball) have been instituted in several states, including California. Such laws impose mandatory life sentences without parole on "habitual offenders": generally persons with three felony convictions. Enormously popular with the public, they have been criticized for eliminating judicial discretion in sentencing, essentially shifting power from judges to prosecutors. See, for example, Andy Furillo, "Sentencing Discretion May Return to Courts," *Sacramento Bee,* April 2, 1996.

6. See Kuhn, "Incarceration Rates . . . "

7. See Maguire and Pastore, *Sourcebook,* p. 487 (showing that as of December 31, 1997, at least 3 percent of state prisoners were held in local jails because of prison overcrowding).

8. See International Covenant of Civil and Political Rights (ICCPR), art. 10(2), but note that in ratifying the ICCPR the United States included a specific reservation to this provision; Standard Minimum Rules for the Treatment of Prisoners, art. 8(b). For further discussion of international standards and the U.S. reservations to them, see chapter III, below.

9. DOS, Torture Report.

10. Another 12,347 persons were in contract facilities, including community corrections centers or "halfway houses." Ibid.

11. See California Department of Corrections, "CDC Facts," October 1999. Available: http://www.cdc.state.ca.us/factsht.htm (December 1999). Texas Department of Criminal Justice, Institutional Division, "Divisional Overview," December 1999 (available at http://www.tdcj.state.tx.us/id/id-home.htm (December 1999)).

12. DOS, Torture Report.

13. Maguire and Pastore, *Sourcebook,* p. 79; DOS Torture Report. "Design capacity" refers to the number of inmates that planners or architects intended the facility to house, while "rated capacity" refers to the number of beds assigned by a rating official. Among the most overcrowded prison systems, in 1995, were those of California, Hawaii, Indiana, Iowa, and Ohio.

14. In six states, however, prisons and jails form an integrated system. The states are Connecticut, Rhode Island, Vermont, Delaware, Alaska and Hawaii. Maguire and Pastore, *Sourcebook,* p. 492.

15. Nationally, as of 1998, jails had an overall capacity of 612,780 inmates and were at 97 percent of capacity. Maguire and Pastore, *Sourcebook,* p. 481. These overall numbers, however, mask the fact that numerous jails are jammed far beyond their capacity. See, for example, *Mangan v. Christian County,* Case No. 6–99–03373-JCE, complaint filed October 6, 1999, describing overcrowding and other abuses.

16. Maguire and Pastore, *Sourcebook,* p. 82. See also Eric Bates, "Private Prisons," *The Nation,* January 5, 1998, which states that private prisons hold an estimated 77,500 prisoners.

17. See, for example, Human Rights Watch, *World Report 2000* (New York: Human Rights Watch, 1999), p. 394, describing violence and abuse at privately-operated prison facilities.

18. Justice Policy Institute, "The Punishing Decade . . . "; Maguire and Pastore, *Sourcebook,* p. 4 (giving 1994 figure of $34.9 billion).

19. Camille G. Camp and George M. Camp, *The Corrections Yearbook 1998* (Middletown, Connecticut: Criminal Justice Institute, 1998), p. 13 (data as of January 1998 showing male inmates making up 93.6 percent of the national inmate population).

20. As of mid-1997, some 13 percent of the U.S. resident population identified themselves as black, while some 11 percent were Hispanic. DOS, Torture Report.

21. Anthony Lewis, "Punishing the Country," *New York Times,* December 21, 1999.

22. See *World Report 2000,* p. 394.

23. See, for example, Connie L. Neeley, "Addressing the Needs of Elderly Offenders," *Corrections Today,* August 1997; Robert W. Stock, "Inside Prison, Too, a Population Is Aging," *New York Times,* January 18, 1996 (citing national survey finding that 6 percent of U.S. inmates were 55 and older).

24. Between 1992 and 1998, at least forty U.S. states adopted legislation to facilitate the prosecution of juvenile offenders in adult courts, which typically means that they are detained in adult jails pending trial. Human Rights Watch, *No Minor Matter: Children in Maryland's Jails* (New York: Human Rights Watch, 1999), p. 16. The federal government's Office of Juvenile Justice and Delinquency Prevention (OJJDP) documented a 14 percent increase in the number of juveniles held in adult jails from 1985 to 1995. *OJJDP Annual Report* (Washington, D.C.: OJJDP, 1998), p. 44. For an analysis of what this means for juvenile offenders, see generally Margaret Talbot, "The Maximum Security Adolescent," *The New York Times Magazine,* September 10, 2000.

25. U.S. Department of Justice, Office of Justice Programs, Bureau of Justice Statistics, *Correctional Populations in the United States, 1995* (Washington, D.C.: Bureau of Justice Statistics, 1997).

26. See, for example, Vincent Schiraldi and Jason Zeidenberg, "The Risks Juveniles Face When They Are Incarcerated With Adults," Justice Policy Institute, 1997.

27. Eileen Poe-Yamagata and Michael A. Jones, *And Justice for Some: Differential Treat-*

ment of Minority Youth in the Justice System (Washington, D.C.: Youth Law Center, April 2000), p. 25 (available at http://www.buildingblocksforyouth.org/justicefor-some/).

28. National Institute of Corrections, "Offenders under Age 18 in State Adult Correctional Systems: A National Picture," 1995, p. 5.

29. See *World Report 2000*, p. 394.

30. *Ruiz v. Johnson*, 1999 U.S. Dist. LEXIS 2060, at 236–37 (March 1, 1999).

31. Marilyn D. McShane and Frank P. Williams III, eds., *Encyclopedia of American Prisons* (New York: Garland Publishing, Inc., 1996), p. 379.

32. *The Corrections Yearbook 1998*, pp. 30, 40.

33. Laura M. Maruschak and Allen J. Beck, "Medical Problems of Inmates, 1997," Bureau of Justice Statistics Special Report, January 2001, pp. 1, 4.

34. David E. Eichenthal and Laurel Blatchford, "Prison Crime in New York State," *Prison Journal*, vol. 77, no. 4, December 1997, pp. 458–59.

35. McShane and Williams, *Encyclopedia*, p. 213.

36. Cory Godwin, *Gangs in Prison: How to Set Up a Security-Threat Group Intelligence Unit* (Horsham, Pennsylvania: LRP Publications, 1999), p. 4.

37. McShane and Williams, *Encyclopedia*, p. 215. Human Rights Watch's communications with prisoners have suggested to us that gang activity pervades many prison systems.

38 . McShane and Williams, *Encyclopedia*, p. 215.

39. McShane and Williams, *Encyclopedia*, pp. 111–14, 379.

40. A number of prisoners who had been raped sent Human Rights Watch copies of letters that they has sent to local law enforcement officials reporting the crime. None of them resulted in a criminal investigation, let alone the filing of criminal charges. See also McShane and Williams, *Encyclopedia*, p. 299 (stating that "[a]s a practical matter, few prosecutions result from complaints made by prisoners"). As the *Encyclopedia* points out, the time and expense of prosecution deter most local officials, who have other competing priorities, from focusing on prison abuses.

41. McShane and Williams, *Encyclopedia*, p. 299. Of the 26,005 assaults that were reported to have been committed by inmates against other inmates during 1997, only 1,306 were referred for prosecution. *1998 Corrections Yearbook*, p. 40. It is likely that only a small fraction of this number were in fact prosecuted, although precise figures are not available.

42. Human Rights Watch, *World Report 2000*, p. 394.

43. McShane and Williams, *Encyclopedia*, p. 163. Accumulated good-time credits allow a prisoner to leave prison sooner than he otherwise would.

44. Different prison systems have different types of classification schemes with variations in terminology. For example, the Federal Bureau of Prisons has established five security levels: minimum, low, medium, high and administrative. Federal Bureau of Prisons, *State of the Bureau* (Washington, D.C.: U.S. Department of Justice, 1995), p. 67.

45. McShane and Williams, *Encyclopedia*, p. 377.

46. *Lee v. Washington,* 390 U.S. 333 (1968).

47. For example, a 1995 Department of Justice investigation of conditions at the Musco-gee County Jail in the state of Georgia found that African American inmates were housed separately from white inmates there. Letter from Assistant Attorney General from Civil Rights Deval L. Patrick to Acting City Manager Iris Jessie, Columbus, Georgia, June 1, 1995. In 1997, a just-released California prisoner drew press atten-tion to the striking degree to which that state's prisons were segregated by race. See Daniel B. Wood, "To Keep Peace, Prisons Allow Race to Rule," *Christian Science Mon-itor,* September 16, 1997 (describing how "nearly every activity—sleep, exercise, and meals—is determined by race"); Emanuel Parker, "White Former Con Says State Prison Practices Segregation," *Los Angeles Sentinel,* May 16, 1996.

    A concurring opinion in the *Lee* case did, however, appear to leave the door open to some forms of racial categorization. It stated:

    > In joining the opinion of the Court, we wish to make explicit something that is left to be gathered only by implication from the Court's opinion. This is that prison authori-ties have the right, acting in good faith and in particularized circumstances, to take into account racial tensions in maintaining security, discipline, and good order in prisons and jails.

    Lee, 390 U.S. at 335 (Black, J., Harlan J., and Stewart, J., concurring).

48. Camp and Camp, *Corrections Yearbook 1998,* p. 26.

49. *Ruiz* at 215 (stating that as of December 1, 1998, there were 2,592 safekeeping beds and 128 protective custody beds in the Texas prison system). An expert witness testi-fying on behalf of the plaintiffs in the *Ruiz* case asserted that these numbers were insufficient given the size of the Texas prison population.

50. *Palmigiano v. Garrahy,* 443 F. Supp. 956, 965 (D.R.I. 1977).

51. Under the Supreme Court's current interpretation of constitutional protections on due process, the changed conditions must impose an "atypical and significant hard-ship on the inmate in relation to the ordinary incidents of prison life." *Sandin v. Con-ner,* 115 S. Ct. 2293 (1995). This standard, which cuts back significantly on earlier protections, essentially grants prison officials full discretionary power in classifying inmates.

52. See, for example, McShane and Williams, *Encyclopedia,* p. 379; Seth Mydans, "Racial Tensions in Los Angeles Jails Ignite Inmate Violence," *New York Times,* February 6, 1995; Wood, "To Keep Peace . . ."; Rick Bragg, "Unfathomable Crime, Unlikely Figure," *New York Times,* June 17, 1998 (quoting a spokesman for the Southern Poverty Law Center as saying, "The level of racism in prison is very high. The truth is, you may go in completely unracist and emerge ready to kill people who don't look like you.")

53. Letter to Human Rights Watch from T.B., Texas, September 3, 1996.

54. Letter to Human Rights Watch from W.M., Texas, October 31, 1996.

55. Letter to Human Rights Watch from V.H., Arkansas, November 17, 1996.

56. See, for example, "Inmate Dies and 8 Are Hurt as Riot Erupts in California Prison," *New York Times,* February 24, 2000. This article, which described a riot involving

some 200 inmates at California's Pelican Bay State Prison, quoted one prison official as saying, "It was black and Hispanic inmates fighting. We've had racial incidents in the past."

57. "Ride" is Texas prison slang for paying protection to another prisoner; "turn them out" is slang for raping them.

58. Letter to Human Rights Watch from T.B., Texas, November 15, 1996.

59. The act provides: "[n]o action shall be brought with respect to prison conditions under [42 U.S.C. §] 1983 . . . , or any other federal law, by a prisoner . . . until such administrative remedies as are available are exhausted." 42 U.S.C. § 1997e(a).

60. Standard Minimum Rules for the Treatment of Prisoners, art. 55; Penal Reform International, *Making Standards Work* (The Hague: Penal Reform International, 1995), pp. 161–65.

61. In 1999, only about a quarter of state prisons and 5–7 percent of local jails were accredited with the ACA. In contrast, all of the facilities operated by the Federal Bureau of Prisons were accredited or in the process of receiving accreditation. Human Rights Watch telephone interview, Mike Shannon, assistant director for standards and accreditation, ACA, Lanham, Maryland, March 14, 2000.

62. In New York, for example, the Correctional Association of New York has statutory authority to visit state prisons.

CASE HISTORY OF R.G

1. Human Rights Watch interview, California, May 1998.

2. The "softie tank" is inmate slang for the separate housing area reserved for weak or vulnerable prisoners.

3. Ibid.

4. "Plaintiffs Notice of Motion and Opposition to Defendant Motion for Summary Judgment," *R.G. v. Haskett*, October 1, 1996.

CHAPTER III. LEGAL CONTEXT

1. Typical of this view were the words of a federal court in 1949:
   This Court . . . is not prepared to establish itself as a "co-administrator" of State prisons along with the duly appointed State officials . . . . [I]t is not the function of a Federal Court to assume the status of an appellate tribunal for the purpose of reviewing each and every act and decision of a State official.
   Siegel v. Ragen, 88 F. Supp. 996 (D.C. Ill. 1949).

2. *Hudson v. McMillian*, 503 U.S. 1, 17 (1992) (Thomas, J., dissenting).

3. See, for example, *Estelle v. Gamble*, 429 U.S. 97 (1976); *Dothard v. Rawlinson*, 433 U.S. 321 (1977).

4. See, for example, Francis A. Allen, "The Decline of the Rehabilitative Ideal in American Criminal Justice," *Cleveland State Law Review,* vol. 27, 1978, p. 147.

5. The criticisms of Supreme Court Justice Clarence Thomas—who complained that prisons conditions rulings from the 1970s effectively "transform federal judges into superintendents of prison conditions nationwide"—are emblematic of this attitude. *Farmer v. Brennan,* 511 U.S. 825, 839 (1994) (Thomas, J., concurring).

6. See, for example, Amnesty International, "United States of America: Florida Reintroduces Chain Gangs," AMR 51/02/96, January 1996; Human Rights Watch, *Cold Storage: Super- Maximum Security Confinement in Indiana* (New York: Human Rights Watch, 1997), pp. 17–20 (describing national trend toward super-maximum security prisons); Amnesty International, "Rights for All. Cruelty in Control? The Stun Belt and Other Electro-Shock Equipment in Law Enforcement," AMR 51/54/99, June 1999 (discussing the use of stun weapons in prisons and jails). An indicator of the strength of continuing public antipathy toward prisoners can be found on the website of the Florida Department of Corrections. The site includes the results of a public opinion poll on prison issues and a page called "Eight Misconceptions about Florida Prisons." The poll concludes that 96 percent of Florida's public approve of requiring prisoners to do unpaid work and that 73 percent approve of the use of prison chain gangs. The "misconceptions" that the page forcefully dispels include the notion that prisoners are not made to work, that they are allowed cable television, and that prisons are air-conditioned. Available: http://www.dc.state.fl.us/pub/annual/9798/myths.html (October 1999).

7. In the mid-1990s, in particular, it seemed that politicians' outrage over inmate litigation knew no bounds. Ignoring real prison abuses, they publicized only the most factually absurd lawsuits, creating what one commentator described as "the meta-narrative of the frivolous." Henry F. Fradella, "A Typology of the Frivolous: Varying Meanings of Frivolity in Section 1983 Prisoner Civil Rights Litigation," *Prison Journal,* December 1998, p. 470. See, for example, Paula Boland, "Prisoners Deserve Punishment, Not Perks," July 1996 (position paper by member of the California Assembly, complaining that "inmates receive three meals a day, free medical, dental and vision care, free stationary, postage and free laundry services!"), available: http://www.calgop.scvcr/pb0796.htm (September 1996); "Lance to Testify against Frivolous Inmate Lawsuits," January 1996 (position paper by Idaho attorney general), available: http://www.state.id.us/ag/middle/releases/0126friv.htm (September 1996); Gregg Birnbaum, "Vacco wants restrictions on inmates' petty suits," *New York Post,* October 19, 1995 (on attempts by New York Attorney General Dennis Vacco to impose filing fees on inmate lawsuits).

   As generally portrayed in the media, inmate litigation was reduced to stories of prisoners who went to court over broken cookies and lukewarm soup. See, for example, Sandra Ann Harris, "Crime: Inmate Lawsuits Costly to Taxpayers," *Detroit News,* October 23, 1995. Especial emphasis was placed on the cost to taxpayers of defending against frivolous lawsuits filed by inmate litigants. The NBC Nightly News reportedly aired a segment in 1996 on the "The Fleecing of America," focusing on this issue, while the April 1996 issue of Reader's Digest contained a similar piece. D. Van Atta, "The Scandal of Prisoner Lawsuits," *Readers's Digest,* April 1996, p. 65; Nat Hentoff, "Our 'Overprivileged' Prisoners," *Washington Post,* March 29, 1997. Unfortunately, stories of legitimate inmate lawsuits—challenging horrendous conditions of incarceration, unchecked violence, and custodial sexual abuse—rarely received such coverage.

8. *See* 18 U.S.C.A. § 3626.

9. The PLRA provision on filing fees provides that if a prisoner has brought three or more lawsuits that have been dismissed as frivolous, malicious, or as having failed to state a claim, that prisoner is barred from obtaining *in forma pauperis* (indigent) status, a prerequisite for the reduction of filing fees. As the courts have explained it, "Congress enacted the PLRA with the principal purpose of deterring frivolous prison litigation by instituting economic costs for prisoners wishing to file civil claims." *Lyon v. Krol,* 127 F.3d 763, 764 (8th Cir. 1997). Yet it is clear to Human Rights Watch that numerous prison suits are dismissed as frivolous because prisoners lack legal skill and, in some case, because judges simply lack interest in their claims, not because the prisoners' claims actually lack merit. By imposing filing fees on prisoners who have no money to pay them, the provision has the effect of creating a class of poor prisoners for whom the courthouse door is closed.

10. *See Inmates of Suffolk County Jail v. Rouse,* 129 F.3d 649 (1st Cir. 1997); *Plyler v. Moore,*100 F.3d 365 (4th Cir. 1996), *cert. denied,* 117 S. Ct. 2460 (1997); *Dougan v. Singletary,* (11th Cir. 1997); *Rivera v. Allin,* 144 F.3d 719 (11th Cir. 1998); *Wilson v. Yaklich,* 148 F.3d 596, 606 (6th Cir. 1998); *Gavin v. Branstad,* 122 F.3d 1081 (8th Cir. 1997).

11. Courts have relied upon other constitutional amendments to resolve a limited range of prison issues. Prominent among them is the Fourth Amendment prohibition against unreasonable searches and seizures, which has been interpreted as granting inmates a limited right to privacy. See, for example, *United States v. Hinckley,* 672 F. 2d 115 (D.C. Cir. 1982); *Frazier v. Ward,* 528 F. Supp. 80 (S.D.N.Y. 1981). The First Amendment, in addition, has been used in the prison context in cases involving religious freedom and free expression. See, for example, *O'Lone v. Estate of Shabazz,* 482 U.S. 342 (1987); *Pell v. Procunier,* 417 U.S. 817 (1974); *Cruz v. Beto,* 405 U.S. 319 (1972). All of these provisions, and the Eighth Amendment as well, are not directly applicable to the actions of state governments, but are instead applied to the states via the Fourteenth Amendment.

12. Because the Eighth Amendment bars cruel and unusual *punishment,* and because pretrial detainees are not supposed to be subject to any punishment at all, the courts have ruled that the Eighth Amendment is not directly applicable in cases involving pretrial detainees. Yet, in practice, the standards applied to pretrial detainees under the Fifth Amendment's Due Process Clause have followed those applied to convicted prisoners under the Eighth. See generally *Bell v. Wolfish,* 441 U.S. 520 (1979).

13. *Farmer*, 511 U.S. at 832 (internal quotations omitted).

14. *DeShaney v. Winnebago County Dept. of Social Services*, 489 U.S. 189, 199 (1989).

15. *Whitley v. Albers*, 475 U.S. 312, 319 (1986).

16. *Hudson v. McMillian*, 503 U.S. 1, 14 (1992).

17. *Wilson v. Seiter*, 501 U.S. 294, 298 (1991).

18. *Hudson*, 503 U.S. at 10; *Whitley*, 475 U.S. at 320–21.

19. *Wilson*, 501 U.S. at 303. The Supreme Court did not define "deliberate indifference" in *Wilson*. In the 1994 *Farmer* decision, however, it ruled that prison officials must know of the risk and fail to take reasonable measures to prevent it.

20. See *Hudson v. Palmer*, 468 U.S. 517 (1984).

21. *Farmer*, 511 U.S. 825.

22. Ibid. at 834 (quoting *Rhodes v. Chapman*, 452 U.S. 337, 347 (1981)) (internal quotations omitted).

23. *Farmer*, 511 U.S. at 837.

24. See *Wilson v. Seiter*, 501 U.S. 294 (1991).

25. Ibid. at 311 (White, J., concurring in the judgment).

26. *Wilson*, 501 U.S. 294.

27. Ibid.

28. The requirement of "under color of state law" means that a state official must be using his or her authority as a state official when the violation occurs. A state official may still be acting under color of law even if the conduct violates state law. *Screws v. United States*, 325 U.S. 91, 109 (1945). In order to be actionable, the misuse of power must be made possible by the actor's authority under state law. Ibid.

29. Sections 241 and 242 are both general civil rights provisions, and their application is not limited to abuses within prisons. Title 18, United States Code, Section 241 provides, in relevant part: "[i]f two or more persons conspire to injure, oppress, threaten, or intimidate any person in any State . . . in the free exercise or enjoyment of any right or privilege secured to him [or her] by the Constitution or laws of the United States, or because of his [or her] having so exercise of the same . . . [t]hey shall be fined or imprisoned not more than ten years, . . . or both."

    Section 242 provides, in relevant part: "Whoever, under color of law, statute, ordinance, regulation, or custom, willfully subjects any person in any State . . . to the deprivation of any rights, privileges, or immunities secured or protected by the Constitution or laws of the United States . . . shall be fined under this title or imprisoned not more than one year, or both; and if bodily injury results from the acts committed in violation of this section or if such acts include the use, the attempted use, or threatened use of a dangerous weapon, explosives, or fire, shall be fined under this title or imprisoned not more than ten years, or both; and if death results from the acts committed in violation of this section or if such acts include . . . aggravated sexual abuse, or an attempt to commit aggravated sexual abuse, . . . shall be fined under this title, or imprisoned for any term of years or for life, or both, or may be sentenced to death."

30. *Screws,* 325 U.S. at 103 (18 U.S.C. Section 242); *United States v. Guest,* 383 U.S. 745, 760 (1966) (18 U.S.C. Section 241).

31. *Screws,* 325 U.S. at 101–03.

32. See Paul Hoffman, "The Feds, Lies and Videotape: The Need for an Effective Federal Role in Controlling Police Abuse in Urban America," *Southern California Law Review,* Volume 66, p. 1522 (1993).

33. DOS, Torture Report.

34. 42 U.S.C. Section 1997 *et seq.*

35. See, for example, *Canterino v. Wilson,* 538 F. Supp. 62 (W.D. Ky. 1982); Senate Reports Number 96–416, 96th Congress, Second Session (1980), *reprinted in* 1980 United States Code Congressional and Administrative News, pp. 787, 797.

36. The investigation itself must be triggered by a published report or information from a source with personal knowledge about allegations that constitutional rights are being violated.

37. Ibid.

38. *United States v. Michigan,* 868 F. Supp. 890 (W.D. Mich. 1994).

39. Courts prior to the Michigan decision repeatedly upheld DOJ requests to enter institutions and conduct investigations. See *U.S. v. County of Los Angeles,* 635 F. Supp. 588 (C.D. Cal. 1986); *U.S. v. County of Crittenden,* Civil Action No. JC89–141, 1990 WESTLAW 257949 (E.D. Ark. December 26, 1990).

40. Human Right Watch telephone interview, Mellie Nelson, Deputy Chief, Special Litigation Section, Civil Rights Division, Department of Justice, March 30, 2000.

41. Besides remedying abusive prison and jail conditions, the Special Litigation Section is also responsible for the enforcement of legal standards covering conditions in mental institutions, protecting clinics providing reproductive health services, and remedying patterns or practices of police misconduct.

42. As of March 2000, the section planned to hire eight additional staff attorneys. Human Right Watch telephone interview, Mellie Nelson, Department of Justice, March 30, 2000.

43. Human Right Watch telephone interview, Mellie Nelson, Department of Justice, March 30, 2000. The section also filed a consent decree for a case involving prisons and jails in the Northern Mariana Islands.

44. The Eleventh Amendment bars suits in federal court against a U.S. state as such, unless the state has waived its immunity. *Welch v. Texas Dept. of Highways and Public Transportation,* 483 U.S. 468, 472–473 (1987). In addition, Section 1983 grant of federal jurisdiction does not extend to suits against states or state officials acting in their official capacities. *Will v. Michigan Dept. of State Police,* 491 U.S. 58 (1989).

Cases involving conditions in federal prisons, where Section 1983 does not apply, are generally based on the precedent established by the case of *Bivens v. Six Unknown Federal Narcotic Agents,* 403 U.S. 388 (1971). In *Bivens,* the Supreme Court ruled that officials of the federal government may be held personally liable for actions undertaken in their official capacity.

45. See *Monroe v. Pape*, 365 U.S. 167 (1961). Section 1983 was initially passed to protect African Americans in the South from reprisals during Reconstruction. It was known as the Civil Rights Act (originally the Ku Klux Klan Act) of 1871 and was later recodified as 42 U.S.C. Sec. 1983. It provides: "Every person who, under color of any statute, ordinance, regulation, custom, or usage, of any State or Territory, or the District of Columbia, subjects or causes to be subjected, any citizen of the United States or any person within the jurisdiction thereof to the deprivation of any rights, privileges, or immunities secured by the Constitution and laws, shall be liable to the party injured in an action at law, suit in equity, or other proper proceeding for redress."

46. *Cooper v. Pate*, 378 U.S. 546 (1964) (reinstating complaint of Muslim inmate denied permission to purchase religious publications).

47. Unlike lawyers in most other countries, U.S. lawyers may work on a contingency fee basis, typically taking a quarter to a third of any damages award won in a lawsuit. In essence, such lawyers are betting on the success of their clients' claims to damages. This practice allows many plaintiffs to obtain legal counsel who would otherwise be unable to afford it.

48. Section 504(a)(15) of the 1996 appropriations act for the Legal Services Corporation (LSC), Public Law 104–134, 110 Stat. 1321 (1996), prohibits the participation of LSC recipients in any litigation on behalf of prisoners. Not only does the law bar legal services lawyers from taking on new prison cases, its passage disrupted numerous ongoing court cases, such as a New Hampshire class action asserting that the state had relegated mentally ill prisoners to harsh high-security cells. Nina Bernstein, "2,000 Inmates Near a Cutoff of Legal Aid," *New York Times*, November 25, 1995.

49. Class action litigation refers to cases in which an entire class of similarly situated plaintiffs, as opposed to a single plaintiff, files suit. The ACLU National Prison Project (NPP), based in Washington, D.C., is perhaps the best known of the organizations that specialize in inmate class action suits, having litigated some of the most important prison cases of the past few decades. Among its many critical interventions, the NPP represented the inmate plaintiff in argument before the Supreme Court in the case of *Farmer v. Brennan*, the first case in which the Court faced the issue of sexual abuse in prison. Some local ACLU affiliate offices also handle prison cases.

50. The situation of Prisoners' Legal Services, established in the wake of the brutal suppression of the inmate uprising at the prison of Attica, N.Y., is all too typical. In the past few years, the organization's funding has been cut; it has been forced to lay off staff, and its very survival has been threatened. At one point, its legal department consisted of little more than the executive director. See Clyde Haberman, "Attica's Ghost in the Shadow of Pataki Veto," *New York Times*, July 28, 1998.

51. Roger A. Hanson and Henry W.K. Daley, "Challenging the Conditions of Prisons and Jails: A Report on Section 1983 Litigation," U.S. Department of Justice, February 1995 (providing data showing that 96 percent of prisoners proceed pro se).

52. Ibid.

53. For example, the landmark case of *Farmer v. Brennan*—the only prison rape case to

be heard by the Supreme Court—was filed by an inmate acting pro se; legal counsel was not provided until the case was on appeal. Other precedents involving inmate pro se plaintiffs include: *Risley v. Hawk*, 918 F. Supp. 18 (D.D.C. 1996); *Jones v. Godinez*, 918 F. Supp. 1142 (N.D. Ill. 1995); *Blackmon v. Buckner*, 932 F. Supp. 1126 (S.D. Ind. 1996). More commonly, however, courts summarily dispose of cases filed by inmates via unpublished memorandum opinions. See, for example, *Collier v. Zimmerman*, 1988 WL 142788 (E.D. Pa. 1988) (dismissing complaint of rape as frivolous even though the plaintiff made several statements indicating that his claim was valid); *Ginn v. Gallagher*, 1994 U.S. Dist. LEXIS 16669 (E.D. Pa. 1994) (granting summary judgment for the defendants in case alleging prison rape); *Hunt v. Washington*, 1993 U.S. Dist. LEXIS 681 (N.D. Ill. 1993) (dismissing complaint of attempted rape).

54. Numerous prisoners have mailed Human Rights Watch their handwritten legal documents. Some of these legal briefs—meticulously drafted, complete with supporting affidavits, citing to all of the relevant legal precedents—are twenty or thirty pages long. One wonders about the reception of such documents in the courts: particularly whether anyone takes the time to read and understand them.

55. Two important such resources are the *Jailhouse Lawyer's Manual*, published by Columbia University, and the *Prisoners' Self-Help Litigation Manual*. Columbia Human Rights Law Review, *A Jailhouse Lawyer's Manual*, 4th ed. (New York: Columbia University School of Law, 1996); John Boston and Daniel E. Manville, *Prisoners' Self-Help Litigation Manual*, 3rd ed. (New York: Oceana Publications, 1996).

56. Hanson and Daley, "Challenging the Conditions . . . " (stating that more than 94 percent of prisoner lawsuits are unsuccessful).

57. Typical of such cases is *Collier v. Zimmerman*, 1988 WL 142788 (E.D. Pa. 1988), in which the plaintiff alleged that he had been raped on two separate occasions by different inmates. The court acknowledged that the several of the plaintiff's statements indicated that he had a valid claim—that the prison authorities might have wrongly failed to protect him from rape. It found the plaintiff's allegations lacking in the proper specificity, however, and thus dismissed the complaint.

    Discussing such cases, a recent article notes that "'frivolous' is not the same as 'nonmeritorious.' A claim could be dismissed as frivolous because some technical requirement of constitutional law was not met, but such a disposition is not necessarily a reflection on the merit or lack thereof of the substantive allegations raised in any given complaint." Henry F. Fradella, "A Typology of the Frivolous: Varying Meanings of Frivolity in Section 1983 Prisoner Civil Rights Litigation," *The Prison Journal*, December 1998, p. 474.

    Describing the handicaps facing pro se inmate litigants, one federal judge noted:
    A collection of books is never a substitute for a lawyer. We should not romanticize what even a jailhouse lawyer, much less a poorly-educated inmate, can accomplish by rummaging for a few hours in a limited collection. Many intelligent prisoners can pick up the lingo of the law; very few of them can put it all together and present a persuasive petition or claim.
    Toussaint v. McCarthy, 926 F.2d 800, 815 (9th Cir. 1990).

58. *Bounds v. Smith,* 430 U.S. 817 (1977).

59. A 1996 Supreme Court decision, *Lewis* represents a huge step backwards from the principles enunciated in *Bounds.* In *Lewis,* a divided Court ruled that even the total absence of a prison law library does not violate the Constitution unless a prisoner can show that he or she was effectively barred from pursuing a "nonfrivolous" legal claim as a result of the deprivation, and thus suffered "actual injury." *Lewis v. Casey,* 516 U.S. 804 (1996). The practical effect of *Lewis* is to make it much more difficult for prisoners to challenge a lack of legal services or facilities. See David W. Wilhelmus, "Where Have All The Law Libraries Gone?" *Corrections Today,* December 1999, p. 153.

60. See, for example, Larry Fugate, "New Law Cracks Down on Frivolous Inmate Lawsuits," *Daily Reporter* (Columbus, Ohio), July 19, 1996; Elisa Crouch, "Sue at Your Own Risk," Missouri Digital News, September 1, 1995; "Pa. House Approves Legislation That Would Curb Inmates' Lawsuits," *Philadelphia Inquirer,* January 21, 1998.

61. ICCPR, art. 10(1).

62. ICCPR, art. 10(3).

63. See, for example, the U.N. Human Rights Committee's decision in *Mukong v. Cameroon,* in which it cites various violations of the Standard Minimum Rules as evidence showing that the complainant was subject to cruel, inhuman and degrading treatment. *Mukong v. Cameroon* (No. 458/1991) (August 10, 1994), U.N. Doc. CCPR/C/51/D/458/1991. The authority of the Standard Minimum Rules has also been recognized in U.S. courts, which have cited them as evidence of "contemporary standards of decency" relevant in interpreting the scope of the Eighth Amendment. See *Estelle v. Gamble,* 429 U.S. 97, 103–04 & n. 8 (1976); *Detainees of Brooklyn House of Detention for Men v. Malcolm,* 520 F. 2d 392, 396 (2d Cir. 1975); *Williams v. Coughlin,* 875 F. Supp. 1004, 1013 (W.D.N.Y. 1995); *Lareau v. Manson,* 507 F. Supp. 1177, 1187–89 & n. 9 (1980) (describing the Standard Minimum Rules as "an authoritative international statement of basic norms of human dignity and of certain practices which are repugnant to the conscience of mankind").

64. Body of Principles, art. 5.

65. U.N. Human Rights Committee, General Comment 21, paragraph 3. The Human Rights Committee, a body of experts established under the ICCPR, provides authoritative interpretations of the ICCPR though the periodic issuance of General Comments.

66. See, for example, *Aydin v. Turkey,* Eur. Ct. of H.R., Judgment of 25 September 1997, paras. 62–88; *Prosecutor v. Furundija,* ICTY, Case No. IT-95–17/1-T, Judgment of 10 December 1998, paras. 163–86.

67. Judgment, International Criminal Tribunal for Rwanda (ICTR), *Prosecutor v. Jean-Paul Akayesu,* Case No. ICTR-96–4-T (2 September 1998), para. 38 (hereinafter Akayesu judgment). In the Akayesu decision, which involved a Rwandan official who encouraged the rape of Tutsi women during the genocide, the court went on to explain that: "coercive circumstances need not be evidenced by a show of physical force. Threats, intimidation, extortion and other forms of duress which prey on fear or desperation may constitute coercion."

The Elements of Crimes corresponding to the Statute of the International Criminal Court include a similar definition of the "war crime of rape." It too speaks of the physical invasion of a person with a sexual organ, or of the penetration of a person's anal or genital openings with any object or part of the body, when such an act is committed during wartime. It requires that the invasion be committed "by force, or by threat of force or coercion, such as that caused by fear of violence, duress, detention, psychological oppression or abuse of power . . . or by taking advantage of a coercive environment," or that the invasion be committed "against a person incapable of giving genuine consent." Article 8(2)(b)(xxii)-1, Elements of Crimes, Report of the Preparatory Commission for the International Criminal Court, U.N. Doc. PCNICC/2000/INF/3/Add.2 (6 July 2000), p. 34; see also "Crime against humanity of rape," article 7(1)(g)-1, ibid., p. 12. These regulations also specifically note that "the concept of 'invasion' is intended to be broad enough to be gender-neutral." Ibid., fn. 15.

Also instructive is the definition of rape employed by the U.N. special rapporteur on rape during armed conflict. She describes rape as "the insertion, under conditions of force, coercion or duress, of any object, including but not limited to a penis, into a victim's vagina or anus; or the insertion, under conditions of force, coercion or duress, of a penis into the mouth of the victim." Significantly, she points out that: "Rape is defined in gender-neutral terms, as both men and women are victims of rape." Report of the Special Rapporteur on systematic rape, sexual slavery and slavery-like practices during armed conflict (hereinafter "U.N. sexual slavery report"), U.N. Doc. E/CN.4/Sub.2/1998/13 (22 June 1998), para. 24.

68. See, for example, Human Rights Watch, *All Too Familiar,* pp. 52–53. In the Akeyesu decision, the court explained: "Sexual violence, including rape, is not limited to physical invasion of the human body and may include acts which do not involve penetration or even physical contact." Akayesu judgment, para. 38.

69. Convention against Torture, arts. 1(1) and 16(1).

70. For a discussion of this point in the context of specific prison visits, see the reports of the European Committee for the Prevention of Torture and Inhuman or Degrading Treatment or Punishment (CPT), the prison monitoring organ of the Council of Europe. In a 1993 report on Finland's prisons for example, the CPT expressed concern over the high level of inter-prisoner violence and criticized the "low level of supervision by staff of the activities of inmates in some areas of [Helsinki Central Prison]." Concluding that the prison authorities had to do more to counter the problem of prisoner-on-prisoner violence, it emphasized: "The duty of care which is owed by custodial staff to those in their charge includes the responsibility to protect them from other inmates who wish to cause them harm." CPT, "Report to the Finnish Government on the visit to Finland carried out by the European Committee for the Prevention of Torture and Inhuman or Degrading Treatment or Punishment from 10 to 20 May 1992," 1 April 1993, CPT/Inf (93) 8.

71. See U.N. sexual slavery report, paras. 27–28.

72. Ibid., para. 28.
73. Ibid. (quoting the Slavery Convention, art. 1(1)).
74. Slavery Convention, arts. 2 and 6.
75. ICCPR, art. 8; see also Supplementary Convention on the Abolition of Slavery, the Slave Trade, and Institutions and Practices Similar to Slavery.
76. See U.N. sexual slavery report, paras. 29–31 ("Implicit in the definition of slavery are notions concerning limitations on autonomy, freedom of movement and power to decide matters relating to one's sexual activity . . . . Sexual slavery also encompasses most, if not all forms of forced prostitution.").
77. By contrast, in 1929, when the U.S. ratified the Slavery Convention, it only attached one reservation—a reservation that had the effect of giving a more generous interpretation to the treaty's protections.
78. Among other U.S. reservations and understanding to the ICCPR are the following:

    That the policy and practice of the United States are generally in compliance with and supportive of the Covenant's provisions regarding treatment of juveniles in the criminal justice system. Nevertheless, the United States reserves the right, in exceptional circumstances, to treat juveniles as adults, notwithstanding paragraphs 2 (b) and 3 of article 10 . . . . The United States further understands that paragraph 3 of article 10 does not diminish the goals of punishment, deterrence, and incapacitation as additional legitimate purposes for a penitentiary system.

79. See, for example, Statement of Sweden, June 18, 1993; Statement of Spain, October 5, 1993; Statement of Portugal, October 5, 1993; Statement of Norway, October 4, 1993; Statement of Netherlands, September 28, 1993. Available: http://www.un.org/Depts/Treaty/final/ts2/newfiles/part_boo/iv_boo/iv_4.html (December 1999).
80. Vienna Convention on the Law of Treaties, art. 19(3).
81. Human Rights Committee, Comments on United States of America, U.N. Doc. CCPR/C/79/Add 50 (1995).
82. For further discussion of Human Rights Watch's position on U.S. reservations to these treaties, see Human Rights Watch, *All Too Familiar*, pp. 47–50.
83. See, for example, *White v. Paulsen*, 997 F. Supp. 1380 (E.D. Wa. 1998). The U.S. government did enact implementing legislation under the Convention against Torture to allow persons tortured outside the United States to file suit in U.S. courts. Torture Victim Protection Act of 1991 (TVPA), 18 U.S.C. Sec. 2340 *et seq.*
84. The Human Rights Committee consists of eighteen experts acting in their individual capacities who are elected by states parties to the ICCPR. The Committee against Torture consists of ten experts acting in their individual capacities who are elected by the states parties to the Convention against Torture.
85. The Working Group consists of five independent experts from the membership of the Sub-Commission on the Promotion and Protection of Human Rights. Meeting for the first time in 1975 as the Working Group on Slavery, the group was renamed in 1988.
86. In a section outlining areas of concern in the criminal justice system, the govern-

ment's 1999 report to the Committee against Torture made a brief reference to "sexual assault and abuse of prisoners by correctional officers and other prisoners." Although the report went on to discuss the custodial sexual abuse of women prisoners in some detail, it contained no further mention of the problem of prisoner-on-prisoner sexual abuse. See DOS 1999 Torture Report. The 1994 report included an even more allusive reference to the problem in its discussion of prison classification rules, which noted that "it would be dangerous to house young, inexperienced, non-violent offenders with older men who have spent a great deal of their lives in prison for the commission of violent, predatory crimes." Consideration of Reports Submitted by State Parties Under Article 40 of the Covenant, Initial report of state parties due in 1993, Addendum, United States of America, U.N. Doc. CCPR/C/81/Add.4 (1994), para. 294.

87. The Human Rights Committee last reported on U.S. compliance in 1995. With regard to prisons, the Human Rights Committee expressed concern over overcrowding, custodial sexual abuse of women inmates, and conditions in high security prisons. Human Rights Committee, Comments on United States of America, U.N. Doc. CCPR/C/79/Add 50 (1995).

CASE HISTORY OF RODNEY HULIN

1. Testimony of Rodney Hulin, September 27, 1997.
2. Human Rights Watch telephone interview, Beaumont, Texas, October 30, 1999.
3. Complaint, *Bruntmyer v. TDCJ*, date unknown.
4. Human Rights Watch telephone interview, Beaumont, Texas, October 30, 1999.

CHAPTER IV. PREDATORS AND VICTIMS

1. See *Farmer v. Brennan,* 511 U.S. 825 (1994). Farmer's feminine characteristics included silicone breast implants.
2. Previous studies and analyses agree on this point. See, for example, Daniel Welzer-Lang, Lilian Mathieu and Michael Faure, *Sexualités et violences en prison* (Lyon: Aleas, 1996), pp. 150–53; Carl Weiss and David James Friar, *Terror in the Prisons: Homosexual Rape and Why Society Condones It* (Indianapolis: Bobbs-Merrill, 1974), p. 74 (explaining that "[n]o age escapes prison rape, but youth is hit the hardest). Accounts of minors imprisoned with adults often make reference to sexual abuse. For example, Amnesty International, in its 1998 report on juvenile justice in the United States, quoted a letter from an incarcerated fifteen-year-old in which the boy stated that adult inmates were "talk[ing] to me sexually." He said: "They make moves on me. I've had people tell me I'm pretty and that they'll rape me . . . I'm even too scared to go eat." Amnesty International, "Betraying the Young: Children in the U.S. Justice Sys-

tem" (AMR 51/60/98), 20 November 1998. Available at: http://www.amnesty.org/ailib/aipub/1998/AMR/25106098.htm (December 1999).

3. See case history described above.

4. Human Rights Watch telephone interview with J.Q., Arkansas, August 25, 1998. The woman said that her son, age twenty, was incarcerated for burglary, while four of the inmates who raped him had life sentences.

5. Letter to Human Rights Watch from R.P., Arkansas, September 14, 1998.

6. Letter to Human Rights Watch from R.P., Arkansas, October 5, 1998.

7. Letter to Human Rights Watch from W.W., Florida, February 19, 1999.

8. Letter to Human Rights Watch from D.A., Nebraska, October 31, 1996.

9. Letter to Human Rights Watch from R.H, Utah, September 10, 1996.

10. Letter to Human Rights Watch from C.B., Minnesota, July 19, 1999.

11. Other studies have also found that both the victims and perpetrators of sexual abuse tend to be young, although perpetrators in mixed-age institutions may be slightly older than victims. See, for example, Lockwood, *Prison Sexual Violence*, p. 28.

12. Letter to Human Rights Watch from R.B., California, September 1, 1996.

13. Letter to Human Rights Watch from J.C., Texas, December 16, 1998.

14. Human Rights Watch interview, Texas, March 1999.

15. Human Rights Watch interview, California, May 1998.

16. Letter to Human Rights Watch from R.B., Texas, October 13, 1996.

17. It is estimated that between 6 and 15 percent of prison and jail inmates are seriously mentally ill. See Editorial, "Jails and Prisons—America's New Mental Hospitals," *American Journal of Public Health,* December 1995, p. 1612.

18. Letter to Human Rights Watch from B.S., Indiana, June 16, 1999.

19. Human Rights Watch interview, Texas, March 1999.

20. Letter to Human Rights Watch from L.V., Arkansas, September 25, 1996.

21. Letter to Human Rights Watch from J.G., Minnesota, August 8, 1996.

22. Among the judicial decisions discussing the problem of "homosexual predators" are: *Cole v. Flick,* 758 F. 2d 124 (3d Cir. 1985) (upholding prison regulations limiting inmates' hair length, in part because allowing inmates to wear long hair could lead to an increase in attacks by "predatory homosexuals"); *Roland v. Johnson,* 1991 U.S. App. LEXIS 11468 (6th Cir. 1991) (describing "gangs of homosexual predators"); *Roland v. Johnson,* 856 F. 2d 764 (6th Cir. 1988); *Ashann-Ra v. Virginia,* 112 F. Supp. 2d 559, 563 (W.D. Va. 2000) (mentioning "inmates known to be predatory homosexuals" who "stalk other inmates in the showers").

23. The homophobia that may underlie the judicial stereotype of the inmate "homosexual predator" also shows itself in cases involving gay victims of rape. See, for example, *Carver v. Knox County,* 753 F. Supp. 1370, 1380 (1989) (pointing out that a witness admitted on cross-examination that "the rape he witnessed was of a known homosexual whose cries for help may not have been as vigorous as those of a heterosexual inmate under the same circumstances").

24. Letter to Human Rights Watch from P.E., Illinois, October 28, 1997. See also Stephen

Donaldson, "A Million Jockers, Punks, and Queens: Sex among American Male Prisoners and its Implications for Concepts of Sexual Orientation," February 4, 1993. Donaldson explains that "the sexual penetration of another male prisoner by [a dominant prisoner] is considered a male rather than a homosexual activity, and is considered to validate the penetrator's masculinity." Ibid., p. 5. He later goes on to emphasize that "[f]or the majority of prisoners, penetrative sex with a punk or queen remains a psychologically heterosexual and, in the circumstances of confinement, normal act." Ibid., p. 12.

25. Previous studies have similarly concluded that gays face a higher risk of sexual assault and abuse. See, for example, Wayne S. Wooden and Jay Parker, *Men Behind Bars* (New York: Plenum Press, 1982), p. 18 (finding that 41 percent of homosexual were sexually assaulted, as opposed to 9 percent of heterosexuals); see also *Gregory v. Shelby*, 220 F. 3d 433 (6th Cir. 2000) (gay jail inmate sexually abused and killed by another inmate).

26. Letter to Human Rights Watch from M.P., Arkansas, September 24, 1996.

27. See, for example, Leo Carroll, "Humanitarian Reform and Biracial Sexual Assault in a Maximum Security Prison," in Anthony M. Scacco, Jr., ed., *Male Rape* (1982); Alan J. Davis, "Sexual Assaults in the Philadelphia Prison System," in *Male Rape*; Daniel Lockwood, *Prison Sexual Violence* (1980); Hans Toch, *Living in Prison* (1992); C. Scott Moss, Ray E. Hosford and William R. Anderson, "Sexual Assault in a Prison," *Psychological Reports*, vol. 44 (1979); David A. Jones, *The Health Risks of Imprisonment* (1976).

28. Human Rights Watch's sources of information were almost entirely made up of white, African American, and Hispanic inmates; we did not receive enough information from members of other minorities to be able to reach any conclusions as to their general situation.

29. Letter to Human Rights Watch from W.M., Texas, October 31, 1996.

30. Letter to Human Rights Watch from T.D., Texas, March 14, 1997.

31. See, for example, Lockwood, *Prison Sexual Violence*, pp. 105–06.

32. See, for example, Anthony M. Scacco, Jr., *Rape in Prison* (Springfield, IL: Charles C. Thomas, 1975).

33. Leo Carroll, "Race, Ethnicity, and the Social Order of the Prison," in Johnson and Hans Toch, *The Pains of Imprisonment* (1982), p. 194.

34. Letter to Human Rights Watch from V.H., Arkansas, November 17, 1996.

35. See, for example, Davis, "Sexual Assaults," pp. 14–15; Nobuhle R. Chonco, "Sexual Assaults among Male Inmates," *The Prison Journal*, vol. 68, no. 1 (1989), p. 74.

36. Human Rights Watch interview, Texas, October 1998.

37. Letter to Human Rights Watch from L.V., Arkansas, September 3, 1996.

38. Letter to Human Rights Watch from D.G., Texas, January 15, 1998.

CASE HISTORIES OF L.O. AND P.E.

1. Psychological Evaluation, Texas Department of Criminal Justice, Institutional Division, October 9, 1995.

2. Letter to David Barron, District Attorney, Madisonville, Texas, from L.O., August 19, 1996 (including notarized affidavit of L.O. dated August 18, 1996).
3. Letter to Human Rights Watch, September 27, 1998.

CHAPTER V. RAPE SCENARIOS

1. Letter to Human Rights Watch from V.H., Arkansas, November 17, 1996.
2. Letter to Human Rights Watch from B.H., Florida, October 22, 1996.
3. Gilligan, *Violence,* p. 165.
4. See the international definitions of rape discussed in chapter III, above. Although there is a critical difference between consensual and nonconsensual sex in terms of whether an inmate's rights have been violated, it is worth noting that all forms of sex, even consensual sex, are uniformly forbidden under prison disciplinary codes.
5. International protections of prisoner's rights demonstrate an implicit recognition of this problem by barring medical or scientific experimentation even on prisoners who purport to consent to it. See article 11(2) of Protocol I to the Geneva Conventions, prohibiting experimention on prisoners of war. Protocol Additional to the Geneva Conventions of 12 August 1949, and Relating to the Protection of Victims of International Armed Conflicts (Protocol I), 1125 U.N.T.S. 3, entered into force December 7, 1978. The U.N. Human Rights Committee, the body charged with monitoring implementation of the International Covenant on Civil and Political Rights (ICCPR), has a similar reading of the ICCPR's protections. It has explained:

   > Article 7 [of the ICCPR] expressly prohibits medical or scientific experimentation without the free consent of the person concerned . . . . The Committee also observes that special protection in regard to such experiments is necessary in the case of persons not capable of giving valid consent, and in particular those under any form of detention or imprisonment.

   Human Rights Committee, General Comment 20, Article 7 (Forty-fourth session, 1992), U.N. Doc. HRI\GEN\1\Rev.1 at 30 (1994).
6. Human Rights Watch, *All Too Familiar,* p. 43.
7. Letter to Human Rights Watch from J.D., Colorado, October 12, 1997.
8. A landmark 1982 study of prisoner-on-prisoner sexual abuse in Philadelphia specifically mentions this problem, along with describing the difficulty, in the prison context, of distinguishing rape from consensual sex:

   > [I]t was hard to separate consensual homosexuality from rape, since many continuing and isolated homosexual liaisons originated from a gang rape, or from the ever-present threat of gang rape. Thus, a threat of rape, expressed or implied, would prompt an already fearful young man to submit. Prison officials are too quick to label such activities "consensual."

   Davis, "Sexual Assaults in the Philadelphia Prison System," p. 13.
9. Allan Turner, "Mother probes son's death in prison," *Houston Chronicle,* June 4, 1995.
10. Human Rights Watch interview, Texas, March 1999.

11. Ibid.

12. Letter to Human Rights Watch, October 13, 1996.

13. Human Rights Watch interview, Texas, October 1998.

14. Letter to Human Rights Watch from R.L., Arizona, August 26, 1999.

15. Letter to Human Rights Watch from W.M., Texas, December 26, 1997.

16. Human Rights Watch interview, Texas, October 1998.

17. Letter to Human Rights Watch from M.H., Florida, October 29, 1996.

18. Letter to Human Rights Watch from J.S., Tennessee, September 5, 1996.

19. Letter to Human Rights Watch from G.H., Texas, December 1, 1998.

20. Human Rights Watch interview, Texas, October 1998.

21. Letter to Human Rights Watch from P.S., Texas, October 17, 1996.

22. Human Rights Watch interview, Texas, March 1999.

23. Letter to Human Rights Watch from C.K., Texas, October 28, 1996.

24. Letter to Human Rights Watch from W.M., Texas, October 31, 1996. The prisoner attributed this belief to African American inmates in particular, but Human Rights Watch has found it to be fairly widespread among prisoners generally.

25. In doing so they echo the views of prison experts from earlier times. One such commentator, writing in 1934, warned:

> Every year large numbers of boys, adolescent youths, and young men are made homosexuals, either temporarily or permanently, in the prisons of America . . . . These newly born perverts, in turn, corrupt others.

Joseph Fishman, *Sex in Prison* (New York: National Library Press, 1934), p. 83. Even certain contemporary writers have held to this idea, asserting: "Repeated homosexual rape causes the inmate victims to develop a new sexual identity. They now harbor a raped female in their male bodies." Weiss and Friar, *Terror in the Prisons,* p. 74. (But see Lockwood, *Prison Sexual Violence,* p. 94, stating "there is no evidence that homosexual rape actually causes changes of sexual identity.") The language of another expert—speaking of a sexually abused inmate as having "part[ed] with his manhood"—similarly suggests that raped inmates somehow become female. Alan J. Davis, "Report on Sexual Assaults in a Prison System and Sheriff's Vans," in Leon Radzinowicz and Marvin E. Wolfgang, eds., *Crime and Justice,* 2d ed. (New York: Basic Books, 1977).

26. Letter to Human Rights Watch from M.B., Indiana, October 10, 1996.

27. Letter to Human Rights Watch from R.E., Florida, March 5, 1999.

28. Human Rights Watch interview, Texas, March 1999.

29. Letter to Human Rights Watch from J.O., Utah, February 18, 1997.

30. See, for example, Human Rights Watch, "Getting Away with Murder, Mutilation, and Rape: New Testimony from Sierra Leone," *A Human Rights Watch Short Report,* vol. 11, no. 3(A), June 1999. The report states: "Several girls and women abducted during January described pairing up and attaching themselves to one rebel so as to avoid gang-rape, be given a degree of protection, and be subjected to less hardship." Ibid., p. 34.

31. Letter to Human Rights Watch from W.M., Texas, October 31, 1996.

32. The phenomenon of renaming raped men has also been reported in the context of armed conflict. A *New York Times* article on Russia's conflict in Chechnya, for example, includes an account of how two men allegedly raped by Russian soldiers were given female names after the rape. Michael Wines, "Chechens Report Torture in Russian Camps," *New York Times,* February 18, 2000.

33. Letter to Human Rights Watch from J.D., Texas, November 5, 1996.

34. Letter to Human Rights Watch from T.B., Texas, October 23, 1996.

35. Letter to Human Rights Watch from T.D., Texas, March 14, 1997.

36. Letter to Human Rights Watch from G.H., Texas, December 1, 1998. The responsibility for household chores, typical in such accounts, is consistent with the idea that these victimized prisoners are substituting for women (in the most traditional sense). Another such prisoner, for example, spoke of being forced into sex and into "performing other duties as a woman, such as making his bed." M.P., Arkansas, pro se federal civil rights complaint filed August 2, 1996.

37. Letter to Human Rights Watch from C.D., Indiana, November 20, 1996.

38. The amendment, adopted in 1865, states:

    Section 1. Neither slavery nor involuntary servitude, except as a punishment for crime whereof the party shall have been duly convicted, shall exist within the United States, or any place subject to their jurisdiction.

    Section 2. Congress shall have power to enforce this article by appropriate legislation.

    U.S. Constitution, Thirteenth Amendment.

39. Rideau, "The Sexual Jungle," p. 75.

40. The view of rape as a crime of violence rather than sexual passion found its most prominent exponent in Susan Brownmiller, whose work *Against Our Will: Men, Women and Rape,* is a touchstone for work on the topic. Susan Brownmiller, *Against Our Will: Men, Women and Rape* (New York: Simon & Schuster, 1975).

41. The opinion of a federal court in Pennsylvania, for example, in a case involving sex between inmates, betrays the assumption that rape is sexually motivated. The court stated: "Prison rapes are a serious problem . . . Perhaps forward-looking legislative and administrative reforms with respect to conjugal visits will alleviate the problem of prison rape." *United States v. Brewer,* 363 F. Supp. 606, 608 (M.D. Pa. 1973).

42. See, for example, Lee H. Browker, *Prison Victimization* (New York: Elsevier, 1980), p. 7; Anthony M. Scacco, Jr., *Rape in Prison* (Springfield, Illinois: Charles C. Thomas, 1975), p. 47; Rideau, "The Sexual Jungle," pp. 74–75; Victor Hassine, *Life Without Parole: Living in Prison Today* (Los Angeles: Roxbury Publishing, 1996), pp. 111–12.

43. Rideau, "The Sexual Jungle," p. 74.

44. Letter to Human Rights Watch from D.G., Virginia, November 17, 1996.

45. Letter to Human Rights Watch from D.A., Nebraska, September 6, 1996.

46. Letter to Human Rights Watch from D.W., Kansas, February 23, 1998.

47. Letter to Human Rights Watch from J.O., Utah, February 18, 1997. A letter from a prisoner to the editor of *Prison Life Magazine* similarly illustrates the use of "punk" as the ultimate term of opprobrium:

> Dear [editor], You're a fucking punk! . . . . you take it up the ass, pole smoker! I'd bust
> your fucking grape open if I could get my hands on you . . . . Don't be a punk . . . .
> *Prison Life Magazine* (October 1996), p. 11.

48. Letter to Human Rights Watch from J.G., Colorado, January 31, 1999.
49. Lockwood, "Issues in Prison Sexual Violence," p. 101.

CASE HISTORIES OF S.H. AND M.R.

1. Letter to Human Rights Watch, September 10, 1996.
2. Ibid.
3. Human Rights Watch interview, Texas, October 1998.
4. Ibid.
5. Note to Sergeant W., April 19, 1999.
6. Ibid.
7. Ibid.
8. Letter to Human Rights Watch, September 10, 1996.
9. Human Rights Watch interview, Texas, October 1998.
10. Ibid.
11. Letter from Warden J. Cockrell to M.L.H., August 15, 1994. (Compare the date of this letter to the date of the inter-office memorandum cited in the following footnote.)
12. The counselor's report on the situation said: "According to Inmate S.H., W. is forcing him (S.H.) to perform sexual favors, because he does not have any money to pay protection." Texas Department of Criminal Justice, Inter-Office Communications, August 10, 1994.
13. Complaint, *S.H. v. Scott,* July 12, 1996.
14. Texas Department of Criminal Justice, Inmate Grievance Form, Step 1, June 22, 1994.
15. Ibid., July 11. 1994.
16. For example, one affidavit stated:

> I knew that Plaintiff was being sexually assaulted by other inmates, spacifically: R.J.,
> E.D., and others. Plaintiff talked with me about these problems and I was like his confidant to him, and he was pretty upset, and stressed out. Plaintiff spoke with numerous
> prison officials about his situation, namely W.S., L.S., C.B., and others. I know this,
> because plaintiff spoke to me regarding these conversations.

Affidavit dated March 11, 1997 (names omitted).
17. Letter to Human Rights Watch, August 4, 1999.
18. Letter to Human Rights Watch, September 24, 1996.
19. Ibid.
20. Ibid.
21. Ibid.
22. M.R., Arkansas, federal civil rights complaint filed July 25, 1996.
23. Ibid.
24. M.R., Arkansas, pro se federal civil rights complaint filed July 25, 1996.

CHAPTER VI. BODY AND SOUL

1. Excerpt of a *pro se* complaint filed in federal court by a prisoner in Arkansas, January 14, 1998.

2. Letter to Human Rights Watch from W.M., September 13, 1996.

3. In January 1998, a federal jury rejected Blucker's argument that two prison staff members, including a prison doctor, had been "deliberately indifferent" to the risk that Blucker would be raped. The previous August, a different jury had ruled in favor of five other prison employees in Blucker's suit. Carolyn Starks, "Former Inmate with AIDS Virus Loses Suit against Prison Officials," *Chicago Tribune*, January 24, 1998. Blucker, who is married, was paroled from prison in 1996.

4. Few prison inmates can afford to pay for legal counsel in suits challenging ill-treatment in prison. (See chapter on legal context.) The vast majority of prisoners' claims, therefore, are filed *pro se,* as attorneys do not generally find prison litigation on a contingency basis to be financially viable. This reflects both the legal obstacles to such litigation and the lack of sympathy for prisoners among the public and the judiciary, which, from a lawyer's perspective, translates into low prospective damage awards. Indeed, in Human Rights Watch's experience, the only individual cases in which prisoners have succeeded in finding private lawyers to represent them are those involving HIV transmission, suggesting that only when prisoners' lives are directly and unequivocally at issue is there much hope that their injuries will be legally recognized.

5. *K.S. v. Sargent,* 149 F. 3d 783, 785 (8th Cir. 1998).

6. *See K.S. v. Sargent,* 149 F.3d 783 (8th Cir. 1998). A related decision is *Billman v. IDOC,* 56 F.3d 785 (1995), in which the court stated that a prison official could be held liable for assigning an inmate to a double cell with another inmate who was known to be a rapist and was HIV-positive. Ibid., pp. 788–89.

7. Letter to Human Rights Watch, December 13, 1996.

8. Lawrence K. Altman, "Much More AIDS in Prisons Than in General Population," *New York Times,* September 1, 1999 (describing results of study commissioned by the National Commission on Correctional Health Care).

9. U.S. Department of Justice, Bureau of Justice Statistics, "HIV in Prisons and Jails, 1995," February 1998.

10. See Elizabeth Kantor, "AIDS and HIV Infection in Prisoners," in *The AIDS Knowledge Base* (Lippenkott, Williams & Wilkins: New York, 1999) (available online at <http://hivinsite.ucsf.edu/akb/1997/index.html>); Nancy Mahon, "New York Inmates' HIV Risk Behaviors: The Implications for Prevention Policy and Programs," *American Journal of Public Health,* vol. 86, no. 9, September 1996, p. 1211.

11. Recognizing this, the European Court of Human Rights has declared that the abuse "leaves deep psychological scars on the victim which do not respond to the passage of time as quickly as other forms of physical and mental violence." *Aydin v. Turkey,* Judgment of 25 Sept. 1997, Eur. Ct. of H.R., para. 83.

12. Letter to Human Rights Watch, March 28, 1999.

13. Letter to Human Rights Watch, October 31, 1996.

14. Letter to Human Rights Watch, November 4, 1996.

15. Letter to Human Rights Watch, October 12, 1997.

16. Letter to Human Rights Watch, September 10, 1996.

17. Letter to Human Rights Watch from E.R., October 10, 1996. Another inmate with similar fears said, "I feel like I am no longer a 'man', at least not recognized as one on the inside." Letter to Human Rights Watch from P.E., March 6, 1999.

18. Letter to Human Rights Watch, March 30, 1999.

19. Letter to Human Rights Watch from J.D., November 5, 1996.

20. See, for example, Burgess and Holmstrom, "Rape Syndrome," *American Journal of Psychiatry,* vol. 9 (1974), pp. 981–86.

21. Letter to Human Rights Watch, September 23, 1996.

22. L. Cohen and S. Roth, "The psychological aftermath of rape: Long-term effects and individual differences in recovery," *Journal of Social and Clinical Psychology,* vol. 5 (1988), pp. 525–34; Stephen Donaldson, "Rape Trauma Syndrome in Male Prisoners" (undated) (available on the internet at <http://www.spr.org/docs/rts.html>).

23. The 1994 Nebraska prison study reported that over one-third of inmates targeted for sexual abuse had thoughts of suicide after the incident. Struckman-Johnson, "Prison Sexual Coercion," p. 74.

24. Letter to Human Rights Watch from D.E., May 14, 1998.

25. Letter to Human Rights Watch from R.H., September 10, 1996.

26. Lindsay M. Hayes, "Prison Suicide: An Overview and Guide to Prevention," National Institute of Corrections, June 1995, p. 1.

27. Ibid., p. 32.

28. Ibid., p. 70. The rate of jail suicide, approximately nine times that of the general population, far exceeds that of prison suicide. Ibid., p. 1. Yet a number of precipitating factors exist in the jail context—including the initial crisis of incarceration and shame over the alleged offense—that distinguish it from the prison context. Although prison rape, or the fear of rape, may play a role in some prisoners' suicidal response to detention, it is only one of many factors that come into play during these first stages of incarceration.

29. Letter to Human Rights Watch from W.W., December 31, 1996.

30. Letter to Human Rights Watch from W.M., September 13, 1996.

31. See, for example, Lockwood, "Issues in Prison Sexual Violence," p. 98.

32. Letter to Human Rights Watch, September 21, 1996.

33. Letter to Human Rights Watch from L.Q., December 3, 1997.

34. Letter to Human Rights Watch from J.D., November 5, 1996.

35. Daniel Lockwood, *Prison Sexual Violence* (New York: Elsevier, 1980), pp. 53–54.

36. James Gilligan, *Violence: Our Deadly Epidemic and its Causes* (New York: Grosset/Putnam, 1996).

37. Letter to Human Rights Watch from B.E., October 26, 1996.

38. Human Rights Watch telephone interview, October 22, 1999. When describing the rape of one woman, he added, "I remember being extremely angry."

39. Letter to Human Rights Watch from R.L., October 21, 1996 (emphasis in original).

40. Michael Berryhill, "Prisoner's Dilemna," *The New Republic,* December 27, 1999; *see also* Joseph L. Galloway, "Into the Heart of Darkness: A Texas Prison's Racist Subculture Spawned the Grisly Murder in Jasper," *U.S. News & World Report,* March 8, 1999 (noting that one defendant's lawyer stated that he believed his client was raped in prison).

41. Stephen Donaldson, the late president of Stop Prisoner Rape, as quoted in Ellis Henican, *Special Report: Prison Rape—Every Man's Worst Fear Becomes a National Scandal,* Penthouse Magazine (August 1995), p. 30; *see also* Robert W. Dumond, "The Sexual Assault of Male Inmates in Incarcerated Settings," *International Journal of the Sociology of Law,* vol. 20 (1992), p. 147 (asking "is it not reasonable to assume that some [raped inmates] will leave prison more embittered, angry and violent? . . . . How many innocent victims will fall prey to inmates full of rage and anger at a system that did not protect them?"); Wooden and Parker, *Men Behind Bars,* p. 116–17 (expressing concern over "the potential ramifications to society" of releasing raped inmates, and urging that such inmates receive proper psychological care "to stem the possibility of their becoming future assaulters"); Heilpern, *Fear or Favour,* p. 18 (stating that "[t]hose who have been sexually assaulted in prison will be released as time bombs, waiting to obtain their revenge in inappropriate and destructive ways").

42. Daniel Lockwood, "Issues in Prison Sexual Violence," *in* Michael C. Braswell, Reid H. Montgomery, Jr., and Lucien X. Lombardo, eds., *Prison Violence in America,* 2nd edition (Cincinnati: Anderson Publishing, 1994), p. 99.

43. *LaMarca v. Turner,* 995 F.2d 1526, 1534, 1543 (11th Cir. 1993).

CASE HISTORIES OF P.N. AND L.T

1. Affidavit, September 1, 1996.

2. Complaint, *N. v. Woods,* civil action filed October 3, 1995.

3. Human Rights Watch interview, Texas, October 1998.

4. Letter to Human Rights Watch, February 19, 1997.

CHAPTER VII. ANOMALY OR EPIDEMIC

1. To date, the U.S. Bureau of Justice statistics has not included prisoner-on-prisoner rape or other sexual abuse in its annual crime surveys (available on the internet at http://www.ojp.usdoj.gov/bjs/pub/pdf/sisfcfq.pdf).

2. Carl Weiss and David James Friar, *Terror in the Prisons: Homosexual Rape and Why Society Condones It* (Indianapolis: Bobbs-Merrill, 1974), p. 61.

3. See Lockwood, "Issues in Prison Sexual Violence," p. 97 (calling prisoner-on-prisoner rape "a rare event," but noting that sexual harassment in prison affects "large numbers

of men"); Robert W. Dumond, "Ignominious Victims: Effective Treatment of Male Sexual Assault in Prison," August 15, 1995, p. 2 (stating that "evidence suggests that [sexual assault in prison] may a staggering problem").

4. Letter to Human Rights Watch from Manuel D. Romero, deputy secretary of operations, New Mexico Corrections Department, July 9, 1997.

5. Letter to Human Rights Watch from Harold W. Clarke, director, Nebraska Department of Correctional Services, July 10, 1997.

6. For Florida, see letter to Human Rights Watch from Fred Schuknecht, inspector general, Florida Department of Corrections, July 30, 1997 (94 reported sexual batteries or assaults in 1995, 92 in 1996); letter to Human Rights Watch from Fred Schuknecht, inspector general, Florida Department of Corrections, July 8, 1998 (93 allegations of sexual battery reported in 1997); letter to Human Rights Watch from E.A. Sobach, chief of investigations, Florida Department of Corrections, December 8, 1999 (89 allegations of sexual battery in 1998, 91 in 1999 (through December 7)).

For Ohio, see letter to Human Rights Watch from Norm Hills, north region director, Ohio Department of Rehabilitation and Correction, May 8, 1997 (one reported rape since January 1, 1997); letter to Human Rights Watch from Norm Hills, north region director, Ohio Department of Rehabilitation and Correction, July 16, 1998 (two additional sexual assaults since May 1997); letter to Human Rights Watch from Rhonda Millhouse, administrative assistant, Ohio Department of Rehabilitation and Correction, December 30, 1999 (fifty-five alleged sexual assaults in 1999, of which eight have been confirmed, the rest being deemed acts of consensual sex or fabrications).

For Texas, see letter to Human Rights Watch from Debby Miller, executive services, Texas Department of Criminal Justice, May 19, 1997 (average of 110 sexual assaults investigated annually since 1993, with four cases being criminally prosecuted); letter to Human Rights Watch from Debby Miller, executive services, Texas Department of Criminal Justice, June 29, 1998 (123 reported sexual assaults in 1997, and fifty-nine in the first five months of 1998); letter to Human Rights Watch from Darin Pacher, administrator, Texas Department of Criminal Justice, April 17, 2000 (enclosing table showing eighty-four alleged sexual assaults in 1994, 131 in 1995, eighty-four in 1996, eighty-seven in 1997, eighty-nine in 1998, 237 in 1999, and sixty-two in the first three months of 2000).

For the Federal Bureau of Prisons, see letter to Human Rights Watch from Renee Barley, FOIA adminstrator, Federal Bureau of Prisons, June 30, 1997 (forty-four alleged sexual assaults in 1996, six of which were confirmed); letter to Human Rights Watch from Elizabeth M. Edson, chief, FOIA/PA Section, Federal Bureau of Prisons, October 19, 1998 (sixty-six reported sexual assaults in 1997); letter to Human Rights Watch from Katherine A. Day, chief, FOIA/PA Section, Federal Bureau of Prisons, April 18, 2000 (stating that the FBOP does not maintain statistics on inmate-on-inmate rape).

7. Struckman-Johnson, "Sexual Coercion," p. 67. The survey had a 30 percent return rate, so it is possible that overall rates of victimization were lower than 22 percent. But

for several reasons, including the fact that staff and inmate estimates of the incidence of these abuses correlated closely with the actual numbers found, the researchers believe that the 22 percent figure is reasonably accurate. Ibid., p. 74.

8. Ibid., p. 71.

9. See chapter II for a discussion of the numbers of prison inmates nationally. Stephen Donaldson, the late president of Stop Prisoner Rape, made a similar estimate in 1995 on the basis of previous academic studies. He concluded that 119,900 male prison inmates—as well as many thousands of jail inmates—had been anally raped. Stephen Donaldson, "Rape of Incarcerated Americans: A Preliminary Statistical Look," July 1995 (available on the internet at: http://www.spr.org/docs/stats.html).

10. Letter to Human Rights Watch from R.B., Kansas, September 28, 1996.

11. Letter to Human Rights Watch from G.M., Ohio, June 27, 1997.

12. Letter to Human Rights Watch from S.K., Washington, February 18, 1997.

13. Even witnesses who inform on the perpetrators of rape are likely to suffer violent retaliation. See, for example, *Gullatte v. Potts,* 654 F. 2d 1007, 1009 (5th Cir. 1981) (inmate who witnessed rape of cellmate informed prison officials, and was later murdered by other prisoners in retaliation).

14. Letter to Human Rights Watch from J.D., Colorado, October 12, 1997.

15. Letter to Human Rights Watch from W.M., Texas, November 24, 1996.

16. Letter to Human Rights Watch, October 22, 1996.

17. Struckman-Johnson, "Sexual Coercion," p. 75; see also Peter L. Nacci and Thomas R. Kane, "The Incidence of Sex and Sexual Aggression in Federal Prisons," *Federal Probation,* vol. 47, no. 4 (1983), p. 31 (finding that only 32 percent of targets of sexual aggression had done something "official" to remedy the problem).

18. Helen Eigenberg, "Male Rape: An Empirical Examination of Correctional Officers' Attitudes Toward Rape in Prison," *Prison Journal,* vol. LXIX, no. 2, Fall-Winter 1989, p. 47.

19. Davis, "Sexual Assaults," p. 13.

20. Human Rights Watch sent an initial request for information to all corrections authorities on April 20, 1997. We sent an additional letter to corrections authorities on June 17, 1998, to request 1997 statistics. Finally we contacted such authorities again on November 16, 1999, to request 1998 data, and on January 19, 2000, to request 1999 data. Follow-up letters were sent and phone calls were made to those authorities who failed to respond to any of these letters. Where necessary, we also filed official requests for information under state freedom of information laws.

Four state corrections department—in Alabama, Louisiana, Nevada, and Utah—never responded to Human Rights Watch's queries, even though they were contacted on several occasions. For example, Human Rights Watch wrote to the Alabama Department of Corrections on April 20, 1997; June 26, 1997; September 8, 1997 (via fax); February 28, 1998; July 10, 1998 (official request for information under the Inspection and Copying of Records Act (ICRA), section 36–12–40 of the Alabama Code); November 16, 1999, and March 15, 2000 (official request under ICRA).

21. Letter to Human Rights Watch from Cora K. Lum, Deputy Director for Corrections, Hawaii Department of Public Safety, Honolulu, Hawaii, March 19, 1998.

22. Letter to Human Rights Watch from John Gifford, Information Officer, New Hampshire Department of Corrections, July 17, 1997. In a subsequent letter, state officials said that there were no recorded prisoner-on-prisoner rapes or sexual assaults in 1998 or 1999. Letter to Human Rights Watch from Mark L. Wefers, Chief, Internal Affairs, New Hampshire Department of Corrections, December 20, 1999. Similarly, in the state of Alaska (where, it should be recognized, there is a very small prison population), officials responded: "Our Department has not seen a sexual assault between prisoners in over 10 years. We, luckily, have no need to keep statistics, as this has not been a problem." Letter to Human Rights Watch from Denise Reynolds, Deputy Director of Institutions, Alaska Department of Corrections, December 15, 1999. Washington state officials told us that they do not maintain such statistics on inmate-on-inmate sexual assault, "as this type of assault seldom occurs within our institutions." Letter to Human Rights Watch from Tom Rolfs, Director, Division of Prisons, Washington Department of Corrections, May 7, 1997.

23. Letter to Human Rights Watch from Steve Crawford, Facility Captain, Institution Services Unit, California Department of Corrections, Sacramento, California, June 18, 1997; Human Rights Watch telephone interview with Art Chung, Data Analysis Unit, Information Services Branch, California Department of Corrections, Sacramento, California, June 24, 1998.

24. See letters cited above.

25. The Oregon corrections authorities, to be precise, stated that they had received eleven reports of inmate-on-inmate rape or sexual abuse between 1995 and August 1997, which would average out to three to four cases per year. Letter to Human Rights Watch from David S. Cook, Director, Oregon Department of Corrections, August 18, 1997.

26. The Arizona numbers averaged out to more than ten a year, but in 1999 only nine sexual assaults were recorded (compared to nineteen in 1998 and thirteen in 1997). Letter to Human Rights Watch from Richard G. Carlson, Deputy Director, Administration, Arizona Department of Corrections, March 9, 2000.

    The Virginia corrections department provided Human Rights Watch with the following information: five of seventeen allegations of "nonconsensual sexual activity" in 1993 were "founded"; four of twelve allegations in 1994; six of eleven in 1995; nine of twenty-two in 1996; five of ten in 1997; seven of fourteen in 1998; and three of thirteen in 1999. Letter to Human Rights Watch from Ron Angelone, Director, Virginia Department of Corrections, May 27, 1997.

27. Illinois informed Human Rights Watch that 130 and 188 inmate-on-inmate sexual assault allegations were reported in 1998 and 1999, respectively, but pointed out that only eight of the 1998 cases had been substantiated, and only twelve of those from 1999 (with four still pending as of April 2000). It also stated that ninety-seven allegations were reported during the two year period before May 1997, only twelve of which had been substantiated. Letter to Human Rights Watch from Odie Washington, Director, Illinois Department of Corrections, May 6, 1997. The letter included the

definition of sexual assault under Illinois state law: "any contact between the sex organ of one person and the sex organ, mouth or anus of another person, or any intrusion of any part of the body of one person or object into the sex organ or anus of another person by the use of force or threat of force."

28. Letter to Human Rights Watch from Rhonda Millhouse, Administrative Assistant 4, Office of Prisons, Ohio Department of Rehabilitation and Correction, December 30, 1999.

29. Statistics provided in chart sent by Texas Department of Criminal Justice on April 17, 2000. Viewed another way, the numbers show 162 alleged sexual assaults per 100,000 prisoners in 1999.

30. Eigenberg, "Male Rape," p. 47 (the remainder were undecided).

31. Struckman-Johnson, "Sexual Coercion," pp. 70–71.

32. See Davis, "Sexual Assaults" (Philadelphia); Lockwood, *Prison Sexual Violence* (New York); Wooden and Parker, *Men Behind Bars* (California); Nacci and Kane, "Sex and Sexual Aggression" (federal prisons); Richard Tewksbury, "Measures of Sexual Behavior in an Ohio Prison," *Sociology and Social Research,* vol. 74 (1989), p. 34; Christine A. Saum, Hilary L. Surratt, James A. Inciardi, and Rachael E. Bennett, "Sex in Prison: Exploring the Myths and Realities," *The Prison Journal,* vol. 75, no. 4 (1995) (Delaware); Struckman-Johnson, "Sexual Coercion" (Nebraska); Cindy Struckman-Johnson and David Struckman-Johnson, "Sexual Coercion Rates in Seven Midwestern Prison Facilities for Men," *The Prison Journal,* vol. 80, no. 4 (2000), p. 379 (four midwestern states).

33. Davis, "Sexual Assaults," p. 9.

34. Lockwood, *Prison Sexual Violence,* pp. 17–18. The author defined rape as being forced to participate in oral or anal sex. Ibid., p. 36.

35. Wooden and Parker, *Men Behind Bars,* p. 227.

36. Tewksbury, "Measures of Sexual Behavior," p. 36; Saum et al., "Sex in Prison," p. 427.

37. Struckman-Johnson, "Sexual Coercion Rates," pp. 383, 385.

38. The studies cited are not exhaustive of the research on prisoner-on-prisoner sexual abuse, but in general represent the most comprehensive and direct examinations of the topic. Several other studies have been conducted; their findings are equally inconsistent. For example, a study of state prisons in North Carolina, based on the records of disciplinary hearings and interviews with prison superintendents, found an extremely low rate of sexual assault, but its methodology is obviously vulnerable to criticism. Dan A. Fuller and Thomas Orsagh, "Violence and Victimization within a State Prison System," *Criminal Justice Review,* vol. 2 (1977), p. 35. A study of an unnamed maximum security prison in an Eastern state, in contrast, concluded that there were at least forty sexual assaults per year in the facility, which had a daily population of some 200 inmates. The data on assaults in that study, however, came from a small number of inmates, as well as from a review of prison records and conversations with staff and other prisoners. Leo Carroll, "Humanitarian Reform and Biracial Sexual Assault in a Maximum Security Prison," *Urban Life,* vol. 5, no. 4 (1977), p. 417.

39. Saum et al., "Sex in Prison," p. 421.

40. Ibid., p. 427.
41. Letter to Human Rights Watch from A.C., Arizona, March 23, 1997.

CASE HISTORY OF B.L.

1. Letter to Human Rights Watch, September 5, 1996.
2. Affidavit of James Agan, November 14, 1990.
3. Affidavit of Philip Bagley, December 6, 1990.
4. Letter to Human Rights Watch, September 5, 1996.
5. Florida House of Representatives, Ad Hoc Subcommittee on Management Oversight of the House Committee on Corrections, Probation and Parole, Final Report, October 1980, p. 4.
6. Ibid.
7. The officer continued: "[E]verybody that is willing to tell the truth knows this to be the truth and the man doesn't have any chance at all unless he's willing to fight . . . . [Unless he has friends to protect him,] why he'll get raped within the first 24 to 48 hours. That's about standard." Another officer explained: "A young, slim, slender kid, probably his first time in an institution like that, after he's been there two or three days, he's bound to get raped." Several officers used the words "a daily occurrence" when asked about the frequency of rape in their facility. Ibid.

CHAPTER VIII. DELIBERATE INDIFFERENCE

1. E-mail communication to Human Rights Watch, July 28, 1997.
2. Although few past studies have specifically examined correctional authorities' response to prisoner-on-prisoner rape, most commentators agree that little has been done to address the problem. See, for example, Robert W. Dumond, "Inmate Sexual Assault: The Plague That Persists," *The Prison Journal*, vol. 80, no. 4 (2000). Dumond notes: "Although the problem of inmate sexual assault has been known and examined for the past 30 years, the body of evidence has failed to be translated into effective intervention strategies for treating inmate victims and ensuring improved correctional practices and management." Ibid., p. 407.
3. Arkansas corrections authorities give a course "designed to train correctional personnel to recognize and prevent potential sexual abuse among the inmate population and to intervene quickly and efficiently in instances of suspected, actual, or on-going abuse." The staff training manual on the topic is clear, detailed, and includes extremely useful guidelines as to how prison employees should react to instances of known or suspected sexual abuse. Arkansas Department of Correction, "Sexual Aggression in Prisons and Jails: Awareness, Prevention, and Intervention" (undated manuscript). The manual itself says the course is eight hours long, although the training academy manual says it lasts four hours.

The Nebraska correctional authorities, in their response to our 1997 survey, stated that they were "in the process of defining and implementing a formal sexual assault prevention program for both inmates and staff." Letter to Human Rights Watch from Harold W. Clarke, Director, Nebraska Department of Correctional Services, July 10, 1997. The department did not respond to any of our subsequent requests for information.

4. Massachusetts is one of the few states that provided such a protocol, titled the "Inmate Sexual Assault Response Plan," which came into effect in October 1998. It covers the appropriate staff reaction to incidents of sexual assault, evidence collection, inmate medical care, reporting procedures, witness interviewing, seeking of criminal charges, and psychological evaluation and counseling. Massachusetts Department of Correction, "Inmate Sexual Response Plan," 103 DOC 520 (October 1998). In a welcome step, the department trains certain staff members to be Certified Sexual Assault Investigators.

  The Federal Bureau of Prisons, charged with the management of one of the largest prison populations in the country, has also established a comprehensive protocol of this sort. It is designed to "provide guidelines to help prevent sexual assaults on inmates, to address the safety and treatment needs of inmates who have been sexually assaulted, and to discipline and prosecute those who sexually assault inmates." Federal Bureau of Prisons, "Program Statement: Sexual Abuse/Assault Prevention and Intervention Programs," PS 5324.04, December 31, 1997.

  Connecticut has a sexual assault response protocol that was drafted in December 1996. The protocol covers staff response, evidence collection, medical treatment, mental health treatment, and inmate housing placement. It is aimed at prison medical practitioners, however, rather than the correctional officers who are generally responsible for the initial response to claims of sexual abuse. "Health Services: Inmate Sexual Assault/Rape Protocol," December 11, 1996.

5. The survey found that only six correctional departments—Idaho, Michigan, New Mexico, North Dakota, Oregon and Tennessee—had specifically proscribed sexual harassment among male inmates. In addition, a few states generally barred harassing behavior, and several other states barred certain forms of harassment. Arizona and Nebraska were alone in punishing inmates for "pressuring" others for sex. See James E. Robertson, "Cruel and Unusual Punishment in United States Prisons: Sexual Harassment among Male Inmates," *American Criminal Law Review,* vol. 36 (Winter 1999), p. 45.

6. See Human Rights Watch, *All Too Familiar,* p. 5.

7. Arkansas Department of Correction, "Sexual Aggression in Prisons and Jails: Awareness, Prevention, and Intervention" (undated manuscript), p. 4.

8. *Farmer v. Brennan,* 511 U.S. 825, 841 (1994).

9. See, for example, *Ginn v. Gallagher,* 1994 U.S. Dist. LEXIS 16669 (1994) (summary judgment for defendants granted); *Dreher v. Roth,* 1993 U.S. Dist. LEXIS 209 (1993) (summary judgment for defendants granted).

10. North Carolina General Statutes, Chapter 143B-262.2.

11. Letter to Human Rights Watch from G.M., Ohio, June 27, 1997.

12. Undated attachment to Letter to Human Rights Watch from Ron Angelone, Director, Virginia Department of Corrections, August 21, 1997.

13. Unfortunately, included in the Arkansas materials is a sentence that perpetuates the myth that male victims of rape thereby lose their "manhood." In a section aimed at warning potential rapists against committing the act, it says: "Put yourself in the [victim's] place for just a minute. No matter who he is, the most valuable thing a man has is his manhood, and you want to rob him of this." Arkansas Department of Correction, "Sexual Aggression in Prisons and Jails: Awareness, Prevention, and Intervention" (undated manuscript), p. 48.

14. It was not clear, however, whether this handbook was only used in a single facility, or more generally. Attachment to letter to Human Rights Watch from Donald N. Snyder, Jr., Director, Illinois Department of Corrections, April 7, 2000.

15. Letter to Human Rights Watch from R. Alan Harrop, Mental Health Director, Division of Prisons, North Carolina Department of Correction, September 16, 1997.

16. Human Rights Watch has previously documented abuses that occur in supermax prison units, including the fact that a lack of due process in assignment to such units means that prisoners may wrongly end up in them. See Human Rights Watch, *Cold Storage: Super- Maximum Security Confinement in Indiana* (New York: Human Rights Watch, 1997). In other words, not all prisoners housed in supermax units are actually the "worst of the worst," as proponents of such units like to claim. Indeed, Human Rights Watch has even found rape victims taking refuge in such units, having purposefully broken prison rules in order to escape to a highly regulated and secure environment.

17. Mark Arax, "Ex-Guard Tells of Brutality, Code of Silence at Corcoran," *Los Angeles Times*, July 6, 1998.

18. Ibid.

19. Mark Gladstone and Mark Arax, "Prison Guards Can Consult Lawyers Prior to Questioning," *Los Angeles Times*, September 25, 1998.

20. Letter to Human Rights Watch from B.J., Connecticut, September 23, 1996.

21. Letter to Human Rights Watch, November 7, 1996.

22. Human Rights Watch telephone interview, August 6, 1997.

23. Jim Yardley, "Escape Prompts Scrutiny of Texas Prison System," *New York Times*, January 11, 2001 (quoting Brian Olsen, deputy director of the American Federation of State, County and Municipal Employees, which represents roughly one-sixth of the state's correctional officers).

24. Letter to Human Rights Watch from K.M., Florida, June 18, 1999.

25. Letter to Human Rights Watch from D.A., Texas, September 18, 1998.

26. Human Rights Watch interview, Texas, March 1999.

27. Letter to Human Rights Watch from L.T., Texas, February 19, 1997.

28. Letter to Human Rights Watch from J.G., Florida, September 4, 1996.

29. Letter to Human Rights Watch from S.H., Texas, September 10, 1996 (excerpt from legal pleadings).

30. See Nacci and Kane, *Sex and Sexual Aggression in Federal Prisons*, p. 16.

31. Past studies confirm this point. See, for example, Lockwood, *Prison Sexual Violence*, p. 55; Helen M. Eigenberg, "Rape in Male Prisons: Examining the Relationship Between Correctional Officers' Attitudes toward Rape and Their Willingness to Respond to Acts of Rape," in Michael Braswell et al., 2d ed., *Prison Violence in America* (Cincinnatti, Ohio: Anderson Publishing, 1994), p. 159 (stating that prison staff "seem to offer little assistance to inmates except the age-old advice of 'fight or fuck'"); Lee H. Bowker, *Prison Victimization* (1980), p. 13 (noting that correctional staff tell inmates "to fight it out"); Weiss and Friar, *Terror in the Prisons*, p. 25 (describing how an officer advised an inmate, "Go back . . . and fight it out").

32. Letter to Human Rights Watch from D.A., Nebraska, September 6, 1996.

33. Letter to Human Rights Watch from L.L., Ohio, August 10, 1997.

34. Texas was the only state that provided precise numbers regarding criminal prosecutions. In 1997, the Texas correctional department stated: "Since 1984, Internal Affairs has investigated a total of 519 cases [of inmate-on-inmate sexual assault]. Four cases have resulted in prosecution, with the guilty party receiving an additional prison sentence." Letter to Human Rights Watch from Debby Miller, executive services, Texas Department of Criminal Justice, May 19, 1997. The department did not provide specific numbers in response to our 1998 and 1999 queries. In 1998, for example, Human Rights Watch was told that "our Internal Affairs Division is not always notified by the prosecuting attorneys as to the outcome of these cases, [so] we do not have the precise number of cases that are prosecuted and result in an additional prison sentence." Letter fromDebby Miller, executive services, Texas Department of Criminal Justice, Juny 29, 1998.

35. Letter to Human Rights Watch from Terry Carlson, Adult Facilities Support Unit Director, Minnesota Department of Corrections, August 26, 1997.

36. Typical is the response of Oklahoma correctional authorities: "Our reports do not list the felony charges filed in district court so we cannot confirm whether charges have been filed, but it does not appear to be routine." Letter to Human Rights Watch from James L. Saffle, Oklahoma Department of Corrections, June 5, 1997. Similarly, Rhode Island correctional authorities told us that they had no statistics on actual convictions. Letter to Human Rights Watch from Ashbel T. Wall, II, Director, Rhode Island Department of Corrections, April 25, 2000.

37. Letter to Human Rights Watch from J.C., Texas, December 16, 1998.

38. *Billman v. Indiana Department of Corrections*, 56 F. 3d 785, 790 (1995). For an instructive shock, change the word "prisoners" in that sentence to denote any other group—women, Native Americans, or homeowners, for example.

39. *Farmer v. Brennan*, 511 U.S. 825, 839 (1994) (Thomas, J., concurring in the judgment) (quoting *McGill v. Duckworth*, 944 F.2d 344, 348 (7th Cir. 1991)).

40. *See LaMarca v. Turner*, 662 F. Supp. 647 (S.D. Fla. 1987) (granting $201,500 in damages, as well as injunctive relief, in class action brought by inmates who were gang raped at the Glades Correctional Institution), *aff'd in part and vacated in part*, 995 F. 2d 1526 (11th Cir. 1993), *cert. denied*, 510 U.S. 1164 (1994); *Redman v. County of San*

Diego, 896 F. 2d 362 (9th Cir. 1990) (affirming district court direct verdict that a small, eighteen-year-old inmate who was raped by his cellmate and others did not prove that he had been treated with deliberate indifference), *aff'd in part, rev'd in part,* 942 F.2d 1435 (1991) (en banc) (reversing district court, finding that a reasonable jury could have concluded that prison officials had acted with deliberate indifference), *cert. denied,* 502 U.S. 1074 (1992).

41. *Chandler v. Jones,* 1988 U.S. Dist. LEXIS 693, *3 (E.D. Mo. 1988). It thus absolved the prison officials of responsibility, stating that the officials "made the best of a bad situation."

42. See, for example, *McGill v. Duckworth,* 944 F. 2d 344 (7th Cir. 1991) (reversing verdict in favor of raped prisoner, reasoning that legislatures, architects, taxpayers and judges all bear a share of the blame for prison abuses). The decision in *Kish v. County of Milwaukee* reflects similar thinking. Ruling against two inmates who were sexually assaulted, the court suggested that sexual assault was extremely common in the overcrowded jail under consideration, but that prison officials could not be blamed for the problem. It explained: "the assaults were a result of the physical layout and overcrowding of the jail, both matters beyond the control of the defendant." *Kish v. County of Milwaukee,* 441 F. 2d 901, 905 (7th Cir. 1971).

43. *Butler v. Dowd,* 979 F. 2d 661 (8th Cir. 1992).

44. *James v. Tilghman,* 194 F.R.D. 408 (D. Conn. 1999). At the suggestion of defense counsel, the court revised the award, giving the plaintiff one dollar in nominal damages.

CASE HISTORY OF W.H.

1. Human Rights Watch interview, Texas, October 1998. The expression "ride," in Texas prisons, means to pay protection money or sexual favors or both to another inmate.

2. Inmate Grievance Form, December 4, 1996. The grievance concluded: "I fear for my life here on [this unit] and request that I be placed in ad seg protective custody for my own protection. Thank you! Your prompt response to this matter would be greatly appreciated."

3. Human Rights Watch interview, Texas, October 1998.

4. Ibid.

5. Ibid